Life and Death
in
Historic
Atlantic City, Wyoming

Barbara Townsend

Fine Nib Publishing

Life and Death in Historic Atlantic City, Wyoming

Hardcover: ISBN 979-8-9929682-0-0
Paperback: ISBN 979-8-218-47979-4
Ebook: ISBN 979-8-9929682-1-7

Library of Congress Control Number: 2024922607

With a Foreword by Todd Guenther

Cover photos:
Top, left to right: Franz Alwes: courtesy of the Betty Carpenter Pfaff Collection,
     South Pass City State Historic Site; Miss Ellen Carpenter, and Martha Dohm:
     courtesy of C. E. Carpenter IV; Lawrence Giessler: courtesy of the Atlantic City
     Historical Society Collection, Wyoming State Archives
Center: East Cemetery
Bottom, left to right: James Carpenter, James Cassie, and Joseph Barbett:
     courtesy of the South Pass City State Historic Site

Each photograph is accredited unless it is the author's
or the photographer is unknown.
Color and quality were adjusted to ensure clarity by the printing process.
Minor damage to some photographs were electronically repaired.

Quoted passages have retained the misspellings
of the original documents.

First Edition

To our Atlantic City people
who turned a gold rush camp
into a community

and to Betty Carpenter Pfaff
who recorded their stories
and preserved them for history
1923-2024

Poll List

Of an Election held at Atlantic City Sweet Water County Wyoming Territory on the third day of September A.D. 1872

1	John Atkinson	36	Louis Pauly
2	Barna McCabe	37	Robert Dyer
3	C. Meglin	38	E. Dikens
4	Wm Hartman	39	Jos. M. Ramsey
5	Eli Coapy	40	Hugh McLean
6	Wm Laben	41	Rufus McKidrick
7	Thos McClausey	42	Joseph De Corey
8	Oliver Belscalagen	43	Chris Smith
9	Herman Kirl	44	V. D. Harris
10	Ben DeCorey	45	B. Frank Lowe
11	Peter Ward	46	John McTurk
12	J. L. Bowman	47	Abram Fischer
13	Geo A Lewis	48	Robt McCauley
14	J. A. Smith	49	Joseph Bucher
15	J. Nelson	50	P. T. Murphy
16	Jno W Anthony	51	Alvin Heyrott
17	Ed Lawn	52	Louisa E. Heyrott Mrs
18	H. A. Davison	53	Thomas Shroden
19	AC Stephens	54	Annie Schlesting Mrs
20	Thos Havara	55	James Forest
21	Enoch Joy	56	Jos W Menefee
22	Daniel McRea	57	John Stump
23	George Longeon	58	Peter Dick
24	John Fischer	59	Charles J Isaacson
25	L. C. Bills	60	Peter Wison
26	Frank Brandon	61	Jules Timmereux
27	Theopler Rodrigas	62	Mary Bucher Mrs
28	Santiago Cresta	63	Charles F Freire
29	Jose Lopez	64	Charles Chapin
30	Alonzo Harvey	65	
31	John R Smith	66	
32	F. A. Weber	67	
33	John Fritter	68	
34	H. Baldwin	69	
35	Richard Young	70	

Contents

Foreword   vii

Preface   ix

Acknowledgments   x

Illustration, Territory of Wyoming, 1879   xii

1 How This Project Started and How it Ended   1

2 From Government Lands to Private Property   11

   Illustration, regional plat map, 1884   16

3 Buried in Atlantic City, Gravesite Unknown   19

4 East Cemetery   30

   Map   35

   Marked Burials and Family Plots   36

5 East Cemetery, People Buried Here, Gravesite Unknown   101

6 East Cemetery, Dowsed Graves of Unknown Persons   119

7 West Cemetery   152

   Map   157

   All Burial Sites   158

8 Buried Outside of Atlantic City   170

9 Burial Sites Unknown   222

10 Cadaver Dogs   249

11 Dowsing for Graves   252

Notes   261

Bibliography   293

Index   302

About the Author   308

Poll Book, Atlantic City precinct. General Election on November 21, 1880. Tick marks annotate people included in this book. –Courtesy of the Sweetwater County Historical Museum

POLL BOOK

Of an Election, held in *Atlantic City* Precinct, in Sweetwater County, Territory of Wyoming, on the 2d day of November A. D. 1880, at which time *John McPurk. Chas Washington Joseph 4 Ansell. G.I. Bishop* were Judges and *Joseph Weber*

were Clerks of said Election, the following named persons voting thereat :

No.	NAMES OF VOTERS.	No.	NAMES OF VOTERS.
1	N. L. Turner	34	John Werlen
2	A. J. Daugherty	35	Herman Karl
3	H Rucker	36	Ellen. Huff Mrs
4	Charles. Townsend	37	John T. Huff
5	Wm Gratut	38	Henry. Do Wolf
6	F. C. Lewis	39	Louis Poire
7	Alonzo Harrey	40	Oliver Baialargou
8	Robert. McAuly	41	William Shell Sworn
9	Samuel. Spangler	42	James A Smith
10	Wm Schlisting	43	Solow Wells Sworn
11	Wm Laun	44	
12	Mary. Washington Mrs	45	
13	William Shark	46	
14	Mrs Elizebeth Harsch	47	
15	Phillip. Harsch	48	
16	H. H. Bruning Sworn	49	
17	Geo. Langlois Sworn	50	
18	Thomas Mackie Sworn	51	
19	Orrvis Smith Sworn	52	
20	Edward. Laun	53	
21	Lizzie. Dewolf. Mrs	54	
22	Liddie E McAuly Mrs	55	
23	Josephine. Werlen Mrs	56	
24	Burt. Smith	57	
25	John. McPurk	58	
26	George. Bishop	59	
27	Helena. Smith Mrs	60	
28	Joseph. H. Ansell	61	
29	Joseph. Weber	62	
30	Charles. Washington	63	
31	Alvin ; Heyroth Sworn	64	
32	A. Schlichting Jm Sworn	65	
33	Agnes Ansell Mrs	66	

FOREWORD

After serving the nation during a career in the U.S. Air Force, Barbara Townsend is now serving the people of Wyoming, past and present, by documenting the lives and end-of-life stories of pioneers who answered the call of gold at South Pass and thus helped create the state and build a home for those of us here today.

Townsend, one of the few people who live in the near-ghost town of Atlantic City, shares stories of frontier warfare, childbirth, accidents, violence, childhood maladies, disease, and myriad other causes of death including plain old age that filled Atlantic City's cemeteries and dotted the surrounding sagebrush hills with tiny clusters of graves.

Her engaging anecdotes and short biographies bring to life the people who walked the streets of this Old West gold-mining boom town.

What began as an effort to satisfy her own curiosity became a years-long labor of love and a daunting undertaking due to scanty information about ordinary working people who often labored in near-anonymity.

To find and mark the forgotten graves and tell the stories of the people buried in them she utilized the tools of history: online, public and family archives, old newspapers, oral histories, and field archaeology methods on the ground. Where graves could be discerned but no information could be found she secured trained cadaver dogs and dowsers to leave no stone unturned in her efforts to resurrect the names of previously forgotten pioneers who settled the central Rockies.

The historical tales are interwoven with intriguing accounts of the twists and turns involved in research and the experiences of people who helped with the project. Their efforts to unravel old mysteries and compare sometimes conflicting lines of evidence including US Census manuscripts, mortality schedules, and coroner interviews, then relate that information to archaeological clues make a compelling read.

"Dust to dust," we say as we bury friends and loved ones and then consign them to the past. Yet, the old saw applies here: "No one truly dies until the last person speaks their name." Townsend is speaking the long-forgotten names of those who have gone before us.

For those interested in the beauty and brutality of frontier life for the children, women, and men who lived it, not the rich or powerful but the workers and voters who dug Wyoming's mines, drove the freight wagons, clerked the stores, homesteaded the ranches, and raised the children, *Life and Death in Historic Atlantic City, Wyoming,* provides rare insight into a traumatic part of life.

Todd Guenther
Professor Emeritus, Anthropology and History
Central Wyoming College
and Former Curator, South Pass City State Historic Site

PREFACE

In 1867, a gold boom launched at the tip of the Wind River Mountains in the Dakota Territory. Thousands flocked to this region. South Pass City came into being.

The next year, a few miles away, Atlantic City and Hamilton City were founded and the first Atlantic City death was reported. Since then, there have been many more deaths, often under tragic circumstances.

Through the following 157 years in this wilderness area, many of these deaths have been forgotten.

This book started out thousands of hours ago as a database with the simple intent to list the information carved on the headstones in Atlantic City's two cemeteries. After all, the information on those headstones was all we needed to know, right?

To document their deaths and their burial sites, fantastic facts about our people emerged. As discoveries grew, the database's sections grew into multiple sections which included maps and indexes and hundreds of photographs and knowledge gleaned from museums, old newspaper sites, and genealogy sites.

Visits by a college anthropologist and students, a cadaver-seeking dog and his handler, and three expert dowsers who search for graves led to the mind-blowing discovery of 87 unmarked burial sites.

While this work has been profoundly enlightening, information on many of our Atlantic City people remains elusive. Despite dedicated seeking the names and stories of many who lived and died here cannot be discovered. It saddens me many of our people in this unique community are lost to history.

Of the people listed here, I am heartened we know their names, we know their stories, and we remember them.

Through this journey, I received the most amazing gift. My comprehension of these people shifted from the technical information of their deaths to the celebration of their lives.

One long-term resident of Atlantic City described this work is about "working to restore and preserve the history in those hills, the trials we went through, the heartbreaks and hard work."

Acknowledgments
With Gratitude

The depth and breadth of this information would not be possible without the trust and permission by a few individuals to whom I give great gratitude. These individuals' generosity enabled the knowledge of valuable Atlantic City history which was nearly lost to time.

Our Atlantic City cemetery landowners of these *private* properties, without hesitation and with infinite patience, each granted my prowling, the activities of scholars, a search-and-rescue dog handler and her dog, dowsers, the placing of grave markers, and my unknown hours documenting burial sites.

To the owner of the East Cemetery, who additionally gifted innumerable permissions for visitor tours, one of which led to my recognizing an 1875 wood grave marker in a pile of boards. The owner granted permission to reinstall this treasure and for a moving memorial ceremony to honor this pioneer and to all who rest in the cemetery.

To Kee Dunning and Kori Dunning Klein, and Cassidee Thornhill and Laurel Thornhill, previous and current owners of the West Cemetery, who were and are most generous and enthusiastic with their permissions for the access, research, and grave documentation.

For each of you, I am deeply grateful for your generosity and your patience. Your trust in me with your sacred land is the highest gift I've ever received.

To Robert K. Townsend for your encouragement through these years. Your unwavering support, patience, and profound insights for this long-term project and this book have enabled Atlantic City people and its history to come to light.

To those who searched the cemeteries for clues of burials, search-and-rescue dog handler K. T. Irwin and border collie Blue, and dowsers Don Schooley, Ann Noble, and Sam Drucker whose findings filled the void of knowledge about our cemeteries. Your dedicated and selfless work revealed information never before imagined.

To Betty Carpenter Pfaff whom I give highest regards for her sharing the knowledge of this region's history and its lore. I am deeply saddened by her recent death. We often hear, "Someone should get with the old-timers and write down their stories." Betty did that. She collected knowledge before it faded away. Her books reveal not only historical facts but also the personalities—*the life*—of these individuals. I thank her for her generous permissions through the years to include her information, research, and photographs. Her generosity added a depth of humanity to our comprehension of our early people.

To the Atlantic City Historical Society for granting support under its auspices for my early work. Furthermore, on December 23, 2016, at a point when I had finalized the original database thinking I had found all information possible, I donated my rights to the ACHS, printed the database, and distributed it to a few research facilities. In 2023, after collecting a fresh store of new information, the ACHS board returned my rights.

The ACHS generously paid for dog handler K. T. Irwin's fee, and reimbursed my expenses for the original database's printing and for the stainless steel plaques for Casimer Melin's grave.

To Jonita Sommers and Emmett Williams, descendants of Atlantic City's pioneer Williams and Huff families, who granted permission to share the vast store of information about their family, and thus Atlantic City, history. Jonita provided the information about dowsing for graves and of our three dowsers' capabilities. Her generosity and their results caused an explosion of knowledge.

Others whose generosity allowed for our Atlantic City history to be explored are Reverend Don A. Sanford, Reverend Nicholas Kersten, and the estimable Seventh Day Baptist Historical Society, with the permission of the Council of History of the Seventh Day Baptist General Conference. I thank you all for your support and generosity to share Harden "Pardon" Davis' powerful story.

So many persons made this project successful. Many generously gave permission to include photographs, book excerpts, information, or their perspectives. Some performed an important service. Some gave moral support. I appreciate you all.

I gratefully appreciate and thank Marjane Ambler; Terry Appleby; C. E. Carpenter IV; Reverends Charles Clarke, Pamela Glasser, and Bonnie Deyo, and the congregation of our St. Andrew's Episcopal Church; Charlotte Dehnert; Matthew Dobson and the Jay Historical Society; Joan Earl; William Elder; Joe Ellis; David Geible; Todd Guenther; Steve Gyorvary; Carl Hallberg; Philippina Halstead; Alicia Hamilton; Jean Mathisen Haugen; Steve Hockett; Field Iiams and the Mount Hope Cemetery staff; Erin Ivie and the Fremont County Coroner's Office staff; Carole Justice; Kennedy; Opal Kiyomi; Jon Lane; Susan and David Layman; Tammy and Steve Lee; Julia Lenocker; Amy McClure; Verne Meredith; John Mionczynski; Carmela and William Moore; Laura Norman; Donna Sue Ratliff; Rick Reynolds; Dr. Phil Roberts; Bonnie and Scott Robinson; Lorna Ruebelmann; Patricia Saltgaver; Eiko Sherlock, James E. Sherlock, Kevin Shields and the *Riverton Ranger*, Bill Sniffin and the *Wyoming State Journal*; Pam Spencer-Hockett; Mark Stratmoen; Judy Taylor; Jo and Rod Trumble; Loretta Tschirgi; Martha Walrath; Terry Wehrman; and Lynn Zerbe.

And finally to the Wyoming Historical Society. The Society and its members supported and honored my project about our people in this humble ol' mining town with its Outstanding Historical Preservation Award in 2022.

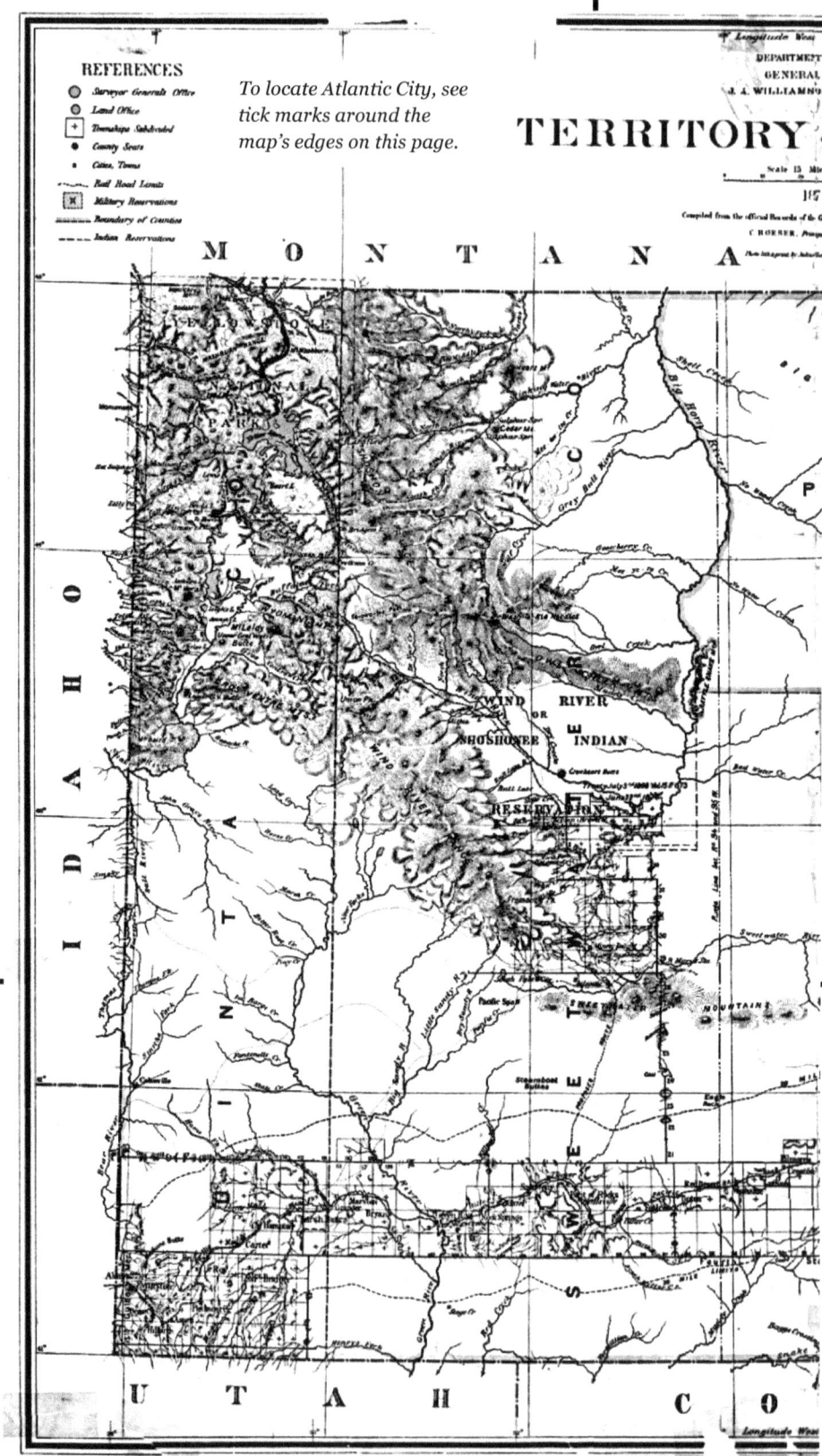

To locate Atlantic City, see tick marks around the map's edges on this page.

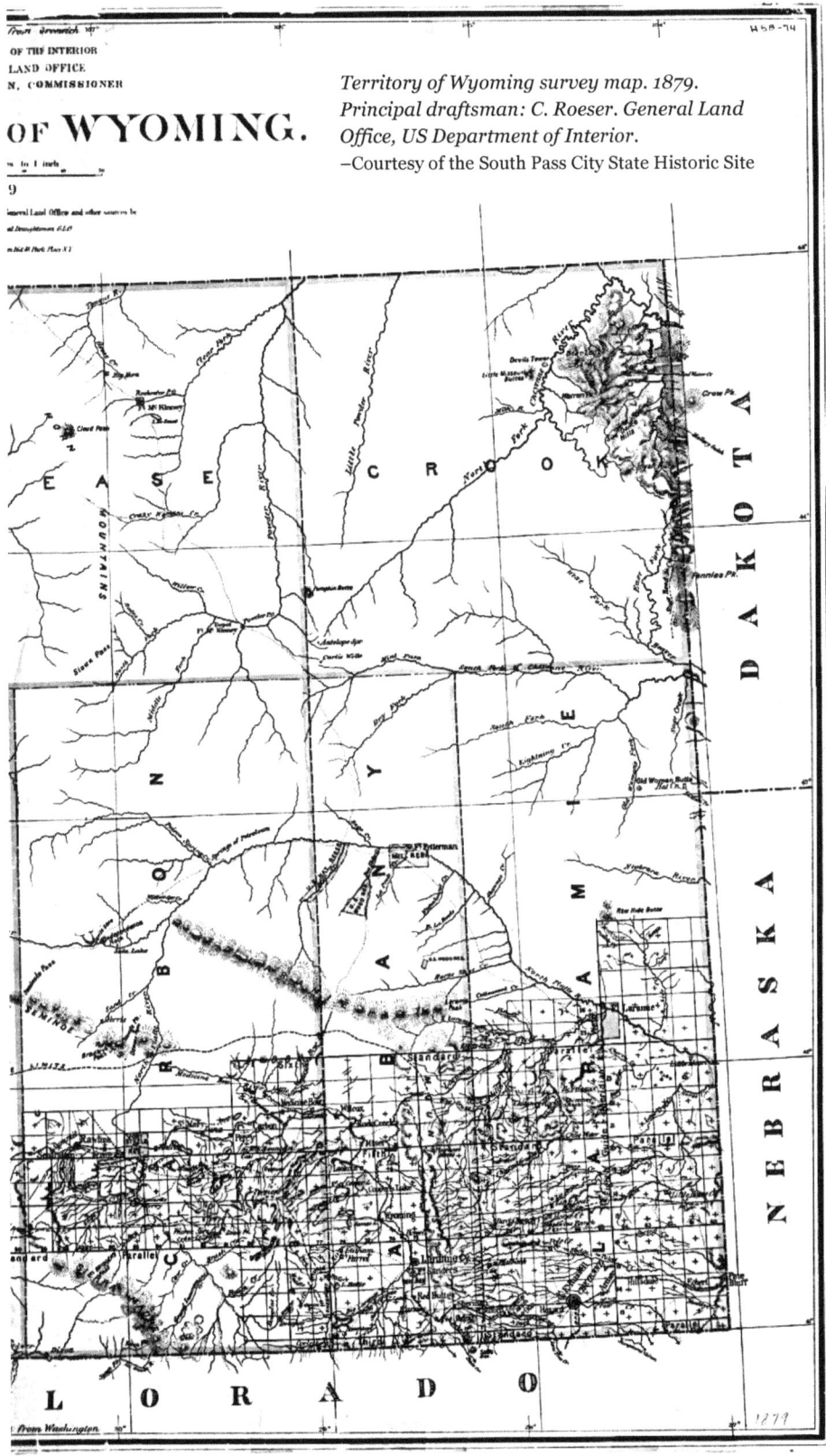

Territory of Wyoming survey map. 1879.
Principal draftsman: C. Roeser. General Land
Office, US Department of Interior.
—Courtesy of the South Pass City State Historic Site

Atlantic City, Wyoming, July 1894. The unknown photographer faced northeast.
—Courtesy of the Sweetwater County Historical Museum

ONE

How This Project Started
and How It Ended

First, what makes Atlantic City so fascinating?

One visitor summed up what makes Atlantic City so intriguing. He arrived from England to conduct research for a play about the American Old West he was writing for the London stage with the Royal Shakespeare Company.

Before he made his reservation at the Miner's Delight Inn, his initial research was to find the one place in the United States where everything to do with the Old West occurred such as the overland trails, pioneers, cowboys, soldiers, Native Americans, and gold miners. He discovered everything to do with the Old West *all happened right here.*[1]

He was right. We have all those and more. Wilderness. Elevation of 7,500 feet. Wild animals. Fights in the saloons. Cattle. Mountains. Plains. Forests. The Red Desert. Guns on the hip. Temperatures down to -40. Big snow. Winds to blow you off the porch. Independent and self-reliant people. Peace.

When Atlantic City was founded in April 1868, notable pioneer H. G. Nickerson said "during the height of its prosperity its population was variously estimated from 1,500 to 2,000."

One can be forgiven for imagining those early years as a rough-and-tumble mining camp where plenty of hard and dirty work, boozing, and female companionship of the floozy kind took place. While those activities did occur, my study of the 1870 Atlantic City census depicted a different scenario. Of the 332 residents enumerated, 90 were females, many of the domestic or married and motherly kind. Children under 18 numbered a surprising 62.[2]

Those early glory days didn't last long. In 1870 the Army established a camp northeast of Atlantic City to protect miners from Indian attacks. Many people included in this book were victims of those attacks. This same year, the Army camp was named Camp Stambaugh in honor of First Lieutenant Charles B. Stambaugh who was one of the persons killed.

By 1873, a Mr. R. H. Hall, a telegraph operator at Camp Stambaugh, declared "Atlantic City was already called an abandoned or ghost city."[3]

After a hard day of work, pastimes and relaxation were essential. Carter County issued the first license for an Atlantic City saloon to John Murphy on

June 28, 1869, license number 16. Five other Atlantic City entrepreneurs were later licensed for a saloon. The first licensed liquor dealers were men named Fosher (possibly Abraham or John) and Charles H. Collins with license number 44 on September 25.

Atlantic City is the first town in Wyoming Territory to open a brewery. Atlantic Brewery was issued retail liquor license number 173 on January 2, 1871. While the "Nature of Business" was listed as "Retail Liquors," just like the earlier and staggering number of issued retail liquor licenses, this was the first license issued to a Carter County brewery.[4]

Now, during the summer the town bursts with hops plants grown from the cuttings from the original hops plants used for brewing beer. The trick is keeping the cows from eating them in this free-range wilderness. Yes, we're one of the few places where it's "open range." Cattle roam the roads and trim our yards unless the owner fences them out. A "back easterner" asked me if my cattle guard was for decoration. No.

Our water is clean from mountain snowmelt. One drop right from the well can be added to a dram of top-shelf single malt Scotch.

To continue with their needed "R and R," in the old days, they made their own fun. Dancing and card playing was popular as were cribbage parties.[5]

Even in the rough-and-tumble Old West, they had the arts. The first opera house was here, located in the unique stone two-story building built by John W. Anthony in 1869 and later owned by Robert McAuley. This structure can't be missed in the half-mile drive through town.

The first story held a general store and people gathered for dances in the second story. In later years, the structure became known as Hyde's Hall after the new owner Thomas H. Hyde. "They used to have some high-powered dances in the Hyde's Hall," said Mel Freeburgh.

This structure now has one story. An earthquake caused damage, making the structure unsafe and the top floor was removed. Oddly, the exact year of the earthquake and when the second floor was removed is unknown. I've heard a range from 1902 to 1916.[6]

Information from the US Geological Survey for earthquakes in Atlantic City listed fascinating, yet inconsistent, information. A 1984 map of Wyoming's earthquake epicenters listed three at Atlantic City: December 12, 1923, with an intensity of V; October 30, 1935, intensity III; and August 22, 1959, intensity IV. At this time, for perspective, the intensity scale (degree of shaking) was I–XII.

Surprisingly, more research revealed listings from a state resource which included the same data above except that the October 30, 1935, earthquake actually occurred in 1925. Another source from the University of Wyoming also stated this earthquake occurred in 1925. The 1935 date did not match any other source and all other sources stated this occurred in 1925.

It's possible that the 1923 earthquake, while considered moderate, was intense enough for the owner to remove the second story.[7]

Returning to the arts and making our own fun in modern times, the local legend Buffalo Chips, a band renowned for its old-time tunes, could turn dancing and stomping into a glorious pastime. They drew so many enthusiasts the owner of the Atlantic City Mercantile was forced to shore up the century-old floor to support the weight and rhythmic stomping of packed dancers.

For arts for the quieter and more sober patrons, in 1983 David Geible wrote, edited, and arranged a play which covered more than hundred years of Atlantic City history, *That Gold Mine in the Sky*. He and other Atlantic City actors performed in the play which was staged throughout the state.[8]

In the 2010s, Jo and Rod Trumble led and taught novice players for our homegrown band, the Strumlords. We mainly played for each other betwixt helpings of our pot-luck meals. Eventually we became competent and confident enough to play in public here in town and at South Pass City State Historic Site's Gold Rush Days.

Back in pioneering days, sports included a Fourth of July rodeo along with drilling contests. Cowboys and miners could show off their talents. School children entertained with a program of recitations and songs followed by a dance. One event earned the children a day off from school the next day as "the young folks had to have a nap."[9]

Today, sport is the annual "One-Hole Golf Tournament" with its par-72 fairway through sagebrush hazards. ATVs carry sustenance to the intrepid players.

In the early days, a "red light district" known as French Town consisted of "quite a few houses" down Rock Creek, many in dugouts. The location for brewing beer was Beer Garden Gulch, immediately northeast of Atlantic City. In 1869, *licensed* saloons and liquor dealers numbered six and four, respectively. At one point, there was an estimate of "maybe ten or twelve saloons."

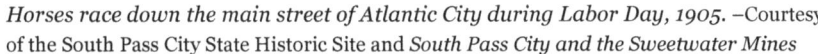

Horses race down the main street of Atlantic City during Labor Day, 1905. –Courtesy of the South Pass City State Historic Site and *South Pass City and the Sweetwater Mines*

Our two current drinking holes, the Atlantic City Mercantile and the Miners Grubstake offer beer, spirits, and raucous good times. The now-closed Miner's Delight Inn had boasted a stunning collection of single malt Scotch and held monthly tastings. French Town no longer exists. Only remnants of the dugouts down Rock Creek survive.[10]

Our roads are still dirt. It can be an annoyance during the annual spring Mud Season though I find the protective layer of mountain mud preserves the finish on my car. One day this loud city slicker who had stayed in our local watering hole too long demanded to every local as they entered, "You should pave these roads. You'd get a lot more business!" Every local responded with the same answer, "Why would we do that?"

Even movie star Robert Redford lingered in Atlantic City in 1975. During a journey financed by National Geographic, he followed the Outlaw Trail which runs from north Montana to the Mexico border. He described Atlantic City as, "everything seemed to have been preserved as in an old tin type. A few cabins stood like wooden sentries against stark, brown-and-white slopes."

At Terry Wehrman's Atlantic City Mercantile, basically the town center, he described "the Merc" as being

> instantly cast back to the era of suspendered store clerks with rumpled cowboy hats, high collars, moustaches and haircuts that left the ears naked (and quite a bit of scalp around them) and the wide-eyed stares of people who looked on a camera as some crazy new invention.

Atlantic City, 1944. Bisecting the center: *The tailings piles from the dredge which collected gold from Rock Creek in the 1930s.* Left: *The Sypes house is the large white structure.* Left middle: *The Carpenter Hotel.* Background: *The Granier Ditch slices the distant hillsides.*
–Courtesy of the Atlantic City Historical Society Collection, Wyoming State Archives

Redford also spent time with resident Renaissance man John Mionczynski. He admired "the evidence of John's ingenuity everywhere" in the handmade cabin and wind generator. Redford's book, *The Outlaw Trail*, included a massive photo of John and Redford sipping beer on the steps of John's porch.[11]

Like "the good ol' days," life is slower here. We're self-sufficient. We leave people to their solitude if that's their thing. We help when help is needed. Gunfire is for sighting in and practicing or celebrating.

Of the many things continued since the pioneer days one is personal freedom. In 1869, the Wyoming territorial legislature passed the unprecedented law in the Union to allow women residents at least 21 years of age to vote and to hold public office.

Women did enjoy more freedom here. As Laura Green Marrin stated, "All the women in Atlantic had their own personality and could do what they liked." In 1929, Laura's own sister Zoie Green drove a truck to move the Dexter mill out of Atlantic City over to what would become the Carissa mill just outside of South Pass City.[12]

In the morning, I watch the alpenglow and marvel how the sunrise in the east makes even the western sky magnificent. In the evening, I watch the fast-moving shadow slither eastward as the sun sinks behind the mountains.

And peace descends on our tiny ol' town.

How this project started

The first surprise in the beginning of this project was that Atlantic City, with its double-digit population, has two cemeteries. The second surprise is that they are *private* property.

The nearest public cemeteries are both four miles from Atlantic City and are owned by the Bureau of Land Management. To the southwest a windswept cemetery stands watch above South Pass City. Only a minority of its former occupants remain as many have been disinterred and buried elsewhere.

To the northeast the first sight of Hamilton City/Miners Delight is its fenced cemetery. This small site has one marked grave, Anna Anderton, 1837-1875. This ground is also pitted from exhumations or possibly collapsed graves.

For our two Atlantic City cemeteries, the owners have generously granted their permission and bestowed their trust in me with their sacred land to conduct research and to invite other researchers. Their trust is forefront in my mind.

This project started thousands of hours ago with a simple intent: to document with photographs and in a spreadsheet the inscribed information on the meagre number of headstones. This would also update the 2007 compilation by Philippina Halstead, charter member of the Atlantic City Historical Society.

To begin this project, I stumbled through the East Cemetery. This space was described by Mary Lou Pence and Lola M. Homsher as:

The tilting cemetery of the frontier village attests to the underlying tragedy that gripped those who shared the heartaches, hardships and sudden death which were all part of the settlement's pulse beat.[13]

This is not a manicured city cemetery. This is wild land, a fenced one-acre specimen of this untamed country stretching miles in all directions. Here, visitors usually have four feet.

I skirted thick sections of sage and stepped over dead branches and bits of decayed wood to make my way to the row of Carpenters, a renowned family whose former hotel I was honored to own. I plucked some blooms from nearby plants and placed them on a headstone.

Listing the text on the headstone and typing it into a spreadsheet should take a few hours. Then I expected to proclaim, "Here are our people buried in Atlantic City." Easy peasy.

After all, the engraved information on those headstones were all we needed to know, right?

One headstone has sections eroded to the point they were illegible. I researched to fill the information gaps because leaving incomplete information in a database didn't make sense. Alwin Heyroth died in 1884 and his grave has the earliest placed headstone in this cemetery. Soon, fantastic facts about him emerged. Then came the addiction to find more information, not just about him but about everyone in the cemetery.

Before long, the two-page database grew so ponderous it couldn't even be emailed. The database was split into two sections. As the number of discoveries grew the number of sections swelled.

While the store of information grew, I turned my attention to the cemeteries.

As a rank amateur trying to study what may be graves in a wild land, I needed guidance from experts. With permission by the owners of both cemeteries and under the auspices of the Atlantic City Historical Society, I requested an anthropological visit from the Central Wyoming College.

William Elder and two students arrived on October 3, 2015.

They discussed indicators of a gravesite and other indicators that it may not be. William pointed out signs of some unmarked graves. Then he explained how to study the terrain and how the terrain could cause an appearance of a grave. He described how the hillside's gullies and snowmelt could cause the water to pool and swirl in a low spot then drain away leaving a site which suspiciously resembled a grave.

At one spot William knelt and stared at a bare patch of crushed rock for a long time. "There's a pendant here."

Indeed, a small, worn silver-colored pendant, like a child's pendant that had escaped its chain, lay on the ground, likely eroded up from the rocky soil. He then taught the students how to document the artifact according to scientific practices and handed the piece to me. After notifying the owner of this precious find the pendant is in the hands of the ACHS curator.

Meanwhile, the names of people said or thought to be buried here multiplied. I intended to find as many persons and their graves as possible.

The thought of ground-penetrating radar came to mind. The radar would allow us to find disturbed soil and thus burials. However, major issues arose. With our thick and tall vegetation, steep hillsides, the unknown cost, and the consideration of finding an agency to attempt the effort was daunting.

A happenstance article in the *Casper Star-Tribune* announced a cadaver-seeking dog found a 150-year-old grave on an overland trail.

A dog, mobile, agile, with a knowledgeable handler: perfect. John Mionczynski knew a search-and-rescue dog handler.

Soon, K. T. Irwin and border collie Blue explored the cemeteries to detect human remains while John recorded their actions. K. T. and Blue's teamwork was mesmerizing. Blue downed on thirteen sites which K. T. confirmed as human remains, one in the West Cemetery and twelve in the East Cemetery.

Some of the confirmed human remains were in known graves as evidenced by the fallen and decaying wooden fences surrounding the sites. The discovery and location of unknown burials added to the knowledge of our buried people.

The next searches involved a technology dating back thousands of years. Many of us have heard of dowsing, or "witching," using a y-shaped wood branch or metal rods to find water. Jonita Sommers, descendant of Atlantic City's pioneer Williams and Huff families, told me about people who can dowse for graves. Some can even determine the sex of the buried person.

One thing I know about myself is I tend to be gullible, and even I didn't believe this fantastical ability. After my own research I found this practice is a real skill.

Arriving first was Don Schooley, a county sexton and dowser with decades of experience. Weeks later and twice Ann Noble, an award-winning Wyoming historian. Then Sam Drucker, an archeologist for the Bureau of Land Management.

Preparing for their arrivals was complex. I didn't know what to expect, how they worked, or how many burials they'd find.

Don arrived first and meticulously dowsed the East Cemetery. When he finished, with me following behind to document each grave and plant a colored and marked pin flag at each site—blue for males and pink for females, I turned to see the totality of his findings. I was stunned at the sea of waving pin flags.

Then Don repeated his work on the hillside of the West Cemetery. We know there were many burials on that hillside thanks to the knowledge collected by John Mionczynski from the old-timers in the 1960s. The problem was there was no sign of any other graves on that massive hillside other than its three lonely known burials. We had no idea where to look. Don found no other burials.

Ann Noble arrived and she also meticulously dowsed the East Cemetery during two days and found twelve more burials. Then she dowsed the West Cemetery and found one lone male.

Sam Drucker, the third dowser, arrived to concentrate on the West Cemetery's boundless, steep hillside. His efforts rewarded us with 15 gravesites.

One could be excused to think any grave would be noticeable. Yet here, with our rugged terrain, wilderness, and harsh conditions, any sign of a grave can quickly disappear. In fact, we have two instances where a grave was dug and that place was occupied. While excavating a grave in 1961 the diggers discovered the space was already inhabited. In 2016 one site was discovered to contain two overlapping bodies. More on these in the following chapters.

For specific information for the dowsers' actions, results, and my preparations see chapters 4, 6, 7, and 11.

How it ended

All total, K. T. and Blue, Don, Ann, and Sam discovered 87 gravesites or spread cremains. The number of their discoveries was—and still is—mind boggling.

I feel vindicated at the numbers. Before the dog and dowsers discovered these graves, the number of people found through myriad resources was so much higher than the scant suspected graves in the cemeteries. The rough number of those who are or may be buried here drew closer.

Information about our people came from scouring maps, indexes, hundreds of photographs, newspaper articles, original documents gleaned from museums and archives, oral histories by our treasured old-timers, books, friends and neighbors, libraries, county clerks' offices, county coroners, old newspaper sites, genealogy sites, and US and Territorial censuses to locate any elusive nugget from those gold mines of information.

One disturbing and infuriating news article came to light about vandalism in the cemeteries. The article wasn't specific about the damages but it might explain the many bullets in the 1875 wood grave marker in the East Cemetery or perhaps why many of the metal and wood grave markers are missing.[14]

Moving forward, while searching I also discovered fascinating tidbits and magical moments about the people in this humble ol' busted gold mining town.

One surprising find was the oral history by Jacob Booth who spoke about mercury poisoning from the fumes produced during the process of recovering fine gold. According to Jake, "Suddenly everybody was sick and dying of mercury

Vandalism Deplored At Cemeteries Of South Pass City, Atlantic City

The Fremont County chapter of the Wyoming State Historical Society met May 14 in the banque room of the Masonic Temple in Lander.

A carry-in dinner was enjoyed by 23 members, seven guests and four officers.

Attention of the chapter again was directed toward the vandalism that has taken place at the South Pass and Atlantic City cemeteries. Such acts are punishable by law and the members hope it will not be necessary to take such action.

35 From Lander At Toastmasters Meeting

The District 55 Toastmasters Convention held a week ago Saturday in Riverton with about 190 members and wives attending.

The Fremont County chapter of the Wyoming State Historic Society discussed vandalism at our two cemeteries and at South Pass.

–Courtesy of the Wyoming State Journal, May 23, 1961

poisoning. ... And it scared everybody else, and everybody threw up their hands and left." He also described a couple, possibly in the 1920s, in their Atlantic City home when the husband put his "fines" and his copper plate scrapings in a frying pan on the "good and hot" stove. "Both died, right there on the spot." He did not recall their names. A search of Wyoming newspapers about poisoning or deaths caused by mercury or this cooking method revealed no articles.[15]

In the Sweetwater County Historical Museum I held the earliest original voting poll book they possessed, 1880, and searched for familiar names. I saw a woman's name. And another. *Women voted.* Though 1880 was not the first election where Wyoming women could vote the impact of their ground-breaking history made me dizzy. Nine Atlantic City women cast their ballots that year.

Discouragingly, I cannot locate the September 6, 1870, mid-term election poll register when women first could vote. According to Robert Morris, son of legendary Esther Hobart Morris, we know many women voted. In his letter to his cousin Frankie on September 8, several women voted in Atlantic City, eight women voted at South Pass City, and all thirteen women voted at Hamilton City.[16]

Thanks to Carl Hallberg at the Wyoming State Archives, I received available electronic and paper copies of the 1869, 1871, and 1872 poll register. Sadly, some election files did not have the poll book register which would reveal the names of voters.

In the earliest known election with a polling register since women could vote, three named Atlantic City women cast their vote, Louiza E. Heyroth, Annie Schlisting (Schlichting), and Mary Bucher on September 3, 1872.

Purpose for this book

First, it's to share rare and hard-to-find knowledge and stories of our early people who built this boom-and-bust town and who turned it into a community.

Second, to encourage and assist people interested in researching their own town's people or cemeteries but may not know where to start. Here you can find myriad places and ideas to begin.

Third, it's a demonstration in creativity, the "thinking outside of the box" to find extraordinary means to discover information.

Lastly, tips are sprinkled throughout to ease finding information and a few cautionary tales to prevent errors.

With creativity and stick-to-itiveness, the resources and discoveries can be endless and the findings jaw-dropping.

Atlantic City main street with an unknown horse rider. According to old-timers, Butch Cassidy would stop at the Green Saloon [center] after a train robbery. He always asked about one woman, a widow, and he would leave her a large amount of money. Butch was generous to anyone in need.

Butch was supposedly killed in 1908 yet old-timers insisted he was alive and had returned to Atlantic City. Interestingly, the old-timers would hold heated arguments about the year Butch had returned, 1938 or 1939. –Source: John Mionczynski, August 15, 2024.

Handwritten on the back of the photograph, "Stone McAuley Building [left], Green Saloon. 1904. Given B. Pfaff by Verla Sommers." –Courtesy of the Fremont County Pioneer Museum

TWO

From Government Lands
to Private Property

Ownership history of Atlantic City

This land that would become our tiny town and our two cemeteries started out as wilderness occupied by ancient peoples. Then Europeans showed up and claimed the wilderness for king and country. For decades, the land became a commodity traded at a furious rate.

In 1803, Thomas Jefferson made a great deal with Napoleon Bonaparte for the Louisiana Purchase, known as the Louisiana Territory. This land mass consisted of 530,000,000 acres or, in "smaller" terms, 828,000 square miles.[1] Its $15,000,000 price tag, also in "smaller" terms, amounted to $0.04 an acre.

The dot of land where Atlantic City would later sprout was included within this vastness by a mere 13 miles from the territory's western border. Territory #1.[2]

In 1812, when the State of Louisiana was carved out of the Louisiana Territory, to prevent confusion the territory was renamed Missouri Territory. Territory #2.[3]

In 1854, the Missouri Territory was split to form two new territories. Our section containing the future Atlantic City was renamed Nebraska Territory. The other section became Kansas Territory. Territory #3.[4]

In 1861, Nebraska Territory was split. Our south portion remained as the Nebraska Territory. Our new shape was much like Nebraska as it appears today except the panhandle extended further west. The north portion was called the Dakota Territory, forming what would later become the North and South Dakotas.[5]

In 1863, our west-most part of the Nebraska panhandle was carved from Nebraska Territory, and we became part of the new Idaho Territory. This great land mass encompassed today's Wyoming, Idaho, and Montana. Territory #4.[6]

In 1864, this great Idaho Territory split into three parts. The Idaho and the Montana Territories became their own entities, shaped much as we know them today. Our area formed a shape close to our future State of Wyoming except our northeast corner was attached to the southwest corner of Dakota Territory, which absorbed us. We looked much like the tail pinned on the donkey. Territory #5.[7]

In 1867, a gold rush boomed, people swarmed, and South Pass City sprouted. Our Wyoming portion of Dakota Territory was sectioned into four counties. On December 27, our region was designated as Carter County with South Pass City as the county seat. County #1.[8]

In 1868, the Wyoming Organic Act sliced the tail off the Dakota Territory, and Wyoming Territory came into its own. Territory #6.[9]

During this year, Atlantic City and Hamilton City, now more commonly referred to as Miners Delight, came into being.

In 1869, Carter County was renamed Sweetwater County. County #2.[10]

Between the years 1873 and 1875, because of the shrinking and difficult-to-reach South Pass City, the legislature chose Green River as the county seat. Stubbornness of South Pass City's residents to remain as county seat caused a ping-pong transfer of documents and government workers between Green River and South Pass City. The Territorial Legislature finally settled the issue with a law flatly declaring Green River as the county seat.

In 1886, the Legislature split Sweetwater County in two sections, and our northern section became Fremont County. County #3.[11]

The final and most significant change came on July 10, 1890, when the Territory of Wyoming entered the Union as the 44th state, Wyoming.[12]

Tip: A seemingly inconsequential phrase on a history website stated *"much of"* Wyoming was in Dakota Territory. To determine how much of Wyoming was in Dakota Territory led me to delve into the exact territorial borders, which led to the surprising fact that Atlantic City had belonged to six territories.

Why the name Atlantic City?

This is an oft-asked question. I've heard two answers. Choose the one you like.

The first claim was, in the pioneer days, there was a man who had wanted this settlement named for his home town, the "back east" Atlantic City. If this was true, this unknown man carried a lot of power to name this town.

My preference is the second claim because of the nearby Continental Divide. From our eastern slope of the Divide, the "Atlantic" slope, water flows to the Atlantic Ocean via the Gulf of Mexico. Water from the western slope, or the "Pacific" slope, flows to the Pacific Ocean.[13]

This settlement is on the Atlantic slope, hence it was named Atlantic City.

Bolstering this claim, at the South Pass where the water changes from its eastern flow to the western flow there was a settlement known as Pacific Springs.

Private ownership of the cemeteries

Determining when territorial land turned to private property proved extremely difficult because much of the original documentation can't be located. These papers may be "out there," but not where a professional researcher or I could locate them.

On May 20, 1862, when this piece of land destined to become Atlantic City was part of Nebraska Territory, President Abraham Lincoln signed the Homestead Act into law. This act encouraged western expansion. For a filing fee of $18, a person could obtain a 160-acre plot of public land, with some requirements of residence and improvements.[14]

As difficult as it was to find the old records, we do know one thing: it's a thankfully short lineage from government to present-day owners.

Note: Included here is the ownership from the US Government to private companies to the individuals owning the cemeteries. Private property owners will not be named out of respect for their privacy.

According to the historical information from the National Park Service during its Historic American Buildings Survey in 1973, Atlantic City was stated to have been laid out by Charles W. Tozier (sometimes spelled Tozer or Tosier), Colonel Charles Collins, and H. A. Thompson in 1868.

We know an early map or plat of Atlantic City existed as many early deeds mention one. Despite diligent searching, no early map or plat has been located.[15]

The earliest document found for private ownership of this area was a claim by Wilbert B. Teters on November 10, 1884, which included the right of way to Granier Placer on Rock Creek that runs through Atlantic City, and the right of way from Christina Lake for "constructing a flume or water ditch from Willow Creek stream to the 'Willow Creek' Placer on Willow Creek, and to the 'Granier' Placer on Rock Creek and other placers along said stream...." The claim was recorded on November 25, 1884.[16]

On November 22, Wilbert B. Teters granted an indenture to Emile Granier for the Teters Placer and the Granier Placer which included other lands. The indenture encompassed the main townsite of Atlantic City and the land of both cemeteries.[17]

Teters tightened his control with land ownership, and he claimed area water rights on August 3, September 3, and October 7, 1884, and on November 30, 1888.[18]

East Cemetery

This fenced one-acre piece was part of the Teters claim which became a patented claim from the US Government to Emile Granier. He was renowned in the region because of his Granier Ditch to bring water from Christina Lake, six miles away, to use for mining here. Remnants of the ditch can still be seen slicing through our hillsides.

This property was part of the Teters Patented Mining Claim that the US Government issued a patent to Granier, number 115682 on December 2, 1885. The patent was finally recorded in the Fremont County Land Records Office 43 years later on February 14, 1928.[19]

On January 23, 1928, the Timba-Bah Mining Company signed a lease/purchase agreement for this property. The agreement was recorded in the Fremont County Land Records Office on March 30.[20]

The Timba-Bah Mining Company continued ownership of the land until it was transferred to a private owner on December 28, 1998.[21]

West Cemetery

This hillside was originally part of the Granier Placer Mining Claim granted to Emile Granier by Wilbert B. Teters. This piece made up the bulk of the Atlantic City Townsite.

The US Government issued Granier patent number 115683 on January 28, 1889. This patent was recorded 39 years later on February 14, 1928, in the Fremont County Land Records Office.[22]

The West Cemetery is made up of two halves owned by different people and both halves have burials.

The west half

This piece of land was surveyed and sold out of the Granier Placer Mining Claim which makes up the bulk of the Atlantic City townsite. This half is renowned for its most visible burials, Lydia McAuley's striking headstone and fenced grave and Baby Williams' marked and mounded grave.

The original land ownership is nearly identical to the East Cemetery's. Signed by President Grover Cleveland, the US Government patented this part of the Granier Placer Mining Claim, number 115683 on January 28, 1889. It was recorded 45 years later in the Fremont County Land Records Office on February 14, 1928.[23]

Likely, this patent was only recorded in time for the receivership when the Timba-Bah Mining Company received this property in 1928.

A Quit Claim Deed created this specific piece of property from the Timba-Bah Mining Company dated May 8, 1978, to a private owner. The deed includes a covenant: "Nothing will be erected or placed upon the above described property as the same is, in part, a cemetery and is to be preserved, in toto, as it exists on the date hereof."[24]

The east half

This land ownership is identical to the western half. It was a part of the Granier Placer Claim in 1889, then was passed on to the Timba-Bah Mining Company in 1928.[25]

A Quit Claim Deed transferred three lots from the Timba-Bah to a private owner on July 31, 1968. Then, on March 31, 1971, a fourth lot was deeded to the same owner.[26]

Ownership of the general area

While this book concentrates on our people and our cemeteries, as research went on curiosity grew as to the property ownership of our townsite. We know now of the Teters and the Granier patent claims.

About the topic of early street names, a mystery kicked in during a cemetery tour when I mentioned Casimer Melin's estate probate paperwork stated he owned property on "C St ?." A tour participant stated that there were no such street names in Atlantic City.

While searching original land deeds, I discovered many deeds proved Atlantic City's original layout did have street names. East-west streets were named A Street on up to H Street and in the north-south direction streets were named by ordinal numbers, such as First Street.

As a last-ditch effort to find such a map, I even traveled to Sweetwater County Clerk's office with professional land researcher David Geible. We hoped to find an original map there since I've exhausted every other avenue. We searched but could find nothing at the Clerk's records because they did not have original documents from the Carter County era.

At the Sweetwater County Land Records Office and the Engineering Office, Andy Hooten conducted a thorough search of land records, filed maps, and engineering records, but found nothing.

Something he said made me wonder if any map is in either private hands or lost or destroyed like so much of our history.

There had to have been a map or plat because many of the old deeds even specified lot numbers. One example is a mechanic's lien placed by William Glover on John W. Anthony's property on February 22, 1870: "Lot No (44) forty four on First Street between C and D Streets according to the original plat of said town."

Not all deeds mentioned specific locations such as a lot number. Some deeds described their place such as "a house, a stable, a corrall [sic] and fence, known as the Ricketts house situate [sic] on the flat of Rock Creek at Atlantic."[27]

There is a 1908 map of Atlantic City drawn by John Linn, which is similar to modern-day Atlantic City; however, there are differences in the lots and the placement of one avenue.[28]

While Dave, Andy, and I discussed the issue of not finding the original map or plat, Dave brought out the 1965 map of Atlantic City.

Andy pointed out that this map by the Timba-Bah Mining Company was not a "plat." This is a huge difference. We know what a map is, but a plat, to scale, depicts boundaries and easements, and must be approved by the county.[29]

Andy added that this map likely was accepted by government officials as a plat. As this map is older than 40 years, by law, this is settled law.

The original plat or map of the Atlantic City townsite I cannot locate.

In 1983 Albert Mann, a long-time Atlantican, stated:

Timba-Bah, ... It was a mining company—they came through and bought up the whole town. ... And then when Timba-Bah folded they sold it out that

Survey map, 1884, Township 29, Range 100, and Sections 1-36. Map by Edward C. David. US Surveyor General's Office. –Courtesy of the Wyoming State Archives

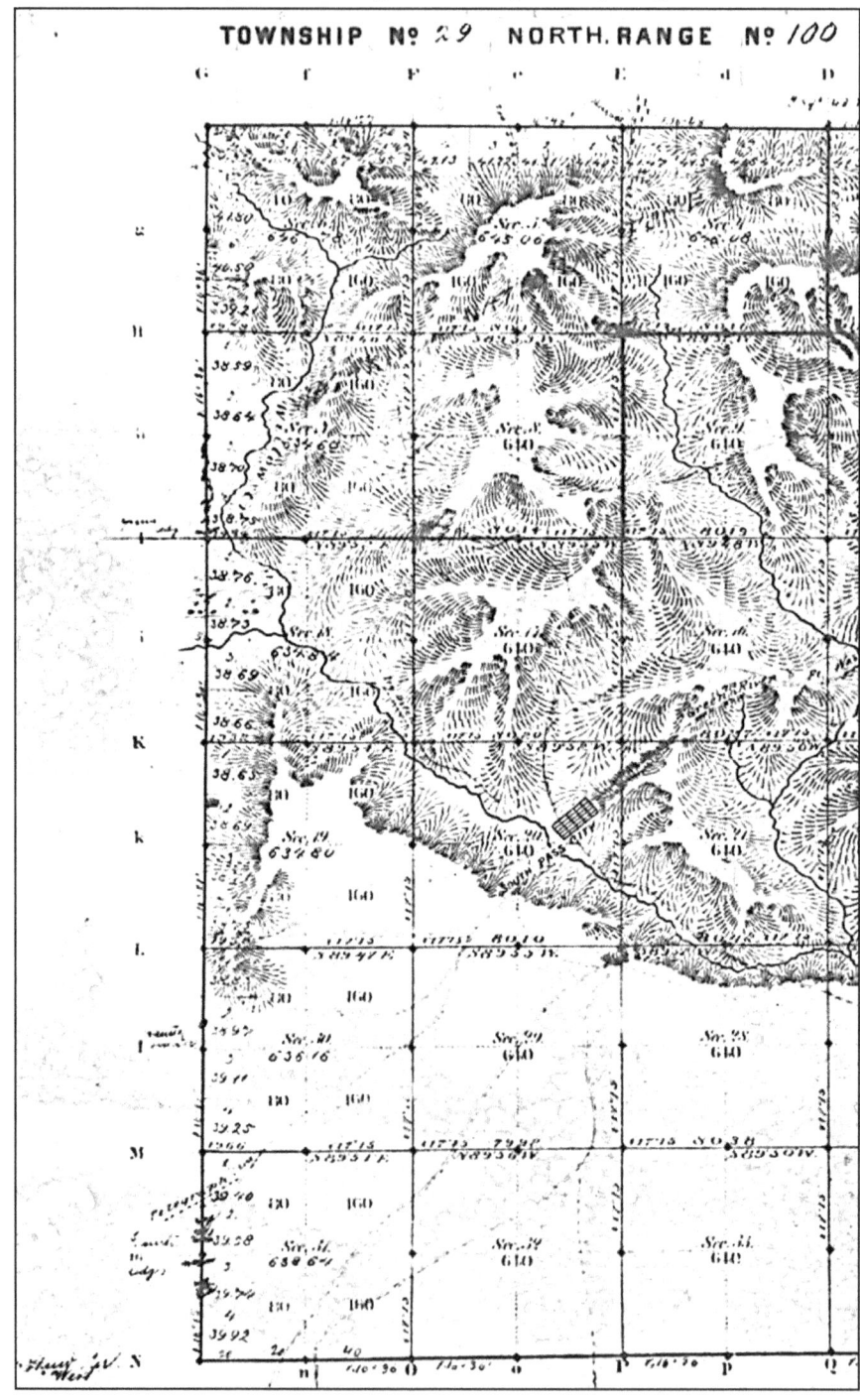

To locate Atlantic City, see tick marks around the map's edges on this page. Note Atlantic City is placed south of Rock Creek.

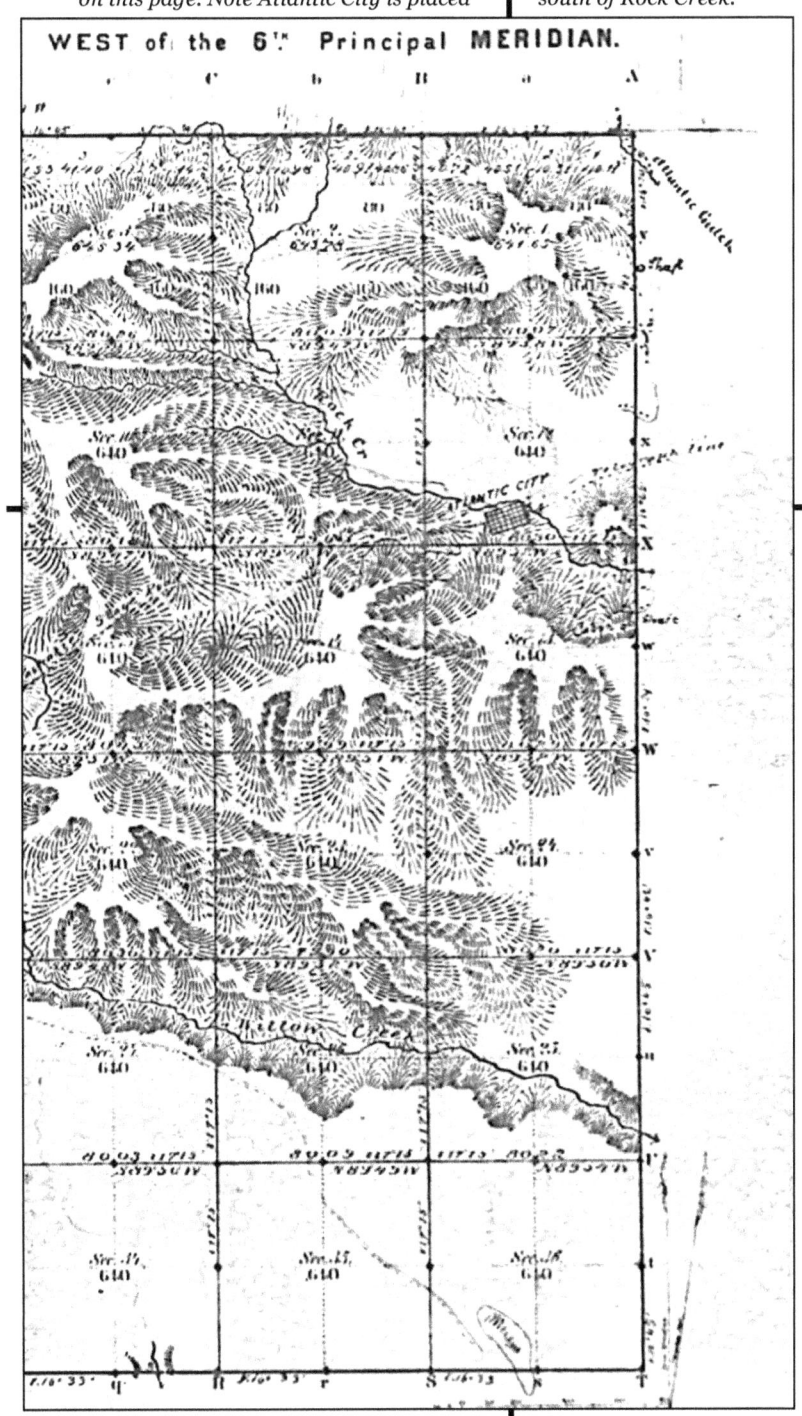

was all patented binding claims. So as that company closed up, they sold people title to their grounds. That's why most of the ground runs right along Rock Creek, because they patented the placer claim from the dredge companies that have been through. And they just within the last 3 to 5 years sold off the last of it. The company offices are out in New Jersey. But that's how people got title to the ground is through that mining company.[30]

Lyle Moerer worked at the US Steel Corporation's iron ore mine outside of Atlantic City in 1962 and owned the Atlantic City Mercantile. He said:

When we first bought, shortly after that, about a year after we bought, Timba-Bah Mining started selling lots, and they had the old survey of Atlantic City, and they started selling lots. And the lots were 25 by I think 125 or 150 feet long. They were selling at that time for $150 each, and in the first two years the lots really sold. All of the very good lots sold immediately, in the first two years.[31]

Lyle's phrase, "the old survey," caught my attention. I emailed Rick Reynolds, the grandson of the owner of the Timba-Bah Mining Company, and asked about the old documents.

He kindly responded he had helped his grandfather on occasion, and "doing much Timba-Bah correspondence. ... When [grandfather] passed, much of what was in his house was thrown out. ... I am sure we lost a lot of Timba-Bah documentation."[32]

THREE

Buried in Atlantic City, Specific Gravesite Unknown

When researching our Atlantic City pioneers and those who followed them, each person was sorted into chapters by their known or suspected burial sites.

Many were buried in Atlantic City. Some we know are buried in the East or the West Cemeteries. Some are buried in or around Atlantic City, but their specific burial site is unknown.

Many were buried away from Atlantic City in another city or state.

Through our 157 years, many death notices or news articles of a death stated only the person was "buried in Atlantic City." Many other articles made no mention of a burial place.

Those who have been "buried in Atlantic City" and a few who are strongly believed to be buried here are included in this chapter.

These people may very well be buried in the East Cemetery, which makes sense. For most intents and purposes it was the city burial ground though no formal recognition was located. The sheer number of unmarked graves supports this belief.

There are many who may have been placed in the West Cemetery. The numbers of unmarked graves there supports this too.

Perhaps some were buried in these hills where they were found, where they fell, or were buried on the property they owned at the time of their death.

Maybe they were indeed buried in Atlantic City but later disinterred to be returned to their families, like First Lieutenant Charles B. Stambaugh. He was killed in an Indian battle on May 4, 1870, and buried in Atlantic City, likely in the East Cemetery. Judging from one newspaper account, soon after burial he was disinterred in order to ship his body for burial in Lancaster, Ohio, on May 15.

Supporting the likelihood of disinterred remains in the East Cemetery is an overturned concrete base for a headstone. I believe the headstone was removed and the base was flipped out of the way in order to disinter the body. It's impossible to know whose headstone rested on this base.

For our people listed in this chapter, the only truth we know is they were buried in this vicinity, even if it was only temporary.

Atlantic City's main street. 1903. —Courtesy of the South Pass City State Historic Site and the Wyoming State Archives Photo Collection. Photographer: Joseph Elam Stimson. *The town dump was located below the road, as seen on the left side of the photograph.* —Source: John Mionczynski. October 16, 2024.

Belcher, Alvin E.
Unknown–February 12, 1909

Belcher had been traveling overland to Rock Springs with Granville T. Smith, Smith's unnamed wife, and their 3-year-old son when he was killed in a fight. Near Seven Lakes, about 18 miles northwest of Atlantic City in the vicinity of Atlantic Canyon, Belcher insulted Mrs. Smith's cooking. Apparently during the journey his habit was to insult her food.

This night, Belcher and Smith argued. In a wagon the argument escalated until Belcher grabbed a .45 Colt revolver, and Smith fought him. As they rolled out of the wagon the gun discharged.

The bullet penetrated Belcher's neck and caused his death.

Smith turned himself in to Atlantic City Deputy Sheriff Giessler. Twice the coroner's jury traveled the 18 miles through snow to where the dead man lay.[1]

After the inquest, Belcher was interred in Atlantic City as "he had no relatives in the country and is originally from New York State," according to an article in the *Wyoming State Journal* published on February 26, 1909.

The inquest found Granville Smith had committed felonious intent to kill Belcher because Belcher died not just from the gunshot wound. It also found Belcher had suffered a fractured skull.

The 24-year-old Granville Smith was charged. His 19-year-old wife and their child then became charges of the county.[2]

Smith's District Court trial began May 20, 1909. A week later, on May 28, he was acquitted.[3]

The knowledge of Belcher's killing came to light solely from a handwritten note added to a document compiled of information from the Wyoming 1870 Mortality Schedule: "Alvin Belcher – shot in scuffle. February 12, 1909."

Who wrote this note is unknown but based on the handwriting on cemetery photographs she gave me in 2015, I suspect Belcher's story was discovered and this note was written by notable historian Jean Mathisen Haugen.[4]

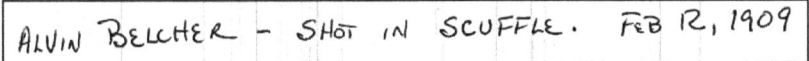

The scanned segment of the handwritten text of Alvin Belcher's death
–Courtesy of the Mount Hope Cemetery Office, City of Lander

Boston, James R.
Circa 1855–December 7, 1885

James' life and death came to light while reviewing a deeds record book in the Fremont County Courthouse. He died in Atlantic City on December 7, 1885.

This deed was signed on December 21, 1885, by James' parents Martha E. Boston and A. J. Boston, as James' heirs. They had signed the deed for James' "Fairview Lode Claim" in the Atlantic Mining District to transfer ownership to James' younger brother, G. C. Boston.[5]

James was born to parents Martha Elizabeth Dunlap and Andrew Jackson Boston "Abt 1855" in Liberty, Clay County, Missouri. They lived in Silver Creek, Mills County, Iowa.

In the 1870 Silver Creek, Iowa, census, James was listed as 14 years old.[6] G. C. Boston was James' next oldest sibling of eight children and the initials stand for either Grant Collier or George Carl.[7]

The Boston family has a family burial section, Section 1, Lot 185, in the Malvern Cemetery, Mills County, Iowa, where his parents and several siblings are buried.

James is not included there so I believe James was buried in Atlantic City.[8]

The deed signed by James Boston's parents to his brother G. C. on December 21, 1885.
–Courtesy of Fremont County Clerk. Land Recording Office.

Godfrey, John
Circa 1838–July 23, 1868

John's death was the first reported in Atlantic City when he died July 23, 1868. According to an article in the *Sweetwater Mines*, John was from Marysville, California, and died at the age of "about 30 years."

The newspaper article stated he died suddenly from hemorrhage of the lungs (possibly pneumonia or altitude sickness).[9]

I can't find any other information about him. With the article below seeking his friends or relatives and with no follow-up for any who were found to retrieve his body, I believe he is buried here in Atlantic City. If so, he may be the first to be buried in Atlantic City and possibly in the East Cemetery.

John Godfrey's death notice in the Sweetwater Mines newspaper, August 1, 1868.
—Courtesy of the University of Wyoming and Wyoming State Library

John Godfrey, Esq.. died very suddenly on July 23d, at Atlantic City, from a hemorrhage at the lungs. He had had several attacks of bleeding at the lungs, previous to the one that proved fatal, and that day felt much better than usual, but after the last attack only spoke once and then asked that a doctor be sent for. The deceased was formerly of Marysville, Cal., and any information his friends or relatives may wish to obtain concerning him, can be had by addressing John Frank, Esq., Hamilton City, Carter County, Wyoming Territory. (California papers please copy.)

Hayes, John Hammond
Circa 1852–May 3, 1899

According to the coroner's inquest, John died of natural causes on May 3, 1899, in his cabin in Atlantic City. Hayes had complained he had eaten something which didn't agree with him to Reginald C. Hunt, the Atlantic City drug store owner.

After a dose of Ipecac, the next day Hayes was found dead, thought to be from pneumonia.[10]

A newspaper account stated Hayes had lived in Atlantic City for six years, and before then he had lived in Lander a number of years.

> The deceased was 58 years old and was born in York state but little is known of his birth place or his parents. The funeral took place the 4th of May and was largely attended.

Since he was buried the day after he died, and he's not buried in Lander's Mount Hope Cemetery, it's reasonable to believe he was buried in Atlantic City.

Two weeks after his death, an article in the *Clipper* disclosed a rumor circulated from Denver and from Salt Lake City with the belief John had starved to death. This same edition contained an adamant denial from the people in this region. John

> had some money in his pockets, and should he have been out of money, the people of that land of peace and plenty wouldn't allow any one to suffer for the necessaries of life. The report certainly does these good people an injustice.[11]

Left: *John Hayes' death notice in the* Clipper *on May 19, 1899.* Right: *The report John Hayes starved to death was refuted in the same* Clipper *edition.*
−Courtesy of the University of Wyoming and Wyoming State Library

A Death at Atlantic City.

A sudden death occurred in Atlantic City May 3, 1899. This time king reaper called on Mr. John Hayes to visit the great unknown. Mr. Hayes had lived here six years, he came here from Lander where he had lived for a number of years, he was well and favorably known in Fremont county. The deceased was 58 years old and was born in York state but little is known of his birth place or his parents. The funeral took place the 4th of May and was largely attended. Mr. R. C. Hunt conducted the services in a very impressive manner.

Our friends of the mines are some what exercised over the report which was sent out from here to the Denver and Salt Lake City papers concerning the death of John Hayes in which was stated that it was the belief of the people that he had died of starvation. This they wish to deny for Mr. Hayes at the the time of his death had some money in his pockets, and should he have been out of money, the people of that land of peace and plenty would n t allow any one to suffer for the necessaries of life. The report certainly does these good people an injustice.

Kennedy, Michael
1865–November 18, 1913

On or about November 19, 1913, night watchman Michael was found dead in the Duncan mine by the oncoming day shift.

The inquest returned a verdict of natural causes, suspected heart failure, and his death was not from foul play.

He left behind a wife and seven children in Ireland.

He was an "above middle age" night watchman for the Duncan mine a mile west of Atlantic City, and he worked at various occupations around here. He was well liked and enjoyed a good reputation.

"The remains will be interred at Atlantic."[12]

From the death certificate of "Mickel" Kennedy, his year of birth was 1865. His birthplace was Cork County, Ireland. He was aged 49. His date of death is listed as November 18, 1913, and was caused by heart failure.

He was buried in Atlantic City on November 20, 1913.[13]

Also spelled Mickel.

Duncan Mine shaft house west of Atlantic City. 1974.
–Courtesy of the Wyoming State Archives. Photographer: Jack E. Boucher.

Knight, Emma
Circa 1868–October 1870

Emma was only two years old when she was killed by a horse in October 1870, as stated in the compilation of the Wyoming Mortality Schedule which ended in June 1870.[14]

Her parents were Martha Martina Marechal Knight and Alexander Knight.

The 1869 Wyoming territorial census for Carter County was taken "from May 29 to July 30, 1869." The listing included "Knight A," "Knight Martha," and "Knight Emma" (below).

Father Alexander was listed as 29 years old, his occupation was "restaurant," had lived in the US for 17 years, and had resided in the territory for 18 months. His place of birth was Canada and he declared his intention to become a citizen.

Mother Martha was 19 years old and had lived in the US her whole life, and she had resided in the territory for 18 months and declared to become a citizen.

Emma was 19 months old and, like her mother, had lived her whole life in the US and had an 18-month-long residence in the territory.[15]

Note: I do not believe the date of her October 1870 death is correct.

First, the above Mortality Schedule ended in June 1870, yet it listed Emma had died in October 1870. If Emma actually died in the month of October, her year of death could only be 1869.

Supporting this, the 1870 US census for Atlantic City (opposite page), which was enumerated on June 10, listed only Martha and Alexander. Emma was not listed. If she were living, excluding her from the census makes no sense.[16]

Since the 1870 Mortality Schedule is an official document listing her death as October 1870, it remains listed above.

Emma Knight and her parents, Martha and Alexander Knight, are listed on lines 1421-23 in the Wyoming territorial census for Carter County. 1869.
–Courtesy of Wyoming State Archives, Ancestry.com

Side note: On July 16, 2016, at the West Cemetery, dowser Don Schooley sexed the known and small mound of rocks near Baby Williams' grave. His rods indicated a burial and was dowsed as a female (designated F3 in chapter 7, *West Cemetery Burials).*

I wondered if this could be Emma and if she may have been the first burial in the West Cemetery instead of Lydia McCauley. Lydia was one year old when she died of unknown causes on April 19, 1874. Her grave has the white marble gravestone and hers is the oldest marked burial in Atlantic City.

Before I'd had even started this project, I came across a 1982 article in the *Wyoming State Journal.* It was the tragic story about Baby Williams and the Williams family told by Alma Williams Golliher. Alma was the older sister to Baby Williams who was born on February 26, 1903. The newborn boy was "born blue" and did not survive.

Alma recalled:

I knew there was a little grave up on that hillside—a little girl who died a long time ago had been buried there. I guess her mother wanted her where she could keep an eye on her, and I instinctively knew that was where they were going to put Mama's little baby.[17]

I wondered if this grave may have led to this grouping of little ones and this place becoming known as the "Children's Cemetery."

On October 9, 2016, Ann Noble dowsed this grave. Her rods confirmed the body was a female.

If this particular grave is not Emma or another little girl who died in those early days, then Lydia McAuley would certainly be the "little girl who died a long time ago."

Martha and Alexander Knight are listed on lines 30 and 31 in the US census but Emma is not. Other individuals are listed above and below them. June 10, 1870.
–Courtesy of Wyoming State Archives, Ancestry.com

29			Belmore Jeremiah	27	M/W	Teamster	·	500	Canada
30	105	86	Knight Alexander	30	M/W	Laborer	·	300	Canada
81			— Martha	21	F/W	Keeping house	·		Missouri
82	106	87	Viatt Philip E	27	M/W	Carpenter	·		Canada

Lamoureux, Oliver
Circa 1846–June 17, 1870

Some of the first pioneers to arrive in this region, Oliver arrived with brother Jules and his family, sister Lea, and brother Moses. Oliver was a younger brother of Jules Lamoureux who would become a notable figure in this area.

On October 16, 1868, Oliver Lameraux [sic], along with Sage Miller and James Pardee, signed an indenture to "B&S DeCory[sp?] & Co." for $100 for the "Quartz Bearing Lode known as … Smoker State Lode. Situated in the California Mining District."[18]

The June 1870 US census for Atlantic City listed Oliver as 24 years old, his occupation was teamster, and his place of birth was Canada.[19]

In a remembrance article printed in 1928, on that fateful day in 1870 Oliver was searching for horses which had gone missing. He headed to Point of Rocks and followed "the trail as far as the last crossing of the Sweetwater."

There he met John Pelon and they continued together toward Point of Rocks. Near a ranch, they were attacked by eight Indians. Oliver was killed but Pelon managed to escape but not before killing one of the attackers.

Additionally, the Indians who killed him "took from his body a fine gold watch, considerably [sic] money and two horses. … Lamoureaux [sic] was killed by a volley fired by the Indians in ambush."[20]

The next day, Lieutenant F. U. Robbenson, Troop B from the 2nd Cavalry, "sallied out to bring in the body of the slain Lamoreaux, which was accomplished and the remains of the brave frontiersmen were interred at Atlantic City on the following day."[21]

Other perspectives discovered about Oliver's death and burial place:
- He was killed by Indians on June 17, 1870, at Point of Rocks Road 30 miles south of Atlantic City, and was returned for burial by family—site unknown, but "near Atlantic City."[22]
- He was killed on June 17, 1870, at Burnt Ranch, about 10 miles south of Atlantic City, "while freighting from the UPRR [Union Pacific Railroad] at Point of Rocks across the Red Desert to Atlantic City."[23]
- In another reference to his murder in the *Wyoming State Journal* the article stated he was killed in 1871.[24]

Side note: This message was written by an unknown person on a document compiled from the Wyoming 1870 Mortality Schedule: "South edge of Harsh [sic] plot midde [sic] of fence Dick Larmareaux [sic]."[25]

Handwritten text added to the compilation of the 1870 Wyoming Mortality Schedule
–Courtesy of the Mount Hope Cemetery Office, City of Lander

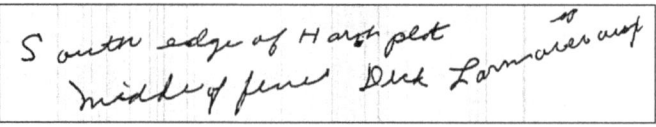

Oliver's brother Richard Lamoureux, born in 1865 and died in 1953, is buried in Lander (see chapter 8). I can find no person here who fits this name.

I can only guess the handwritten note states if this may be where Oliver was buried; however, there are no remnants of a marker in this area. Furthermore, the note locates the burial plot by a direction from the middle of the south fence of the Harsch plot. The confusing point is the first Harsch family member buried in the Harsch plot was Martha who died in 1899, 29 years after Oliver's death.

Also spelled Lameraux, Lamoreau, Lamoreaux, Lamoreux, and Lamoureaux.

Lamoreaux, Robert
Unknown–Unknown

A *Wyoming State Journal* article stated Robert Lamoreaux was buried in the Atlantic City cemetery.[26]

No records in the old Wyoming newspapers or various online genealogy sites revealed anything. I cannot find the relationship between Robert and the Atlantic City Lamoureux family.

Winn, Infant
Circa December 15, 1904–January 25, 1905

The infant boy was six weeks old when he died on January 25, 1905, of pneumonia. He was interred in the Atlantic City cemetery. His parents were Mrs. and Mr. John Winn.[27]

I can't help but wonder if he's buried in the West Cemetery, also known as the "Children's Cemetery."

Infant Winn's death notice on February 9, 1905 –Courtesy of the Pinedale *Roundup and Sharon Lass Field*

The infant son, six weeks old, of Mr. and Mrs. John Winn died on the 25th and was buried on 27th. Death was caused by pneumonia and it was only sick four days. The funeral was a sad affair and was well attended. "Safe in the Arms of Jesus," "Some Sweet Day," "What a Friend We Have in Jesus," and "Nearer My God to Thee," were the songs sung at the funeral. Interment was made in the Atlantic City cemetery.

FOUR

East Cemetery
Marked Burials and Family Plots

In the Old West, life was hazardous in the easiest of times, but even more so in the grueling days of an Old West mining camp. Indian attacks, accidents, illnesses, suicides, and murders were not uncommon. No matter the cause, deaths will happen and the bodies must be buried.

Exactly when the East Cemetery was established and its first burial is unknown. It's likely 1868 when Atlantic City officially sprouted and the first death occurred. On July 23, John Godfrey died of "hemorrhage of the lungs."[1]

The sloping land to the east of town was close enough to Atlantic City to be convenient. The cemetery is also easily observed from town to monitor for Indian or animal grave scrounging. It's a beautiful location to inter loved ones.

I first thought this cemetery had no name. While compiling information on people buried here, Hazel Carpenter's 1911 obituary stated she was "laid to rest in St. Andrew's cemetery, Atlantic City, Tuesday. February 21." This title was a surprising first. There has never been any known church ownership of any of the regional cemeteries.[2]

The Episcopal Church had a long and strong following in this region. Since the members had no official church structure, itinerant pastors and bishops preached in various locations around town. In 1911, concerted actions took place to build one. Hazel's family, the Carpenters, a renowned family in this region, was part of the planning, construction, and long-term support.

The following year, parishioners and townspeople built the log church. In 1913 the church was consecrated. Through the following years many people were buried in what was referred to as "St. Andrew's cemetery."[3]

In 2023, the humble little log church standing watch over the town took its place on the National Register of Historic Places.

Sometime in the 1960s or 1970s when the property was owned by the Timba-Bah Mining Company, the Bureau of Land Management (BLM) enclosed the cemetery's one acre with a post-and-rail fence.

Of the 91 buried or memorialized people here, only 19 have permanent markers. These 19 include buried remains or placed cremains. Those marked with permanent stones are made up of eleven males and eight females.

Left: *Easily visible is the Harsch family plot surrounded by a metal fence.* Right: *The leaning fence posts of an unknown male, M47, whose grave was confirmed by two dowsers. Beyond the Harsch family plot is the standing wood fencing and headstone of Alwin Heyroth (difficult to see through the pickets). Just beyond Alwin Heyroth's fenced grave is Casimer Melin's gravesite with its tall wooden fence and the spire of his wooden grave marker. The photographer faced west. 1956.*
–Courtesy of the Henderson Collection, South Pass City State Historic Site; and the American Heritage Center, University of Wyoming. Photographer: Harold A. Titcomb, A. E. Blair, or Barney N. Tibbals

A descendant of the pioneering Williams family wrote, "There are not many marked graves even though there was a lot [*sic*] people buried in the cemetery."[4]

Two non-grave entities included on the cemetery map and its index are the Carpenter family monument (Map Index #2) and the fenced plot enclosing the Harsch family (Map Index #9).

On June 7, 2016, a cadaver-seeking border collie named Blue, owned and handled by K. T. Irwin, downed in several locations indicating he scented human remains. Out of his seventeen downs, K. T. confirmed twelve human remains.

In this black-and-white cemetery's map, confirmed human remains are marked by black stars and the unconfirmed downs are white stars. In any color map confirmed remains are green stars and the unconfirmed downs are indicated by yellow stars.

One of Blue's confirmed downings, at the grave of Jared Williams (Index #21), was not listed on K. T's final report. Jared's confirmed finding was reasonably not included as his grave was already a known and named grave. I chose to include the black star on the map because, frankly, it tickled me to no end to do so. See Jared's story below why Blue's finding was cause for celebration.

Furthermore, I chose to include the five unconfirmed sites because K. T. stated it's possible there may be human remains there. The dog's actions led her to decide otherwise. By including these sites, perhaps future technology or information might be able to confirm or refute human remains.

K. T. and Blue's actions were videographed by John Mionczynski. Copies of the videos are held by the Atlantic City Historical Society and me. Gaps in the videos were caused by the need to replace filled SD cards and drained batteries.

To delve deeper about Blue and the abilities of cadaver dogs and specifics of his and K. T.'s actions and decisions see chapter 10.

On July 16, 2016, grave dowser Don Schooley corroborated the dog's confirmed detections. Of the 60 gravesites Don discovered with his six-foot-wide grid, he also determined the person's sex, 44 males and 16 females. He also verified there were remains at the Carpenter family stone (Map Index #2), later determined to be the placed ashes of Anne Carpenter Robinson (Index #20).

Then Don made a discovery about Miss Ellen Carpenter's grave (Map Index #4) which led to a jaw-dropping revelation which proves how our harsh weather and vegetation obscures gravesites.

Gravesite M35 is another site which must have been obscured. A second grave was dug so close to the first the bodies overlapped.

Each dowsed grave is marked with a wood stake. The top is painted blue for males and red for females, and has a hand-painted designator (i.e., M2 or F12).

On September 29 and October 9, 2016, dowser Ann Noble confirmed Don Schooley's findings and, with her three-foot-wide grid, found 12 more burials and determined the sex of the persons, 8 males and 4 females.

For more information on dowsing and how to dowse refer to chapter 11.

Once each grave was documented and platted on a map, a rough pattern emerged. I had suspected the early burials began in the southwest corner, then new graves were placed northward and eastward. Newer graves with headstones were placed more eastward.

In late August 2024, new neighbor Loretta Tschirgi studied the cemetery and its southwest area with fresh eyes and made a keen observation.

She stated the Atlantic City road heading north out of town traveled within 1,100 feet of the cemetery. She pointed out it made no sense to travel the mile-long and rough BLM two-track road that dropped down to the cemetery from the north. A short road would be a straight shot to the cemetery's southwest corner.

Approaching the cemetery on this cutoff road from the southwest made more sense since mourners could trudge behind the wagon bearing the coffin across the narrow Beer Garden Gulch and up the short drainage.

I remarked only a small bridge would likely be necessary to cross the spring at the gulch. If this were the case, mourners could stop at the hilltop at the southwest corner of the cemetery then bury their dead just immediately north of this trail. Thus, this would support my suspicion the southwest corner was the starting point of the early burials.

A study of an internet satellite mapping site revealed an overgrown and abandoned two-track road which ran due east from Beer Garden Gulch. If you didn't know about this road you'd likely never notice it.

The road traveled up the short hill and passed immediately south of the cemetery. This would place burials a mere 20 feet from the road. The road was so close, the southeast corner of the BLM's circa 1960s wood fence was constructed across the overgrown road. The road then continued east.[5]

In the 1907 photograph of the Carpenter Hotel on page 42, this road and the cemetery can be seen in the upper right corner.

A few weeks after Loretta's observation, Susan and David Layman led me up the hill on this old road. Susan and David know this gulch well. While overgrown, the remains of a two-track road are noticeable. The hill is a bit steep, but not steeper than many roads here and it's very short.

Susan believed this road was the original road to Camp Stambaugh and it would meet up with the current Stambaugh Loop Road further east.

At my mention of a bridge at the gulch, David asserted a driver could easily just drive through the gulch.[6]

A slightly different view from the previous photograph. June 1956. Foreground: The Carpenter family monument with Hazel Carpenter in the center. Behind the monument is the fallen fence remnants for grave F4, which was confirmed by a cadaver dog and its handler and two dowsers. Middle right: A metal fence surrounds the Harsch family plot.

Beyond the Harsch family plot are the standing fencing and headstone of Alwin Heyroth. His tan headstone is barely visible between the tall white headstones of Elizabeth and Philip Harsch. Beyond that is Casimer Melin's grave with his tall fence and the spire of his wooden grave marker with its intact cross jutting high and leaning slightly to the left.

The photographer faced west.

–Courtesy of the Henderson Collection, South Pass City State Historic Site; and the American Heritage Center, University of Wyoming. Photographer: Harold A. Titcomb, A. E. Blair, or Barney N. Tibbals

After the discovery of the dowsed graves and the sites were mapped, the row of graves in the west north-south line have no markers, likely from deterioration or from not having a marker at all. A few sites have remnants of thick wooden fences which once surrounded it to confirm there is a grave.

The exception was my 2021 find of Casimer Melin's 1875 wood grave marker (Index #15). With its letters still legible, it is no doubt a state treasure. It's now the earliest marked grave in this cemetery, a record which replaced Alwin Heyroth's 1884 marked grave (Index #13). Alwin's burial was the first to have a headstone, a sandstone marker which has severely eroded.

On the map, some burials were quite separate from the main grouping and were clustered in their own area. These suggested a small family, a couple, or those who may have been considered "outsiders."

Most burials here were in the Christian or Western method of burial with the head toward the west, feet to the east.

Six people were buried north-to-south and four were separated far from the main group. It's also possible some of these graves weren't burials at all but were placed or spread cremains.

Listed in this chapter are those buried in this cemetery with grave markers.

Technical information:

For each grave with a stone or wood marker, the text from those markers are included in the person's segment. The text in the original 2016 database served to document the marker's text and condition. Thus, the documentation of those texts are carried forward in this book.

Lat/Long coordinates indicate the spot at the headstones and the markers.

The coordinates' format is in the Degrees and Decimal Minutes format: DDD° MM.MMM' (WGS 84 map datum).

Map, East Cemetery

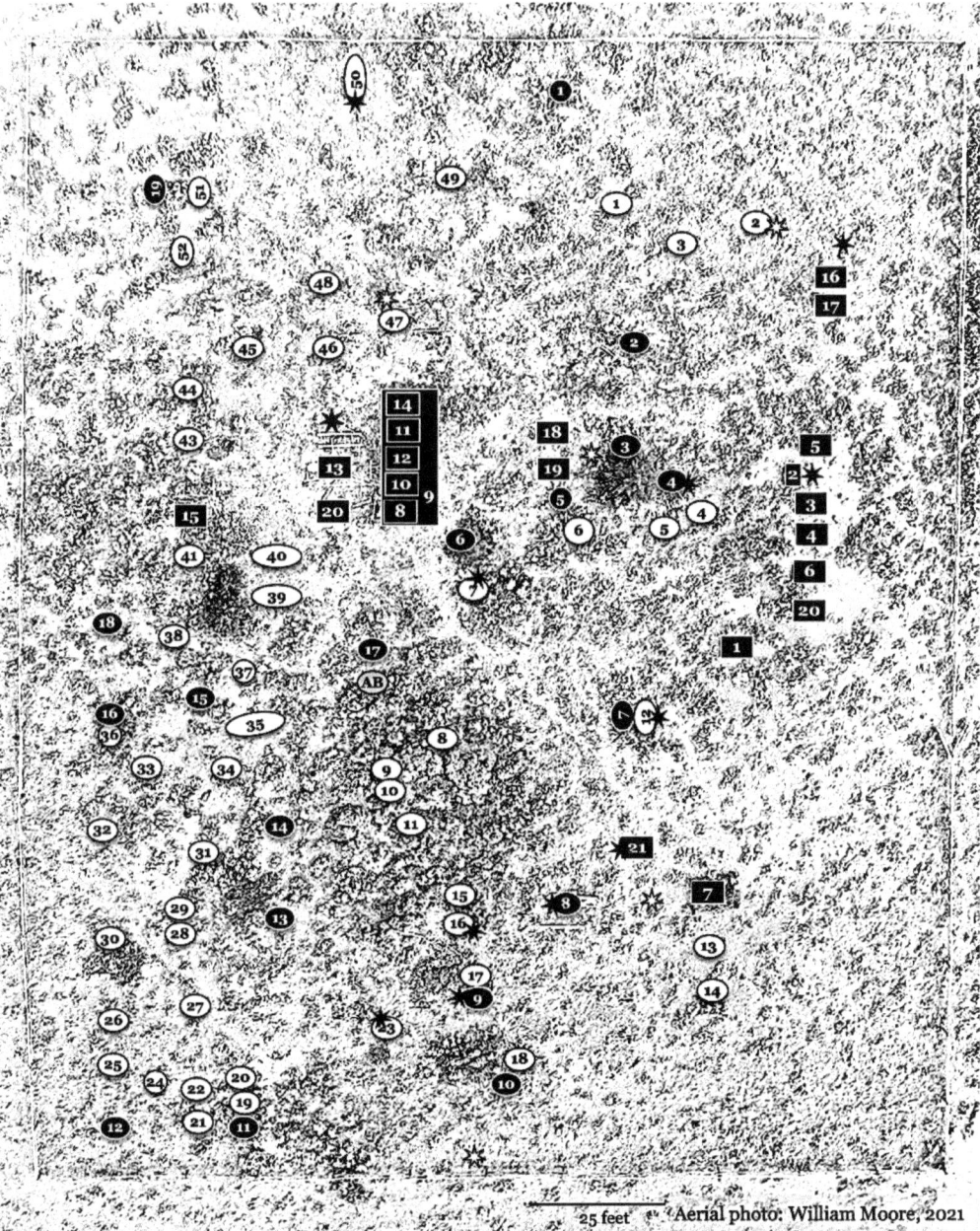

25 feet   Aerial photo: William Moore, 2021

A named person or marked by a permanent marker and its index number

A dowsed burial site of an unknown person. The site is marked with its index number and is colored by sex (white for male, black for female). Ovals depict the direction of burial; circles depict an infant or small child.

Cadaver dog downings (locations approximate)
✳ Confirmed human remains (12)
✶ Unconfirmed human remains (5)

(AB) Abandoned headstone base

35

Barbett, Joseph "Joe"
December 30, 1869–June 1, 1960

Joseph's obituary stated he came to Fremont County in 1904 and lived in Atlantic City year-round until five years before his death. In those final years he moved to Lander during the winters.[7]

His dates of birth and death and his place of birth, France, came from his death certificate.[8]

Joe was described as "a small, wiry and muscled fellow with short, white, curly hair made you notice how dark his skin looked."[9]

The US censuses for Atlantic City listed Joe three times. In 1910, "Barbett, Louis J." was 40 years old, single, and from France.

The 1930 census listed "Barbette, Joseph L." as 60 years old and a miner from France. In 1940 "Barbett Louis" was 70 years old, and he had an occupation of gold miner.[10]

Friend Jacob "Jake" Booth described Joe as "an extremely interesting man, ... He had a very colorful history."

Joe's photograph below was included in an article from the county Pioneer Museum's magazine *Wind River Mountaineer*. Its caption stated, "Joe Barbet sought gold in the 1920's-1930's as many had before him—with a gold pan."[11]

As a young man, Joe worked his way to Canada, remained and worked there for "travel money," headed to Colorado to work the mines, then came to this area.

During World War I, James Sherlock said:

Joe Barbett. Location and date is unknown.
–Courtesy of the South Pass City State Historic Site

Joe wanted to enlist in the Army. He was a very patriotic fellow and he wanted to enlist in the Army. And he wasn't very big, and he wasn't hardly suitable material, they figured. ... I think his height was one thing against him. ... And he told [the investigator] that he was a good man physically, and that he could take any of these "cheese-asses" sitting around here down and sit on them.[12]

Not accepted by the Army, Joe moved to east-central Wyoming to mine for chrome. After the war and "the bottom dropped out" for the price of chrome, "about 1920," he returned to Atlantic City.

Jake spoke how Joe

was quite instrumental in shaping some of the history with Timbah Bah [Mining Company] ... with geologic information that Timbah Bah was able to take advantage of in their successful placer operation down the creek. So they named a block, a group of their claims, after him, in recognition, the Barbette Gold Placer.[13]

Joe voted in the 1926 primary election as the 11th voter and for the Republican party. He voted in both 1930 elections. For the August 19 primary, he was the 19th voter and voted in the Republican party. For the November 4 general election, the poll book indicated "L. J. Barbett" was the 5th voter, was 62 years old, and born in France.[14]

Partner James Cassie (a notable 1900s Atlantic City fixture and included in this book) said, "Joe used to say, 'I tell you, brother, we were working fools!' "

When Joe was 64 years old, Zoie Green Fuller described his cabin as a

little cabin up, oh, like you're going to South Pass and you get on what we call a lily bend, ... when you're up on that high bench that goes between the two draws [Little Beaver Creek and Rock Creek]. ... That little log cabin along the left-hand side down there in the trees. ... Joe Barbett lived there for years. ... Then he moved over there on big Atlantic Gulch.[15]

Intrepid regional mailman Clarence Roe said he would

haul Joe Barbet [sic] to town. He'd go down one day and come back up the next day. He would always needs some tobacco and he'd cash his little check of ... thirty dollars a month for something ... and get some groceries.[16]

Joe suffered a traumatic injury when a truck accidently crushed him into an embankment which left him "terribly crippled" and with a severe stoop.[17]

Devoted friends Aurlein and Jake Booth watched over Joe. He had "claims up here," and he lived alone in the summer and "in town" in winter.

As Joe's back had been broken, Aurlein and Jake would help with "things" and fix him a meal. By this time, Joe was "close to 90 then."

After his death, Aurlein and Jake ensured Joe was buried and they provided his headstone.

Later, Aurlein and Jake realized Joe had left a will and gave Jake Booth all his possessions.[18]

To see more photographs of Joseph, see *Fine Gold, Changes,* and *Atlantic City Nuggets.*[19]

Also spelled Barbet, Barbette, Louis J., and Joseph L.

Cemetery map index #: 1
Headstone Lat/Long: N42° 29' 49.1" W108° 43' 17.9"

Headstone inscription:
JOSEPH BARBETT
1869 [engraved pick and shovel] 1960

Carpenter Family stone and plot

The Carpenter family members at this stone are buried in a north-to-south line. From the north lies Hazel Winifred Carpenter, the Carpenter family stone marks the unfenced family plot, Eleanor Louise Wallace Carpenter (Mother), Ellen McKisson Carpenter, James Herron Carpenter, and Anne Cecelia Carpenter Robinson.

In shocking moves, on June 7, 2016, during a cadaver-dog search of the cemetery, dog Blue twice "downed" in front of the family stone indicating he scented human remains. K. T. Irwin, the dog's handler, confirmed the remains. These actions were videographed and are in file *5 Search* with time stamps at 4:54 and at 6:58. In her final report, the dog handler's waypoint is #246.

Days later, on June 26, I called family matriarch and former long-term Atlantic City resident Betty Carpenter Pfaff to report this surprising find. She stated the ashes were of Anne Carpenter Robinson, one member of the family who arrived as a child in 1890. She died in New York in 1979. Her cremains were placed at this family marker. See Anne Robinson's segment below.[20]

On July 16, 2016, as dowser Don Schooley approached the line of Carpenters, I informed him the cadaver dog had twice downed on this site. He "witched" this marker, his rods indicated remains, and then indicated the remains of a female. The site number for his work is DF132.

Cemetery map index #: 2
Family stone Lat/Long: N42° 29' 49.4" W108° 43' 17.8"

The Carpenter family members in the family plot in this panoramic photograph. Left to right: *Anne Carpenter Robinson, James Herron Carpenter, Ellen McKisson Carpenter, Eleanor Wallace Carpenter, the Carpenter family stone, and Hazel Winifred Carpenter.*

Marker inscription:
CARPENTER

Carpenter, Eleanor "Nellie" Louise Wallace
January 9, 1865–August 18, 1930

This renowned hotel owner's obituary stated she was "one of the best known and most highly esteemed residents of that community."

Her obituary went on to state Nellie was born in Cleveland, Ohio. Her name was listed as "Nellie Wallace Carpenter" and she died as a "result of stroke." Her "Interment was made in St. Andrews churchyard cemetery" on August 20, 1930.[21]

She was described as "one of the 'kingpins' of the area." She was of English-Irish descent. Her father, William Wallace, had died of pneumonia contracted when he stood guard for Abraham Lincoln's casket.[22]

Nellie married Clarence Emmett Carpenter on August 3, 1882, at Fort Niobrara, northern Nebraska. Her first child, Ellen McKisson, was born on June 23, 1883, at Fort Sidney, west Nebraska. Anne Cecilia followed on January 18, 1885, and son James Herron arrived on January 12, 1887.

Fourth child Edith Lucy arrived on March 4, 1890, just months before the family departed Nebraska to head for Oregon.

Albert Wallace was born October 7, 1891. Hazel Winifred was born June 23, 1894. Clarence Emmett, Jr., arrived on January 14, 1897. Her final child, Ruth Marguerite, was born on December 13, 1902.[23]

The family had left Nebraska by covered wagon with their destination being Oregon. On their way, in October, fate dealt them a blow. They traveled the wrong road toward this area instead of their intended destination of Rock Springs. Their horses drank alkali water, which killed at least one or two horses. Stranded and with snow falling, Nellie broke up an old trunk for firewood.

Just as the family was running out of food and living in a tent, they were rescued by Henry Williams, a pioneer. He assisted the family to Atlantic City.

Eleanor Louise Wallace Carpenter. Undated.
–Courtesy of Betty Carpenter Pfaff and C. E. Carpenter IV

The family arrived and decided to remain. Their home became a "little old log house ... and it had a dirt roof on it." Clarence got a job in a mine and was often partially paid in flour. With the flour, Nellie opened the Carpenter Restaurant. In 1904 it grew into the Carpenter Hotel with guest rooms and a large dining room in a one-story log building.

Initially, this one-story structure had been built at Camp Stambaugh. After the camp closed in 1878, the Huff family removed the structure to Atlantic City and opened it as the Chief Hotel on Main Street. When the Huff family left Atlantic City, the Carpenters moved the building to its present location as the Carpenter Hotel.[24]

Nellie owned and ran this renowned hotel for 30 years.

She was confirmed into the St. Andrew's Episcopal Church on July 30, 1910, before the log church on the hill had even been built. She and other family members and locals helped raise funds for the hand-made structure which was built in 1912.[25]

Birthing and raising several children, running a hotel and a restaurant, and doing so in a tough environment, Eleanor must have been a strong woman.

Eleanor Carpenter, undated photos at the Carpenter Hotel, ca. 1910s.
–Courtesy of C. E. Carpenter IV

The Carpenter family held on in Atlantic City during one of its bust years. –Courtesy of the *Wind River Mountaineer*, November 8, 1918

The Carpenter family are holding down the hotel and waiting for the good times that will sometime come to the old camp. Among the old-time faces I saw Sam Spangler, Wesley Westfall, Jerrod Williams, Laurence Giessler and John Alberg.

She was "less than five feet tall with expressive brown eyes. ... and had an erect carriage and one thought 'lady' when you looked at her." From photographs of her, it's easy to believe "pretty hats were one of her weaknesses."[26]

The 1900 US census listed "Ellen" as born in January 1865, aged 35, and born in Ohio. In 1910, she was listed as head of household, aged 45, divorced, and a hotel keeper.

In 1920, the census listed "Nellie W. Carpenter" as head of household, aged 55, from Ohio, owned her mortgage-free home, and was a hotel keeper. In 1930, she was listed as head of household, aged 65, divorced, and had an occupation as "none," possibly because she had been afflicted by a stroke.[27]

Nellie also owned a mine, the Philistine, located 1.5 miles west-southwest of Atlantic City. On October 5, 1918, Nellie granted the Philistine mine to "The

The Carpenter Hotel and barn. Distant right: the Dexter mine and mill. Extreme upper right corner: Beyond the mill, the road from Beer Garden Gulch leads up to the East Cemetery. Distant center: The white Sypes house. My favorite part of this stunning photograph is the hanging laundry. 1907.
–Courtesy of the W. B. D. and Annette B. Gray Collection, American Heritage Center and the University of Wyoming. Photographer: W. B. D. Gray

Public" and the deed was filed in the courthouse the same day. The instrument used was "Notice to hold cl [*sic*]". Other listings in this book spelled out the "Cl" as "Claim."

The bulletin *The Atlantic Gold District and the North Laramie Mountains; Fremont, Converse, and Albany Counties, Wyoming* included an article about our region's geological formations and it also included specific maps. One map depicted local mines which included her Philistine mine, #73.[28]

For more photographs of Nellie from the early 1900s, see *Fine Gold*, chapter 17, page 2; chapter 41, pages 1 and 8; chapter 43, page 3; and chapter 52, page 5; and *Changes*, page 120.[29]

Nellie's official cause of death was determined to be cerebral hemorrhage.[30]

Side note: To nominate both her Carpenter Hotel and the St. Andrew's Episcopal Church to the National Register of Historic Places was my honor.

On December 12, 2012, the Carpenter Hotel Historic District was approved and took its deserved place as one of the "historic properties worthy of preservation" and "provides recognition of the property's historic significance."

On December 11, 2023, the St. Andrew's Episcopal Church for which Nellie worked toward also joined its prestigious place on the Register.[31]

Cemetery map index #: 3
Headstone Lat/Long: N42° 29' 49.3" W108° 43' 17.7"

Headstone inscription:

MOTHER
1865 – 1930.

Carpenter, "Miss Ellen" McKisson
June 23, 1883–May 13, 1961

Like any news article concerning Miss Ellen or the Carpenter Hotel, her obituary was front-page news. She was a legend in this region.

She was born at Fort Sidney in western Nebraska. She died in the Lander hospital and was buried in "St. Andrew's Cemetery" on May 17, 1961.[32]

This tiny indominable woman never married. She had been instrumental in raising funds to build the St. Andrew's Episcopal Church. She also performed repair work and ensured the minister had all items he needed for the services. Miss Ellen was confirmed on July 15, 1913, and taught Sunday School.[33]

Betty Carpenter Pfaff remembers her Aunt Ellen:

> She was the oldest of the children, ... she was the one who really got the least attention because she ... had taken care of all the other children. She's the only one that didn't go through college or go through high school. At that time high school was incorporated with college. She only went through the fifth grade and then she had to go home and take care of the other children and help her mother with feeding the boarding house. ...
>
> The one time she did go away, she went with my dad to Greeley [Colorado] one winter. My dad [James Herron Carpenter] and Aunt Annie [Anne Cecilia Carpenter Robinson], and I think it was Uncle Pete [Albert Wallace Carpenter] were in Greeley at that time and she was to housekeep for them and she took a sewing course, but she was called back that year

Miss Ellen Carpenter, left, *and Maude Huff Williams in a photograph on a postcard. Undated.* –Courtesy of the Henry Williams Family

because her mother had another baby ... and this was the history of her life, she's taken care of the babies that came along and her mother was sick after that so she more or less stayed home and took care of the Hotel. ...

She was engaged to Philip Harsch [Jr.] and this didn't come about. She changed her mind and decided not to marry him. ... Aunt Ellen liked to sing and liked to dance, and ... she did a lot of embroidery work and a lot of sewing. She was an excellent seamstress.[34]

After mother Eleanor died in 1930, Miss Ellen owned and managed the Carpenter Hotel. Friend Zoie Green Fuller recalled Miss Ellen:

She was so afraid of charging people. Golly, you'd pay probably four or five dollars for a meal down here [Lander] and you'd go up there and get it for a dollar. And a book was for 50¢. A room was for 50¢ or a dollar. ... But she was just too good, she didn't want to beat anybody. ... But she—a dollar for a good meal, everything you could eat, and set up family style.[35]

In Atlantic City's bust years, likely during the 1950s, the Carpenter Hotel was the only business open in the area and the population consisted of Miss Ellen and brother James.[36]

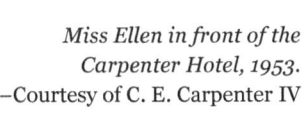

Miss Ellen Carpenter stands behind Edna Nations, ca. 1910.
−Courtesy of Betty Carpenter Pfaff

Miss Ellen in front of the Carpenter Hotel, 1953.
−Courtesy of C. E. Carpenter IV

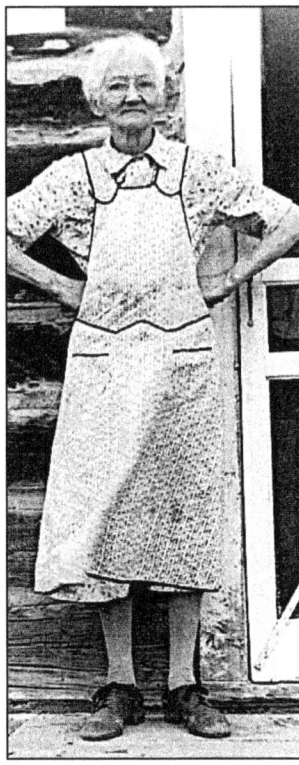

She was also the postmistress for Atlantic City. The post office was located in the hotel's dining room, across from the public telephone. In this room, she held dances. For music, Pearl Parker remembered:

I know we had a fiddle. Somebody fiddled, and somebody played a Jew's harp. ... We used to dance those old fashioned dances. Virginia Reel, and all that kind of stuff.[37]

Miss Ellen's hard work ethic, generosity, fearlessness, and kindness were renowned. She had earned authority and respect.

When she spoke, people listened. There's one springtime tale of when she heard the county road graders were coming to open the roads of the snow drifts. She made them hold off.

Mailman Clarence Roe said:

They'd be visitors from out of town in the summer time. In the winter she'd say, "Don't have nobody come. Don't have them open the road till I get my house cleaned."

I said "I'll probably walk another month then."

"Well, you won't mind," she said. "I don't want them down here while I'm oiling my floors."[38]

For more photographs of Miss Ellen, see *Fine Gold*, chapter 17, page 2; chapter 29, page 4; chapter 41, pages 8 and 9; chapter 45, page 2; chapter 52, page 5; with Miss Ellen as post mistress in chapter 23, page 5; and *Changes*, pages 115, 116, and 120.[39]

Miss Ellen voted in the special election on May 10, 1921. She was the 7th voter. In the primary election on August 17, 1926, she was the 20th voter and she voted in the Democratic party. She also voted in the November 4, 1930, general election as the 30th Atlantic City voter.[40]

The 1900 census listed her as born in June 1883, aged 16, and was born in Nebraska. In 1910 she was aged 26, and a dress maker. The 1920 census listed Miss Ellen, aged 36, and hotel cook.

In 1930 she was at age 47 and a hotel manager. The 1940 census listed her as head of household, 57 years old, and her occupation as (illegible) hotel.[41]

Zoie Green Fuller said of Miss Ellen, "She was a wonderful person. She was good to everybody. ... She'd give them the last dollar she had and the last cookie she had in the house."

Nearing the end of her life and suffering from poor health, Miss Ellen became very ill and was hospitalized in Lander.

Clarence Roe described the effort to get help for this strong woman. "She ran [the Carpenter Hotel] all the time until she had to go to the hospital. They hauled her out in the truck. We shoveled the road all the way from the hotel all the way up on that hill."

Miss Ellen Carpenter in front of the Carpenter Hotel, ca. 1920s.
—Courtesy of C. E. Carpenter IV

Zoie worked in the hospital laundry, and she visited Miss Ellen who was "sick at her stomach." Zoie

> held her and had my arms around her, holding her. She just kind of went like that and I thought, oh good, she's going to rest, but she was dead. So it was after all the years and all we went through that I would be with her when she died, which I was glad of.

Clarence Roe recalled, "I was at her bedside when [she] died down at the hospital. Zooie [*sic*] Fuller and I were there when she passed away that day. She had an awful time."[42]

Miss Ellen's death certificate stated her cause of death was "myocardial failure, acute," and she had suffered from a heart-wrenching seven contributing conditions which led to the death of this small, iconic powerhouse.[43]

Special notes:

1. While Bob and I owned the Miner's Delight Inn (formerly the Carpenter Hotel), former guests and even one former worker told priceless stories of Miss Ellen and the hotel's history.

One elderly former worker described her duties back in her day. As the youngest and newest worker for the hotel, her job was to empty the chamber pots and to sanitize them with boiling water.

Quite a few boarders and friends spoke of Miss Ellen's strict teetotalling, likely as a result of her father's alcohol use.

My favorite story came from a guest of Miss Ellen's who boarded at the Carpenter Hotel in 1957 for three weeks while working on a drilling crew. Electricity hadn't yet arrived in Atlantic City, so the hotel still used lamps.

In 2008 John returned to Atlantic City and stayed in the renamed Miner's Delight Inn. This time he brought his companion Bonnie.

He spoke how "Missus Carpenter" and her brother Jim (James Herron Carpenter) changed his life. Their ethics of decency, kindness, and of hard work impacted him so much he had always felt compelled to return.

When John arrived, he was thrilled. His memory of his time with the Carpenters was vivid. He walked into the one-story structure from the south end, which then and still does house the dining room. He headed straight for the north portion which had, back in the day, contained the six bedrooms with a hallway down the center. Now, this space housed the inn's saloon, the guest kitchen, and two bathrooms.

John immediately walked over to the west wall's center window, stopped, raised his arms, and proclaimed, "I'm standing in my room!"

He recalled when Missus Carpenter opened the bedroom door to show him into his room, rats scurried away.

Seeing John's shocked reaction to the rats, Miss Ellen calmly opened a drawer and handed him some corks from the drawer. "Just plug the holes. It'll take them a couple days to chew through."

Miss Ellen was a strict teetotaler and would not allow any alcohol on her property. One day John had a case of beer with him.

With arm raised pointing toward South Pass City Miss Ellen commanded, "If you want to drink, take it to South Pass."

John carried his case of beer to South Pass City.

He recalled he asked Missus Carpenter where he could take a bath. Being on a drilling crew was a dirty business.

Miss Ellen pointed to Rock Creek. "In the creek."

John said those were the coldest baths he'd ever taken. That evening he and Bonnie walked to the Atlantic City Mercantile for dinner. When they returned, John said as he walked over the bridge he got the shivers just remembering those cold baths.

2. On July 16, 2016, grave dowser Don Schooley determined Miss Ellen's grave was six feet wide to which he stated made no sense.

I told him information from an earlier conversation with Betty Carpenter Pfaff, Miss Ellen's niece.

When Miss Ellen's grave was being dug in 1961, the diggers *discovered the body of a red-haired woman.*

Shocked to my core, I asked her what had happened to the woman. She replied, "I don't know, but my brother Wally (James Wallace Carpenter) was one of the grave diggers."

With this information, Don suspected the grave was dug wider in order to remove the first woman's remains.

Two months later, I happened to be in a gathering with Wally. I asked him about the story and his finding her body. He said, "Yeah, that actually happened." I asked what had happened to her. He said he didn't know and "the other men took care of her and they're both gone."[44]

*Miss Ellen Carpenter in her
kitchen, ca. late 1950s.
Photographer: Paul Newman.
–Courtesy of C. E. Carpenter IV*

3. The Carpenter Hotel Miss Ellen and mother Eleanor were devoted to and worked so hard for was recognized and listed on the National Register of Historic Places. For 13 years Bob and I had the honor to own this amazing place and I felt great pride to nominate it.

The Carpenter Hotel Historic District took its deserved place as one of the "historic properties worthy of preservation" which provided "recognition of the property's historic significance" on December 21, 2012.

Additionally, the humble log structure of the St. Andrew's Episcopal Church, cherished by Miss Ellen, took its place on the Register on December 11, 2023.[45]

Cemetery map index #: 4
Headstone Lat/Long: N42° 29' 49.3" W108° 43' 17.7"

Headstone inscription:

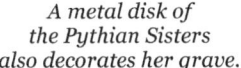

ELLEN McKISSON
1883 – 1961

*A metal disk of
the Pythian Sisters
also decorates her grave.*

Carpenter, Hazel Winifred
June 23, 1894–February 12, 1911

Born in Lander to Nellie and Clarence E. Carpenter, owners of the Carpenter Hotel, Hazel suffered from heart trouble. In late 1910, Hazel's mother took her to California's lower altitude in an attempt to improve her health. After a brief improvement Hazel died suddenly in Long Beach. She was only 16 years old.[46]

Older brother James traveled to California to assist in bringing her home. Dr. August Schepp, Episcopal Church rector in Lander, left Lander at 6 a.m. to officiate her funeral. Because of deep snow and drifts reaching 30 feet, the trip took two days. James met them at the Old Stage Station, above the "Boss Tweed Ranch." They arrived the next day in sub-zero weather. This information came courtesy of Charlotte Dehnert with her private letter.[47]

In Hazel's obituary, the article was the first to refer to this cemetery as "St. Andrew's cemetery." The St. Andrew's Episcopal Church's "Record Book for Atlantic City" listed she was interred in "St. Andrews' Cemetery" on February 21, 1911. Despite the harsh conditions, 62 people attended her funeral.[48]

Right: *In front of the Carpenter Restaurant, Hazel Carpenter holds the hand of Maurice "Casey" Lewellyn;* background: *her father, Clarence E. Carpenter, Sr. Ca. 1903.*
–Courtesy of Betty Carpenter Pfaff and Miss Ellen Carpenter. The source for the names is *Fine Gold*, chapter 29, page 1. See footnote 48 for more information.

Below: *Hazel Carpenter with brother "Bud" [Clarence], ca. 1905.*
–Courtesy of C. E. Carpenter IV

The 1900 census listed Hazel as born in June 1895 [*sic*], aged 4, and born in Wyoming. The 1910 Census listed her as aged 15.[49]

Betty Carpenter Pfaff's book *Fine Gold* devotes chapter 17 to Hazel and includes more photographs of her in chapters 29 and 52.

Hazel wrote lovely poetry and stories about her life. Two poems are included in *Fine Gold*'s chapter 14, page 11.

Personal note: In the early years of the original 2016 database, it only included photographs of the markers or headstones to document its appearance and condition. Then, only photograph of Hazel I had seen was in Betty Carpenter Pfaff's book *Fine Gold*. The photograph showed a lovely young woman with a solemn countenance which was likely the norm for photographs. Later, after an epiphany of adding photographs of our people to this document, discovering and including these photographs of her happy and playing were so moving.

Left: *Hazel Carpenter with baby sister Ruth, ca. 1905. Hazel with a calf in front of the Carpenter Hotel barn, ca. 1909.*
–Courtesy of C. E. Carpenter IV

Cemetery map index #: 5
Headstone Lat/Long: N42° 29' 49.4" W108° 43' 17.7"

Headstone inscription:

HAZEL WINIFRED
1894 – 1911.

Carpenter, James "Jim" Herron
January 12, 1887–February 2, 1968

As with any news about the Carpenters, Jim's obituary was front-page news in the *Wyoming State Journal*. Born in Fort Robinson, northwest Nebraska, he was 3 years old when he and his family arrived in Atlantic City in 1890.

Jim died in Kemmerer. He was buried in the Atlantic City's East Cemetery on February 5, 1968. His was the final burial in Atlantic City.

Renowned for his knowledge of local geology, history, hunting, and fishing, his helpfulness is evident as told in numerous books and oral histories.

The 1900 US census listed him as born in January 1887, aged 13, and born in Nebraska. The 1910 census listed him as aged 23, single, and a hotel keeper.[50]

In 1917, he registered for the draft. A year later on July 5, 1918, he was conscripted as a private in the infantry and stationed at Camp McArthur in Texas. By August 16, he was promoted to sergeant. When the Army demobilized after World War I, Jim was honorably discharged on January 24, 1919. His character was rated "Excellent."[51]

The 1920 census listed James, aged 32, and as a miner in a quartz mine. In 1930 he was listed as head of household, aged 43, married, and a caretaker for a gold mine. The 1940 census listed him as 50 years old, single, and a watchman for a gold mine.[52]

He voted in the August 17, 1926, primary election as the first voter and also served as Clerk of the election. He served as judge in the November 4, 1930, general election, was 43 years old, born in Nebraska, and voted 19th.[53]

James Carpenter in June 1938
–Courtesy of the Betty Carpenter Pfaff Collection, South Pass City State Historic Site

James Carpenter is assessor in our vicinity this year.

James Carpenter as the Atlantic City assessor.
–Courtesy of the *Wyoming State Journal*, June 27, 1928

In the 1962 elections, in the primary, James served as Election Judge and Clerk of Elections. In the general election he was listed as voter #2, though he was included on the supplemental "List of Absent Voter Ballot Envelopes." Possibly, he relinquished his unused absentee ballot in order to vote in person or, depending on the state law at the time, he may have turned in his absentee ballot at the polling place.[54]

James died on February 2, 1968. His death certificate stated he died aged 81 years old, and he was a gold miner. His cause of death was coronary occlusion, a sudden death.[55]

To see more photographs of James, see *Fine Gold*, chapter 1, pages 1 and 2; chapter 25, page 2; chapter 30, page 3; chapter 42, page 2; chapter 45, page 2; and chapter 52, page 5; and *Changes*, pages 113, 115, and 116.[56]

In celebration of electricity coming to Atlantic City, James holds an electric toaster. 1958. The caption [bottom left] *reads "Jim Carpenter beside stove from Camp Stambaugh."*
–Courtesy of Betty Carpenter Pfaff

James Carpenter and older sister Miss Ellen Carpenter in a quiet moment on the Carpenter Hotel porch. 1954. –Courtesy of the Henderson Collection, South Pass City State Historic Site, and the American Heritage Center, University of Wyoming. Photographer: Harold A. Titcomb, A. E. Blair, or Barney N. Tibbals

Cemetery map index #: 6
Headstone Lat/Long: N42° 29' 49.2" W108° 43' 17.7"

Headstone inscription:
JAMES HERRON CARPENTER
1887 – 1968

Garrison, John
August 23, 1841–March 23, 1913

A pioneer to the region, in 1897 as the locator John was granted the water rights to a "stream named Big Hermit Creek for mining and milling purpose, ni [sic] connection with the King Soloman [sic] Mine."[57]

He was listed in the 1900 census for South Pass City, which stated he was head of household for wife Katherine. There are discrepancies between the censuses and his headstone carvings.

The census included he was born in August 1848 (the headstone states 1841), was 51 years old (his headstone's 1841 would make him about 59 years old). He and Katherine were in their first marriage and had been so for eleven years. His father had been born in New York and his mother in Canada. He was a quartz miner.

Katherine was stated to be 55 years old, was born in March 1845, and was born in New York to parents born in Pennsylvania and Vermont.[58]

The discrepancies continue in the following 1910 census for South Pass City. He was listed as head of household, 61 years of age, had been married for 19 years, was born in Canada to Canadian parents, immigrated to the US in 1873, and was a quartz miner.

The next line, listed wife Catharine Garrison, aged 77 (having aged 22 years in 10 years), was on her second marriage and she and John had been married 19 years, was born in Ireland to an English father and a mother born in Scotland. She immigrated to the US in 1849, and her profession was "none."[59]

To determine if John's wife Catharine was a second marriage, a search through Fremont County's *Marriage Record* books *A*, *B*, and *C*, starting in 1884 through November 4, 1914, revealed nothing.

Pioneer Passes Away.

John Garrison, one of the old timers of the South Pass-Atlantic City region, died at Atlantic City on Sunday, March 23. His demise was caused from the ailments of old age. Mr. Garrison was one of the men who were in the camps at the time when they were booming and his faith has never wavered for an instant, but he has always waited for the rehabilitation of the camps and the making of one of the best camps in the west.

John Garrison's notice of death in the Miner, *March 28, 1913*
—Courtesy of the University of Wyoming and Wyoming State Library

In 1912, John had traveled to Lander with L. L. Giessler "for a few days to enjoy the sights and see if some of our local Drs. couldn't put him on his feet again."[60]

The death of this pioneer came on March 23, 1913. The notice stated "his demise was caused from the ailments of old age. ... and he was one of the men who were in the camps at the time when they were booming."

For his funeral, "Ed. Farthing, representing the local lodge of Odd Fellows left Tuesday for Atlantic to take part in the funeral arrangement of John Garrison who died Sunday."[61]

The chain links and letters carved into John's headstone signify his membership in the Independent Order of Odd Fellows. The initials F, L, T stand for Friendship, Love, and Truth. The headstone is held up by wire because the base of the headstone has a vertical crack, likely caused by swollen, rusted rebar.

His plot is surrounded by a wrought iron fence with a gate.

Five years after his death, in 1918 weekly legal articles in the *Wyoming State Journal* reported a "Notice of Forfeiture" of John's claims by a partner with the Houdan Group of claims." It appears the individual was seeking reimbursement for payment of $266.67 from John's estate to hold the claims. The article referred to the location of the mining claims "on Pages 248, 249, 250, 251, and 252 in the office of the County Clerk of said County."[62]

John Garrison's fenced burial plot is at the cemetery's southeast corner. Photograph taken while facing southwest. 2024.

Note: In the search for a possible second marriage, a John C. Garrison, on June 1, 1908, married Rose Simmons in Thermopolis where they both resided. Other than this name I see no correlation between the two families.[63]

Cemetery map index #: 7
Headstone Lat/Long: N42° 29' 48.6" W108° 43' 18.0"
Footstone Lat/Long: N42° 29' 48.6" W108° 43' 18.1"

The marble base is engraved [hidden by vegetation]
GARRISON

Headstone inscription:
[engraved three chain links and the
letters F, L, T within the links]
JOHN GARRISON
AUG. 23, 1841
MAR. 23, 1913
Footstone: It's barely visible in the vegetation and it is unknown if the stone has any engraving.

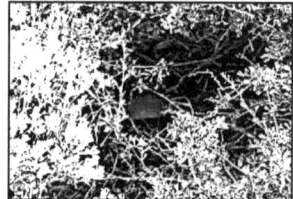

Gustafsen, Peter Magnus
April 5, 1868–December 25, 1949

Peter's death was reported on the front page in the *Wyoming State Journal*. He was the son-in-law of pioneers Elizabeth and Philip Harsch, and he joined them in the Harsch family's fenced plot.

Peter emigrated from Norway in 1904 and arrived in Atlantic City. He worked at the Dexter mill in Atlantic City.

Soon after his arrival, he became involved in many activities around the area. With his skill as a driller, he won South Pass City's Fourth of July drilling contest in 1904 or '05 with teammate Michael "Emmett" Connell. The drilling stone now stands near South Pass City's Masonic Lodge #2.[64]

As ice sawyers, he and sawing partner Emmett were an undefeated team.

James Sherlock described Peter as a "kind of hot headed fellow, but he was a real good honest person. ... A likeable man that loved to play cards ... and he was a good solo player."[65]

When Peter was 44 years old, he married 28-year-old Martha Elizabeth Harsch on February 7, 1912. The ceremony took place at the bride's home in Atlantic City.

He and Martha had no children.[66]

For a time, Peter and his sister-in-law Lenora Harsch Hunt lived with her older sister Katherine and husband Emmett and their four children in De Pass, Wyoming. While they were all there, Peter assisted Emmett at Copper Mountain to sink a "very deep shaft." De Pass is 80 miles northeast of Atlantic City, east of Copper Mountain.[67]

He was also a member of the South Pass City Wyoming Masonic Lodge #2.[68]

Peter was civic minded. He was the 8th voter in the May 10, 1921, Atlantic City special election. During the August 17, 1926, primary election, he served as Clerk of the election and was the second voter. He also performed as Election Judge in the November 6, 1928, general election. Peter signed the Oath of Judges and spelled his last name "Gustofson."[69]

Peter Gustafsen and Martha Harsch's Certificate of Marriage. 1912.
–Courtesy of Fremont County Clerk's Office. Land Recording Office.

In both the 1930 primary on August 19 and the general election on November 4, Peter voted and also served as Election Judge.[70]

The 1910 census for South Pass City listed him as aged 42, single, a quartz miner, and he immigrated to the US in 1882 from Norway.[71]

In 1920, the census for Atlantic City listed him as head of household, aged 52, immigrated from Norway in 1889 and naturalized in 1895, and a gold miner. The 1930 census listed him as head of household, aged 62, married, immigrated in 1883, and a gold miner. In 1940, he was listed as 72 years old, and the space under "Occupation" was blank.[72]

He died in the family home on Christmas Day, 1949. His cause of death was coronary occlusion with an antecedent cause of arteriosclerosis.

According to his death certificate, Peter's birthplace was Nancy, Norway.[73]

Most often spelled Gustafson, and also spelled Mangus.

Cemetery map index #: 8
Headstone Lat/Long: N42° 29' 49.4" W108° 43' 18.6"

Headstone inscription:

PETER M. GUSTAFSEN
1868 – 1949

IN LOVING
MEMORY

Harsch Family plot, surrounded by wrought iron fence and gate

Burials within the fence are in a north-to-south line.

From the north, they are Lenora Angelina Harsch Hunt, Henry William Harsch, Philip Harsch, Elizabeth Schulka Harsch, and Peter Magnus Gustafsen.

In 2015, Central Wyoming College anthropologist William Elder studied the fence. He pointed out the original fence appeared to have been placed around the first family burial, Elizabeth, who was buried in 1899.

As burials were added, the north and south fence sections were moved outward. A remnant of a metal brace juts from the ground between Philip and Henry's burials sites.

The expanded sections were filled in with newer fencing.

Cemetery map index #: 9

The Harsch family plot in a panoramic photograph. Left to right: *Peter Gustafsen, Elizabeth Harsch, Philip Harsch, Henry Harsch, and Lenora Harsch Hunt. 2024.*

Harsch, Martha Elizabeth Schauke Hess
Circa 1844–August 25, 1899

The death of pioneer Martha was reported in the *Wind River Mountaineer* on August 29, 1899. "She had been ill for several months previous and had lately contracted typhoid fever."[74]

She was said to have arrived in South Pass City in 1868. In 1869, she married Frederick Hess. He worked a mine in Big Hermit Gulch west of Atlantic City along with partner Philip Harsch.

The discovery of the 1870 census for Hermit Gulch was exciting. "Eliza" Hess was 20 years old and was "keeping house." She was born in Prussia. Specifically, son Henry Harsch's death certificate stated his mother was from Hesse Castle, Germany, a Prussian province.

Listed above Martha on the census is Frederick Hess, listed as head of household. He was 33 years old, a miner, and from "Baden," Germany.[75]

After this June 12 census, Martha had a daughter, Katherine "Kate" Elizabeth on the Big Hermit Gulch.[76]

Between 1870 and 1872, Hess abandoned Martha and Kate at Fort Washakie. Martha was pregnant with second daughter Caroline "Carrie," who was born on Christmas Day in 1872. Martha worked as a laundress after he deserted them. Family lore stated Hess was "a poor husband, neglectful and mean of disposition." One terrifying instance occurred when "Hess attempted to take the child Caroline away from her mother after the separation but failed."[77]

Martha Elizabeth Harsch. This portrait is half of a joint portrait with husband Philip Harsch.

The back of the portrait is dated 1869, which I do not believe is correct. In 1869, she married Frederick Hess and they were said to have divorced in 1872. On June 30, 1873, she married Philip Harsch.
—Courtesy of the Fremont County Pioneer Museum

Family lore also stated Martha divorced Hess in Green River and she returned to South Pass City. For newly discovered information on her divorce case, see Note #2.

In South Pass City on June 30, 1873, she married Philip G. Harsch, Hess' former mining partner. The marriage certification stated Martha was 30 years old (three years earlier the 1870 census stated she was 20 years old) and he was 38 years old. Another source stated they were married on June 21, which is an error. Martha's two daughters, Kate and Carrie, took the Harsch name.[78]

Martha settled into her new life with Philip. She gave birth to son Philip Junior on June 12, 1874. On April 28, 1876, second son Henry William followed while they lived at Camp Stambaugh.[79]

After the family moved to nearby Atlantic City in 1876, three daughters followed: Lenore "Nora" on October 30, 1881; Martha on December 16, 1883; and Anna Regina "Jean" on October 26, 1885.

Family members listed on the 1880 Atlantic City census was Philip at 44 years of age, Martha was 35 years old from Hesse Cassel, Katie was 10, Carrie was 8, Philip was 5, and Henry was 4 years old.[80]

Back in 1869, the Wyoming territorial legislature granted women the right to vote. In the November 2, 1880, general election, Martha was the 14th voter in Atlantic City's precinct. She was the 9th voter in the midterm election on June 14, 1881.[81]

In a 1980 article about Fremont County cemeteries, Myra Connell spelled Martha's maiden name as "Schaake."[82]

Elizabeth Schauke and Philip Harsch were married in South Pass City on June 30, 1873.
–Courtesy of the Sweetwater County Clerk and the South Pass City State Historic Site

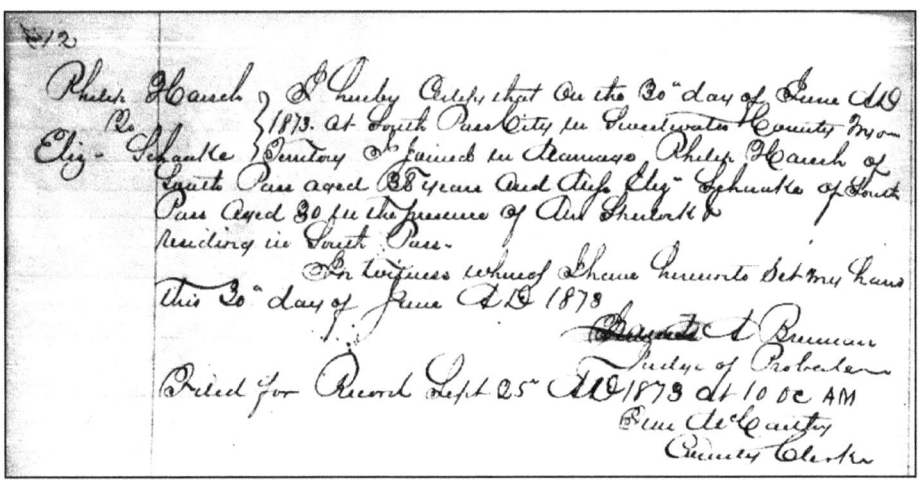

ATLANTIC.

Mrs. Philip Harsch has opened the Atlantic hotel. Mrs. Harsch is thoroughly competent and will give the traveling public satisfaction. Everything is neat and clean and the table is unsurpassed and the beds are first-class.

Elizabeth Harsch opened the Atlantic Hotel to great reviews. –Courtesy of the *Clipper*, July 29, 1898, and the University of Wyoming and Wyoming State Library

Mrs Philip Harsch is running an eating house in Atlantic.

Elizabeth Harsch opened a small restaurant. –Courtesy of the *Wind River Mountaineer*, September 7, 1898

Her death notice in the *Mountaineer* also reported Martha "was respected and beloved by all who knew her." She was buried in the hillside of the East Cemetery. Hers was the first burial in the Harsch family plot.

In the 1913 death notice of her husband Philip, her year of death was incorrectly stated as 1898.

Also spelled Schaake, Schake, Schakie, Scheeka, Schualke, Schulka, and Hesse.

Note #1: While researching Martha many years ago, the initial sources referred to her as Elizabeth, which is how she was referred to in the original database. Only later did other sources refer to her as Martha. Very recently I found out Martha was her actual first name. From researching her, the names Martha and Elizabeth were commonly interchanged.

Note #2: From reading the family history, knowledge about when her divorce from Frederick Hess took place appeared to be uncertain. Finding this information became a goal. After much research online, in person, and by telephone, I then reached Donna Sue Ratliff, the Sweetwater County Deputy Clerk of Court. She conducted her own research to find the Hesses' divorce case.

On June 17, 2024, via the deputy clerk, the archivist at the Wyoming State Archives sent a pdf of the scanned page of the original divorce docket.

The divorce case officially began on April 18, 1872, with the petition from Elizabeth "Hesse," as annotated in the district court ledger in Green River.

On May 20, Sheriff John McGlinchy deputized John Boyd of Salt Lake City to serve Frederick Hesse the summons. On that same day, Deputy Boyd read the summons to Hess and left him a certified copy.

On October 7, 1872, the case was dismissed.

The Wyoming State Archives have no other documents for this case.[83]

Since Hess was served the summons in Salt Lake County, Utah Territory, it was possible he had filed for divorce in Utah and this may have been the reason Martha's case was dismissed.

A search of the State of Utah's Archives revealed a District Court, Third District, for civil cases such as divorce for his area. All indexes for the court's ledgers revealed no case by Hess or Hesse was ever filed.[84]

Elizabeth Hess' divorce case against Frederick Hess was dismissed. October 7, 1872.
–Courtesy of Donna Sue Ratliff, the Sweetwater County Deputy Clerk of District Court, and the Wyoming State Archives

203

Elizabeth Hesse
vs
Frederick Hesse

Divorce

1872   Paid 5.00

1872		
April 18	Docketing & entering app. of Atty. Indexing suit	1 75
"	Praecipe & Petition filed. Summons issued and one copy	1 25
"	Summons retd & filed "no service made"	30
May 16	Alias Summons issued & copy	1 30
25	Alias Summons retd & filed with the following return endorsed thereon	

At the request of the plaintiff I hereby deputize John Boyd of Salt Lake City to serve the within Summons & make due return thereof. John McClinchy Sheriff. I certify that I received the within Summons on the 20th day of May A.D. 1872, and served the same by reading and leaving a certified copy with the defendant Frederick Hesse this the 20th day of May 1872. Salt Lake City, Salt County, Utah Ter. John Boyd Dep Sheriff. Sworn and subscribed to before me this 20th day of May A.D. 1872. [Seal] Wm S. Walker, Clerk 3rd Jud. Dist. Court. Utah Territory

June 10	Motion filed. Answer filed Issue joined. Entg app. of Deft.	1 00
1872 October 7	Entg on Judge Trial & Bar Dockets. Bringing record into court	1 25
"	James A Brennan appointed Special Master in Chancery	2 00
"	Searching records Entg order dismissal	50

65

Cemetery map index #: 10
Headstone Lat/Long: N42° 29' 49.5" W108° 43' 18.6"
Footstone Lat/Long: N42° 29' 49.5" W108° 43' 18.6"

Headstone inscription:

[engraved scrollwork]
In Memory
Mrs. Elizabeth Harsch
Beloved Wife
Philip Harsch
DIED
AUG. 25, 1899.
AGED 54 YRS.
6 MOS. 15 DAYS.

Marble base inscription:

HARSCH

Footstone inscription:

E. H.

Harsch, Henry William
April 28, 1876–May 2, 1928

Henry was born at Camp Stambaugh, Wyoming Territory, and the fourth child to pioneer parents Martha and Philip Harsch.

The 1880 census stated Henry was 4 years old and born in Wyoming. In 1900, he was listed as born in April 1876, aged 24, and born in Wyoming.

Like his father, Henry was a blacksmith. After his father retired, he took over his father's blacksmith shop.[85]

The 1910 census listed him as 34 years old; his occupation was listed as blacksmith. In 1920, he was listed as head of household, aged 43, and a blacksmith in a mining camp.[86]

Henry was known for loving horses. Though he didn't have a ranch he once owned 300 head of horses and 400 head of cattle. He had mining claims on the Big and Little Atlantic Gulches and Smith's Gulch, all to the east.

Joseph Cook spoke of Henry:

Oh, Henry was a wonderful fellow! He was just a wonderful man. Everybody liked him. And he runs a few horses and a few cattle up there around Atlantic City.

Joseph spoke how, when he was about 16 years old, one December in "the hard winter," (ca. 1914) his uncle received word from Henry. "We've got a bunch of horses snowed in out at Lovell Meadows," (likely Level Meadows, 5.5 miles east-southeast) and wanted us to come help and rescue his horses. The horses could not get out from the belly-deep snow.

Joseph and Henry made their way to "old miner" Charles Jackson's place. Henry and Joseph trekked their way to the trapped horses three miles away. With a halter-broke stallion, they broke a trail out to return to Charles' place on a rescue mission which took the entire day. "I tell you, we about froze to death."[87]

Henry voted in the August 17, 1926, primary election as the 17th voter and voted the Republican ticket.[88]

He was a member of the South Pass City Wyoming Masonic Lodge #2, and was a devout Christian Scientist.

He had been a life-long bachelor. At one time he was engaged to Miss Ellen Carpenter, but she had changed her mind about marriage.[89]

Henry's notice of death was printed in the *Wyoming State Journal*. His obituary stated he died from flu complications. Another article reported he had been "quite ill the past week" and he died of a sinus infection. New research revealed his death was caused by something else as seen in the note below.[90]

On the day of his funeral, the road to Atlantic City was opened for the first time that spring. Atlantic City Masons and others from Lander attended his funeral at the Harsch house, and he was buried beside his father.

Henry was "held in high esteem as a citizen, trustworthy, dependable and a man who made the world better with his life."[91]

Note: His handwritten death certificate, dated May 2, 1928, stated his cause of death was "Abscess-(illegible)" with a contributory cause of (illegible). A typed government note card of his death stated his cause of death was "nephritis," which is an inflammation of the kidneys.

Speaking with Fremont County coroner Erin Ivie and staff, they studied the writing, dissected the wording, and reviewed the government note card stating nephritis. After much discussion they concluded Henry died of "Abcess-Umbilicus" with a contributing cause of "Nephritis, Chronic."

She explained an infection, such as a urinary tract infection, could travel up the tract and to his kidneys and cause nephritis (inflammation of the kidneys).

Untreated nephritis (chronic nephritis) may progress to more serious conditions or weaken the immune system making the body more vulnerable to infections and abscesses. It is likely that the untreated "chronic nephritis" led to pyelonephritis, an actual acute infection, and caused the formation of renal/abdominal abscesses.

She summed up that pyelonephritis can cause all of the "flu complications" the family described in Henry's obituary, such as coughing, vomiting, and aches and pains.[92]

Cemetery map index #: 11
Headstone Lat/Long: N42° 29' 49.6" W108° 43' 18.6"

Headstone inscription:

HENRY W. HARSCH
1876 – 1928

Harsch, Philip G.
July 2, 1832–July 7, 1913

The death of this stellar pioneer was reported in the *Wind River Mountaineer* and in the *Wyoming State Journal*. The record for St. Andrew's Episcopal Church listed he died of acute asthma and was interred in "St. Andrew's Cemetery" on July 9, 1913.

Philip was born to Angelica and Adam Harsch at Luxemberg, Germany. His father was a blacksmith, like Philip was destined to become. He immigrated to the US in 1855 and was immediately naturalized as a citizen.[93]

The 1890 Veterans' Schedule listed Philip as a Civil War veteran. He enlisted in August 1861 at St. Louis, Missouri, and family history stated his enlistment had a term of three months. After his discharge for honorable service, he reenlisted.

He must have enlisted very early in August as he fought at Wilson Creek on August 10, which took place 227 miles southwest of St. Louis. Wilson Creek was the first major battle of the Civil War to take place west of the Mississippi River (Missouri, 2,300 estimated casualties on August 10, 1861, for a Confederate victory).[94]

His four-year Civil War service took place while in the Company C, First Regiment, Missouri Light Artillery, and Hancock's Veteran Volunteers. Philip was a soldier who continually saw incredible action. He also fought in the battles of Fort Donaldson [*sic*] (Donelson, Tennessee, 16,537 estimated casualties on February 13, 1862, for a Union victory), Shiloh (Tennessee, 23,746 estimated casualties on April 6,

Philip Harsch. This portrait is half of a joint portrait with wife Martha Harsch.

The back is dated 1869, which is likely not correct. In 1869 Martha was married to Frederick Hess. On June 30, 1873, Philip married Martha.
–Courtesy of the Fremont County Pioneer Museum

1862, for a Union victory), Antietam (Sharpsburg, Maryland, 23,000 casualties in 12 hours on September 17, 1962, for a Union victory), and the Siege of Vicksburg (Mississippi, 37,273 estimated casualties on May 18, 1863, for a Union victory).

He had been a private when he suffered a head injury, for which he was again discharged on November 3, 1864. The specific battle where he was wounded is unknown. The Harsch family history states Philip

> was wounded and knocked unconscious. ... He came to as the Confederate troops were passing by, thinking him dead. He lay very still, then made his way back to the Union lines.

Philip also stood as a guard at the residence of Secretary of State William Henry Seward the night Seward was attacked by a conspirator of John Wilkes Booth, the same night President Lincoln was assassinated on April 14, 1865.

Philip re-enlisted again though the details are unknown. In 1866, he was mustered out of the Army at Alexandria, Virginia.[95]

Later, he was employed by the US Government at Fort Leavenworth, Kansas. After four months, in 1869 he left to head for Wyoming. He arrived in Uinta County and started the first blacksmith shop before heading north to the South Pass area.[96]

"He was among the first to come to Atlantic in the halcyon days when gold was to be found on every side."[97]

On May 7, 1869, Philip purchased a blacksmith shop from E. Steele on the southeast corner of Price and Grant Streets in South Pass City. "At one time Philip worked with Ervin Cheney, a wheelwright, at South Pass."

Philip Harsch and daughter Martha on one of their daily walks. Undated.
—Courtesy of the Betty Carpenter Pfaff Collection, South Pass City State Historic Site

Philip, a powerhouse of a 5-foot, 1-inch man, was "very strong for his size, ... with blue eyes and light hair." He had been raised as a Catholic, and he was a member of the South Pass City Wyoming Masonic Lodge #2.[98]

Also in 1869 on September 2, Philip voted in the Atlantic City precinct in the Wyoming territorial election as the 108th voter.[99]

The 1870 census for South Pass City listed Philipp Harsh [*sic*] as 35 years old, a miner (partnering with Frederick Hess), owning $500 worth each of real estate and personal property, and his place of birth was Luxembourg.[100]

On June 30, 1873, he married Martha Elizabeth Schuake in South Pass City (his obituary and family lore stated they had married on June 21.). He was 38 years old and she was 30 years old.

He also adopted Martha's two daughters by Hess. The daughters "loved Harsch dearly, and [eldest daughter Katie] 'was never reconciled' to the fact he was not her natural father." Together with Martha, he raised seven children.[101]

The tax assessments for 1874 show Philip Harsch owned a business in Atlantic City.[102]

Philip voted in the November 2, 1880, election as the 15th voter. On June 14, 1881, he signed an oath to "support the Constitution of the United States, and the Organic Act of Wyoming Territory, and faithfully and impartially discharge the duties" as Election Judge and was the 6th voter in the Atlantic City election.[103]

The 1880 census for Atlantic City listed him as 44 years old, a blacksmith, and from Lusxumbourg [*sic*]. Atlantic City's 1900 census listed him as born in July 1832, aged 67, and born in Germany. In 1910 the Atlantic City census listed him as 77 years old, his middle initial is "G.," he was from Germany, and his occupation is listed as "none."[104]

His Martha died on August 25, 1899, who was buried in the East Cemetery. His family stated he "was a frequent visitor to the cemetery."

Philip Harsch, left, *and Sam Brady at Philip's blacksmith shop in Atlantic City. 1876.*
–Courtesy of South Pass City State Historic Site

Philip's obituary lauded him as "he was ever kind and considerate. Every one being treated with a kindly courtesy that bespoke a beautiful soul." The funeral took place in his home in Atlantic City. He was buried beside Martha in the Harsch family plot.

> Mr. Harsh [*sic*] was an old soldier and the bier was draped with the flag which he held so dear, and the services ... were conducted by [the Episcopal Church and] the Masonic fraternity, of which he was an honored member.[105]

In *Fine Gold*, chapter 22 is devoted to Philip and the Harsch family.[106]

Also spelled Harsh and Phillip.

Cemetery map index #: 12
Headstone Lat/Long: N42° 29' 49.5" W108° 43' 18.7"
Footstone Lat/Long: N42° 29' 49.5" W108° 43' 18.6"

Headstone inscription:
[engraved backward flying U.S. flag
with seven stars]
In Memory
Philip Harsch
DIED
JULY 7, 1913.
AGED 81 YRS.
5 DAYS.
Marble base inscription: HARSCH

Footstone inscription: P. H.

Heyroth, Alwin
Circa 1838–August 9 or 10, 1884

This pioneer's grave is the second-oldest marked burial in this cemetery and the first to have a headstone. With much of the headstone engraving eroded, I searched for information about him to complete its details for the 2016 database. This search and its findings set in motion this entire project.

Alwin left the port of Bremen (Germany) aboard the ship *Breman* and landed at the port of New York on July 3, 1856. The manifest indicated he was 18 years old, his birth year was 1838, the "country to which they severally belong" is Bolnerswerk (crease down the center obliterates part of the word), his occupation was a "smith," and the "country in which they intend to become inhabitants" is Wisconsin. (Note: the "w" in Alwin would have been pronounced as "v").[107]

The 1870 census listed Alwin as 32 years old, his occupation was "Brewer," and he came from Prussia. Below his head-of-household line is his wife Louisa E., who was 30 years old and came from Austria.[108]

Alwin is possibly one of the first men to own the first brewery in Atlantic City, Wyoming Territory. License number 173 was issued on January 2, 1871, to Atlantic Brewery, the first to own a brewery. As the license was for a business, it's not known if he was the licensee.[109]

He was granted a wholesale liquor license on April 10, 1870. The 1870 tax assessment roll shows Alvin Heyroth owned "Lot 25" on "First Street" valued at "$200." The 1871 tax assessment stated he owned Lot 25 and an "Old Brewery."

His wholesale liquor license was renewed for another year until April 1872. This year's tax assessment indicated he still owned a brewery valued at $300.[110]

Alwin Heyroth's upright headstone [propped up]. 2007. By 1980, the headstone had fallen backward. Photographer: Philippina Halstead.
—Courtesy of Laura Norman

73

Alwin's wholesale liquor license was renewed for another year until April 1873. The tax assessment stated he still owned the brewery, $100, two horses and 1 vehicle. In 1873, his wholesale liquor license was renewed for another year until April 1874.

Today we think government rules are excessive. Renewing liquor licenses are now an annual occurrence; however, studying the Licenses ledger, Alwin was required to renew his license—not just for retail liquor but also for a billiard table—four times a year. Other names in the ledger complied with the same requirement. From August 1, 1877, to February 1, 1880, Alwin renewed his licenses every quarter. In October 1880, Alwin must have started a partnership with Sam Spangler. Come January 14, 1881, Alwin must have quit the business because only Spangler's name was listed for license renewal.

The ledger entries slowed and by 1882 much of the entries stopped except for Ed Lawn who continued his renewals until they stopped on April 22, 1884.[111]

On June 19, 1876, Alwin witnessed a deed between Louis Poire, et al., to Charles H. Schnell. On November 24, 1876, Alwin purchased Lot 44 on Front Street in Atlantic City from John M. Reid in a quitclaim deed. On May 1, 1877, he was granted a license for "one billiard Table." On January 25, 1879, he sold his lode claim "formerly called the Gold-Star lode, now called the Louisa," to Phil Harsch.

Alwin was involved in the community. He was the 31st voter (sworn) in the November 2, 1880, Atlantic City precinct presidential election. On June 14, 1881, he signed an oath to "support the Constitution of the United States, and the Organic Act of Wyoming Territory, and faithfully and impartially discharge the duties" as Election Judge and was the 7th voter in the Atlantic City election.[112]

The 1880 census for Atlantic City listed "Hyeroth [sic], Alvin," aged 35 years old and was a blacksmith from Prussia. Louisa was not listed.[113] I cannot find what became of her.

Sadly, Alwin began "showing signs of insanity." Complaints to Judge Nickerson caused the judge to dispatch Sheriff Lowe.

When Lowe arrived, Heyroth "shot himself."

During the inquest several witnesses, including Philip Harsch, testified they "heard Heyroth asking someone to shoot him; drunk + drugged." The Justice of the Peace found Alwin committed suicide.[114]

The coroner's inquest concluded he "died by his own hand."

For the difference in his date of death, the *Cheyenne Sun* reported on August 15, a Friday, his suicide occurred on Saturday, which would be August 9. A report in 1968 by Daniel Y. Meschter about defunct Wyoming cemeteries described the intact and legible headstone: "Sandstone monument: Alvin Heyroth, aged 46 years, died August 10, 1884."

In her 1980 article about Fremont County cemeteries, Myra Connell wrote of Alwin's headstone: "sandstone monument lying on the ground."[115]

Alwin must have been a highly valued member of the community. His grave was the first in this cemetery to have a headstone placed and with a stout fence surrounding his grave. The remnants of the fence can still be seen today.

An astounding discovery of a copy of a clipped newspaper article in the Pioneer Museum illustrates just how carelessly our history was sometimes treated. The article described how individuals looking through the Anthony building (now known as Hyde's Hall near the center of town) had discovered a rubble-covered ledger with original Atlantic City documents. One of the discovered documents was the original handwritten inquest for Alwin's death.[116]

This copy of the clipped article had been poorly cut from the newspaper, which sliced off information. The paper did not include the publication or the date. After a frustrating search without success, with great thanks to Kennedy, the intrepid Lander librarian tracked down the actual article and publication.[117]

This article contained a transcription of Robert McAuley's handwritten inquest for "Alvin" Heyroth. The article included an itemized cost of the burial and of those who performed those services.

On June 7, 2016, during a cadaver-dog search of the cemetery the dog "downed" about three feet north of Alwin's grave indicating a scent of either human remains or ashes. In the video of the action, Clip #10, time stamp at 1:05, the handler pondered if the dog could be scenting Alwin's remains. In the handler's final report, the site is waypoint #252. It's shown on the cemetery map as confirmed human remains. On July 16, 2016, a dowser did not locate any remains north of Heyroth.

The newspaper article contains the transcription of Robert McAuley's handwritten coroner's inquest in 1884. –Courtesy of the *Wyoming State Journal*, July 2, 1957

REACH TRAGEDY

Another turn of the crumbling pages revealed a tragedy in the isolated settlement—the full report of a coroner's inquest in the case of a man who died by his own hand. The writing is that of Mr. McCauley and below is the document in full and as accurate as the faded writing and somewhat erratic spelling permit:

Estate of Alvin Heyroth	Dr& Cr	
To Robert McCauley Justice of the Peace and Acting Coroner		6.00
Making entry		.15
Issuing Venire		.50
Issuing Subpoenas		.25
Fixing costs		.25
filing papers		2.10
Jury fees for acting as coroners and aiding search		10.00
Wm. Gratrix for helping dress corps dig grave		10.00
Merritt Thompson " " "		10.00
J. H. Cook for helping to dress corps		5.00
Witnesses		4.00
J. H. Cook for watching and anointing corps		5.00
To J. H. Cook for making coffin case		5.00
R. F. Cheney for coffin		30.00
Express Company on " from Lander		1.25
Charles Washington for self and team at funeral		2.50
William Gratrix for acting as special constable		3.50
		$100.60

Members of the jury "searched the body" but unfortunately the amount of money found was recorded on a page which has crumbled away. Taxes for the year 1884 were paid and all personal property sold at public auction. Every item was meticulously recorded and the sale brought $60.95. An so ends another chapter in the colorful history of Wyoming's first-mining area.

Also spelled Heyboth, Hyeboth, Alvin.

Headstone inscription:

_____ HEYROTH
AGED 46 YEARS
DIED
AU_____4

Footstone inscription:

A. H.

Cemetery map index #: 13
Headstone Lat/Long: N42° 29' 49.5" W108° 43' 18.8" (Note: the are at the headstone's base as if the stone were upright.)
Footstone Lat/Long: N42° 29' 49.5" W108° 43' 18.7"

Alwin Heyroth's fallen headstone is eroding quickly, 2024, and his footstone, 2015

Alwin Heyroth's original fence which has collapsed outward. 2015.

Hunt, Lenora "Nora" Angelina Harsch
October 30, 1881–January 31, 1954

Lenora's obituary was printed in the *Wyoming State Journal*. She had traveled to a Christian Science Center at Wheat Ridge, Colorado, to improve her health and hope to find a cure, but she died there.

Nora was born in Atlantic City as the middle daughter of Martha and Philip Harsch. The St. Andrew's Episcopal Church's "Record Book for Atlantic City" noted her baptism date as June 9, 1912, listed her middle name, date of birth, and she was born in Atlantic City.[118]

When Nora was 18 years old, she married 29-year-old Reginald Carew Hunt in Atlantic City on March 7, 1900. The ceremony was performed by Justice of the Peace William B. Gratrix.[119]

Reginald was highly regarded and likely considered to be quite a catch. An immigrant from England, he was said to have had some training as a physician and educated at Heidelberg. His name came up in many newspaper articles as he provided medical assistance. In Atlantic City, he was a pharmacist and was also the postmaster from 1900 to 1903. He was even included in the 1903 tome *Progressive Men of Wyoming*.[120]

The 1900 census stated Nora's birth date as October 1881, she was 18, born in Wyoming, and married to Reginald C. Hunt. As head of household, Hunt was listed as born in January 1871 and was 29 years old. He'd been married one year and his place of birth was England and born to English parents. He immigrated to the US in 1889.

Hunt was described as a "remittance man," an immigrant "who is supported abroad chiefly by remittances from home." Another definition is "Typically a

Lenora Harsch and Reginald Hunt's Certificate of Marriage, March 7, 1900.
–Courtesy of Fremont County Clerk, Land Recording Office

disgraced man of good position or family who has been sent abroad by his family and whose payments depend on his remaining there."[121]

In May 1903, "The sound of Reginald crying woke Nora one night. He wouldn't tell her what was wrong." The next morning, he abandoned Nora and fled to Rock Springs with "a considerable amount of money from the post office."

The "family thinks he became addicted to drugs and died of an overdose in St. Louis but never found out for sure." At one point, his disappearance had been explained he "disappeared in a snowstorm and was never found. Family history stated he never contacted her again.[122]

The amount he stole and the fallout of his behavior was stated

> to have been $6000.00. Lenora received a card from him from Rock Springs and that was the last she ever heard from him. She borrowed money from the Sherlock family to repay the money Hunt had taken, then she went to work to repay the Sherlocks. ... Hunt's fate remains unknown. He was declared legally dead after the proper amount of time had elapsed and Nora received $10,000 from his estate.

One account stated he died in 1903; yet, the "England & Wales, National Probate Calendar (Index of Wills and Administrations), 1858-1995" listed:

> Hunt Reginald Carew of Atlantic City Fremon [sic] county Wyoming United States of America died 10 January 1914 Administration (limited) London 9 March to the reverend Robert Walter Carew Hunt clerk attorney of Lenora Angelina Hunt.[123]

Hunt's burial place is unknown. I found no proof of a burial site.
Nora moved on in her life. She took evening walks with her father and sisters

Lenora Harsch Hunt, left, and younger sister Martha Gustafsen, ca. 1940s
−Courtesy of the Betty Carpenter Pfaff Collection, South Pass City State Historic Site

Martha Gustafsen and Jean Harsch. The family became Christian Scientists.[124]

For a time, Nora lived with sister Katherine and her husband Michael Emmett Connell and their four children in De Pass, Wyoming. De Pass is 80 miles northeast of Atlantic City, east of Copper Mountain.

While there, the 1910 census listed her relationship to the head of household as sister-in-law, 28 years old, being married for the first time and for ten years, and she had no children. Her occupation was listed as "Domestic-small family."

Family history states she was instrumental in saving the life of her infant nephew Emmett Connell. She recognized he wasn't getting enough food and likely fed him canned milk.[125]

The 1920 census listed her as returned to Atlantic City, "sister" to the head of the household, aged 38, divorced, and occupation as "none."[126]

Lenora served as Clerk during the May 10, 1921, Atlantic City special election. In the 1926 Democratic primary election on August 17, Lenora was the 13th voter. For the November 4, 1930, general election, she was the second voter.

Note: What's odd about the 1930 poll book entries is the registration list clearly listed Lenora and sister Martha Gustafsen as aged 21. Lenora was actually 48 years old. Martha, who was born December 16, 1883, was 46. Likely it was a simple acknowledgment they were at least the legal age of 21 to vote.[127]

The 1930 census listed her as aged 48, divorced, and an occupation as "none." In 1940, she was listed as 58 years old, single, living with sister Martha and Peter Gustafsen, and her occupation entry was blank.[128]

The 1950 census listed her as head of household, 69 years old, and her marital status was "wd" for widowed.

Until her death, Nora lived with sister Martha Gustafsen in Atlantic City.

To see more photographs of Nora and sister Martha, refer to Betty Carpenter Pfaff's books, *Atlantic City Nuggets* and *Fine Gold*.[129]

Cemetery map index #: 14
Headstone Lat/Long: N42° 29' 49.7" W108° 43' 18.6"

Headstone inscription:
    LENORA A.
    HUNT
    1881 – 1954
IN LOVING
MEMORY

Melin, Casimer
May 7, 1837–July 7, 1875

The source for Casimer's existence came from a paper which had referenced "History written 1968 by Dan Meschter." Mr. Meschter had traveled Wyoming to document Wyoming's defunct cemeteries.

This document stated: "Emelyn, Casimer: died July ___, 18?? aged 38 yrs. (wooden marker difficult to read)."[130]

Intense searching found no "Emelyn." Considering Dan Meschter copied the name from an old wood marker exposed to extreme weather led me to try many versions of that name. Tip: While searching, misspelling names can help find similarly misspelled names, which may eventually lead to names closer to the correct name and the correct person. Finally, I found versions of "Melin" or "Mellin" which finally pieced together this person.

Searching finally revealed evidence of when and from where Casimer arrived and lived in the US. The ship's passenger manifest listed a "Catina Melin" (with translations of "Casimir Melin" and "Francois Meslin"). Casimir had a birth date of "abt 1837" and his age was 15.

Casimer and his family departed from Le Havre, France, and they arrived in New Orleans on October 21, 1852. The family's destination was "Missouri."[131]

During the Civil War, Casimier Mellin was drafted in 1863 to the Missouri 2nd District. The draft record listed his birthplace of France, he was Class 1 (between 20 and 35 years of age), unmarried, a laborer, and resided in Carondelet, Missouri (an annex of St. Louis in St. Louis City County by the Mississippi River). His age was 26, and he had a birth year of "abt 1837."

After the war, Casimer Melin eventually made his way to Wyoming Territory. The Cheyenne Post Office published a newspaper notice declaring it held his mail.

"Cassimer Melin" left the Cheyenne Bloom's clothing store clerkship accompanied with Bob Beers, and arrived at South Pass City in 1869. In "Early

Casimer Melin's grave, June 1956
–Courtesy of the Henderson Collection, South Pass City State Historic Site and the American Heritage Center, University of Wyoming. Photographer: Harold A. Titcomb, A. E. Blair, or Barney N. Tibbals

AC," "Cash Melin" was stated to have had a mercantile. Additionally, he voted in Atlantic City's September 2, 1869, territorial election as the 108th voter.[132]

The 1870 census for Atlantic City listed "Cassimer Mellin," age 33, his birthplace was France, his birth year "abt 1837," and he was a clerk in a store.[133]

The year 1871 was a good year. On January 1, "Mellin" married Leah Lamouraux [sic] in Atlantic City.

On June 29, "Casimer Melin" was mentioned in a store ad in the *South Pass News*.[134] Later, Judge Brennan appointed "C. Melin, of Atlantic" as a member of the Board of County Commissioners.[135]

The 1871 tax assessment roll indicated "C. Melin" owned a lot worth $15, $500 in "cap. merch" (believed to read he owned $500 worth of capital in merchandise) on "(C St?)." The busy year continued as he ran for county commissioner in the 1871 special election. With 205 votes cast for four candidates, Casimer came in second and lost by only six votes.[136]

In 1872, the Sweetwater County Tax Assessment listed a "C. Melin" owned "$500 cap. Merch." The 1873 tax assessment stated "Melen" owned an Atlantic City dwelling, $100, $600 in merchandise, and one vehicle. In 1874 "Cash. Melin, Atlantic" was on the Sweetwater County Democratic Ticket.[137]

Unexpectedly, on July 5, 1875, Casimer signed his Last Will and Testament leaving his estate to wife Lea. Oliver Baillargon and William Gratrix witnessed his signature.

Casimer died on July 7, 1875.

No newspaper article of his death or of his obituary was discovered. Casimer's estate was probated on August 5, 1875, and the judge designated Lea Melin to manage his estate.[138]

Casimer Melin signed his last will and testament bequeathing his property to his wife, Lea Melin. July 5, 1875. His signing of his will was witnessed by Oliver Baillargon and William Gratrix. –Courtesy of the Wyoming State Archives

Left: *Casimer's gravesite as it appeared before the board* [angled to 1 o'clock] *at the time of suspicion that it was his original grave marker.* Right: *That board at the time of lifting it to verify that it was the grave marker. July 29, 2021.*

Special note: I knew this gravesite well with its pile of boards and thick fence posts. For years I searched for and studied photographs from the State Archives. This grave had been photographed through the decades because it was so picturesque. Those photos were taken for its beauty. None showed the marker clearly enough to read the name, even with manipulation by electronic software.

In July 2021 after a tour of the cemetery, I stood with a woman beside this grave as we discussed dowsing. The sunlight hit one plank among the fallen boards on his grave. In a blinding realization I recognized this plank was actually his original grave marker.

This remarkable find of the original then-146-year-old wooden marker kicked off three months of painstaking research about Casimer and to find the best solution to re-erect his marker and to protect this Old West treasure.

With approval from the cemetery owner, to reset the marker and to protect it from the weather Steve Hockett constructed a case made of old snow fence and redwood planks from the old deck at the Miner's Delight Inn. The cremains and memorials of the inn's former owners, Georgina and Paul Newman, are in this cemetery. The case was attached to 6" posts set in concrete.

Steve and I scraped the grave to locate the buried wood remnant of his marker. We chose to set the grave marker further west from the original placement because of our desire not to take a chance getting too close to the body. We had no idea how deeply—or shallowly—he was buried.

We dug to find the exact spots where the original fence posts once stood. Handmade bricks from the early 1900s are set in place to mark the exact corners. The remnants of the grave's original fence were placed to line the grave.

Digging the 24"x18"x18" hole felt like we were digging in concrete. When the hole was the correct size and depth, Steve, a contractor, made the comment, "That's the hardest dirt I've ever dug." I was relieved I wasn't the only one who had trouble digging.

The hard work made me consider the people who dug these graves by hand. Possibly they were traumatized or distraught at burying their family member or a dear friend in this unforgiving earth and perhaps doing so in harsh weather. I also considered how deeply or how shallowly they labored to dig the grave. This thought also made me feel better about moving the marker further west.

A stainless steel plaque depicting the text of his marker is mounted on the front of the case. With help from this plaque, a visitor can easily read the marker. A second plaque is mounted to the case's back which depicts my representation of how the grave appeared in its earlier days.

The back of the case is 23'11" from the west fence, and the front of the case is 2'0" west of the original M42 stake which marked and identified the Unknown grave. This stake was 27'2" from the west fence and 35'0" from the southwest corner of the Harsch family fence (Index #9).

On October 10, 2021, on a magnificent fall day, we townspeople and two pastors from our St. Andrew's Episcopal Church held a re-memorial ceremony to honor and to bless Casimer, his grave and marker, and to all who are buried in the cemetery.

Steve Hockett inspects his nearly complete case that would house Casimer Melin's grave marker. The painted stake in the center of the grave, marked M42, marks the spot where the marker originally stood. Two bricks that flank the center stake mark the exact spots of two of the original corners of the fence. September 28, 2021.

To conclude the ceremony, I was honored and deeply moved to remove his wood stake marked M42 which had designated his Unknown grave.

The grave known as M42 no longer existed as Casimer Melin took his place among the marked graves.

Also spelled Casimier, Casimir, Cassimer, Catina; nicknames Cash and Casper; Emelyn, Melen, and Mellin.

Cemetery map index #: 15
Marker Lat/Long: N42° 29.825/6' W108° 43.319'
Original wood marker inscription:

CASIMER MELIN
DIED
JULY 7, 1875
AGED
38 YEARS

Casimer Melin's wood grave marker is re-set, the remnants of the original fence line the grave, and plaques are in place before his memorial ceremony. October 9, 2021.

A stainless steel plaque is mounted to the back of the case. The hand-drawn representation is how his gravesite looked back in the day and to show and honor the detail with which his grave marker and fence were constructed.

Townspeople gathered to honor Casimer Melin, those who worked hard to construct his intricate marker and fence in 1875, and to all who rest in the cemetery. October 10, 2021.
–Courtesy of Pam Spencer-Hockett

Philippina Halstead's watercolor-and-ink depiction of Casimer Melin's gravesite. 2000. Her dream was to see his marker replaced, and she earned the honor to conclude Casimer's segment. –Courtesy of Carole Justice and Laura Norman

Newman, Georgina "Gina" Dewey
June 10, 1920–September 8, 1998

Before her arrival to Atlantic City, Georgina had already achieved celebrity status. She was the first woman stylist at General Motors, the executive editor for the *Living for Young Homemakers* magazine, and was a Condé Nast editor in New York City.

Gina was a guest on the TV game show *To Tell the Truth* in season 1971–72. She fooled two of the four panelists. To see her move and to hear her voice was a thrill. She also became a temporary Western expert while proofreading radio scripts for *Death Valley Days*.[139]

In 1958 husband Paul Newman, a notable Fifth Avenue advertising executive, suggested a vacation to Wyoming. For years thereafter, they were regulars at Miss Ellen Carpenter's Carpenter Hotel.

After hearing of Miss Ellen's death in 1961, Paul suggested they bid on the hotel. In 1963 they owned it. They modernized the hotel, removed the hotel rooms in the former Camp Stambaugh one-story log building, and installed a restaurant, bar, and a second kitchen.

Gina spent six weeks in cooking classes at the James Beard Cooking School in Greenwich Village, and four weeks at the Dione Lucas Cooking School.

They decided their restaurant would have no menu and have a limit of 36 people. They obtained a liquor license. They changed the name Carpenter Hotel

Left: *Georgina Newman, ca. 1960s.* Right: *Gina Newman, ca. 1980s.*
–Courtesy of C. E. Carpenter IV

to the Miner's Delight Inn out of respect for Miss Ellen Carpenter, who was a strict teetotaler. The Carpenter Hotel would never serve alcohol.

On June 10, 1967, they opened the doors to their new restaurant—to two people. Undaunted, their success grew and their gourmet restaurant was highlighted in newspapers and magazines throughout the country.[140]

With its stunning success, Wyoming's US Senator Gale McGee entered the Miner's Delight Inn into the *Congressional Record* on September 29, 1971.[141]

Active in voting, Gina cast ballots in all primary, general, and special elections from 1964 through 1978. In the primaries she voted for the Republican party, and in 1968 through 1978 she also ran unopposed for Precinct Committeewoman and was elected each time. Her age in the 1964 primary was 44 or 45 (the number had been changed). In the general election her age was listed as 40, and the 1968 primary her age was listed as 43.[142]

Before Paul's death in 1986, he and Gina had agreed they would not allow themselves to be embalmed but to be cremated. During this period, the only crematorium in the state was in Cheyenne.

State law required Paul's body to be embalmed in order to take him to Cheyenne. According to local rumor, to comply with Paul's wish Gina loaded his unembalmed body in the trunk of her car and drove him there. From the many stories I've heard of the Newmans, I believed it.

Gina's friend Lorna Ruebelmann confirmed this story. She stated this information came from Gina's mouth to her ears. As Lorna wrote as she graciously permitted this story:

Getting *him* into their Cadillac trunk is just one small example of her indefatigable determination to make their retirement in AC as worldly and sophisticated as possible. She was an icon![143]

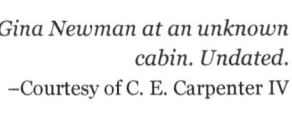

Gina Newman at an unknown cabin. Undated.
—Courtesy of C. E. Carpenter IV

After Paul's death, she continued to run the restaurant. Later, one winter while she brought in firewood Gina fell and hit her head.

While snow fell the next day, neighbor Bob Bell noted no signs of Gina, no footprints, and no smoke coming from the chimney. He took action and obtained a key to the inn.

He found Gina, nearly frozen and hypothermic. Her dog Penelope had snuggled with her to help keep her alive.

Gina was hospitalized and survived her ordeal. She sold the hotel and entered a Lander nursing home. For her great nursing care, she "just wanted to give something back." Gina left a bequest of $391,000 in funds and property to the Central Wyoming College Community Foundation. With these funds, she established the Georgina D. Newman Memorial Scholarship for Fremont County nursing students.[144]

When she died in 1998, Gina's obituary was published in the *Wyoming State Journal*. According to townsfolk statements, Georgina was cremated and her ashes spread in the cemetery.[145]

In her obituary, she had requested memorials be made to CWC's Foundation for nursing scholarships.[146]

At CWC, on the second floor of the JoAnne Youtz McFarland Health and Science building is a large display of scholarship donors. There, a smiling Gina holds her beloved dog Penelope.

On June 7, 2016, a cadaver dog "downed" just north of her memorial marker. It can be seen on video *5 Search* at 12:29. It's possible the dog detected her spread cremains, and the handler determined the remains to be confirmed. The finding is in K. T. Irwin's final report as waypoint 248.

Cemetery map index #: 16
Marker Lat/Long: N42° 29' 49.7" W108° 43' 17.7"

Memorial inscription:

GEORGINA DEWEY NEWMAN
JUNE 10, 1920   SEPT. 8, 1998
DECORATOR   STYLIST
BORN CROSS CREEK, N. C.

Newman, Paul Edwin
March 14, 1900–May 10, 1986

Before his permanent arrival in Atlantic City in the 1960s, Paul was an advertising executive in New York City. One of Paul's claims to fame was his famous slogan "wide-track Pontiac" for the Pontiac Bonneville, General Motors.

A 1961 Bonneville was made for the Pontiac General Manager Semon Knudsen, including unique Beige Metallic paint and leather bucket seats. Paul purchased the car which had inspired the slogan and he drove it in Atlantic City. Decades later, this car was the subject of an article in the Pontiac aficionados magazine *High Performance Pontiac*.[147]

To read much about Paul's history, a stunning full-page article written by Carolyn B. Tyler, published by the *Riverton Ranger* in 1968, explores his life. Crowning the article is the title: "Wide-Tracking Man Follows Pioneer Tracks to His Miner's Delight."

While born in New York, Paul's family moved to the Hawaiian Islands where his father opened Hawaii's first drugstore. This time and place inspired Paul's love of art, and he trained in commercial art.

In 1958, because of medical issues likely caused by the stress of "Fifth Avenue," he suggested to wife Georgina they take a vacation to Wyoming.

Although they had reservations at a dude ranch at Encampment, a friend in New York insisted they make a side-trip to Atlantic City to visit Miss [Ellen] Carpenter and see her hotel and the ghost town. They caught the fever of the town and stayed for six weeks.[148]

Paul Newman on the cover of Scribner's Magazine, *August 1937. Cover by Henry Waxman.*

They became regulars at the Carpenter Hotel. With his artist's eye, his are photographs are commonly seen here. His series of photographs captured Miss Ellen baking a cherry pie. My favorite photo of Miss Ellen is in her segment.

Upon hearing of Miss Ellen's death in 1961, Paul suggested they bid on the hotel. In 1963, they owned it. They modernized the hotel and installed a restaurant and bar.

Gina and Paul took six weeks of cooking classes at the James Beard Cooking School in Greenwich Village, and four weeks at the Dione Lucas Cooking School.

Paul went on to take a six-week sauce class at the famed Cordon Bleu in Paris. They decided their restaurant would have no menu and a limit of 36 people. They obtained a liquor license. Out of respect for Miss Ellen's teetotalling ways, they changed the Carpenter Hotel name to the Miner's Delight Inn to ensure the Carpenter Hotel would never have served liquor.

On June 10, 1967, they opened the doors to their new restaurant—to two people. Despite the slow start, their success grew. It was celebrated for fine dining and highlighted in newspapers and magazines throughout the country.[149]

With the impressive success of the inn, Wyoming's US Senator Gale McGee entered an article about the inn into the *Congressional Record*.[150]

Like his wife Gina, Paul was active in voting. He cast ballots in all primary, general, and special elections from 1964 through 1978. In the primaries he voted for the Republican party, and in 1968 through 1978 he also ran unopposed for Precinct Committeeman and was elected each time. His age in the 1964 primary was 61, in the general election his age was listed as 59, and the 1968 primary his age was listed as 61.[151]

Paul died on May 10, 1986. His obituary ran in the *New York Times*. Paul was cremated and his ashes spread in the cemetery.[152]

Paul Newman. Undated, ca. 1980s.
–Courtesy of C. E. Carpenter IV

The 1961 Bonneville that inspired Paul Newman's famous slogan "Wide-Track Pontiac." Undated.
–Courtesy of the Atlantic City Historical Society Collection, Wyoming State Archives

*Paul and Georgina Newman in the
Miner's Delight Inn's bar, ca. 1980s.*
–Courtesy of C. E. Carpenter IV

Cemetery map index #: 17
Marker Lat/Long: N42° 29' 49.7" W108° 43' 17.7"

Memorial inscription:

PAUL EDWIN NEWMAN
MAR. 14, 1900   MAY 10, 1986
ARTIST   WRITER
BORN GENOA, NEW YORK

"Our Mother"
Unknown–August 28, 1904

A 1980 *Wyoming State Journal* newspaper article by Myra Connell contains all the information known about her:

> The mother of a family who were emigrating across the country in 1904 became ill and died at Atlantic. The grave remained unmarked until the 1940s when a Mr. Anderton appeared in Atlantic, stayed at the Carpenter Hotel and had the stone placed.[153]

Exhaustive searches of genealogy and old newspaper sites revealed no information. With the stone placed decades after the woman died, it's possible the date is not correct. Searches using different decades, months, days, and even searching out-of-state newspaper sites revealed nothing.

On June 7, 2016, a cadaver dog "downed" between her and neighboring Alonzo Richardson (Map Index #19). In video *6 Search* at 00:44, the exact location is obscured by an evergreen tree though it appears the dog is nearer to her site. The downing is shown on the map as unconfirmed human remains.

A close examination of the stone reveals the front of the vertical section may have had an inscription, but if so it has sloughed off and is illegible. On the angled surface, the engraving "Our Mother" is sharp in places, though erosion is taking a serious toll.

The headstone for "Our Mother" is sandstone. Weathering has taken a serious toll. 2024.

In 1968, Daniel Y. Meschter documented this cemetery. His report described her marker only as: "Red sandstone: 'Our Mother, Died Aug. 28, 1904'."[154]

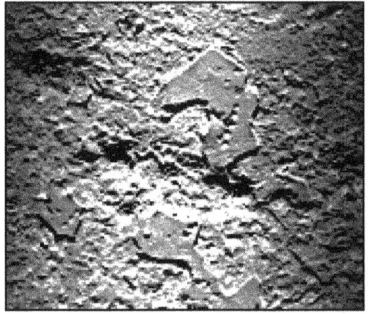

Tip: A woman participating in a cemetery tour in 2016 recommended, in the dark, to shine a flashlight across the surface to better detect engravings.

At dusk on August 22, I followed her great suggestion. With a flashlight facing across the marker's front vertical surface, numerous "grouped poke points" became visible. I could not discern letters or numbers. I could not determine if the grouped poke points were part of a design, vandalism, or a shaping tool.

It is mysterious Daniel Meschter's report stated nothing of a name or even the eroded remnants of one. When he documented the cemetery in 1968, the stone had been in place only around thirty years.

Now, up to roughly 84 years since the stone's placement, the date on the horizontal surface is sharp, the angled surface with "Our Mother" is either sharp or at least legible, but there is no sign of text on the vertical surface.

Inexplicably, there is a definite date of her death yet no name. Perhaps Mr. Anderton had the stone engraved with all the information available to him, and this stone was a loving tribute and memorial to a mother.

Cemetery map index #: 18
Headstone Lat/Long: N42° 29' 49.5" W108° 43' 18.3"

Headstone inscription:

(horizontal surface)
DIED
AUG 28 1904

(angled surface)
OUR
MOTHER

Richardson, Alonzo
Unknown–Unknown

Alonzo was said to have been an Army scout in the 1870s.

A large part of his headstone and its engraving are below ground and are not visible. An exhaustive search revealed numerous "Alonzo Richardson," but it was impossible to determine if any of them were our Alonzo Richardson.

The only information about him came from Betty Carpenter Pfaff's book, *Atlantic City Nuggets*. In it, Betty's father, James Carpenter, relayed the story told to him by Alonzo in 1895. Jim would have been around eight years old.

This story below is paraphrased.

In 1870 during a time of numerous Indian raids in the region when 14 local people were killed, Sioux Indians were killing the miners to protect their hunting grounds. The Army was in the area to protect the miners. Alonzo was present during this time. During a major battle north of Miners Delight, First Lieutenant Charles Stambaugh was ambushed and killed. Alonzo told Jim that Stambaugh was "well liked by his men as was his wife."[155]

Note: Stambaugh's obituary listing his next of kin made no mention of a wife.

The footstone is a large chip which appears to match the missing piece from the upper-right corner of the headstone. The distance from the headstone to the footstone is 5'11", which indicates the buried person is an adult.

On June 7, 2016, a cadaver dog "downed" near this site between him and "Our Mother" (Map Index #8). In video *6 Search* at 00:44, the exact visual location is obscured by an evergreen tree. The handler determined this downing is unconfirmed human remains. This finding is shown on the map as such.

Cemetery map index #: 19
Headstone Lat/Long: N42° 29' 49.5" W108° 43' 18.3"
Footstone Lat/Long: N42° 29' 49.4" W108° 43' 18.2"

Headstone inscription:

ALONZO,
RICHARDSON
DIED
[text buried]

Footstone inscription:
(It's unlikely to have one, but it's
unknown as it's buried too deep.)

Robinson, Anne "Annie" Cecelia Locke Carpenter
January 11, 1885–July 2, 1979
Marker placed possibly: August 17, 1985

Ann was one of the Carpenter children who arrived by wagon with her parents, Nellie and Clarence E. Carpenter, and her three siblings in 1890.

She's listed in the 1900 census as born January 1885, was 15 years old, born in Nebraska, and had an occupation of "At school."

Annie married Montgomery Robinson on June 27, 1910, in Reno, Nevada. Robinson was a "prominent mining man of Lovelock, Nevada, and has a number of splendid claims in that rich section."[156]

Baptized into the St. Andrew's Episcopal Church on October 18, 1916, the church's record listed Anne's full name as Anne Cecelia Locke (Carpenter) Robinson. Her date of birth was listed as January 11, 1885, and she was born at Fort Robinson in northwest Nebraska.[157]

To see a photograph of Anne, see *Changes*.[158]

The 1950 census listed Anne C. Robinson, aged 65. The remaining columns were filled with codes. For example, race was "I" for Indian, Male/Female was "2" and status of married/divorced/widowed/never married was "3."[159]

The Carpenter family history indicates Anne died in 1979 in Ithaca, New York. Her burial was stated as August 17, 1985, in this cemetery.[160]

On June 7, 2016, during a cadaver-dog search of the cemetery, twice the dog "downed" in front of the Carpenter family monument indicating a scent of human remains. The video of the action is in the video *Clip #5*, time stamps at 4:57 and at 6:58. In her written report, the dog handler's waypoint is #246.

On June 26, 2016, Betty Carpenter Pfaff explained Annie's ashes were placed at the Carpenter family monument. It's possible Annie's memorial marker was placed on August 17, 1985, as she was stated to have her burial on this date.[161]

Cemetery map index #: 20
Marker Lat/Long: N42° 29' 49.1" W108° 43' 17.8"

Marker inscription:
    ANNE
    CARPENTER
    ROBINSON
    JAN. 11, 1885
    JULY 2, 1979

Williams, Jared
August 9, 1847–September 8, 1919

An early Western pioneer, Jared was a teamster and a rancher. His obituary was printed in the *Wind River Mountaineer* on September 26. He was said to have died of hardening of the arteries.

Jared was born in Wales. In 1851, his family, consisting of parents Mary and William and sisters, immigrated to the US when he was a child. They traveled west in a covered wagon during the time of Indian trouble. They reached Brigham City, Utah Territory, and lived there for nine years.

Church records show Jared was baptized by his father as a member of the Reorganized Church of Jesus Christ of Latter-day Saints on August 7, 1862. The membership records states his date of birth was August 9, 1847, and his place of birth was Monmonthshire, Wales.

The family never "took up the practice [polygamy] of the Mormons as it was in the early days ... that custom was what made them decide to go back to Iowa."[162]

In Alma Williams Golliher's oral history, she corroborated the story of how the William Williams family left Wales in the 1850s, then headed to Brigham City in Utah. The family consisted of his parents, Jared, and his three young sisters. The parents were urged to arrange plural marriages to older men. The family escaped Utah in 1860 along with others fleeing the state.

Jared Williams. Date and location are unknown.
—Courtesy of the Henry Williams Family

They were pursued by "Returning Angels," men who would stop escapees and force them to turn back. The "Angels" said they'd let the fugitives go on the condition one man would return to Utah.

To save the refugees, Henry Watkins, a single man, volunteered to return. When asked what would happen to Watkins:

> The 'Returning Angels' said he would be tied to the wagon tongue and skinned alive. Someone rode hurriedly to the soldiers at the Platte River Station who came to their aid. They [soldiers] took all the guns from the 'Returning Angels' except one, with enough shells for game for food, and sent them back to Utah.

Jared didn't stay in Iowa. In 1872, he traveled to Montana with his brother John to be a freighter. Later, their father joined them.

At one point, he heard of "Fort Stambow" (Stambaugh) and he and his father traveled to this area. He left in a wagon, accompanied by a wife.

In 1886, Jared soon had a ranch on the Sweetwater River, 6 miles southeast below Atlantic City where Rock Creek runs into the Sweetwater River. One statement was Jared "married in Atlantic but the marriage lasted only a short time and there were no children." Another statement was the woman, believed to be named Liza, was described as a Mormon woman with four children.[163]

One description of Jared was

> He was gruff and chewed tobacco but always carried a big sack of hard candy to treat any child who came by. He used to say "That ar is mighty touchin' " when he heard sad songs played on the Old time Victrola.

From left: *Zoie Green, Laura Green, and Jared Williams in Atlantic City, ca. 1917*
–Courtesy of the South Pass City State Historic Site

Atlantic City Nuggets includes another photograph of Jared.[164]

For his ranch on the Sweetwater River, in 1909 Jared filed a final five-year proof for a homestead. Jared was issued a serial patent for 160 acres which encompassed the confluences of Willow and Rock Creeks to the Sweetwater River on March 3, 1910. His land patent is shown on page 100.[165]

Oddly, the only census found for Jared was in the 1910 census for Big Sandy Town. It listed "Jerd" as head of household, was 62 years old, married one time and for 20 years. It stated he was born in Wales to Welsh parents, had immigrated in 1851, and was naturalized in 1905. His occupation was listed as farmer, and the general nature of his business was "General farm." He could read and write, and owned his home, and had no military service. His wife was not listed on this census. Below him were listed Henry and Maude Williams and their six children.[166]

Jared had been "Well thought of and respected." His nieces and nephews tell of him being a

> gentle, kind man he was, one who wouldn't hurt man or beast. When asked
> if he ever killed an Indian, his answer was one followed him, he shot but
> didn't go back but he was no longer followed.

Zoie Green Fuller and Laura Green Marrin tell a story when Jared fell asleep with his mouth open and they poured ice water in his mouth. It was the only time they ever remember seeing him mad. "People told of how large his upper arms were, like ham is hanging from his shoulders."[167]

Note: After Jared's death and burial, a wooden marker was placed. Years later, relatives of Jared arrived to pay respects, but his marker was missing. They didn't know if it had decayed or if it had been stolen.

In 2012 great-nephew Emmett Williams constructed a replacement marker. To place the marker, the family couldn't recall the exact spot of his grave, so they did the best they could.[168]

On June 7, 2016, cadaver-seeking dog Blue "downed" right in front of this marker, confirming the marker was correctly placed. Dog handler K. T. Irwin confirmed the remains. The video of the action is in video *5 Search*, time stamp at 8:56. The marking of the confirmed remains with orange tape can be seen on video *11 Marking* at 05:11.

Personal note: When dog Blue was searching for remains, watching him bypass Jared's marker, stop, then turn back to decisively down at the marker is one of my favorite memories of this project.

On July 16, 2016, dowser Don Schooley "witched" Jared's grave. His rods indicated remains of a male. On October 9, dowser Ann Noble dowsed the grave.

Her rods indicated the remains of a male, and the gravesite extended east from the marker an appropriate length for an adult, proving again the marker had been placed in exactly the right spot.

Special note: Jared's nephew, Baby Williams, is buried in the West Cemetery.[169]

Also spelled Jerd and Jerrod.

Cemetery map index #: 21
Headstone Lat/Long: N42° 29' 48.7" W108° 43' 18.2"

Marker inscription:

JARED WILLIAMS
BORN
AUGUST 9 1847
WALES
DIED
SEPT. 8 1919

Jared Williams' land patent granted him 160 acres on the Sweetwater River. March 3, 1910.
—Courtesy of the Bureau of Land Management, U.S. Department of the Interior

FIVE

East Cemetery
Specific Gravesite Unknown

The people listed in this chapter are known to have been buried in the East Cemetery. Their interment here is documented in newspaper articles. For any number of reasons, their graves have no marker. They are here in one of the dowsed gravesites.

Whether federally then privately owned, the East Cemetery appears to have served as the city cemetery. This belief is supported by the sheer number of graves, either marked with a headstone or by the vast number of unmarked graves discovered by a cadaver-seeking dog and by experienced dowsers.

There are many reasons for the numerous unmarked graves.

First, the grave may not have been marked at all. Perhaps the deceased was not respected and not worthy of the effort to construct a marker. It's also possible tough weather conditions such as a winter storm may have thwarted the attempt.

Second, the grave was indeed marked and with a wooden marker. Our weather is harsh. Frigid temperatures, gale-force winds, deep and heavy snows, erosion from the crushed rock on the hillsides, and brutal sun damage from being exposed at 7,600 feet can cause wood objects to quickly deteriorate. In my several years of working in the cemeteries, I've seen a marked degradation in the condition of wood remnants. They won't be around much longer.

Our great exception is the treasured 1875 wood grave marker for Casimer Melin. His marker was constructed with great care and his grave was surrounded by a magnificent fence of thick posts. Much of it still exists, though the fence is decaying rapidly.

Third, the population in this town is transient. People flocked here, made or lost their fortunes, then departed or fled. A grave might lose its marker for any reason and there was no one there who remembered the person or their burial site to replace the marker. This person's final resting place is lost to history.

Fourth, there have been instances of vandalism here. I've heard a story by a person who had lived here in the 1960s and recalled seeing many markers, metal funeral home markers, or wood markers, which are gone. There's no telling how many have been stolen by despicable criminals who thought an Old West grave marker would make a great souvenir.

Special note about the "Red-haired Woman":

On December 22, 2015, Betty Carpenter Pfaff mentioned to me in a telephone conversation when brother James "Wally" Wallace Carpenter and others were digging Miss Ellen Carpenter's burial site in 1961, they discovered the remains of a red-haired woman.

On September 30, 2016, I happened to meet Wally at a gathering. I asked him about finding the woman. Wally confirmed, "Yeah, that actually happened."

I asked what had happened to her. He didn't know. "The two other men took care of her, and they're both gone."

This is a harsh example of our environment. Any sign of this woman being buried in this spot had been obliterated, which led to the innocent and shocking discovery during the excavation of this spot for another burial.

I don't know where this unnamed woman was reinterred, but I believe it to be in this cemetery. It's highly doubtful she was taken to South Pass City or to Lander for burial.

Alwes, Franz "Uncle Always" August
Circa 1840–circa April 14, 1919

Affectionately known as Uncle Always, he owned a cabin on "Willow Creek from Deep Creek. Had a dugout there." An additional description for the location of his cabin is "above the Carpenter Hotel on Little Beaver Creek, going south. Here, he loved to garden & often gave friends some produce."[1]

He also owned property in Basin, Wyoming, about 173 miles north.

The 1910 census listed him as head of household, his age as 70, divorced, place of birth as Germany, he immigrated in 1868, and he was a farmer.[2]

On April 14, 1919, he departed an Atlantic City store with provisions and headed for home before a snowstorm struck.

Uncle Always didn't make it home.

He was missed for a week and a search party found him near his home "where he had fallen from exhaustion in an endeavor to reach shelter." He died from extreme exposure at the venerable age of 79. His cause of death was listed as "exposure, lost in storm" after he was found "fifty rods" (825 feet) from his cabin.

Reverend Lewis Smith arrived from Lander to conduct his funeral service.[3]

To see another photograph of Franz at his cabin "on Willow Creek up from Deep Creek," see *Fine Gold*, chapter 18, page 4.[4]

He was buried in "St. Andrew's Cemetery" on April 23, 1919.[5]

Uncle Always came from Minnesota years earlier, but no heirs were likely found as "it is thought that he has no relatives in this country."

The photograph of Franz Alwes with a caption "Raking in front of cabin" with an unknown person kneeling. Judging from the remaining snowdrifts in the distance, they were likely preparing the garden in spring. Undated.
–Courtesy of the South Pass City State Historic Site

Left: *Franz Alwes stands beside oxen hitched to a wagon.* Right: *The identity of the man is unknown.* Bottom: *Handwritten "The Oxen."* Far right: *The vertical caption reads "How is this for a souvanier [sic]." This photograph is of an original postcard. Undated. The back is blank.*
—Courtesy of the South Pass City State Historic Site

Franz Alwes' death notice was published on April 25, 1919.
—Courtesy of the
Wyoming State Journal

PERISHED IN SNOWSTORM

August Alwes, an old time pros-pector of Atlantic City, was found dead last Monday about fifty rods from his cabin near that place. Death was from extreme exposure during a snow storm which raged in the mountains on Monday, April 14th.

Alwes, who was past 70 years of age, had been at the Atlantic store on that day for provisions. Just about the time he started for home a severe snowstorm broke. No one in the store noticed the old man leaving, and after having been missed a week, and it be-ing discovered that he had never reached his cabin since the day of the storm, a searching party was form-ed. The body was found very near the old man's home where he had fallen from exhaustion in an endeavor to reach shelter.

Rev. Lewis D. Smith, of Lander, went up to the mines Monday and con-ducted funeral services that afternoon.

An effort is being made to locate the relatives of the deceased. He came to Wyoming from Minnesota many years ago, and it is thought that he has no relatives in this country. J. H. Sharp of this city acted as agent for him, and a very short time ago was instructed to sell a piece of prop-erty at Basin belonging to the de-ceased. He also had some property at Atlantic which will revert to the county if no heirs can be found.

Anderson, James Frederick
March 17, 1855–July 1, 1916

James arrived to the South Pass mining district from Illinois. He

was [schooled?] as an engineer of some sort, and worked at a variety of places including on the Granier Ditch, a mill at Lewiston, and was supposedly a foreman at the Carissa mine.[6]

He married Atlantic City resident Martha Bernice Godward on January 31, 1900, in Atlantic City. From the marriage license, Anderson married when he was 45 years old and living in Lewiston.[7]

In the 1900 census at Lewiston, James was described as 45 years old, was born February 1855, his occupation was a quartz miner, and from Illinois.

The 1910 Lewiston census listed James' middle initial "F.," head of household, married, with six children, aged 55, born in Illinois, and was a laborer in the mines.[8]

On July 1, 1916, James died of pneumonia, leaving nine orphans. He was interred in "St. Andrew's Cemetery" on July 2, 1916, alongside his wife Martha, who had died two months earlier on May 4 soon after giving birth.[9]

James' date of birth shown above came from his death certificate, though there are differing dates in the censuses and family history. His middle name above, Frederick, came from his death certificate and from the St. Andrew's

This photograph is of a drawing entitled "John Anderson, according to Martha Walrath descendant." Undated. Artist is unknown.
–Courtesy of and with permission by Martha Walrath and the South Pass City State Historic Site

Episcopal Church's records. Family history stated it to be Ford, likely his mother's maiden name as written on the death certificate.[10]

Martha Walrath, a descendant of the Andersons, stated they had had twelve children. Nine survived. Martha's newborn was one of the surviving children.[11]

Later, their nine surviving orphaned children were split between aunts and uncles in Illinois and Lucerne, Wyoming.[12]

The drawing of James entitled "John Anderson, according to Martha Walrath descendant" had been donated to South Pass City State Historic Site. It's possible the artist, Martha, is the daughter of James, born circa 1904 or a granddaughter. The research to discover this information continues.[13]

James Anderson's death certificate, July 2, 1916 –Courtesy of the Wyoming State Archives

Anderson, Martha Bernice Godward
August 1, 1874–May 4, 1916

Martha was born in Cheyenne on August 1, 1874. By 1900, she and her family were living in Atlantic City.[14]

When she was 25 years old she married James F. Anderson, a Lewiston miner, on January 31, 1900. She moved to Lewiston with him.[15]

The 1900 census listed her birth month as August 1874 and she was living in Wyoming.

In 1910 for the Lewiston census, she was listed as "Martha B.," wife, married for 10 years, had six living children out of eight, aged 35, born in Wyoming, and no occupation was listed. Her children were James W., 9 years old; Lyman B., aged 8; Martha B., 6 years old; Lewis E., 5 years old; Christina A., 3 years old; and Fredrick F., 2 years old.[16]

Martha died at Lewiston on May 4, 1916, after having given birth to what the newspaper stated was her eighth child on April 16. Her funeral was held on May 6 in St. Andrew's Episcopal Church with interment in "St. Andrew's cemetery at Atlantic."[17]

Martha's heartbreaking obituary stated:

This photograph is of a drawing entitled "Martha Godward-Anderson, according to Martha Walrath descendant." Undated. Artist is unknown.
–Courtesy of and with permission by Martha Walrath and the South Pass City State Historic Site

107

Mrs. Anderson has raised this family under real pioneer conditions. Living in an out of the way place and having to take care of the family in sickness and in health. She was a good mother and did the best she could. Although her death was caused by complications which arose after the birth of the last child she has been a sick mother for the last six years. She never gave in, with the result that she went to her place of rest with the fortitude of a martyr.[18]

In the early days of this project, I learned the initial cause of Martha's death was stated to be "neglect after childbirth" in the St. Andrew's Episcopal Church's "Record Book for Atlantic City."[19]

Years later I spoke with a great-granddaughter of the Andersons and read to her the newspaper article. She rejected the newspaper's article which stated Martha had had eight babies. She adamantly corrected the record Martha had had twelve babies. Nine survived including her newborn, who was named Kenneth.[20]

Martha Anderson's burial information is on line 4; husband James Anderson's burial information is on line 5. –Courtesy of the St. Andrew's Episcopal Church

In 2024, I discovered her death certificate and was shocked to read the official cause of her death: "cirrhosis of liver" with a contributory reason of "pregnancy-delivered April 16, '16."

Her ailment was stated to have begun "about 6 years ago at least."[21]

In modern times, we can be forgiven to assume her cause of cirrhosis of the liver was alcoholism. After mulling Martha's hard work as a woman birthing and raising many children in a tough environment in Lewiston, I absolutely do not believe this. I looked into natural causes of this disease.

Without going deep into medical science, natural factors can cause cirrhosis of the liver which can lead to a high-risk pregnancy which contributed to her death. Cirrhosis of the liver is also caused by parasites, hepatis, nonalcoholic fatty liver disease, high blood pressure, and infection.[22]

Too much aspirin can cause liver failure. Willows line our waterways and willow bark contains salicin, a chemical which acts similarly to aspirin.[23]

Martha Anderson's death certificate, May 6, 1916 –Courtesy of the Wyoming State Archives

Additionally, meeting with the Fremont County Coroner Erin Ivie and staff it's quite possible a "geriatric mother" (a term meaning a woman having a baby while 35 years old or older) and one who'd gestated and birthed twelve children had experienced so much stress on her body.

Furthermore, preeclampsia is a life-threatening complication and usually occurs during the late stages of pregnancy or soon after childbirth. Side effects of preeclampsia include acute hepatitis and acute fatty liver disease which can lead to cirrhosis.[24]

With her body continually under stress from pregnancy and raising many children in a harsh environment, Martha never had a chance to recover.

Note#1: Two months after Martha's death, her widowed husband James died on July 1 of pneumonia. Their orphaned children were split between aunts who took "the younger boys and the girls" to Illinois, "the uncles will take the other boys to their ranch at Lucerne, Wyoming," and a social worker.[25]

Note #2: Focusing on Martha and husband James Anderson, one reference stated she and James had died within a week of each other. This reference is confirmed to be inaccurate as Martha died on May 4 and James died July 1, 1916.[26]

Note #3: A week after receiving Martha's death certificate, while searching old newspapers in the Lander library, I came across an obituary with a cause of death I had only seen once before in the many years of researching obituaries: cirrhosis of the liver. Jacob S. Meyer died on July 30, 1898, at his ranch on the Upper Big Popo Agie River. He died aged 42 years, 4 months, and 20 days. He was only seven months older than Martha.[27]

Godward, Frank, "Pard" G.
April 1882–June 29, 1903

Frank was a young man of 21 years of age when he was blasting out rock in Granier Meadow, ten miles northwest, in preparation for a drilling contest for the Fourth of July celebration.

A three-ton stone fell on him.[28]

With both legs broken and with internal injuries, the men made him as comfortable as possible in the wagon for the brutal drive to Lander.

> Although suffering excruciating pain from the jolting of the vehicle, Godward stood it manfully and when some distance this side of Reid's asked for a drink of water, remarking also that he felt suffocating.
>
> Water was given him and the curtains of the rig were raised so as to give more air. ... During the time the spirit of the brave young man took its flight without a sound or struggle.

After the undertaker had prepared Frank's body in Lander, on Tuesday morning Frank was "conveyed back to Atlantic City for burial."

"The burial of Frank Godward, which occured [sic] at Atlantic City, was the largest ever seen at this place." The obituary was very specific in detail and included the songs sung by mourners and listed his pall bearers.

> Every person in Atlantic was present to pay their respects. The deceased was one of the most popular and exemplary young men in the city.[29]

The 1900 census stated Frank was born in April 1882 in Wyoming, and at the time of the census he was 18 years old and a day laborer.

As a tribute to Pard, the boulder with the holes made by drillers in the drilling contest was set on Main Street. It stands across the road from the Atlantic City Mercantile, as told by old-timers to John Mionczynski.[30]

Tip: I hadn't known about Frank Godward. Luckily, a trick learned early in the beginning of this project when I was searching for a specific person in the newspapers was to also search the entire newspaper page(s) for any article about Atlantic City or for any death. One day, an article titled "A Distressing Accident" caught my attention. I learned of Pard's tragic accident.

Jackson, Charles "Charley"
October 25, 1852–December 15, 1939

Charles was born on October 25, 1852, in Canada. He passed away at age 87 in Riverton on December 15, 1939. His death notice was printed in the *Lander Evening Post*. He was

> One of the last of the original settlers of the once-bustling frontier mining town of Atlantic City. He had located to Atlantic City in 1885 and worked on the Christina Lake ditch.[31]

Charley lived in Lewiston and he worked as a miner. From his death certificate, we know his birthdate, his place of birth was Canada, and he had lived in the US for 54 years.[32]

Charley and his wife Eliza opened and owned Lewiston's Palmer House, a hotel. Renowned as an expert marksman, "I have seen him pick off a coyote on the dead run in the sagebrush," Betty Carpenter Pfaff stated.[33]

Lewiston's 1900 census listed his birth date as October 1854. He was married. He had immigrated in 1858 but was never naturalized. The next line includes wife Eliza who was born in December 1846, was 53 years old, and born in England. She and Charley had been married four years.

On April 23, 1904, Charley claimed the water rights to "the Strawberry Stream to the extent of 2000 miners inches, for mining purposes."[34]

The 1910 census for Lewiston listed him as 55 years old, married, and as a laborer in the mines. There was no listing for Eliza.

Charles Jackson lived in Lewiston. Undated. –Courtesy of the Henry Williams Family, and the Davison Collection at the South Pass City State Historic Site

Tip: The Atlantic City 1920 census listed a Charles Jackson but his age is listed as 33. His birthplace is obscured but it appears to be Kansas, so this is not our Charles Jackson.

Atlantic City's 1930 census listed Charley at 77, from "Canada English," divorced, with a year of immigration as 1870, and a gold miner.[35]

He voted in both the primary and general elections in 1930. In the August 19 primary, he was the 3rd voter and voted for the Democratic party. For the November 4 general election, the poll book stated he was the 27th voter, was 78 years old and born in Canada.[36]

"Charlie" worked for the Christina Lake Mining Company. He was described as a "tall, thin man with a high-pitched voice."

From Lewiston, he would walk the 12 miles to Atlantic City to "save his horse." He kept his home immaculate.

Wallace Grosvenor, who claimed the Morris, Hidden Hand, and Casselton Lodes, described Charley:

His table was always set for another person, including napkins, utensils and coffee cup. I used to eat with him quite often but the "place" for the missing person was always set, no matter how many people he had for dinner. Hanging from the wall was an old fashioned bird cage with the door open. He said, "Birdie will come home some day."[37]

Charles Jackson's water rights to Strawberry Stream, April 23, 1904.
–Courtesy of the Fremont County Clerk's Office, Land Recording Office

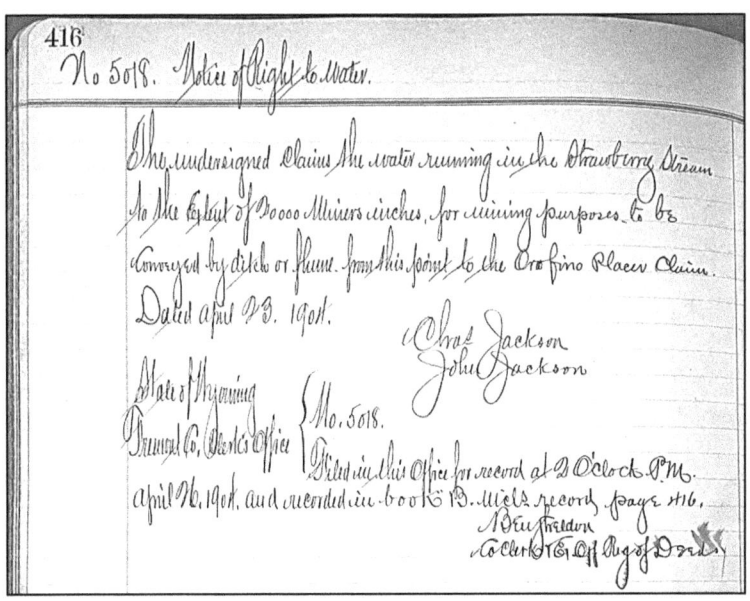

A chapter is devoted to Charley in *Fine Gold* which included he had also cooked for a chuck wagon, joined the Ringling Brothers Circus then left this job to gamble, and was quite "a ladies man."[38]

Charley's death certificate stated he had died of senility with "other condition" of a prostatic abscess. He was divorced and he was a retired laborer as a mine prospector.

His death notice stated:

> Charles Jackson, 87, one of the last of the original settlers of that once-bustling frontier mining town of Atlantic City, died in Riverton last week. He had located at Atlantic City in the spring of 1885 and worked on the Christina Lake ditch. He worked in other parts of the west, returning to Atlantic City to spend the last few winters.[39]

He was buried in Atlantic City on December 18, 1939.

Also spelled Jacome.

Note: We know Charley is in the East Cemetery because of Daniel Y. Meschter's 1968 documentation of defunct Wyoming cemeteries. In it, he described a lone gravesite with a metal mortuary's marker: "Undertaker's marker, glass covered paper: Charles Jackson (?), dates illegible."[40]

It's possible the question mark after Charley's last name indicated a possible misspelling or the name wasn't perfectly legible.

Once I thought Charley's burial site was the grave with the sole funeral home's identifying plate (index # F20). Two items prove this to be incorrect.

First, the same woman who had grown up in Atlantic City and recommended using a flashlight to find markings on "Our Mother's" headstone recalled seeing several of these metal markers throughout the cemetery. The loss of those markers, even without identifying information, was a great loss of knowledge.

Second, on September 29, 2016, a dowser determined this grave held a female.

At least we know Charley is here.

Mr. Charles Jackson, mine host of the Palmer house, is having a good run; the house having been full for the past ten days, and in consequence Charlie wears a broad grin on his pleasant countenance.

Charles Jackson and with wife Eliza, the Palmer house in Lewiston flourished. –Courtesy of the Clipper, *July 29, 1898, University of Wyoming and the Wyoming State Library*

Chas. Jackson walked up from Lewiston Monday to get the mail. Walking is bad and Mr. Jackson has a long way to come but nevertheless he always gets here early.

Local reporting of Charles Jackson walking from Lewiston to Atlantic City. –Courtesy of the Wyoming State Journal, *April 18, 1928*

McCarroll, William
Circa 1861–November 27, 1897

William was a miner for the Carissa gold mine near South Pass City. He had been born in Midway, Utah.

He was killed in a mine shaft explosion on November 27, 1897, aged 36 years old. His death notice stated his "Remains were burried [*sic*] in Atlantic City," and his name was spelled "McCarrol."

"November 28, McCarrol was laid by the side of his intended, Miss Ida Swabes, who was buried at Atlantic City one week ago today."

He had no marker.

Had they both lived, William and Ida were to have been married December 15.[41]

Ida is included in this chapter.[42]

After piecing the information about the deaths of William and Ida and comprehending the entire sequence of the tragedies, I wondered about the possibility if grief caused him to kill himself or if he had been distracted by his grief and this distraction inadvertently caused this accident.

The newspaper article about his death (following page) is included to highlight the daily dangers our men faced in the mines.

Note: Mark Stratmoen, Fremont County's coroner in 2015, studied the proceedings and the finding of the original 1897 coroner's inquest for the accident which killed William. In his book, *Murder, Mayhem, and Mystery: Coroner Inquests in Fremont County Wyoming 1885-1900*, portions of his in-depth commentary about William's inquest profoundly struck me. He wrote:

> The verdict made pains to establish it as accidental. ... As a death investigation, the remarkable thing about it is that it is the only inquest for a mining industrial accident from the period. ... There is no hint as to why this particular incident warranted an official inquest.[43]

When he and I spoke, he said he felt the workers were trying very hard to protect the company owners, something he'd never seen before.

I recalled my earlier thoughts about the possibilities of suicide or he was distracted from grief and made a mistake. I told him about Ida, their engagement, and of her death the week before. I wondered if the men weren't trying to protect the owners—they trying to protect *him*.

Mark became excited and said he had no idea of Ida. Of course, he couldn't know about her since she was not referenced in the inquest. He couldn't know how her loss affected William's thinking and actions. This information gave him a new perspective.[44]

Also spelled McCarrol.

The account of the mine accident that took the life of William McCarroll was published in the Vernal Express, *December 9, 1897.* –Courtesy of the J. Willard Library

William McCarroll Killed in a Wyoming Mine.

South Pass, Wyo., Nov. 27.—This morning when the day shift of the Carriso went on, William McCarroll remarked that one of the shots that he had set off the night previous had not gone, as the cap was bad. Morrice Llowellyn remarked to him, "You are all right; you can fire at noon." McCarroll said, "Yes, I can." At 9 25 a. m the man in the shaft and your correspondent heard something like fifty feet distant on the same level, and in a crosscut just under cover were startled as well as pretty well shaken up, by a terrible explosion Morrice Llowellyn called up the shaft, "That is Bill McCarroll's blast that has gone off, and he is killed."

Your correspondent got to the shaft and called for help on top. Mr Leighton came down, and asked what the matter was; the writer stated that Will McCarroll's shot had gone off and that he must be dead.

Superintendent Leighton then walked to where McCarroll had started the crosscut; the writer followed him; when they reached the spot William McCarroll was breathing; the writer was ordered to ring the bucket up, so that we could get him on top where we could do something for him When we got back McCarroll had quit breathing; he remarked that Will was dead. Mr. Leighton then placed his hand over his heart and said, "Yes, he is dead." We picked him up and carried him to the shaft and lashed him in the bucket and your correspondent then went and got the right hand and arm, which were blown off and lay in the further corner of the west drift. His arm was blown off between the wrist and elbow

The body was then taken down to the Pass, where Daniel Carmody had gone to notify the Justice, William Wygal, who, acted as Coroner, held an inquest, having first come to the mine and impaneling a jury examined the place where the explosion had taken place; then held an inquest with a verdict of accidental death, caused by explosion of giant powder, and exonerating every one. When the body was examined more fully, it was found that McCarroll's right thigh was broken, and a large rock the size of a hen's egg had been blown almost through his chest. His face was badly powder burnt, besides his body was blown full of small particles of rock Nearly a peck of rocks from the size of a pea up to that of a walnut were picked from his body and clothing.

William McCarroll was born in Midway, Utah, thirty-six years ago. His parents are Jess and Amandy McCarroll of Vernal, Utah, he was well known in Midway, Heber City, Mercur and Park City. The old-time boys of the latter place will remember him well, as he drove team for Robert Lindsay at the Ontario mine thirteen or fourteen years ago. He also was known in many of the mining camps of Colorado.

November 28th, McCarroll was laid by the side of his intended, Miss Ida Swabes, who was buried in Atlantic City one week ago to I a j. All the people of the two towns paid their last respects to his memory. Peace to the soul of the brave, noble, generous man —Salt Lake Tribune.

Swabes, Ida
Circa 1879–November 19, 1897

Ida was 18 years old when she died of blood poisoning on November 19, 1897. Albert Mann, a long-term Atlantic City resident spoke of the Swabes family.

> The very early settlers of Miners Delight were the Swabeses. ... When I came in here the old couple, Mr. and Mrs. Swabes, lived in one of those cabins in Miners Delight. ... They were there I guess when soldiers were at Stambaugh.[45]

Ida's obituary explains her lingering, tragic death (following page).

> Hardships and exposure brought on a complication of diseases which resulted in blood poison. That the girl had been failing for weeks there is no question. The remains were followed to their last resting place on earth near Atlantic, by a large concourse of people. ... Supt. Geo. Layton closed the Carissa mine down Sunday that the boys could attend the funeral.[46]

One of "the boys" would have been Ida's fiancé, William McCarroll.

In the *Vernal Express* article about William's death by an explosion in the Carissa mine a week after her death (opposite page), she was included as "his intended" and buried one week earlier.

William was buried by her side. Neither has a marker.[47]

Had Ida and William lived, they would have been married on December 15.

Side note: On December 2, 1896, Ida "Swabs," aged 16, was arrested for pettit [*sic*] larceny.[48]

Also spelled Schwabe, Swabs, and Swapes.

At 4 o'clock p. m. Friday, the 19th inst., Miss Ida Schwabe, aged 18 yrs., soul wended it's way across that dark sea called death. Hardships and exposure brought on a complication of diseases which resulted in blood poison. That the girl had been failing for weeks there is no question. The remains were followed to their last resting place on earth near Atlantic, by a large concourse of people. There was none but what expressed sorrow that one so young should be called away from our midst. Prof. Freeland preached a very impressive funeral service, after which the ladies and gentlemen, led by Mrs. Ella Potter, sang "Nearer my God to Thee" and "The Home over There." The friends of the young lady then wended their way homeward leaving her who in the first blush of womanhood's morn, being weary sank into that eternal slumber while her spirit ship was spreading it's sails and sailing away for the harbor of peace and joy promised by Him who leaving the grand council of Heaven and coming to this earth and donning the mortal robe that by dying on the cross the world could be saved. Knowing that in the care of that loving heart no danger could come to her spirit ship we left her.

Supt. Geo. Layton closed the Caraca mine down Sunday that the boys could attend the funeral.

Ida Swabes' obituary and funeral in the Wind River Mountaineer, *November 29, 1897.*
–Courtesy of the University of Wyoming and Wyoming State Library

SIX

East Cemetery
Dowsed Graves of Unknown Persons

Many of the early graves were marked with a wooden marker which simply deteriorated from our harsh weather. Perhaps the graves weren't marked at all. Additionally, with a large number of single residents and a transient population, or few friends or relatives to replace the marker, no trace of the grave remains.

We may be able to tell a spot is a burial site because of certain signs, but with our weather extremes and vegetation even a true burial site will be obscured.

Thankfully, because of experienced and dedicated individuals, we now know where people are buried in this cemetery. Their efforts allowed the marking of 72 graves with wood stakes painted blue or red, depending upon the sex.[1]

This chapter is a technical listing to document these dowsed graves. It is impossible to know whose body lies in any specific site or if the site contains a body or spread cremains.

For each site, the first paragraph states a brief description of the site and the direction I faced when taking the photograph and the date it was taken. Each photograph was taken with as much background as possible to assist in locating each site.

One important documentation is two measurements from each stake to two differing "hard" items, like a metal fence or a headstone. These measurements would be invaluable in case of fire or vandalism that destroys the stakes. In no way will these graves be lost to history again.

Each site's segment also lists any specifics or miscellaneous information.

While it's sad to see so many unmarked graves, it is heartening to consider many of the people occupying these graves are likely listed in chapter 3, *Buried in Atlantic City, Specific Gravesite Unknown*; chapter 5, *East Cemetery, Specific Gravesite Unknown*; and in chapter 9, *Burial Site Unknown*.

For the remaining graves of unknowns, we will never know their names, but we know someone lies there and we honor them.

First, on June 7, 2016, a cadaver-seeking border collie named Blue, owned and handled by search-and-rescuer K. T. Irwin, detected eleven confirmed human remains on an unknown person's site now designated as F4, M7, F8, F9, M12, M16, M23, M50, and three other locations: the Carpenter family monument, a site north of Alwin Heyroth, and a site north of Georgina Newman.

For information on the abilities of cadaver dogs see chapter 10, *Cadaver Dogs*.

Then, on July 16, 2016, dowser Don Schooley confirmed most of the dog and K. T.'s detections. He dowsed the cemetery and discovered and determined the sexes for 60 burial sites, 44 males and 16 females. They are: F1, M1, F2, M2, F3, F4, M4, M5, F6, M6, F7, M7, F8, M8, F9, M9, F10, F12, F13, M13, F14, M14, F15, M15, M16, F17, M17, F18, M18, F19, M19, M20, M21, M22, M25, M26, M27, M28, M29, M30, M31, M32, M33, M34, M35, M36, M38, M39, M40, M41, M42, M43, M44, M45, M46, M47, M48, M49, M50, and M52.

Don verified the remains confirmed by K. T. and Blue at the Carpenter family stone later said to be the ashes of Anne Carpenter Robinson. He also made a shocking observation about Miss Ellen Carpenter's grave.

On September 29 and October 9, 2016, dowser Ann Noble confirmed all Don's findings and, with her tighter grid pattern, detected 12 more graves and determined the sex for those 12 sites, 8 males and 4 females. They are: M3, F5, M10, F11, M11, M12, F16, F20, M23, M24, M37, and M51.

A few of the dog's and the dowsers' findings can be seen in 1950s cemetery photographs on pages 31 and 33. The photos show remnants of a marker or fence where the dog and dowsers found graves.[2]

Stakes marking each site are colored by sex, red for females and blue for males, and its index number is painted on each stake.

Additionally, the dowsers determined there are six persons buried north-south. The map on page 35 are marked with ovals shown vertically.

To further distinguish these graves from the usual east-west burials, these graves have *two* colored stakes, one at their head and one at their feet with "head" and "foot" included on each stake. Some of the dowsed locations may be placed or spread cremains.

For in-depth information on dowsing and the steps used to document each gravesite see chapter 11, *Dowsing for Graves*.

Technical information:

Since this chapter documents the graves of Unknowns so they will no longer be lost, a photograph shows the stake marking each site. Background was included when possible to help visualize and locate the spot.

In some photographs the appearance of the stake is lost amongst thick vegetation. These photographs have tick marks on each side that lead to the top of the stake to help locate the stake.

Lat/Long coordinates indicate the location of the headstones or markers.

Their format are in the Degrees and Decimal Minutes format: DDD° MM.MMM' (WGS 84 map datum).

Female #1

Her grave is a mound of earth 9 feet from the north fence. Photo taken on August 8, 2021, while facing southwest. The stake is deep into the vegetation but is visible.

Dowser Ann Noble believes she was possibly stillborn and the body was hastily buried. Dirt covers her, but the earth which had been dug out for her wasn't completely replaced.

This infant is located 64'3" from the cemetery's east fence and 8'11" south of the cemetery's north fence.

This point is from the northeast corner post plus four more posts to the west, between the 4th and 5th posts (practically in the middle of the length of the fence, east to west).

Cemetery map index #: F1
Lat/Long: N42° 29.835' W108° 43.302/3'

Male #1

A slight depression of gravel with four white ceramic pieces and a tiny silver-like pendant were found on top of the gravel. Photo taken on August 8, 2021, while facing east.

The stake for this site is located 28'2" from the cemetery's north fence and 41'5" from the northeast corner of the Harsch family fence (Index #9).

On October 3, 2015, anthropologist William Elder from the Wyoming Community College discovered the pendant and documented the finding per their training.

According to the property owner's instructions, the pendant is in the possession of the Atlantic City Historical Society curator for safekeeping.

This tiny pendant was discovered on the ground of this grave by Central Wyoming College anthropologist William Elder. 2015. Left: The face of the pendant.

Cemetery map index #: M1
Lat/Long: N42° 29.832' W108° 43.301/0'

Female #2

The site is slightly sunken with little vegetation. Photo taken on August 8, 2021, while facing east.

It's located 32'8" from the northeast corner of the Harsch family fence (Index #9) and 30'4" from the southwest corner of Paul Newman's marker (Index #16).

Cemetery map index #: F2
Lat/Long: N42° 29.828' W108° 43.301'

Male #2

A gravelly spot with small sages mark this site. Photo taken on August 8, 2021, while facing southeast.

It's located 34'4" from the cemetery's north fence and 14'11" from the northwest corner of Georgina Newman's marker (Index #15).

On June 7, 2016, a cadaver dog downed at this site. It was marked with the orange tape as a confirmed downing. The waypoint number in the handler's report is #248.

Cemetery map index #: M2
Lat/Long: N42° 29.831' W108° 43.297'

Female #3

This is a sunken area, gravelly, with small sages. Photo taken on August 8, 2021, while facing east.

The location is 31'3" from the northeast corner of the Harsch family fence (Index #9) and 8'0" north from the trunk of the evergreen tree to the south.

Cemetery map index #: F3
Lat/Long: N42° 29.825' W108° 43.303/4'

Male #3

A slightly gravelly and slightly sunken area mark this site. Photo taken on August 8, 2021, while facing southwest.

It's located 37'6" from the northeast corner of the Harsch family fence (Index #9) and 30'5" from Georgina Newman's marker (Index #15).

Cemetery map index #: M3
Lat/Long: N42° 29.830' W108° 43.302/1'

Female #4

This fallen and scattered wooden picket fence is immediately east of the large evergreen tree between the Harsch and Carpenter families' plots (Index #9 and #2). Photo taken on August 8, 2021, while facing north-northwest.

This site's "head" is 22'2" from the Carpenter family monument (Index #2), 20'1" from the east face of "Our Mother" headstone (Index #17), and 5' from the trunk of the evergreen tree to the west.

On June 7, 2016, a cadaver dog downed on this site. The waypoint number in the handler's report is #247. The downing was not captured on video. A strip of yellow marking tape marks the site.

Cemetery map index #: F4
Lat/Long: N42° 29.824' W108° 43.301'

Male #4

A flat, gravelly area with rotting boards west of the "head" marks this site. Photo taken on August 8, 2021, while facing north-northwest.

It's located 16'2" from the Carpenter family stone (Index #2) and 11'5" from the trunk of the evergreen tree to the northwest.

Cemetery map index #: M4
Lat/Long: N42° 29.824/3' W108° 43.299/300'

Female #5

The site is surrounded by small sage. Photo taken on August 8, 2021, while facing west.

On September 29, 2016, dowser Ann Noble felt this person was a baby girl or small girl child. She's located 5'2" from Alonzo Richardson's headstone (Index #18) and 22'3" from the southeast corner of the Harsch family fence (Index #9).

Cemetery map index #: M5
Lat/Long: N42° 29.824' W108° 43.305/4'

Male #5

This is a slightly sunken spot with randomly growing small sages. Photo taken on August 8, 2021, while facing west-northwest.

It's located 25'0" from the Carpenter family monument (Index #2) and 36'3" from the southeast corner of the Harsch family fence (Index #9).

Cemetery map index #: M5
Lat/Long: N42° 29.823' W108° 43.301'

125

Female #6

The site is solid with thick bramble bushes. Photo taken on August 8, 2021, while facing west-southwest.

It's located 4'6" from the southeast corner and 13'6" from the southwest corner of the Harsch family fence (Index #9).

Cemetery map index #: F6
Lat/Long: N42° 29.823' W108° 43.309'

Male #6

Three board remnants between the southeast corner of the Harsch family plot and the large evergreen tree mark this site. Photo taken on August 8, 2021, while facing west-southwest.

This is located 12'5" from Alonzo Richardson's headstone (Index #18) and 22'7" from the southeast corner of the Harsch family plot (Index #9). On September 29, 2016, dowser Ann Noble noted the dirt disruption for this grave "was wide."

Cemetery map index #: M6
Lat/Long: N42° 29.823/4' W108° 43.305'

Female #7

This grave is a depression covered with thick vegetation and wood pieces. One piece of timber lies nearby. Photo taken on August 8, 2021, while facing northeast. The grave is marked with two stakes.

On September 29, 2016, dowser Ann Noble noted this burial is north-south. This burial is likely part of a family unit because of their isolation and is alongside a male who was also buried north-south. Refer to Male #12.

This spot is 22'0" from Jared Williams' marker (Index #21) and 14'10" from the corner of Joseph Barbett's headstone concrete base.

Cemetery map index #: F7
Lat/Long: N42° 29.816/7' W108° 43.303'

Male #7

The site is covered with thick sage. Photo taken on August 8, 2021, while facing northeast.

The site is located 14'7" from the southeast corner of the Harsch family fence (Index #9) and 12'0" from the southern edge of Alonzo Richardson's headstone (Index #18).

On June 7, 2016, a cadaver dog downed at this site. It can be seen being marked in video *10 Marking* at 3:14 and can be seen as marked by the orange tape on video *11 Marking* at 05:06. Its waypoint is #251 in the handler's report.

Cemetery map index #: M7
Lat/Long: N42° 29.822' W108° 43.308'

Female #8

Fallen remnants of about seven boards surround a graveled area. Photo taken on August 8, 2021, facing east.

The head is located 25'0" west from the northwest corner and 25'0" west from the southwest corner of John Garrison's metal fence (Index #7).

On June 7, 2016, a cadaver dog downed at this site. The video of the downing action is *Clip #5*, time stamp 20:10. In video *10 Marking* at 00:00 onward, this site can be seen being marked. It can also be seen marked by the orange tape on video *11 Marking* at 05:11. The waypoint number in the handler's report is #255.

Cemetery map index #: F8
Lat/Long: N42° 29.810/11' W108° 43.307'

Male #8

This grave is obscured by very thick sage. Photo taken on August 8, 2021, while facing east-southeast.

It's located 13'8" from the abandoned concrete base (Index #AB), 43'10" from the southwest corner and 43'4" from the southeast corner of the Harsch family fence (Index #9).

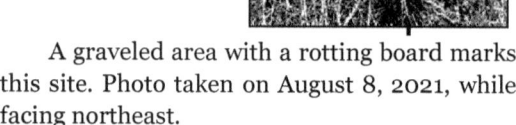

Cemetery map index #: M8
Lat/Long: N42° 29.816' W108° 43.312/3'

Female #9

A graveled area with a rotting board marks this site. Photo taken on August 8, 2021, while facing northeast.

This spot is 37'10" from the cemetery's south fence and 78'4" from the cemetery's west fence.

On June 7, 2016, a cadaver dog downed at this spot. The video of the action is *6 Search*, time stamp of 6:34. This site is possibly the one I'm marking in video *10 Marking* at 00:05. The waypoint in the dog handler's report is #250.

Cemetery map index #: F9
Lat/Long: N42° 29.809' W108° 43.311'

Male #9

This spot is thick with overgrown sage. Photo taken on August 8, 2021, while facing northeast.

It's located 48'4" from the southeast corner and 48'10" from the southwest corner of the Harsch family fence (Index #9), and 18'3" from the abandoned headstone base (Index #AB).

Cemetery map index #: M9
Lat/Long: N42° 29.815' W108° 43.313'

Female #10

A touch of a gravelly area littered with rotting planks indicate this grave. Photo taken on August 8, 2021, while facing southwest.

This burial is likely half of a couple because of their isolation. Refer to Male #18.

The site's location is 17'6" from the cemetery's south fence and 51'9" from the southwest corner of John Garrison's nearby fence (Index #7).

Cemetery map index #: F10
Lat/Long: N42° 29.805' W108° 43.310'

Male #10

A patch of massive bramble bushes and sage cover this site. Photo taken on August 8, 2021, while facing northwest.

The site is located 45'0" from the north post of Jared Williams' marker and 53'10" from the southwest fence corner of the Harsch family plot.

Cemetery map index #: M10
Lat/Long: N42° 29.813/4' W108° 43.314/3'

Female #11

Dead sages and short sages surround this site. Photo taken on August 8, 2021, while facing north-northeast.

On October 9, 2016, dowser Ann Noble stated she was an adult. The site is located 17'1" from the cemetery's south fence and 47'1" from the cemetery's west fence.

Cemetery map index #: F11
Lat/Long: N42° 29.805/6' W108° 43.320/19'

Male #11

This site is a mass of sagebrush. Photo taken on August 8, 2021, while facing northeast.

The stake is 41'5" from Jared Williams' headstone (Index #21) and 70'8" from the cemetery's south fence.

Cemetery map index #: M11
Lat/Long: N42° 29.813' W108° 43.313'

Female #12

This site is slightly gravelly with small sage around its perimeter. Photo taken on August 8, 2021, while facing northeast.

The spot is located 9'5" from the cemetery's west fence and 12'10" from the cemetery's south fence.

Cemetery map index #: F12
Lat/Long: N42° 29.806' W108° 43.328/7'

Male #12

The site is covered with short brambles and sage. Photo taken on August 8, 2021, while facing northeast.

On June 7, 2016, a cadaver dog downed at this site. The waypoint in the handler's report is #249. It can be seen marked by the orange tape on video *11 Marking* at 05:11 and on video *12 Dogs Playing* at 1:15.

On October 9, 2016, dowser Ann Noble stated this person was buried north-south and the gravesite was more than six feet long. This burial is likely half of a couple because of their isolation and with a female also buried north-south. Refer to Female #7.

It's located 14'11" from Joseph Barbett's headstone base (Index #1) and 26'4" from Jared Williams' marker (Index #21).

Cemetery map index #: M12
Lat/Long: N42° 29.816/7' W108° 43.302/3'

Female #13

A flattish spot with sage to the north and small sage to the east-northeast is a sign for this grave. Photo taken on August 8, 2021, while facing north.

This site is 47'2" from the cemetery's west fence and 49'7" from the cemetery's south fence.

Cemetery map index #: F13
Lat/Long: N42° 29.813/2' W108° 43.317'

Male #13

This site is a slight mound of gravel. Photo taken on August 8, 2021, while facing north-northwest.

This spot is 11'9" from the southeast corner and 9'6" from the southwest corner of John Garrison's fence (Index #7).

Cemetery map index #: M13
Lat/Long: N42° 29.809/8' W108° 43.301'

Female #14

A slightly sloping site with large sages to the north and south and with dead sage at the "head" marks this site. Photo taken on August 8, 2021, while facing northeast.

It's located 47'7" from the cemetery's west fence and 71'7" from the cemetery's south fence.

Cemetery map index #: F14
Lat/Long: N42° 29.815/4' W108° 43.317'

Male #14

A gravelly depression surrounded by sage is this grave. Photo taken on August 8, 2021, while facing north-northwest.

It's located at 20'4" from the southeast corner and 18'10" from the southwest corner of John Garrison's fence (Index #7).

Cemetery map index #: M14
Lat/Long: N42° 29.807' W108° 43.302'

Female #15

This site is a slightly sunken and gravelly spot. Photo taken on August 8, 2021, while facing north-northeast.

It's 29'8" from the cemetery's west fence and 19'8" from the trunk of the first evergreen tree to the north.

Cemetery map index #: F15
Lat/Long: N42° 29.819' W108° 43.320'

Male #15

A slightly sunken spot is covered with gravel and sage. Photo taken on August 8, 2021, while facing east.

It's located 44'10" from the northwest corner and 45'2" from the southwest corner of John Garrison's fence (Index #7).

Cemetery map index #: M15
Lat/Long: N42° 29.811/2' W108° 43.311'

Female #16

This gravesite is a solid thicket of brambles. Photo taken on August 8, 2021, while facing east.

It's located 14'1" from the cemetery's west fence and 29'9" from the trunk of the first evergreen tree to the northeast.

On October 9, 2016, dowser Ann Noble believes this female (stake peeks out on the left foreground) is paired with the male infant or child immediately to her south (Male #36, stake is on the right).

Cemetery map index #: F16
Lat/Long: N42° 29.819/8' W108° 43.324'

Male #16

Scattered fallen and rotting timbers cover this sunken site. Photo taken on August 8, 2021, while facing east.

It's located 51'7" from the cemetery's south fence and 45'4" from the southwest corner of John Garrison's fence (Index #7).

On June 7, 2016, a cadaver dog downed at this site. The waypoint in the handler's report is #254. Yellow tape is attached at the site's foot.

Cemetery map index #: M16
Lat/Long: N42° 29.811' W108° 43.311'

Female #17

This is a slight depression with a few rotting timbers. Photo taken on August 8, 2021, while facing west-southwest. The stake is center, mid-foreground.

The stake is located 25'3" from the southwest corner and 27'7" from the southeast corner of the Harsch family fence (Index #9), and 5'4" from the abandoned concrete base (Index #AB).

Cemetery map index #: F17
Lat/Long: N42° 29.820' W108° 43.313'

Male #17

A slightly sunken grave is covered with a rotting board and surrounded by sage. Photo taken on August 8, 2021, while facing east.

The spot is 42'8" from the cemetery's south fence and 45'2" from the southwest corner of John Garrison's fence (Index #7).

Cemetery map index #: M17
Lat/Long: N42° 29.809' W108° 43.311/10'

Female #18

This is an open, flat, and plain site with short sage to the southeast. Photo taken on August 8, 2021, while facing east.

It's located 13'3" from the cemetery's west fence and 23'9" from the trunk of the south evergreen tree to the east.

Cemetery map index #: F18
Lat/Long: N42° 29.823' W108° 43.323'

Male #18

Several wide planks have fallen onto this slight gravelly depression. Photo taken on August 8, 2021, while facing southwest. This burial is possibly half of a couple because of their isolation and closeness. Refer to Female #10.

It's located 23'5" from the south fence and 46'1" from the southwest corner of John Garrison's fence (Index #7).

Cemetery map index #: M18
Lat/Long: N42° 29.806/5' W108° 43.309/10'

Female #19

This site is a gravelly depression. Three timbers lie together to the north. Photo taken on August 8, 2021, while facing north.

This spot lies 23'6" from the cemetery's north fence and 22'4" from the cemetery's west fence.

On September 29, 2016, dowser Ann Noble stated this person is buried north-south. This burial is likely part of a family group because of their closeness and isolation and as all three are buried north-south. See Males #51 and #52.

Cemetery map index #: F19
Lat/Long: N42° 29.835' W108° 43.318'

Male #19

    This sunken spot has a mass of sage at its feet. Photo taken on August 8, 2021, while facing east-northeast.

    The site is 21'1" from the cemetery's south fence and 47'0" from the cemetery's west fence.

Cemetery map index #: M19
Lat/Long: N42° 29.806' W108° 43.318/9'

Female #20

Any personal information which had been inserted in the marker is gone. In August 2016, the marker was upright and intact (below).

A combination of rust at the ground level and flexing by strong wind broke the metal post. Now, the metal marker lies on the ground in front of the stake (right). Photo taken on September 28, 2021, while facing east-northeast.

The marker is 10'1" from the southwest corner and 25'4" from the northwest corner of the Harsch family fence (Index #9).

On September 29, 2016, Ann Noble dowsed this grave and determined the person is a female.

Side note: In the original 2016 database, this grave was included in the *Marked Burials* chapter because of the "permanence" of the marker. The metal marker has since snapped off.

This grave was moved to this chapter in case the marker ever disappears. Being listed here and with a red stake will ensure the gravesite will never be forgotten.

Marker inscription: The personal information is gone and the marker's plate glass is shattered. On the back of the marker is stamped: *PATENTED: 1276798 AUG. 27, 1918* and *1573268 FEB. 16, 1926*

Cemetery map index #: 20
Marker Lat/Long: N42° 29' 49.4" W108° 43' 18.8"

Male #20

This flat, gravelly area has a small sage at its head. Photo taken on August 8, 2021, while facing northeast.

It's 28'3" from the cemetery's south fence and 46'4" from the cemetery's west fence.

Cemetery map index #: M20
Lat/Long: N42° 29.807' W108° 43.318'

Male #21

Sages surround this site. Photo taken on August 8, 2021, while facing east.

It's 16'5" from the cemetery's south fence and 34'7" from the cemetery's west fence.

Cemetery map index #: M21
Lat/Long: N42° 29.806' W108° 43.321/2'

Male #22

This flat spot has small scattered sage. Photo taken on August 8, 2021, while facing east.

It's 22'4" from the cemetery's south fence and 35'10" from the cemetery's west fence.

Cemetery map index #: M22
Lat/Long: N42° 29.807' W108° 43.321'

Male #23

This site is overgrown with sage. The photo was taken on August 8, 2021, while facing east.

This site is 33'2" from the cemetery's south fence and 61'3" from the cemetery's west fence. Another method to find this spot is from the southwest corner post, head east 4 posts, then north 2 posts plus 6'.

On June 7, 2016, a cadaver dog downed at this site. The spot was marked with a bit of cardboard, but later replaced with yellow tape. The video of the action of the dog's downing is video *Clip #5*, at 18:59. The marking of the spot is *Video #9*, time stamp of 00:12. The waypoint in the handler's report is #253.

On October 9, 2016, dowser Ann Noble confirmed this grave is an adult male.

Cemetery map index #: M23
Lat/Long: *about* N42° 29.808' W108° 43.315'

Male #24

This is a flat spot with little vegetation. The photo taken on August 8, 2021, while facing northeast.

This site is 28'9" from the cemetery's west fence and 26'7" from the cemetery's south fence. On October 9, 2016, dowser Ann Noble noted this grave was about two-and-a-half feet long and determined this was a little boy.

Cemetery map index #: M24
Lat/Long: N42° 29.807/8' W108° 43.323'

Male #25

This flat, gravelly area has small sage nearby. Photo taken on August 8, 2021, while facing east.

It's located 13'0" from the cemetery's west fence and 33'0" from the cemetery's south fence.

Cemetery map index #: M25
Lat/Long: N42° 29.809/10' W108° 43.326'

Male #26

This light gravelly area is surrounded by small sage. Photo taken on August 8, 2021, while facing northeast.

It's 12'7" from the cemetery's west fence and 40'6" from the cemetery's south fence.

Cemetery map index #: M26
Lat/Long: N42° 29.811/10' W108° 43.325/6'

Male #27

A slight depression with one rotting board on the gravel and surrounded by sage mark this site. Photo taken on August 8, 2021, while facing east.

It's 38'7" from the cemetery's south fence and 38'5" from cemetery's west fence.

Cemetery map index #: M27
Lat/Long: N42° 29.810/9' W108° 43.320'

Male #28

A slightly sunken space sprinkled with small sage marks this site. Photo taken on August 8, 2021, while facing east.

It's 31'8" from the cemetery's west fence and 48'0" from the cemetery's south fence.

Cemetery map index #: M28
Lat/Long: N42° 29.811' W108° 43.321'

Male #29

This is a flat, gravelly site with sage to the north, south, and east. Photo taken on August 8, 2021, while facing east.

It's 31'5" from the cemetery's west fence and 54'9" from the cemetery's south fence.

Cemetery map index #: M29
Lat/Long: N42° 29.812' W108° 43.321'

Male #30

Short sage grows on and surrounds this sunken grave. Photo taken on August 8, 2021, while facing east.

It's 11'1" from the cemetery's west fence and 51'3" from the cemetery's south fence.

Cemetery map index #: M30
Lat/Long: N42° 29.812' W108° 43.327'

Male #31

The site is slightly sunken and gravelly with one rotting board across it. Photo taken on August 8, 2021, while facing east.

This spot is 31'1" from the cemetery's west fence and 48'2" from the trunk of the first evergreen tree to the north.

Cemetery map index #: M31
Lat/Long: N42° 29.814' W108° 43.321'

Male #32

This is a flattish site with short sage about. Photo taken on August 8, 2021, while facing north. The stake peeks out at 10 o'clock from the foreground bush.

It's 10'6" from the cemetery's west fence and 71'9" from the cemetery's south fence.

Cemetery map index #: M32
Lat/Long: N42° 29.815' W108° 43.325/6'

Male #33

A lone decaying plank remnant lies on top of a slight mound of gravel. Photo taken on August 8, 2021, while facing east.

This spot is 18'0" from the cemetery's west fence and about 9' north of an east-west line from Jared Williams' marker (Index #21).

Cemetery map index #: M33
Lat/Long: N42° 29.817' W108° 43.323'

Male #34

This is a sunken and gravelly site. Photo taken on August 8, 2021, while facing northeast.

It's 32'10" from the cemetery's west fence and 31'3" from the trunk of the first evergreen tree to the north.

Cemetery map index #: M34
Lat/Long: N42° 29.817' W108° 43.320'

Male #35

Little marks this site of a flat spot with little vegetation. Photo taken on August 8, 2021, while facing east.

The head is 92'4" from the cemetery's south fence and 40'4" from the cemetery's west fence.

Dowser Don Schooley detected this site on July 16, 2016. He stated it's about 8' long and 4' wide, though the actual distance between the two stakes is 11'8". The second stake can be seen near the top of the photo.

On October 9, 2016, dowser Ann Noble stated she felt it was two graves, though she could detect no separation between them. She sexed both ends of the grave and the rods indicated male.

It's likely two males are buried here. Essentially, one man overlaps the other. Since there is no separation between the two males they are counted as one burial.

Cemetery map index #: M35
Lat/Long: N42° 29.818' W108° 43.318' at west end and 43.315' at its east end

Male #36

The site is solidly thick with short sage and brambles. Photo taken on August 8, 2021, while facing east-southeast.

It's 14'1" from the cemetery's west fence and 31'7" from the trunk of the first evergreen tree to the northeast.

On October 9, 2016, dowser Ann Noble believes this small boy is paired with the adult female immediately to his north (Female #16, not shown here).

Cemetery map index #: M36
Lat/Long: N42° 29.819' W108° 43.323'

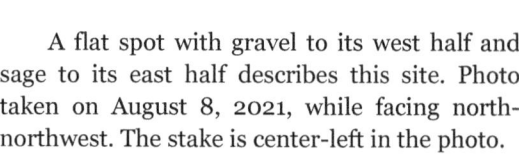

Male #37

A flat spot with gravel to its west half and sage to its east half describes this site. Photo taken on August 8, 2021, while facing north-northwest. The stake is center-left in the photo.

It's located 38'11" from the cemetery's west fence and 37'6" from the southwest corner of the Harsch family fence (Index #9). On September 29, 2016, dowser Ann Noble stated the site was small, likely a child.

Cemetery map index #: M37
Lat/Long: N42° 29.819' W108° 43.319'

Male #38

This site is a depression covered with gravel with sage to the north, south, and east. Photo taken on August 8, 2021, while facing east-northeast.

This spot lies 28'7" from the cemetery's west fence, and 10'0" from the trunk of the first evergreen tree to the northeast.

Cemetery map index #: M38
Lat/Long: N42° 29.821' W108° 43.319'

Male #39

Little vegetation marks this slightly sunken site. Photo taken on August 8, 2021, while facing west.

It's 6'7" from the trunk of the north-most evergreen tree to the west, and 22'9" from the southwest corner of the Harsch family fence (Index #9). Dowser Don Schooley noted this grave was extra-long, at least 8 feet.

Cemetery map index #: M39
Lat/Long: N42° 29.823/2' W108° 43.315/6'

Male #40

This flat site has very little vegetation and is littered with a few tiny shards of purple glass. Photo taken on August 8, 2021, while facing west.

It's 9'5" from the trunk of the north-most evergreen tree to the southwest, and 19'0" from the southwest corner of the Harsch family fence (Index #9). Dowser Don Schooley noted this site was extra-long, about 8 feet long.

Cemetery map index #: M40
Lat/Long: N42° 29.824' W108° 43.315/6'

Male #41

Collapsed and rotting timbers and posts surround this plot. Photo taken on August 8, 2021, while facing northeast.

This spot lies 27'2" from the cemetery's west fence and 10'11" from the trunk of the north-most evergreen tree to the east.

Cemetery map index #: M41
Lat/Long: N42° 29.824' W108° 43.319/20'

Male #42

M42 no longer exists. This photo was taken while facing northeast. This is how this grave appeared on August 8, 2021.

Earlier, on August 4, I identified a plank to be the original and treasured wood grave marker. The identity of the person buried here was confirmed to be Casimer Melin, who died in 1875. At the time of this photo, the marker had been removed from the site for safekeeping until it could be reset.

For information on Casimer Melin (Index #15), his grave, and his re-erected marker, see chapter 4.

Cemetery map index #: Formerly M42, now simply Index #15
Lat/Long: N42° 29.825/6' W108° 43.319'

Male #43

This rotting plank covers a slight depression on this site. Photo taken on October 10, 2021, while facing west.

This grave lies immediately north of Casimer Melin's grave (Index #15). It's 27'2" from the cemetery's west fence and 36'4" from the northwest corner of the Harsch family fence (Index #9).

Cemetery map index #: M43
Lat/Long: N42° 29.827' W108° 43.319'

Male #44

A small area of gravel with sage to the north and south marks this site. Photo taken on August 8, 2021, while facing south.

It's located 29'6" from the cemetery's west fence and 33'10" from the northwest corner of the Harsch family fence (Index #9).

Cemetery map index #: M44
Lat/Long: N42° 29.829' W108° 43.318'

Male #45

This sunken site is littered with decaying sage. Photo taken on August 8, 2021, while facing southeast.

This site is 39'2" from the cemetery's west fence and 26'5" from the northwest corner of the Harsch family fence (Index #9).

Cemetery map index #: M45
Lat/Long: N42° 29.830/1' W108° 43.315'

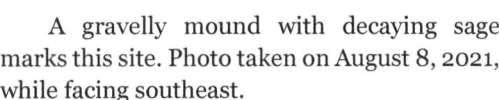

Male #46

A gravelly mound with decaying sage marks this site. Photo taken on August 8, 2021, while facing southeast.

It's 16'4" from the northwest corner of the Harsch family fence (Index #9) and 51'0" from the cemetery's west fence.

Cemetery map index #: M46
Lat/Long: N42° 29.830' W108° 43.313'

Male #47

A sunken site is covered with decaying boards. Photo taken on August 8, 2021, while facing southeast.

It's 10'11" from the northwest corner and 14'6" from the northeast corner of the Harsch family fence (Index #9).

Side note: about 7' north of this stake is yellow tape as the cadaver dog downed on this spot. This information is included here since this grave is nearest to the tape. This downing was determined to be unconfirmed human remains.

Cemetery map index #: M47
Lat/Long: N42° 29.829' W108° 43.310'

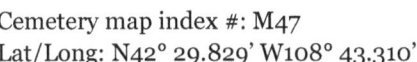

Male #48

This is a deep, sunken area with a few decaying boards and sage remnants. Photo taken on August 8, 2021, while facing south-southeast.

It's located 23'1" from the northwest corner of the Harsch family fence (Index #9) and 42' from the cemetery's north fence.

Cemetery map index #: M48
Lat/Long: N42° 29.832' W108° 43.312/3'

Male #49

A sunken area with dead sage to the south and live sage to the east and west covers this site. Photo taken on August 8, 2021, while facing south.

This site is 24'1" from the cemetery's north fence and 37'3" from the Harsch family fence (Index #9).

On September 29, 2016, dowser Ann Noble stated this site showed signs this was a sloppy burial.

Cemetery map index #: M49
Lat/Long: N42° 29.834' W108° 43.307'

Male #50

This site is a level and open area with gravel and little vegetation. Photo taken on August 8, 2021, while facing north-northwest.

The head is 3'5" from the cemetery's north fence and 54'6" from the cemetery's west fence.

On June 7, 2016, the cadaver dog was working outside the fence. He suddenly turned and immediately dashed under the fence and downed at this spot. The dog's actions were so surprising even handler K. T. Irwin was shocked.

It's possible this is not a burial site but spread cremains. The marking of the spot is video *11 Marking*, time stamp of 00:00. The handler mentions the finding in video *8 Aftermath* at 00:10. The waypoint in the handler's official report is #256.

Dowser Don Schooley noted this grave is 3' wide and 6' long, and it "faces" south. On September 29, 2016, dowser Ann Noble noted his "head" starts about 1' from the north and is buried north-south.

Cemetery map index #: M50
Lat/Long: N42° 29.838/7' W108° 43.310/11'

Male #51

A gravelly area with sage patches to the east and south marks this site. Photo taken on August 8, 2021, while facing north-northwest.

This site is 25'10" from the cemetery's north fence and 29'5" from the cemetery's west fence.

On September 29, 2016, dowser Ann Noble noted this grave ran north-south. This burial is likely part of a family or a close-friend group as all three are buried north-south and because of their isolated location. Refer to Female #19 and Male #52.

Cemetery map index #: M51
Lat/Long: N42° 29.835/4' W108° 43.316'

Male #52

This is a flat, gravelly mound with sage to the west and dead sage to the east. Wide planks, likely from a fence, lie on the ground just outside the gravesite space. Photo on August 8, 2021, taken while facing north-northwest.

This spot lies 31'0" from the cemetery's north fence and 24'5" from the cemetery's west fence. On September 29, 2016, dowser Ann Noble noted this grave runs north-south.

This burial is likely part of a family group as all three are buried north-south and because of their isolation. Refer to Female #19 and Male #51.

Cemetery map index #: M52
Lat/Long: N42° 29.834' W108° 43.317'

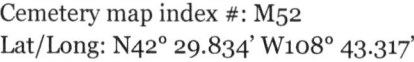

Abandoned Base

A concrete base for a headstone or marker stands alone. I suspect after the headstone was removed, the base was flipped away from the gravesite in order to disinter the body. Photo taken on August 26, 2015, while facing south.

The body must have been exhumed and removed with the headstone. The base's width runs east-west, suggesting the base was moved from its original location—possibly the sunken area to the south of this base.

This base is 23 11/16" wide, 9 5/8" tall, and 14 1/8" deep. Though the lumps of concrete appear to have encircled a headstone, upon closer inspection there are lumps which would have prevented a level and solid base for any headstone. The lumps have no sharp edges which would have braced the bottom outline of any headstone.

Along the outside edges, there are lumps in the concrete likely caused by the dirt hole being scraped out to sharpen the hole's edges.

Initially I wondered if this was the base for Frank Irwin's headstone. Frank was interred in 1870 and disinterred in 1887. He was re-interred in the North Fork Masonic Cemetery, north of Lander. Frank's actual headstone measures 16 5/8" wide and 6 3/32" deep. I do not believe this was his base and it's unlikely concrete would have been used in 1870.

This base is located 30'0" from the southwest corner and 30'6" from the southeast corner of the Harsch family fence (Index #9).

Cemetery map index #: AB
Lat/Long: N42° 29.832' W108° 43.301/0'

SEVEN

West Cemetery Burials

This wide hillside covered with crushed rock is dotted with sage and clusters of other vegetation. With no fence, this place is as open and wild as this entire region. The wind rarely stops.

The wildness is interrupted by two noticeable graves.

One has a white marble headstone surrounded by a metal fence. Lydia McAuley died five days after her first birthday.

The second is a mound of stones marked by a lovingly crafted homemade marker. Baby Williams was a newborn who did not live after birth.

Near Baby Williams' grave, a close inspection reveals a small mound of rocks three feet long smothered by vegetation. It's a small grave for an unnamed child.

This is the West Cemetery, most commonly known in Atlantic City as the "Children's Cemetery."

The West Cemetery with at least four graves. The handwritten text "-The lone graves-Atlantic City, Wyo. Killed by Indians" was written by an unknown person. Whether this comment is a factual statement is unknown. 1900–1918.
–Courtesy of the W. B. D. and Annette B. Gray Papers Collection, American Heritage Center, University of Wyoming. Photographer: likely W. B. D. Gray.

There is no sign of any other grave. The steep hillside, vegetation, and our unforgiving weather obliterated all signs.

There are many people buried here which are confirmed by the stories passed down by the old-timers who had been present in the 1930s-1960s. John Mionczynski, who arrived here in 1967 and has graced this town since, listened to those old-timers who spoke of the tales when several people were buried here.

During John's early days in 1970, old-timer Jacob Booth gave him a driving tour of the town. John recalls what appeared to be three grave markers further east than the ones marked on this cemetery property. One was near the sole neighboring structure. Jake confirmed those markers were grave markers.

John repeated Jake's tale of many people died of typhus in the early 1900s.

At one point while researching numerous documents about this cemetery, I glimpsed the text, "Winter or Children's Cemetery at Atlantic City." At the time, I didn't know what "winter" meant in regard to this cemetery.[1]

Later, John relayed Jake had described when people died in the winter, the bodies, of all ages including babies, were often laid on the hillside and covered with stones until the ground thawed. Come spring, those bodies were either buried here or were removed, possibly to the East Cemetery.[2]

Now it's clear why this land was referred to as the "Winter Cemetery." It was used as a temporary storage for bodies until the spring thaw.[3]

The West Cemetery depicting two graves. Foreground: *Lydia McAuley's grave and its collapsed fence.* Background: *Baby Williams' grave surrounded by a collapsing fence.* Left: *Remnants of a possible third grave's collapsed fence. 1956.*
–Courtesy of the Henderson Collection, South Pass City State Historic Site; and the American Heritage Center, University of Wyoming. Photographer: Harold A. Titcomb, A. E. Blair, or Barney N. Tibbals

Betty Carpenter Pfaff grew up in the Carpenter Hotel and was a regional icon who knew so much about this region. She recalled people being buried there and they had died of influenza. She went on to state "everyone but me was sick."[4]

I searched websites for old newspaper articles for Atlantic City deaths by typhus, typhoid, cholera, diphtheria, influenza, mumps, pneumonia, and measles. Additional searches for deaths by arsenic and mercury poisoning from the gold mining process, as mentioned in Jacob Booth's oral history, yielded no information.[5]

An 1898 South Pass City article stated druggist Reginald C. Hunt was "meeting with good success in his treatment of people who are suffering from mumps...." The column listed many locals stricken with the disease such as "John Sherlock and Wayne Wygal have had the mumps to that extent that a bull dog wouldn't have tackled them." Teacher Mamie Crowley closed the school.[6]

On June 7, 2016, cadaver-seeking border collie Blue and his handler K. T. Irwin searched the western half of the cemetery's hillside and found one site of confirmed human remains, downhill and southeast of Lydia's grave. Blue downed in the three other locations, but those downings were not confirmed. For specifics on Blue and K. T.'s actions, their findings, and the abilities of cadaver dogs see chapter 10, *Cadaver Dogs*.

Three dowsers, Don Schooley, Ann Noble, and Sam Drucker, dowsed this hillside. Combined, they located 16 graves.

On July 16, 2016, Don determined what I had earlier suspected was a burial site actually contained no remains. He then dowsed the known mounded and unnamed gravesite near Baby Williams as a female (F3).

Confirming the name of this child is impossible. His finding of a female child made me wonder if this could be Emma Knight, a two-year-old who was killed by a horse in 1870. Since then, other babies and children were buried on that hillside, leading to this cemetery being known as the "Children's Cemetery."

On October 9, Ann confirmed Don's no-grave decision. She also dowsed the known grave of the unnamed child (F3) and confirmed Don's finding of a female. She then discovered and sexed the grave now known as a male, M12.

On October 22, Sam's task was to focus solely on this hillside. He discovered 15 unknown graves and confirmed the grave at M12. Sam does not sex graves.

Personal note: Before Sam's arrival, I dared to try dowsing here. I imitated Don and Ann's process and my rods crossed at one site. I suspected I had found a grave but as a total novice I was too unsure. I didn't tell Sam. He found it (Index #1).

Of the 15 graves, Sam determined three of the burials were north-south.

On the map, vertical ovals mark those gravesites. It's possible some of the graves may be spread cremains, although the cadaver dog did not respond to those locations.

For information on dowsing see chapter 11, *Dowsing for Graves*.

After the discoveries, each grave had to be marked. On the first day, I initially marked each site with a pin flag. The lone unnamed male was marked with a blue flag. I used pink flags for the Unknowns simply because I had more of those flags. The database and the flags were clearly marked to ensure there was no confusion these were not female but were unsexed graves.

The original 2016 color map was initially marked with red circles or ovals for the unsexed graves and a blue circle for the male grave.

In 2021 to prepare for high-quality overhead photographs by a drone flown by William Moore, assisted by Carmela Moore, I climbed the hillside to replace those pink flags with white flags for clarity and to ensure there would be no confusion as to the sex. Studying the ground, I was horrified to realize most of those pink flags had disappeared.

Thanks to the documented two measurements from a solid point to each stake or flag back in 2016, I could locate the spot to within a square foot of the stake or marker. On a blistering hot day, on my knees with my nose almost touching the dirt, my fingers carefully floated through the dirt to find the hole left by the spike.

I found every spike and the remnants of the pink flags.

Then I realized *why* there are no signs of any burials on this hillside. The eroded rock and steep hillside, our high winds, snows, and snowmelt caused the crushed rock and dirt to roll down the hill and cover the site. During those five years, dirt and small stones covered the majority of the flags and the spikes.

Any burial might have originally left a mark, such as a divot or a mound, in the hillside. Within years the mark would be obliterated and any wood marker decayed. Vegetation would move in. The burial site would be erased.

Now, those unsexed graves are marked with white plastic flags pinned into the earth. On the updated color map, the red markers for the unsexed graves were replaced with white markers.

Below, of the 19 burials listed here two are named and the third had been known but she is unnamed. They are listed first. The remaining list is for the dowsed Unknowns.

According to Daniel Y. Meschter in his 1968 preliminary report of defunct Wyoming cemeteries, in the space around this cemetery:

> Nearby is the wreckage of possibly four or five wooden fences which may have surrounded other unmarked graves. The situation of this cemetery close to the town and the early date of the one marked grave suggests that this cemetery was the earliest one in Atlantic City.[7]

A separate document titled "Pioneer Cemetery and Grave Inventory Form" for the Wyoming State Historical Society stated the "Number of burials discernible at site" is "abt 6."[8]

Also, this cemetery was described "At the date of the lad's murder [Frank Irwin in 1870], nine other men had been killed and their graves are faintly discernible in the desolate little plot."[9]

While these men may be buried in this hillside, I have found no evidence Frank and the other men killed in 1870 are or were buried here. Newspaper accounts rarely mentioned a specific burial place, and if they did, it stated only "in Atlantic City." I've never found any listing of those buried or description of markers with names.

It's unknown which of our two cemeteries was created first, though I suspect it was the East Cemetery. We know Casimer Melin died in 1875, one year after Lydia McAuley's death in 1874. However, the number of unmarked graves in the East Cemetery vastly outnumber what is known to be in the West Cemetery.

Lastly, after plotting the location of all the graves on a map (opposite page), it's interesting to see the placement and grouping of burials, particularly the implied line of the three unconfirmed human remains in a horizontal row with the curve of the hill.

Thanks to those experienced and dedicated dog handler and dowsers, we now know where people are buried in this place.

We will never know their names, but we know they're here and we honor them.

Technical information:

This chapter not only documents the previously known burials, it also documents each Unknown grave so they will no longer be lost. A photograph of each Unknown shows the pinned white flag (blue for M12) which marks each site.

The flags are rimmed with stones to protect the flags from our violent winds which can destroy them. In some photographs the appearance of the flag is lost amongst thick vegetation. These photographs have tick marks on each side of the photograph to pinpoint the spot of the flag.

In the original 2016 database, the text for each grave's stone or marker was included to document the text and the marker's condition. Since this book is to document the markers the texts remain in this book.

Lat/Long coordinates depict the placement of the headstones and markers.

The coordinates' format are in the Degrees and Decimal Minutes format: DDD° MM.MMM' (WGS 84 map datum).

Map, West Cemetery

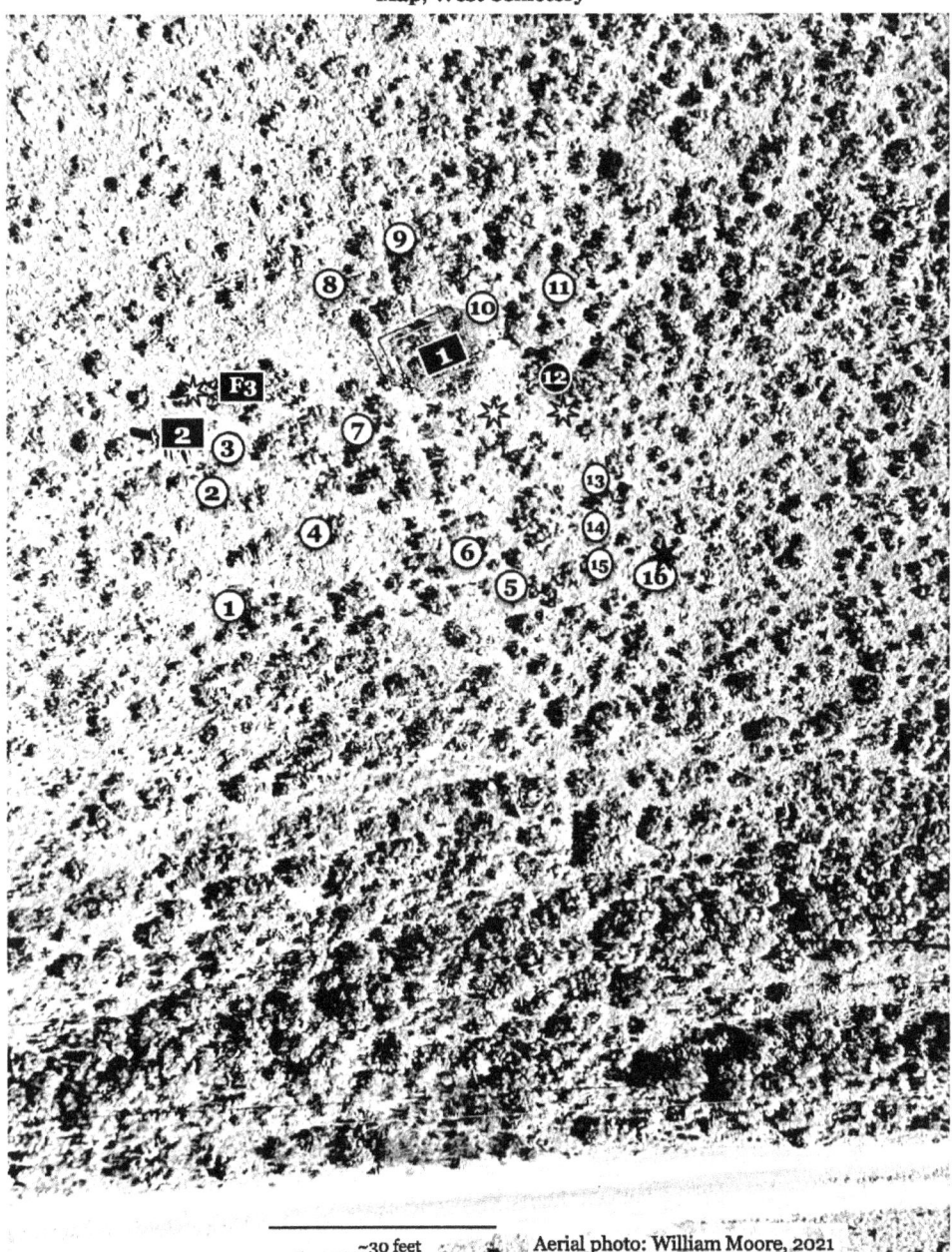

~30 feet   Aerial photo: William Moore, 2021

■ #	Known burial site of a child and its index number
⊕	Dowsed burial site of an Unknown person (sex unknown) and its index number
12	Dowsed burial site of an Unknown male and his index number

Cadaver dog downings (locations approximate)
✹ Confirmed human remains (1)
✲ Unconfirmed human remains (3)

McAuley, Lydia May
April 14, 1873–April 19, 1874

Lydia's grave is the earliest marked burial site in Atlantic City. A wrought iron fence surrounds the site. Four remnants of a wooden picket fence lie within the fence. When the iron fence was placed is unknown. The photo was taken on August 24, 2007, while facing west.

Her cause of death is unknown.

Father Robert McAuley owned "3 lots and Dance House in Frenchtown," down Rock Creek. Her mother was also named Lydia.[10]

On June 7, 2016, cadaver dog Blue, owned by K. T. Irwin, downed as he detected human remains about 8' downhill from her grave. K. T. suspected he scented drained fluids from her grave, though dowser Sam Drucker detected a grave on this spot. The video of Blue's downing is on video *2 Search* at 00:42.[11]

Lydia McAuley's death notice in the Daily Inter-Ocean, *Chicago, Illinois. May 7, 1874.* —Courtesy of the University of Illinois Urbana-Champaign

> ## DIED.
>
> McAULEY—On Sabbath morning, April 19, 1874, at Atlantic City, Wyoming Territory, only daughter of Robert and Lydia McAuley, aged 1 year and 5 days.
> Turner Junction, Ill., paper please copy.

Cemetery map index #: 1
Headstone Lat/Long: N42° 29.818/7' W108° 43.970/69'

Headstone inscription:
  (top horizontal surface)
  LYDIA MAY

  (vertical surface)
  only Daughter of
  R. & L. McAuley.
  DIED
  Apr. 19, 1874,
  AGED
  1 year & 5 days.

Williams, Baby
February 26, 1903

Baby Williams was a boy who did not survive birth.

Older sister Alma Williams Golliher gave a powerful recollection about her family and the death of her brother in a 1982 article by Rosemary Williamson in the *Wyoming State Journal*.[12]

Later articles about the family mistakenly state the infant was a girl.[13]

The remnants of a picket fence, possibly the same fence shown in the photograph below, had been neatly placed on the small pile of stones. In 2015, Emmett Williams, a second cousin of Baby Williams, constructed and replaced the older wooden marker using the same text. The photo (next page) was taken on October 2, 2015, while facing west.

The baby's grave was documented in the undated document "Pioneer Cemetery and Grave Inventory Form" as containing "Baby Girl Williams ... was the child of Henry Watkins Williams and his wife, Maude (Huff)."[14]

On July 16, dowser Don Schooley "witched" this grave. His rods indicated the remains of a male and the disturbed site was about 4–5 feet long, larger than usual for an infant.

Don suspected a bonfire was lit to thaw the frozen ground for burial. In her published recollection, Alma W. Golliher spoke about "the fire I saw through the window. It was about halfway up the hill on the other side of the street."

She quoted her grandmother, Ellen Huff, who explained to her: "The fire was built to thaw the frozen ground so they could dig a little grave."

On June 7, 2016, a cadaver dog "downed" about 4' north of this grave. See the action in video *2 Search*, at 3:22. It's unknown if the dog downed because of this grave, nearby grave F3, or if there is a third unknown burial.

A black-and-white photo (below) of two Williams kin, Barbara and Emmett, stand beside the fence surrounding his grave. [15]

Barbara and Emmett Williams at Baby Williams' grave. The photo was taken while facing east. 1952.
–Courtesy of the Henry Williams Family

Special note: Baby Williams' uncle, Jared Williams, is buried in the East Cemetery.[16]

Cemetery map index #: 2
Headstone Lat/Long: N42° 29.817' W108° 43.976'

Marker inscription:

BABY WILLIAMS
BORN & DIED
BLUE BABY
FEB. 26 1903
PARENTS
HENRY & MAUDE

Female Unknown Grave F3

Situated to the northeast and within feet of Baby Williams' grave, this site consists of a pile of stones obscured by thick vegetation. The dimensions of the pile of stones is 8" in height, 3'10" in length, and 3'3" in width. This latest photo was taken while facing southwest on August 5, 2024.

Tucked within the pile of stones are slices of wood with hand-carved letters (see the two close-ups next page). These photos were taken on September 29, 2015, while facing east.

On the next page, the middle photo was electronically manipulated to better make out the letters. The letters in the bottom piece of wood appear to read "RUNNING." In the bottom photo, the vertical pieces of wood may be the remnants of the fence or pickets.

On June 7, 2016, a cadaver dog downed about 3 feet west of the grave and twice stopped at this spot, though the downing was declared as unconfirmed. It's unknown if the dog downed because of this grave, because of Baby Williams' grave, or if there is a third burial at this spot.

On July 16, dowser Don Schooley "witched" this grave. The dowsing rods indicated the disturbed site was about 5 feet long and likely contained the remains of a child or infant and was a female.

When Don stated this grave was a female, I wondered if she could be Emma Knight, aged 2, who was killed by a horse in 1870, and this grave could be the beginning of this cemetery becoming the "Children's Cemetery."

Foreground: The snow-covered grave of this little girl is obscured by vegetation. Tick marks around the photo's edges lead to the spot of the marker.

Background: Baby Williams' grave. 2024.

This suspicion arose from an newspaper article about the Henry Williams family and the tragic loss of their son on February 26 1903, as recollected by Baby's older sister Alma Williams Golliher."[17]

> I knew there was a little grave up on that hillside—a little girl who died a long time ago had been buried there. I guess her mother wanted her where she could keep an eye on her, and I instinctively knew that was where they were going to put Mama's little baby.[18]

On October 9, 2016, Ann Noble also dowsed this grave and her rods determined the remains were of a female.

If this unmarked grave is not Emma or another unknown little girl, then Lydia McAuley would certainly be the "little girl who died a long time ago." Lydia was one year old when she died of unknown causes on April 19, 1874.

Note: This grave wasn't marked with a flag until this buried person was confirmed as female by both dowsers, which didn't occur until August 6, 2024. The delay was from my error in 2016. Now this little girl's grave is marked with a red pin flag and with her new identifying number. For more information on what happened see the Full Disclosure in chapter 11, *Dowsing for Graves.*

Cemetery map index #: F3
Mound Lat/Long: N42° 29.817/8' W108° 43.974'

Above: *In the electronically manipulated close-up photo, the letters in the bottom piece of wood appear to read "RUNNING." 2015.*

Right: *The vertical pieces of wood may be the remnants of a fence or pickets. 2015.*

Unknown Grave 1

This gravely patch has no vegetation, but sage lies to the east and the south. Photo taken on February 2, 2024, while facing north.

On October 22, 2016, dowser Sam Drucker determined remains at this site. The site was adult length, 6' long and 2'6" wide.

The spot is marked 23'0" from Baby Williams' marker, and 42'3" from the southeast corner and 33'10" from the southwest corner of Lydia McAuley's fence.

Cemetery map index #: 1
Lat/Long: N42° 29.814' W108° 43.974/5'

Unknown Grave 2

This bare space has no vegetation, but sage lies to the east, south, and north. Photo taken on September 28, 2022, while facing north.

On October 22, 2016, a dowser determined remains were at this site.

The spot is marked 8'9" from Baby Williams' marker and 25'10" from the southwest corner of Lydia McAuley's fence.

Cemetery map index #: 2
Lat/Long: N42° 29.816/7' W108° 43.975/4'

Unknown Grave 3

Little vegetation is on this spot. Photo taken on September 28, 2022, while facing northwest.

This site is about one foot east-southeast off the edge of Baby Williams' pile of stones.

On October 22, 2016, dowser Sam Drucker determined remains here and the site is a five-foot-square disturbance. The wide disturbance is possible because of the fire which was required to thaw the ground for this burial or for Baby Williams' grave.[19]

Cemetery map index #: 3
Lat/Long: N42° 29.817/8' W108° 43.974'

Unknown Grave 4

Only a small sage has sprouted at its "foot." Photo taken on September 28, 2022, while facing northwest.

On October 22, 2016, a dowser determined remains here.

This site is 19'5" from the southwest corner and 23'2" from the northwest corner of Lydia McAuley's fence, and also 22'1" from Baby Williams' marker.

Cemetery map index #: 4
Lat/Long: N42° 29.816' W108° 43.972/1'

Unknown Grave 5

There is little vegetation here except for a small sage to the north and south. Photo taken on September 28, 2022, while facing north.

On October 22, 2016, a dowser determined remains here and the site is a five-foot-square disturbance. This large disturbed area could be caused from a requirement to light a bonfire to thaw the space for burial.

This site is 27'6" from the southeast corner and 27'0" from the southwest corner of Lydia McAuley's fence.

Cemetery map index #: 5
Lat/Long: N42° 29.813/4' W108° 43.966/5'

Unknown Grave 6

No vegetation is here except for a small sage immediately to the east. Photo taken on February 2, 2024, while facing north.

On June 7, 2016, a cadaver dog "downed" near this spot (difficult to tell the exact spot in the video). The action is in video *2 Search*, time stamp 00:40. Though doubtful, K. T. suspected the dog reacted to bodily fluids which may have flowed down from Lydia McAuley's gravel.

On October 22, Sam Drucker verified a person was located here. The site was adult length, 6-7 feet long and almost square–a large site. This large disturbance area could be caused from a requirement to burn the ground to thaw it for burial.

The spot is 22'11" from the southeast corner and 20'6" from the southwest corner of the fence surrounding Lydia McAuley.

Cemetery map index #: 6
Lat/Long: N42° 29.814/3' W108° 43.968'

Unknown Grave 7

Dirt with small sage surrounds the site. Photo taken on September 28, 2022, while facing east-northeast.

On October 22, 2016, a dowser determined remains were here. The site is a small square, about 4-5 feet, and likely a child.

This site is 10'4" from the northwest corner and 7'7" from the southwest corner of Lydia McAuley's fence.

Cemetery map index #: 7
Lat/Long: N42° 29.817' W108° 43.970'

Unknown Grave 8

There's very sparse vegetation on this site. Photo taken on September 28, 2022, while facing southeast.

On October 22, 2016, a dowser determined remains here.

This site is 9'10" from the northwest corner and 15'10" from the northeast corner of Lydia McAuley's fence.

Cemetery map index #: 8
Lat/Long: N42° 29.821' W108° 43.970/1'

Unknown Grave 9

Sparse vegetation with a large clump of tall sage and with short sage to the south marks this site. Photo taken on September 28, 2022, while facing south-southeast.

On October 22, 2016, a dowser determined remains here, the grave is east-west and short, about four feet long. This grave may be another child.

This site is 11'1" from the northeast corner and 12'5" from the northwest corner of Lydia McAuley's fence.

Cemetery map index #: 9
Lat/Long: N42° 29.821/0' W108° 43.969/8'

Unknown Grave 10

This site lies to the immediate northeast of Lydia's fence at the path's edge. It is marked by a large sage to the north and a small sage to the east. Photo taken on September 28, 2022, while facing west-southwest.

On October 22, 2016, a dowser determined remains here.

This site is 1'4" from the northeast and 6'11" from the southeast corners of Lydia McAuley's fence.

Cemetery map index #: 10
Lat/Long: N42° 29.819' W108° 43.967'

Unknown Grave 11

Little vegetation marks this site, but there is sage to the north and east. Photo taken on September 28, 2022, while facing west.

On October 22, 2016, a dowser determined remains here and are buried east-west and the site is "not long."

This site is 12'11" from the northeast corner and 13'1" from the southeast corner of Lydia McAuley's fence.

Cemetery map index #: 11
Lat/Long: N42° 29.819' W108° 43.966/5'

Male Unknown Grave M12

A square stone marks this spot. A small sage is to the north and small vegetation is to the west. Photo taken on August 6, 2021, while facing northwest.

This spot may relate to a photograph, ca. 1900-1918, which shows a dilapidated picket-fenced area south of Lydia McAuley's grave on page 152.

On June 7, 2016, a cadaver dog almost "downed" near this spot. See the action in video *2 Search*, at 3:50.

On October 9, dowser Ann Noble detected this spot and the rods indicated the remains were male. On October 22, Sam Drucker verified a person was located here.

The spot is marked 17'6" from the southwest corner and 9'9" from the southeast corner of Lydia McAuley's fence.

Cemetery map index #: M12
At the rock, Lat/Long: N42°29.816' W108°43.966/7'

Unknown Grave 13

Little vegetation marks this site. Photo taken on September 28, 2022, while facing north.

On October 22, 2016, a dowser determined remains here and the grave is north-south and is about five feet long, likely a child or small adult.

This site is 19'2" from the southeast corner, 24'0" from the southwest corner, and 25'5" from the northeast corner of Lydia McAuley's fence.

Cemetery map index #: 13
Lat/Long: N42° 29.816' W108° 43.965'

Unknown Grave 14

A tall, slender sage is to the east. Photo taken on September 28, 2022, while facing north-northwest.

On October 22, 2016, a dowser determined the remains were buried north-south and the grave was 4'7" long.

This site is 23'10" from the southeast corner and 27'4" from the southwest corner of Lydia McAuley's fence.

Cemetery map index #: 14
Lat/Long: N42° 29.815' W108° 43.965/4'

Unknown Grave 15

A small sage dots the site, but with little other vegetation. Photo taken on September 28, 2022, while facing north-northwest.

On October 22, 2016, a dowser determined remains here were buried north-south, and the site is 5'3" long.

This site is 31'3" from the southwest corner and 28'8" from the southeast corner of Lydia McAuley's fence.

Cemetery map index #: 15
Lat/Long: N42° 29.814' W108° 43.965'

Unknown Grave 16

At this site, there is sparse vegetation with a small sage immediately to the east. Photo taken on September 28, 2022, while facing north-northwest.

On June 7, 2016, a cadaver dog "downed" very near this spot. It's hard to tell from the video and from the handler's map of the exact location of the dog's downings. See the action in videos *1 Search* at 00:29 and in *2 Search* at 4:10. In the handler's final report, this downing is designated as waypoint #257.

On October 22, 2016, a dowser determined the remains were buried east-west.

This site is 35'2" from the southeast corner of Lydia McAuley's fence and 38'10" from the southwest corner.

Cemetery map index #: 16
Lat/Long: N42° 29.813' W108° 43.963'

EIGHT

Buried Outside Atlantic City

From the pioneer days to today, Atlantic City has always been a town of transients. Some who live here have stated, "I wasn't born here but I got here as fast as I could!"

The South Pass region has an authentic Old West history with independent, self-reliant people, neighbors who help neighbors, and a powerful appreciation for our wilderness.

Even with our cherished benefits, many residents find they must leave and they move on. Their reasons vary.

Furthermore, many residents of Atlantic City chose to be buried elsewhere, often in Lander's Mount Hope Cemetery.

Each of our pioneers and those who came after them have left a legacy which contributes to this tiny town's character of strength and perseverance. They remain a part of our legacy and lore.

Here are their stories and their final resting places.

Technical information: The abbreviations for the blocks in Lander's Mount Hope cemetery are:
- IOOF: Independent Order of Odd Fellows
- FOE: Fraternal Order of Eagles
- WOW: Woodmen of the World

Baarghoffer, Herman "Harry Burk" M.
April 3, 1847–May 16, 1916

Harry Burk was a pioneer to the South Pass area. He first showed up in the region in the 1869 Wyoming territorial census. His age was listed as 20, and he had an occupation of laborer. His length of residence in the United States is listed as 20 years, and his residence in the territory is listed as 5 months. His place of birth is listed as Missouri, and he declared his intent to be a citizen.[1]

A few years before Herman's arrival, he fought in the Civil War in the Union Army. He was a member of Companies K and D of the 4th Regiment of the Missouri Cavalry. His rank was private.

The only date I could find of his military service was November 30, 1865, and this date was his release. This tidbit stated his birthdate was April 3, 1847. It also included his date of death.

As a result of his Army service, on January 2, 1897, "Herman Baarghafer, Burk, Harry (alias)" filed for a pension.[2]

The 1870 census for Rock Creek Gulch, County of Sweetwater, listed Harry Burk as 23 years old and with an occupation of miner. He's from Missouri. The box is checked for "Male Citizens of U. S. of 21 years of age and upwards."[3]

By 1880, Harry Burke had moved "Near Shushonee and Bannock Indian Agency" (now the Wind River Indian Reservation), County of Sweetwater. He was 34 years old and single. His occupation was freighter. His place of birth is Missouri and he was born to Austrian parents.[4]

Henry Burke showed up at Lewiston by 1900. The census listed his month and year of birth as April 1847. He was 53 years old and single. His place of birth was listed as Missouri. His parents' places of birth was Texas. His occupation was placer miner. He could read and write. He owned his home with no mortgage.[5]

On December 14, 1907, Herman Baarghafer received a Homestead certificate for 160 acres near Strawberry Creek, five miles east-southeast. He had "made payment in full." At the bottom of the certificate is written, "Correct name is Herman Baärghhafer."

Herman Baarghhafer, alias Harry Burk, filed for a pension in Wyoming on January 2, 1897.
–Courtesy of the US Civil War Pension Index

Killed by Lightning.

While working at a lonely prospect several miles from Atlantic, H. M. Baarghafer, aged 70, better known in this vicinity, as Harry Burk, was struck by lightning at the mouth of his tunnel on May 26 and his remains were discovered by Henry Harsch while searching for horses.

At first it was thought that he had been killed by the premature explosion of a blast but three livid marks on the body showed that he had been struck by lightning. The remains were brought to Lander and were buried by the G. A. R. on Monday.

Herman Baarghafer's death notice
—Courtesy of the Miner, June 2, 1916

The next year, Herman Baarghhafer received the formal Record of Patents signed by Theodore Roosevelt on May 21, 1908.[6]

Unexpectedly, Herman was discovered dead at his mine on May 16, 1916. On his death record, Herman Barrghoffer (Harry Burk) was aged 70 years old, and his date of death was listed as May 16, 1916, by a "Stroke of Lightening [*sic*]."[7]

The newspaper article of Herman's death stated he was found by Henry Harsch. In an oral history by Joseph Cook, Joe stated he found the body, and he "rode into Atlantic and reported it in there. But he'd been dead several days, because he was swelled up." He stated Herman's mine was "down on Little Beaver (Creek) and to the south of the Little Beaver, down in what they call the Crow's Nest country [six miles east]. ... He had a straight shaft down."

Joe spoke he testified at the inquest.[8]

Harry was a member of the Grand Army of the Republic (G. A. R.), a fraternal organization for Civil War veterans.

He was buried in Lander's Mount Hope cemetery in Block IOOF, Lot 1B, Space 5.[9]

Also Baarghhafer, Baärghhafer, Barghafer, Barghhafer, Barghofer, Barrghaffer, Berghhafer, Berghoefer, Burke, and Hermann. Middle initial also N.

Note: The Veterans Administration Master Index stated his date of death was May 26, 1916.

Herman Barghafer's military headstone at Mount Hope Cemetery, Company D, 4th Regiment of the Missouri Cavalry. 2024.

Barrett, Silvester Frank
Ca. 1840–ca. April 15, 1924

Silvester was commonly known as Frank. He was a resident of South Pass City and was an employee of the nearby Carissa mine.

His job at the mine was to fire the boilers for steam power to operate the machinery in the mine and the mill.

He lived with bachelor "Rick" Brigham Young Barrows in a cabin thought to go back to the early days of South Pass City.

In James L. Sherlock's book, Frank is described as having a

> Full beard of a bluish-gray color and a very fine texture, with pleasing waves, that reached well down on his bosom over halfway to his waist. His soft blue eyes always held a fascinating twinkle that made them pleasingly attractive.

Frank was further described as being without family, but the 1900 census for South Pass City indicated "Silvester F," lived in South Pass City, was born in 1840 with a current age of 59, and was married and had been for 32 years. He was born in Ohio, and had an occupation of "Mec." [mechanical] engineer. His spouse was not listed in South Pass City.

In the line below Frank was listed Daniel D. Duggan (shown below). Daniel was listed as a partner, was born in 1873, was 26 years old and single. He was born in Michigan.

Frank was not listed in the 1910 census, though his former roommate Brigham Y. Barrows was listed.[10]

Dan Duggan, left, and Frank Barrett, probably near Hermit Creek in South Pass City area. Ca. 1895–1904.
–Courtesy of the Henderson Collection, South Pass City State Historic Site; Legacy of the Plains Museum, Nebraska. Photographer: Harold A. Titcomb, A. E. Blair, or Barney N. Tibbals.

> Word was received here Tuesday of the death of Frank Barrett, caretaker of the Carissa Mine at Atlantic. It is understood that he was an old man and that interment was had at Atlantic.

Frank Barrett's notice of death in the Wyoming State Journal, *April 18, 1924.* —Courtesy of Jon Lane, South Pass City State Historic Site

In 1924, Frank suffered a stroke. He couldn't talk and could only ingest liquids. He died ten days later. Carpenter Ed Walsh built the coffin "from the best lumber available."

James and brother Richard Sherlock worked for two days to dig Frank's grave. The ground was frozen the entire depth to six feet. The pick's point could only be driven two–three inches deep, and then they could only remove a small chip.[11]

Note: I had never heard of Frank until Jon Lane sent me Frank's notice of death. Jon said the mining company's records at South Pass City State Historic Site and Frank's information in *South Pass and Its Tales* stated he resided in South Pass City and worked at the Carissa mine just outside of town. To Jon, that Frank was buried in Atlantic City instead of in South Pass City's cemetery made no sense.

Searching for information I could find nothing.

The newspaper article may have been incorrect. No matter, because of this announcement Frank was originally included in the draft chapter 3, *Buried in Atlantic City, Specific Gravesite Unknown.*

In 2024, a second historian shared this article with me and questioned whether his burial in Atlantic City was true because of his strong association with South Pass City. I gave her all the information I had, which was very little.

Soon after, I read a transcript of an 1986 oral history with James Sherlock. In a master class of conducting oral histories, interviewer Michael Massie specifically asked James who was still buried in the South Pass City cemetery. James' answer solved this mystery and we know where Frank is buried.

> Frank Barrett is buried there, because my brother and I dug the hole to bury him in and it was frozen on the top of that hill, clear down six feet. We had to pick it out with a pick. ... It took us a day and half to dig the darn thing.

The newspaper article was incorrect. Frank's information remains listed in this book because of that death notice and the confusion it caused. His segment was updated and included here to correct the record.[12]

Frank's specific grave in the South Pass City cemetery is unknown. A walk-through of the cemetery revealed several deep depressions, likely from exhumations or collapsed graves, areas strewn with collapsed fencing, and three marked graves of young people between the ages of four and nineteen years old.

In his book, James wrote, "His grave deserves a better marker than the small plain stone that was placed at the head of the grave, which has probably disappeared by now."[13]

Basco, Joseph "Joe"
December 18, 1869–March 23, 1939

Joseph was a "well known character of the South Pass-Sweetwater country." After he fell ill, he was taken to Lander on the stage, but "the hospital had no space so he found care at the home of Mrs. Dave Boston." He died in Lander.[14]

Joe was born in Malence, Yugoslavia (differing information follows). His body was charged to Miss Marie Gramac, La Salle, Illinois.[15]

Close friend Peter Sherlock said Joe was born at Malence, Jugo-Slavia (Southern Slavs), to parents Joseph and Ann Basco.

Joe emigrated to America when he was 20 years old. Initially, he worked with family in LaSalle, Illinois, possibly with Marie Gramac, above.

Peter relayed how Joe came to head west in a remarkably odd story.

> Walking along a road in Nebraska he stopped at a farmhouse by the roadside to ask for a drink of water. The people were evidently suspicious of strangers as they ignored his simple request for water, and pointing westward told him to go on a little further. He accepted their advice literally, continuing on his course until he landed at Green River, Wyoming. There he found employment in the Union Pacific shops as a blacksmith.
>
> He often remarked about the curt manner in which those Nebraska farmers sent him on his way which made him rather angry at the time but turned out to be a great service as he might otherwise have never found his way into Wyoming.[16]

He lived in this region for more than 40 years. Peter stated Joseph's date of birth as December 19, 1869, and spoke of Joseph:

> On the old freight lines he was a blacksmith. He came from Jugo-Slavia where he had learned the trade, ... at Green River and then at Pacific Springs he had a shop. [Later, Joe] took up land on the Sweetwater, one corner of his homestead being within a few hundred feet of the site of the famous Burnt Ranch, on the Oregon trail.[17]

Albert Mann, another long-term Atlantic City resident, stated Joe "had quite a herd."[18]

James Sherlock described the music sessions held at South Pass City in the dance hall and spoke about the musicians:

> Usually it consisted of an organ or a piano and a violin or a concertina or an accordion. ... They had some playing in the band that I never could conceive as being very musical. One of them was the blacksmith, little Joe Basco. ... But they said that he could play pretty good. ... I think it was the cornet.[19]

James went on to talk about Joe's blacksmithing:

Sometimes we'd go down and get [Joe Basco] to shoe them, ... we had the freight team that needed shoeing. Why, there was enough business there that Joe would come up and work every once in a while.[20]

The 1910 census stated he lived in Leckie, at the age of 40, was single, and his birthplace was "Austria Bohemia," he immigrated in 1884, and was a blacksmith.

On the 1920 census, Joe lived at his farm, he was 49 years old, his year of immigration was 1890, became a naturalized citizen in 1919, his place of birth was Tyrol, Austria (written above "Austria" is "German"), and his occupation was a stock farmer.

In 1930, the census stated he was head of household on a place he owned, 60 years old, was from Austria, and he was a stock farmer.

In the 1930 primary and general elections, Joe voted both times in South Pass City. In the primary election he voted the Republican ticket. The general election poll book stated he was 60 years old, and his place of birth was Austria.[21]

Joe voted in the November 6, 1928, general election, likely at South Pass City. The poll book stated he was the 5th voter, was 59 years old, and Austria was his place of birth.[22]

Fine Gold devoted a chapter to Joe, which includes one the best photos of this area as he and Albert Carpenter stand in front of the Carpenter Hotel's barn. Joe worked at the Carissa mine, and he also opened a blacksmith shop and worked for various agencies. He lived in a cabin with a dirt roof and raised horses, cows, and chickens. He was a band member at South Pass City.[23]

Joseph was described as

generous to a fault, he shared his possessions with anyone in need. He was of a kind nature, hospitable and fed and clothed many from whom there could be no return favors. ... A quiet man, inoffensive, keen of mind and known for his quaint philosophy of life which characterized one who thought deeply.[24]

Joe died of "Carcinoma of Prostate" on March 23, 1939, in Lander. He was 70 years old, though the death certificate had no information for his date of birth. The certificate stated his birthplace was Yugoslavia, but the city or town was listed as "Unknown." His parents' names and birthplaces were "Unknown." Joe's trade or profession was listed as rancher.[25]

Joe was buried in Lander's Mount Hope cemetery in Block WOW, Lot 5Y, Space 1. The cemetery's online site stated his birth year was 1869.[26]

Joseph Basco's grave does not have a marker, so a wreath stands in its place.

Burnett, Eliza Ann McCarthy
June 16, 1852–June 6, 1924

Eliza was born aboard a ship transporting her immigrating unnamed Irish mother and her father Michael McCarty (McCarthy) to the US. Her enrollment form for the Wyoming Pioneers stated she was born in New York, New York.

Eliza endured a terrible childhood of hard labor. Around 1865 her father died. Her life became even harder.

Her mother married a Welshman who drank heavily. The circumstances in the home became so unbearable she escaped with a Mrs. Stewart, a friend of her mother's, when Eliza was only 13 years old.

After making their way to Atlantic City, Mrs. Stewart opened a boardinghouse with Eliza as a helper.[27]

Soon, she noticed Fincelius "Finn" Burnett, a handsome boarder. The attraction for both of them was immediate. During their courtship they attended dances and card parties with friends.

On March 2, 1870, Justice of the Peace Dr. James Irwin married them in Atlantic City.

Oddly, Probate Court Judge F. W. Wiswell annotated he had "joined in marriage" Eliza and Finn on this date in his Probate Court ledger. In this certification, Eliza's last name is spelled McCarty.[28]

Eliza McCarty and Fincelius Burnett's marriage certification was written in the Probate Court ledger by Probate Judge F. W. Wiswell, March 2, 1870.
–Courtesy of the South Pass City State Historic Site

Their first home was one-room log cabin with a sod roof, a dirt floor, and one window. With few material goods, they lived simply and constructed their own furnishings. Of the newlyweds' life, Robert Beebe David wrote a most profound description:

> The newlyweds had a pitiful outlook before them if viewed by later more affluent generations, but they were of the stuff that builds frontiers and prepares the way for softer feet to tread.[29]

During those early years, tensions in this region were high from Indian attacks. James L. Sherlock's book *South Pass and Its Tales* included a story illustrating how this stress affected the Burnetts. "A window pane was accidentally broken at Finn's place and had not been replaced, so a pillow was stuffed in the hole."

Eliza woke in the night and became terrified at the sight of a person peering in.

> Arousing Finn from a very sound sleep, she pointed to the window and whispered, "Indians." ... In the slight breeze was the tip of a feather waving in the moonlight. About half awake, Finn ... crawling from his bed, he reached under the bed, and grasped the handle of the old trusty thundermug [chamber pot], ... And with a vigorous swing, took the entire lower sash of the window out. Inspection revealed that the feather was one that had worked out of the pillow.[30]

In the 1870 census for Atlantic City, Eliza was aged 17, her profession was "keeping house," and she was born in New York to parents of foreign birth. Her husband Fincelius, in the line above hers, was 36 years old, his profession was a miner, and his birthplace was Missouri.[31]

Soon, they moved into the "neatest little cabin" belonging to friend James Leighton with the agreement she cooked for him and Eliza and Finn cared for the cabin. Finn worked at the Leighton General Store. He soon became a partner with the Duncan mine, and also discovered a rich placer claim.

As the wealth of the gold mines tapered off, she and Finn decided to leave the "dying town of Atlantic City" on May 1, 1871, for Camp Brown, now Lander. Finn was to be the "boss farmer" at the Shoshoni reservation. She and Finn worked with and on behalf of the Natives and were highly respected. The Shoshone called Eliza *Seezembaugh* for "Rose Flower."

In 1873, alarmed by attacks by Sioux Indians in the region, the family moved to Salt Lake City, Utah, the closest town large enough to be safe from attacks. Two years later, the family returned to Wyoming.[32]

By 1880, in the census for Big Popo Agie Valley, Eliza and Finn lived with five children ranging in age from nine to three years old, and her occupation was "keeping house." Oddly, the census stated Eliza was born in Illinois, though it still reflected her parents were born in Ireland.[33]

In their later years, Eliza and Finn traveled extensively throughout Wyoming. At some point, possibly in the 1920s, they moved to California.[34]

There, Eliza grew weaker.

She died in San Joaquin, California, on June 6, 1924.[35]

Finn joined her in death on May 3, 1934. She and Fincelius lie side-by-side in the plot, ES-D, Lot 341, Row S, in Cypress Lawn Memorial Park, Colma, San Mateo County, California.[36]

Also spelled McCarty.

Eliza McCarthy Burnett and Fincelius Burnett are buried in Colma, California.
–Courtesy of the Cypress Lawn Memorial Park

Burnett, Fincelius "Finn" Grey
Circa 1844–May 3, 1934

Finn's riveting pioneering life was told in his published biography *Finn Burnett, Frontiersman* by Robert Beebe David.

Finn was born in rural Monticello, Lewis County, Missouri, in the northeast corner of the state, not far from the Mississippi River. Most of the people in the area were pro-Confederate slave owners.

The 1850 census for Canton, Missouri, stated Finn was 6 years old and was born in Missouri. Later, Finn attended the Christian University in Canton, but did not graduate.[37]

When the Civil War broke out, he enlisted in the Monticello Grays, Confederate States of America. As a soldier, he served as a private in Company C, 11th Regiment of the Missouri Infantry. In 1862, he was one of the defenders of his hometown from a Union force. "The greater part of [his] army service in which he participated was on the border," which I understand to mean he did not travel beyond his home area or home state.[38]

In October 1864, he learned all young men in Missouri were conscripted into the Union Army. Many men with no dependents, including Finn, promptly escaped to the West.[39]

In 1865, A. C. Leighton, who would later become an important fixture in Atlantic City, hired him for the Powder River expedition against Indians. By the time Finn arrived in the Dakota Territory in 1868, he was about 24 years old and had been involved in many harrowing battles with Indians. These battles include Alkali station, south of Julesburg, Colorado, and the brutal Hay Fields Fight along the Big Horn River at Fort C. F. Smith in southern Montana.[40]

Soon he arrived in the South Pass area. In the June 1869 Wyoming territorial census for "Hallsville & Vicinity," Carter County, F. G. Burnett was 25 years old, a white male, a teamster, and spent his 25 years in the US. His place of birth was listed as Missouri. His time in the territory was 18 days. The column heading of "Intention to become a citizen declared or not," Finn's entry was a single quote mark leading up to the top word, "Citizen."[41]

When he reached Atlantic City, Finn lived at the boardinghouse of a Mrs. Stewart. He immediately fell for a dark-haired, blue-eyed, teenaged woman who worked for Mrs. Stewart, Eliza Ann McCarthy.

His strong feelings matched her own. Friend and Justice of the Peace Dr. James Irwin married them on March 2, 1870, in Atlantic City.

However, I discovered an entry from Judge F. W. Wiswell where he had "joined in marriage" Finn and Eliza on this date in his court ledger. In this certification, Eliza's last name is spelled McCarty. To see this document refer to Eliza's segment.[42]

In the 1870 Atlantic City census, he was 36 years old, his profession was a miner with a birthplace of Missouri. In the line below his is wife Eliza, aged 17, profession of "keeping house," and born in New York to parents of foreign birth.[43]

Finn and Eliza picked their first home, a "strong, well-built cabin ... that was a single room, a sod roof, a dirt floor, and one six-paned window." They furnished the cabin owned by James Leighton with their meager belongings.

He worked in the Leighton General Store, and became a partner in the Duncan mine. Later, with other partners, he "discovered a placer claim just below the forks of Atlantic Gulch which paid from fifteen to forty dollars a day." Later, Finn discovered the Oriental mine.

After Indian attacks in 1870 which resulted in fourteen murders of the settlers and because the wealth of the gold mines tapered off, he and Eliza left the "dying town of Atlantic City" on May 1, 1871. They left for Camp Brown, now Lander, for him to be the "boss farmer" at the Shoshoni reservation.

By the 1880 census, he and Eliza are in the Big Popo Agie Valley with five children ranging in age from nine to three years old. His occupation was farmer. They would come to have eight children.[44]

Finn and Eliza went on to travel in Wyoming and Utah. Finn became friends with Sacajawea and with the legendary Shoshone Chief Washakie. The fort was named Fort Washakie, and the chief called Finn his son. Finn spoke the "Shoshone language and knew the universal Indian sign language." The Shoshone called him *Wingo*, which means Brown Bear.[45]

Finn became of member of the Masons. In 1927, he was elected as a Grand Commander Knight Templar for 1927-1928.[46]

At some point, he and Eliza left for California. There, Eliza died on June 6, 1924. Finn continued to be active. He became president of the Wyoming Pioneers Association, became the oldest living pioneer, and was the oldest Masonic post master in Wyoming.[47]

Finn died in San Diego, California, on May 3, 1934. He joined Eliza in Cypress Lawn Memorial Park, Colma, San Mateo County, California. They lie side-by-side in plot ES-D, Lot 341, Row S.[48]

Also spelled Gray.

Cassie, James "Jimmie"
December 1, 1867–July 22, 1955

James was a beloved Atlantic City figure for decades. He was described as "a short Scotsman with a little burr to his speech, white hair, mustache and with a bit of a bend to his back."[49]

He was born near Aberdeen in New Petaligo, Scotland, in 1867. Because of hard times and with few jobs available, he immigrated to the US. The date is unknown, but eventually he made his way to Colorado.

The 1900 census for Victor Town, Teller County, Colorado, listed he was born in December 1867, he was 32 years old, born in Scotland to Scottish parents, was a miner, and rented his home.[50]

He headed to Cripple Creek to participate in the silver boom. Here, he met Charles Blewett, who would later also become renowned in this region.

From his citizenship naturalization form, Jimmie was naturalized in Cripple Creek, Colorado, on May 31, 1902. His "Country of birth or allegiance" is "Great Britain & Ireland." His "When born (or age)" states simply "Attest." His "Date and port of arrival in U. S." is simply "Not of record."[51]

In 1905, as the price of silver dropped, he and friend Charles made their way to Atlantic City. Jimmie became one-third owner of the Big Chief mine, and used a sluice box and a "single-jack with hand steel"—a hammer and a drilling steel resembling a round chisel.

The Carpenter Hotel, where Jimmie boarded, had a piano and a phonograph in its large dining room where they played music and held dances. Jimmie's favorite song was "Irish Eyes are Smiling."[52]

In the 1910 census, he was a boarder at the Carpenter Hotel, 42 years old, single, he had immigrated in 1888 and was naturalized, and he was a quartz miner.[53]

A younger James Cassie, left, and a man believed to be Charles Blewett. They were old friends from their early 1900s Cripple Creek days. Undated.
–Courtesy of the Betty Carpenter Pfaff Collection, South Pass City State Historic Site

Jimmie was known for being quite the storyteller. Melvin Freeburgh stated:

I liked to use to listen to Jim 'cause when he'd tell you a story or something it's pretty authentic, but he'd add a little bit to it he says to make a good story out of it. He says, "It's not the truth what I'm going to say, but," he says, "it makes a good story any how."[54]

Melvin also spoke how Jimmie

had a knack for panning. He was good. ... He let me go up the canyon there with him and he showed me how to pan ... He made a fairly good living for himself there. He had some fellow in Denver that he used to send [his gold] to—jeweler or something. ... Ellen Carpenter ... used to wash his clothes. She said she would always be sure to turn his pockets inside out because she always got quite a little bit.

Miss Ellen confirmed this story in *Fine Gold*. Whenever Jimmie had worked a rich pocket and she washed "Mr. Cassie's" clothes, she would laugh about panning for gold in the wash water.[55]

Jimmie had a "good a prospect on the Clipper" (group or mine). Its

ore has been milled ... that has paid big money and ... the amount of development is marvelous. They have one six foot vein that is good and another that is small but rich.[56]

Jimmie had a "little sluice box over here on Beaver Gulch and was sluicing. And he said one time he was making four dollars a day, which in '40 wasn't too bad," according to George Klover.

According to Betty Carpenter Pfaff, Jimmie

did do some assessment work for different people. But he usually worked his own claims and I saw him have jars of gold and he was a hard worker,

James Cassie's Record of Naturalization. 1902.
—Courtesy of US Department of Immigration and Naturalization

he liked that kind of life. He was very stooped in later years from doing so much panning."[57]

Even mailman Clarence Roe marveled at Jimmie's abilities:

Jim Cassie, you'd go down there to what we called the Chinaman's [mine] and those riffles and you'd get those rock standing on end. He'd get his tweezers and pick that gold out from the rocks. He had quite a little bit. Jim was pretty old. He must've been 80 at that time.[58]

Jimmie and (Unidentified) Carpenter were contracted by Col. A. M. Adger to dig a fifty-foot tunnel on Peabody Hill, north of Atlantic City. Two years earlier, a Mr. Albertson found some ore which "ran high." A "quantity of this ore now in sight and the company expects to develop it."[59]

In 1917, Jimmie and Joe Barbett were hired to test Rock Creek for the possibility of dredging it. In April 1918, Jimmie obtained a license for the use of explosives in Fremont County.[60] He also conducted assessment work for the Cariboo mine.[61]

James filed for an assessment for the Britannia lode for $100, about a mile to the northwest, on October 1, 1918.[62]

In the 1920 census, he was still a boarder at the Carpenter Hotel, was 52 years old, had immigrated in 1889 and was naturalized in 1902. He and his parents' place of birth, Scotland, was listed as the same.

Later, Jimmie came to own his own house on west Main Street, just west of James Carpenter's house.[63]

James Cassie, left, and James Carpenter at the Carpenter Hotel. Undated.
—Courtesy of South Pass City State Historic Site

In the 1930 census, he was listed in his own place and had a value of $100, his age appears to be 62 (almost illegible), year of immigration is 1889 and he was naturalized. His occupation was miner in a gold mine, and was not a veteran.

James was not listed on the 1940 census, and I could not locate any census for him in the country.

The 1950 census stated he was 82 years old, had never married, and was listed as Retired. Note: Interestingly, all three retired persons on this page had the "Retired" lined out.[64]

Jimmie conscientiously voted. In the 1921 special election on May 10, the poll book stated he was 53 years old, born in Scotland, and he was the 9th voter. In the August 17, 1926, primary election, he voted 6th and in the Democratic party. He also voted in both the 1930 primary on August 19 and in the November 4 general election as the 23rd and 16th voter respectively.[65]

He's described as having

snow white hair smoothed down under a wide brimmed black hat, sporting a light shirt, low button suspenders to hold up his dark pants and topped with a matching vest.

James Cassie holding his gold mining pan in Atlantic City. Ca. 1950s.
—Courtesy of Atlantic City Historical Society Collection, Wyoming State Archives

In exchange for Miss Ellen's foodstuffs she would send home with him, he stacked wood in the fall, picked quarts of wild raspberries, and even churned butter.

James "Wally" Wallace Carpenter recalled Jimmie's twilight years. He

> did a little placering in the summer, and everybody kind of helped him. ... I don't know whether he ever had a pension or not. Probably did in later years. ... Cassie when we was there was very ancient-he would be up at Rock Creek doing a little sluicing in the summer. It didn't take much. Fifty or sixty dollars would buy a winter's grocery.[66]

In 1950, when Jimmie was 83, he moved to his nephew's home, the Scott family, in Little Rock, California.

Jimmy died on July 22, 1955, aged 88. The causes of this strong man's death were senility, cerebral arteriosclerosis, and the general cardiovascular changes of aging.

His death certificate stated he was a hard rock miner from Scotland. His Scottish parents were James Cassie and Ann Smart Cassie. Jimmie had been at the Little Rock, California, address for 5 years.

He was buried in the Pioneer Section, Lancaster Cemetery, Lancaster, California, in plot 5-D-43.[67]

Betty Carpenter Pfaff wrote, "We all missed the kindly old gentleman."[68]

JAMES CASSIE
1867 — 1955
−Courtesy of Antelope Valley Genealogical Society

Former Miner, Jim Cassie, Passes

Jim Cassie, old-time resident of Atlantic City, passed away at 4 a.m. Friday, July 22, at Littlerock, Calif.

Burial will be at Lancaster, Calif. Until his last illness, Mr. Cassie had wanted to "lie on the hill" at the old ghost town in Fremont county where he had lived and labored so many years. But near the end he decided upon burial in the Mojave Desert.

For the last five years years he had been living in Littlerock with a nephew, William Scott. There he leaves a number of relatives.

Jim Cassie was born on a farm at New Pitaligo, Scotland, near the granite city of Aberdeen, in 1867. He was in his 88th year. He came to America and mined at Cripple Creek in the silver boom period. When politics killed the price of silver he roamed over the northwest until he finally holed up in Atlantic City in 1907. Thereafter his life was spent in a cabin on Rock Creek, and in chasing the rainbow of fortune in both lode and placer diggings. Many of the old shafts and tunnels of the district were the toil of Cassie and his partner, Jim Carpenter, who still makes Atlantic City his home. He was a life-long friend of the Carpenter family.

Cassie never found his fortune. The cream had been taken out in the earlier years. The only time Jim ever made a rich strike was when he took out thirty tons of high-grade ore that assayed, according to Jim Carpenter, about a dollar a pound after a crush-up in the mortar. But Cassie never learned what the thirty tons valued. The mill operator departed with the gold only to commit suicide later.

Cassie took it all like the gentle philosopher people knew him to be; and never quit the game until he was too old to beat the rock any longer with hand-steel and single-jack. It was a game that gave him fortitude and strength of character if not fortune. He loved mining. It was not the only thing, however, that he could talk about. He was a great reader and had a memory so tenacious that it astonished even his oldest friends. It was a heritage from a mother who could quote pages of the Bible. Jim usually quoted more from the Reasoners, Thomas Paine or Robert Ingersoll, and amazed hunters and tourists who didn't know "them guys." They also remarked on the miracle of his second-sight when they saw him reading papers in the lobby of the Carepnter Hotel. He'd tossed away his glasses at sixty and read without visual aid thereafter.

Quite likely the fickle promise of fortune caused him to postpone matrimony; but his friends all knew him to be a happy man in spite, or because, of his bachelorhood. They'll miss and mourn him around Lander where the kindly honest old Scot had "mony an auld acquaintance" from the land of kilt and bagpipe.

James Cassie's obituary was a fine tribute to a beloved man.
–Courtesy of the *Wyoming State Journal*, July 28, 1955

Cheney, Ervin Franklin
August 28, 1844–September 29, 1922

Like so many of our early pioneers, Ervin led a storied life. To do justice to this pioneer's history would require a book so his account here is abbreviated.

Ervin was born in New York. The 1850 census for "Free Inhabitants" was enumerated in Conneaut Township, Pennsylvania. The census listed father Eliphalet Cheney, 31 years old and a farmer, and mother Lydia, 28 years old, both born in New York. Ervin was listed as 5 years old and below him was likely brother Elnathan, 3 years old, who would also become a pioneer to this region. Elnathan was listed as "A. S." *Also spelled Alnathan.*[69]

When Ervin was 17 years old, the Civil War broke out. He volunteered as a drummer boy and joined the fight on the side of the Union on August 25, 1861. He was a private with Company H, 83rd Pennsylvania Infantry.[70]

On July 1, 1862, Ervin fought at Malvern Hill in Virginia, one hundred miles south of Washington D.C. At the conclusion of this ferocious battle, more than 5,000 Confederates were dead or wounded in this Union victory. The Union suffered 3,000 casualties killed or wounded, of which Ervin was one of the wounded. He had been shot in the left lung and right hip. He was taken prisoner and held as a prisoner of war. Seven months later, he was paroled and exchanged and taken to the New York General Hospital.

Ervin was discharged for his disability on November 28, 1862, but on June 13, 1863, he re-enlisted, this time in Company B, 21st New York Volunteer Cavalry, and was promoted to Quartermaster Sergeant. He fought at Gettysburg for the three-day battle on July 1–3, 1863. During the battle he witnessed Colonel Strong Vincent killed on Little Round Top. At Cedar Creek, Virginia, he broke a leg "upon General Hunters raid near Martinsburg, Virginia, July 7, 1864."

Daughter Emma Cheney Nottage relayed a charming story of Ervin:

About a month before receiving the injury at Cedar Creek, Ervin Cheney and a comrade were gathering persimmons in Virginia, when a carriage halted on the roadway. Ervin jumped down from a stone-wall and met the carriage.

One of the occupants inquired if the persimmons were ripe. In reply he invited them to partake of those he had in his cap. The persimmons were pronounced fine by the party which included President Lincoln.

While being treated at the Seminary USA hospital at Georgetown for the injury received at Cedar Creek, Virginia [October 19, 1864], Cheney on a cot was recognized by President Lincoln as the lad who had given him persimmons in the early fall.[71]

He continued fighting until the end of the war. He was released from duty on June 23, 1866, at Denver, Colorado.[72]

Brothers Elnathan and Ervin F. Cheney, right, in their Union uniforms during the Civil War. Undated.
–Courtesy of and with permission by Judy Taylor

Ervin's brother, Elnathan "Nathan" Sanderson Cheney, was born on June 27, 1847. Nathan served in Company F, 2nd Pennsylvania Cavalry.

Both men are listed in the same veterans' "Special Schedule" with Ervin on line 16 and Nathan on line 21. After the Civil War, Nathan moved to Lander. He died on January 31, 1934, and was buried in Albion Cemetery, Pennsylvania.[73]

By 1865, Ervin had headed west and lived in Colorado for a short time before he arrived to the South Pass area in 1869. In the territorial census this year, he was 24 years old, a carpenter, and had resided in the territory for three years.[74]

In 1869, he voted in the territory's first election on September 2, in Atlantic City as the 187th voter.[75]

When he arrived in South Pass City, he set up a wagon shop and hired a blacksmith as a partner named Henry Bouck. Ervin also built coffins, and with the Indians battles occurring "he had plenty of work." Another article stated "In April, 1869, E. F. Cheney went to South Pass City, and together with a Mr. Hopper established a carriage shop. ... After a short time they sold out their stock of material and went to Atlantic City."[76]

The 1870 census for Atlantic City listed "Cheney Ervin F." as 26 years old, a wagon maker, owned $300 worth of real estate, and $500 in personal estate. It listed his place of birth as New York.[77]

During this time, Native Americans stalked and murdered many of the miners in the region. Later, Cheney's daughter Mable Cheney Moudy wrote:

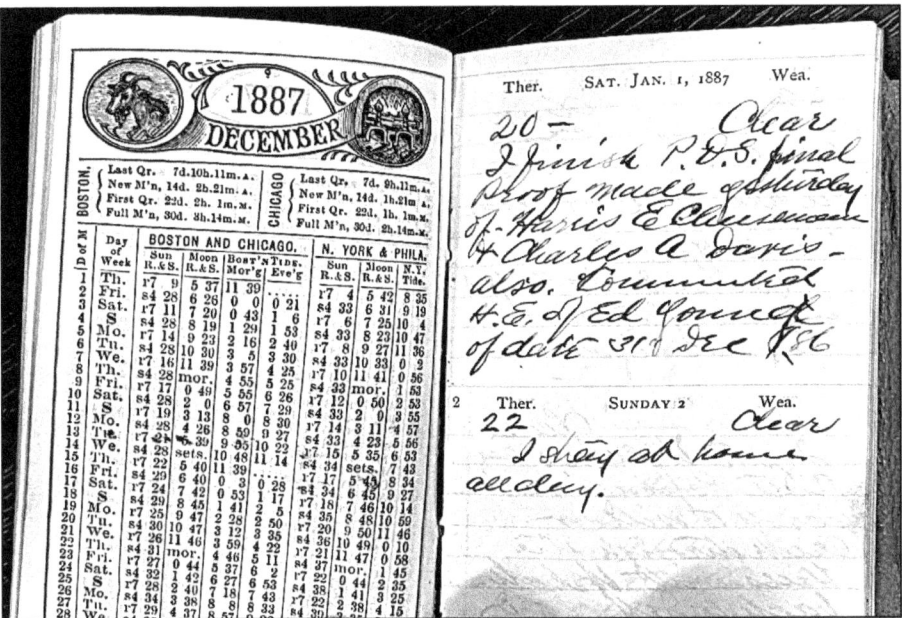

Ervin F. Cheney's journal entries for January 1 and 2, 1887. Many of his journals were tiny in size, and this photo is close to actual size. –Courtesy of the Fremont County Pioneer Museum

On June 20, 1870, Mr. Cheney started at night on horseback to go to Camp Brown a distance of twenty-five miles. Indians were so bad that people traveled at night a great deal. When he was about six miles from Camp Brown his horse reared up, snorted and acted frightened. He finally got off, had to hang onto the reins very tight so the horse wouldn't get away.

He crept along and suddenly came upon the bodies of three of his good friends, Dr. [Rufus S.] Barr, Jerome Mason and Harvey Morgan. All had been scalped. Morgan had the kingbolt out of the wagon driven through his skull. The wagon had been thrown upside down on the ground and a fine team of horses and guns, etc., were taken.[78]

In 1872, Ervin was commissioned by the county to obtain logs and construct the floor for the new South Pass City jail. During his time at South Pass City, Ervin and Jesse Knight had batched together and read law with such diligence Jesse was admitted to the bar. Later, Ervin was admitted to the bar.[79]

In his early years in South Pass City and Atlantic City, Ervin voted in the 1869, 1871, 1872, 1880 special, primary, and general elections. He also ran for county commissioner against and tied with Casimer Melin with 60 votes each. In 1872, Ervin ran for county clerk against Tim McCarty but lost 33-30. He ran for sheriff in 1880, but lost.[80]

Left: *Matilda Jane Henry, 14 years old. 1873. Omaha, Nebraska.*
Right: *Ervin F. Cheney. January 24, 1874. Photography Studio: Currier, Omaha, Nebraska.*
—Courtesy of the Fremont County Pioneer Museum

Ervin's future bride, Matilda, was a young teenager when, in 1873, she had been left in Omaha, Nebraska, until she was notified to join her mother and stepfather at Camp Stambaugh. Before she departed Omaha, she met Ervin. In 1874, Matilda arrived in the camp.

On April 25, 1875, at Fort "Stausbaugh" [*sic*], he married Matilda Jane Henry, who was 17 years old when Ervin was 30 years old and living in Atlantic City.[81]

Ervin and Matilda moved to Lander on November 2, 1878. He set up a wagon shop and built a home. His professional upward trajectory continued. He bought a ranch on the lower North Fork of the Big Popo Agie River. He served as Sweetwater County commissioner. He was elected to the Fifth Territorial Legislature in 1887. He also served as county treasurer. He belonged to numerous organizations: Wyoming Masonic Lodge, No. 2; Thomas A. McCoy Post, Grand Army of the Republic; Fremont County Pioneer Association; and the Stock Growers Association.[82]

By 1910 Ervin and Matilda lived in the voting precinct of Beebe, according to the census. Ervin was 64 and a farmer. Matilda was 51 years old, and was mother to five children with four living. She and Ervin had been married once and for 34 years.[83]

Ervin died on September 29, 1922, of Angina Pectoris with a contributory reason of arteriosclerosis (hardening of the arteries).

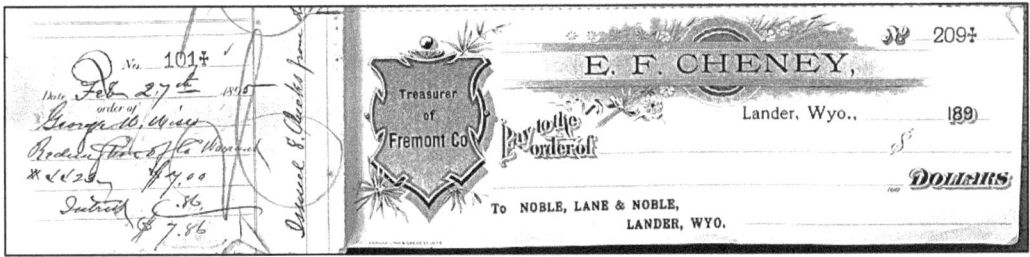

A checkbook and register from Ervin F. Cheney's time as county treasurer. The stub is for check number 101, dated February 27th, 1895, order to George W. Wise. The reason appears to be [illegible] of Co. Warrant #1123; $7.00; Interest .86; for a total of $7.86.
–Courtesy of the Fremont County Pioneer Museum

Ervin was "one of the founders of the Masonic Order in Wyoming and was the oldest live past grand master at the time of his death."

His funeral was held at the Armory and "was one of the largest ever held here." In attendance were members of the Masonic societies, the Grand Army of the Republic, American Legion, and the Pioneers' Society. The notable Reverend John Roberts officiated, and the American Legion held the military salute and a bugler blew Taps.[84]

He was buried in the Mount Hope Cemetery in Lander. Matilda joined him there in 1947. They lie in Block IOOF, Lot 2D, Spaces 7 and 8.[85]

The Cheney family stone stands over the graves of Matilda Jane Cheney and Ervin F. Cheney. 2024.

E. F. Cheney's headstone reads:
Ervin F. Cheney
1844   1922
21 N.Y. CAV. – 83 P.A. INF.

Dohm, Martha Armbruster
February 22, 1886–July 13, 1919

Martha was born February 22, 1886, in New York.[86]

In 1919, Martha's Aunt Emma and her husband Lawrence Giessler invited the widowed Martha and her daughters Edna and Dorothy to Atlantic City.

After arriving in Atlantic City, Martha found "all of these things too much to cope with." On July 13, 1919, aged 33, she committed suicide.[87]

Martha's death certificate stated cause of her death was "probably suicide. Formaldehyde suspected" with a contributory cause of "Melancholia-Brady cardia [slow heart beat]."[88]

The Giesslers later adopted her daughters, Edna and Dorothy.[89]

To see a photo of Edna and Dorothy, refer to the Giesslers' section.

Martha was buried in Mount Hope Cemetery, Block FOE, Lot 6M, Space 5. Emma and Lawrence Giessler are buried 20 feet to the east.

Also spelled Dohn.

Martha Dohm. Undated.
–Courtesy of C. E. Carpenter IV

Giessler, Emma Josephine Stegmiller
June 1869–December 29, 1935

Emma was a notable figure in Atlantic City with her Giessler Mercantile which she ran with her husband Lawrence in the center of town.[90]

She and Lawrence L. Giessler married on June 25, 1889, before their arrival in Atlantic City in 1890.

Emma was half of the duo of the Giessler Mercantile. She was renowned for its cleanliness and for her baking of breads, pies, and cakes.

She and Lawrence enlarged their family by adopting a daughter, Emma Silbers. Afterward, they added two nieces and a nephew, Clara, Lottie, and Fred Armbruster. Later, niece Martha Armbruster Dohm and her daughters Edna and Dorothy Dohm were brought into their fold. After Martha's death in 1919, the Giesslers adopted Edna and Dorothy.

The 1900 census for Atlantic City stated Emma was born June 1869, she was 30 years old, and she and Lawrence had been married for ten years. She was born in Illinois to German parents, and had had "0" children.

The 1910 census stated she was 41 years old, married for 21 years, and despite running a mercantile with Lawrence her occupation was "None."

Like some Atlantic City women, Emma owned "several rich claims."[91]Emma was described in the 1920 census as 55 years of age, able to read and write, but still had the trade or profession as "None."

Emma and Lawrence were married by Reverend John Roberts on June 25, 1889, a year before arriving in Atlantic City.
–Courtesy of the Atlantic City Historical Society Collection, Wyoming State Archives

Lawrence and Emma Giessler with adopted daughters Edna and Dorothy Dohm Giessler. Ca. 1925.
–Courtesy of the Gaylin Carpenter Collection, South Pass City State Historic Site

After husband Lawrence died in 1929, Emma ran the store with Edna and Dorothy's help. Soon after, Emma's health began to fail.

Emma was described in the 1930 census as head of the family, with a value of her home as $1,000, aged 60, and was widowed. The census listed her parents as having been born in "Austria, Vienna." The census included her daughter Edna and Dorothy as "adopted daughter," with ages 17 and 16 respectively, and both had been born in New York.[92]

In 1932, two miners convinced Emma to open a boarding house. This latest venture failed.

She closed the mercantile in 1935. Later, Emma traveled to Thermopolis to enjoy the hot springs. She died there on December 29.

Emma died of bronchial pneumonia and myocarditis. Her death certificate stated she had a contributory cause of septic phlebitis.

She was buried on December 31. One source incorrectly stated she was buried in the Atlantic City cemetery.[93]

Emma and Lawrence are buried flanking the Giessler family monument in Lander's Mount Hope Cemetery.

They rest in Block FOE, Lot 5M. Emma's grave is in Space 7; Lawrence's grave is in Space 5. The Giessler monument stands in Space 6.[94]

Special note: The Giesslers' structure still stands and is active as the Atlantic City Mercantile. This storied city center was listed on the National Register of Historic Places on April 25, 1985.[95]

The Giessler Mercantile in an undated photograph. The persons and photographer are also unknown.
–Courtesy of the Fremont County Pioneer Museum

Emma and Lawrence Giessler are buried flanking the Giessler family monument in Lander's Mount Hope Cemetery.

They rest in Block FOE, Lot 5M. Emma's grave is in Space 7; Lawrence's is in Space 5. The Giessler monument stands in Space 6.

Giessler, Lawrence, L.
July 31, 1855–June 17, 1929

Lawrence was a Renaissance Man of the Old West. He worked as a merchant with his Giessler Mercantile, a Justice of the Peace, a notary, school board member, freighter, a mine owner, rancher, and post master.

Born near the Black Forest, he immigrated from Germany in 1873. He arrived in Wyoming this same year as an 18-year-old cowboy on the Horsetrack Ranch, south of the Sweetwater River.

In 1880, he was listed in the census as an inhabitant of Beaver, County of Sweetwater, State of Wyoming, possibly a small settlement along the Beaver Creek. His brother William was included in the census for Willow Creek. Notable Wyomingite H. G. Nickerson enumerated both censuses, and he listed Lawrence as 24 years old, with an occupation of stock grower, and his place of birth was Baden Baden (Germany). His parents' places of birth were listed as the same town.[96]

Before arriving in Atlantic City in 1900, he married Emma Stegmiller. At one point, Lawrence and Emma bought property south of Atlantic City for a homestead and "proved it up." They ended up owning 160 acres and also leased

Lawrence Giessler. Undated, likely early 1870s.
–Courtesy of the Atlantic City Historical Society Collection, Wyoming State Archives

199

a 640-acre section where a section of the Oregon Trail went through the property. A grave is on the east side of Willow Creek. An old man, a tinker who repaired pots and pans had been caught in a storm and died of exposure.

Lawrence owned about 100 cattle. About 150 wild horses wandered there. His brand was the Bar-73.[97]

Lawrence leased land from Emile Granier, a French capitalist who built the Granier Ditch, for one dollar on Main Street. He removed the existing buildings and built the large building which still stands today. He later purchased the land. The store even had running water from a barrel supplied by a spring.

In its heyday, the Giessler Mercantile had been the town's hub. Decades after the Giesslers' deaths, Jeri and Lyle Moerer purchased the near-collapsed structure in February 1964, and restored it to a tourist shop, complete with gasoline pumps. In 1967 they brought in an antique bar from Hudson. The bar is now the oldest bar in Fremont County.

During the renovations, James Carpenter, who had arrived in Atlantic City in 1890 as a child with his family, relayed an incident to Lyle which had occurred in front of Lawrence Giessler.

In Lyle's oral history, he repeated James' story:

Another thing we were quite interested in, was in the floor while I was cleaning the floor, scraping out through the cracks in the floorboards, I kicked out quite a few shotgun pellets. And right straight up above was a spot in the tin ceiling that was all rusted out. I commented to Jim Carpenter about the shotgun pellets that I was digging out. He was sitting there visiting with me as I was working on the floor so that I could refinish the floor.

And he told me at this time, although I've never heard it repeated since, or before that, that at one time a fellow came in with a shotgun and forced Mr. Giessler behind the counter at the back of the storeroom. And he waited for a fellow to come in, and when the fellow come in, he shot the top of the

> Lawrence Geissler lost a valuable horse last week, it being struck by lightning.

Lawrence Giessler's horse death.
–Courtesy of the *Wind River Mountaineer*, May 25, 1898

> Atlantic was visited Wednesday by a terrible electrical storm. The lightning struck a telephone pole about a hundred yards from L. L. Giessler's store and Mr. Giessler said the wire was one blaze of fire from the pole to the store. The wire sagged to the ground red hot and broke into little pieces, but did no damage to the store.

The Giessler Mercantile escaped a lightning strike.
–Courtesy of the *Wyoming State Journal*, June 27, 1928

fellow's head off. Now I don't know the name of the fellow who did the shooting or the fellow that was killed, but there seems to be quite a lot of evidence, because just this one spot in the building was the only place where the ceiling was rusted. And we could not keep paint on that.[98]

Note: An online search of old Wyoming newspapers revealed no story on this murder. In my years of researching, many major happenings in this region were relayed only by word of mouth and were never reported or printed in the newspapers.

Lawrence Giessler and James Carpenter was renowned as reliable men and not known as tellers of tall tales.

Both Lawrence and Emma were known as great cooks—he was known for his roasts, stews, and for his sausage and butter.

With his brother William they began to move freight. They had a string of up to 16 horses attached to three wagons and traveled from Point of Rocks, about 55 miles to the south, to Atlantic City.

The 1900 Atlantic City census stated he was born in July 1885, he was 44 years old, and he and Emma had been married ten years. He was born in Germany from German parents. He immigrated to the US in 1873, had been in the US for 27 years, and was a naturalized citizen. His occupation was merchant.

In 1904, Lawrence managed the new telephone system in town. Ten phones were stalled with connections with the "business houses," the Dexter mine and Tunnel, and the Garfield mine.

"I remember when [Giessler] was the first one to get an automobile into Atlantic, ... It was a touring car, the top went down, about 1915," recalled Laura Green Marrin, who had been 5 years old at the time.[99]

Lawrence voted in the general election in South Pass City precinct on November 2, 1880. He was the 10th voter. He was the 8th voter in the primary election and voted the Democratic ticket on August 17, 1926.[100]

He was a Mason with the Wyoming Lodge #2 in South Pass City. He would ride together to the meetings with Philip and Henry Harsch, Albert Carpenter, Peter Gustafsen, and Charles Sypes.[101]

Lawrence was 54 years old at the time of the 1910 census and married for 21 years. It showed he had immigrated in 1873, was a naturalized citizen, and was a merchant of a general store.

For Lawrence, the 1920 census stated he was aged 64, immigrated in 1873, his place of birth appears to read "Safen, Ger," with a "mother tongue" of German, and he was a merchant of "General Merch."

After months of ill health, in Thermopolis he died of myocarditis (inflammation of the heart muscle) on June 17, 1929. The death certificate stated he was 73 years old.

The newspaper's obituary described him as

a man of excellent character, and was looked upon as the wise councillor for a large and devoted circle of friends and neighbors. He made no pretense of greatness.[102]

One publication suggested Lawrence was buried in the Atlantic City cemetery; however, the newspaper reported he was to be interred in Mount Hope cemetery.[103]

Lawrence and Emma were buried flanking the Giessler family monument in Lander's Mount Hope Cemetery.

They rest in Block FOE, Lot 5M. Lawrence is in Space 5; Emma is in Space 7. The Giessler monument stands in Space 6.

Note #1: Every article and Lawrence's headstone states he died on June 17, 1929. Lawrence's death certificate states he died on June 16, 1929.[104]

Note #2: While reviewing censuses, in the 1880 census for Willow Creek, Lawrence's brother, William Giessler, 20 years old, a boarder, his occupation was laborer. His place of birth was also Baden Baden (Germany) to parents who were also both born in Baden.[105]

Note #3: Comparing Lawrence and William's death certificates confirmed their parents' information, mother Caroline Himmelsbach and father Loren Giessler, both born in Germany. William died on November 7, 1916, in Thermopolis of heart failure. William's informant for his death certificate was brother Lawrence, Atlantic City, Wyoming.[106]

Also spelled Laurence.

Gratrix, William "Buck" B.
Circa 1846–January 27, 1932

After he was discharged from the Army after serving in the Civil War, Buck traveled to Dakota Territory as one of the first Atlantic City pioneers in 1868.

He was born in England and his parents were born in England. Buck immigrated to the US in 1863 and was living in New York at 17.

While still "back east," Buck was said to have met Ervin F. Cheney, who would also be a pioneer to Atlantic City.

Eighteen-year-old Buck joined the fight in the Civil War with the Army because of a plea from an "out of shape, flabby Jew" desperate to be released from his draft into the Union military service. The federal Enrollment Act of 1863 allowed Union draftees to pay $300 to a substitute to take his place. The man paid Buck $400.[107]

He enlisted on September 22, 1864 and was mustered in the next day. He joined Company B, 21st New York Cavalry on September 24, 1864. Buck served as regimental clerk "because of his clear writing skills and education." He was described as having blue eyes, brown hair, fair complexion, and his height was 5 feet, 5½ inches. He was discharged as a private on June 1, 1865.

The 1890 veterans Special Schedule listed he had incurred a disability of "Wounded in Foot."[108]

Buck was said to have arrived in the South Pass area with Civil War buddy John "Jack" Huff, another notable pioneer who left an Atlantic City legacy.[109]

The 1870 census for Rock Creek Gulch listed Buck was 24 years old, a miner, and born in England to foreign-born parents. The 1880 census for Atlantic City listed him as 34 years old, a gold miner, and born in England to English parents.

On December 8, 1891, 26 years after leaving the Army, he was granted a pension. His pension document was signed by R. McAuley, another notable Atlantic City person, as his attorney in Atlantic City.[110]

Buck's greatest fame was his Atlantic City cabin. Suspected of being the oldest standing cabin in Wyoming, this cabin's earliest documentation is thought to be 1834, and has been called the "Quaking Aspen Hut Crossing." This area was known as a trail for the Shoshoni for thousands of years.[111]

William B. Gratrix's reported as the deputy assessor for E. F. Cheney.
–Courtesy of the *Wind River Mountaineer,* May 25, 1898

The inimitable "Buck" Gratrix, of South Pass, was in the city making his report as deputy assessor for E. F. Cheney. Mr. Gratrix is a jovial, whole-souled fellow who makes many friends wherever he goes. He also has an interesting history a distinguishing feature of which is the fact that he has lived in one state, two territories and three counties and never moved out of town. Since 1865 he has not seen a town larger than Lander.

A man possibly named Richards stands at the Quaking Aspen Hut Crossing cabin. 1943.

–Courtesy of the *Wind River Mountaineer*, Fremont County Pioneer Museum

Photographer: Walter Marsh

According to Alma Williams Golliher, "some old mountain man built it. It formerly had a dirt roof."[112]

One periodical published the photograph of the cabin (shown above). The caption states, "Buck Gratrix (1846-1932), an English immigrant, built this cabin at Atlantic City in 1868. ... The photo above was taken in 1957."

On the back of the original photograph was written "Built before the start of the 'Gold Rush' 1868." Above this notation were "Bucks Cabin" and "Richards." (The man shown in the above photograph may be named Richards.) Above the name Richards was written "Taken by Walter Marsh 1943."

I cannot figure out the discrepancy of the year the photograph was taken, stated to be in the magazine's caption as 1957, and the annotation on the back of the photograph as 1943.[113]

The southeast corner of William Gratrix's cabin showing its V-notch construction. The logs are locked in place by gravity and by each log's point notched in the above log. 2024.
–With permission by Tammy and Steve Lee, and Bonnie and Scott Robinson

Buck lived in the cabin so long, in 1917 he was honored by Wyoming Attorney General Douglas A. Preston. Buck had the distinction of having lived in two territories (Dakota and Wyoming), one state (Wyoming), and three counties (Carter, Sweetwater, and Fremont) without having moved.[114]

This cabin was used as living quarters even as late as the 1960s with new resident John Mionczynski. It was also used as a town meeting site and was Atlantic City's first schoolhouse.

Note: John nominated the cabin for the National Register of Historic Places years ago. A researcher from the Wyoming office inspected the cabin. Because it had been constructed only with V-notch corners, a rare but strong method of construction with no wood pegs or nails, the cabin could not be nominated because there was no construction item with which to date the cabin.[115]

On September 29, 1884, with six other men, Buck signed an indenture granting Merritt Thompson several placer claims: the Sweetwater, the Wyoming, the Fremont, the Antelope, the Wilson, the Pine Grove, and the Junction.[116]

Buck served as a notary in the early 1900s. Additionally, on September 25, 1905, he signed an agreement to possess the Britannia Gold Lode Mining Claim from James Kime. The agreement included a condition Buck had to "do all annual assessment work" … and file proper affidavits for the next three years. Should Buck not uphold the agreement during those three years, the lode would revert to Kime. On November 23, 1908, Buck purchased the Victoria Regina mine from John Huff which was a rich mine. Buck also owned the Diana Lode.[117]

He was also a member of the McCoy Post 34 of Lander of the Grand Army of the Republic, a veterans organization which began after the Civil War. This list mirrored his time in the Army as a private in the 21st New York Cavalry.[118]

In addition, Buck sought elected positions. He voted in the November 2, 1880, general election in Atlantic City as the 5th voter. He sought the positions of justice of the peace against three other candidates, Robert McAuley, Ed Lawn, and Charles Washington. Out of the 43 votes cast in Atlantic City, Buck garnered only 2 votes. In the race for constable, he was up against two others, Sam Spangler and Thomas Mackie. Of the 35 votes cast, Buck earned 9.[119]

William B. Gratrix as Justice of the Peace.
–Courtesy of the Lander Clipper and the Wyoming State Journal, July 21, 1911

John Dillon went to Atlantic last Friday to prosecute a case before Judge W. B. Gratrix in which Stub Farlow was charged with malicious trespass in permitting his sheep to feed across lands belonging to the X L Gold Dredging Company. E. J. Farlow defended his son in court but the Judge finally decided to fine him $10.

For a time, Buck voted in the Miners Delight district and ran for constable. He voted as the 9th voter in the June 14, 1881, election. He again ran for constable against James Kime and Buck won 34-9. Buck also successfully ran as justice of the peace.[120]

The 1900 census for the "Atlantic Precinct" stated Buck was head of the household, he was born in June 1846, was 53 years old, and single. He immigrated to the US in 1863 (and soon enlisted in the Army), had been in country for 37 years, and was a naturalized citizen. His occupation was quartz miner, could read, write, and speak English, and he owned his home.

The 1910 census spelled his name "Garatix." His relationship to the head of the household was "Partner" to Maurice Lewellyn. Buck was 64 years old, single, he immigrated in 1864, and was a naturalized citizen. He was a quartz miner. There was no indication of him owning a home.[121]

The 1920 census for Malibu Township, County of Los Angeles, California, showed "Gratrix, William B." as an "inmate" (believed to mean resident or patient) at the National Military Home. Multiple government facilities had sprung to become home to disabled or elderly veterans.

Buck was 74 years old and single. His immigration status was an odd code, "'008 prior," and was naturalized. His birth and parentage remained as England. His trade—like all the other inmates—was "None."

Buck's final census was in 1930 and his residence had been renamed to the Pacific Branch National Military Home.

Note: Buck's final census in 1930 contained a staggeringly major error. It listed "Gratrix-William B" on line 86, but all the information on his line was wrong. There was no way Buck was 46 years old, married for 30 years, and born in Massachusetts to Massachusetts-born parents.

Additionally, a major column titled "Veteran-Whether a veteran of U.S. military or naval forces" contained two subordinate columns. The first column had the heading "Yes or No" to whether this person was a veteran. Buck's line was annotated "No." The second column had the heading "What war or expedition?" Buck's space was blank.

The only rationale for these inconsistencies is this man was not our Buck, but an unknown William B. Gratrix.

Looking above to line 85, which listed "Brady-Jacob," the personal information matched nearly every piece of Buck's information. Listed on Jacob Brady's line: the man was 84 years old, single, and born in England to English parents. In the column "Yes or No" to being a veteran: *"Yes."* In the "What war ..." column: *"Civ"* (Civil War). Out of the 50 men listed on this page, *this man was the only one listed as a Civil War veteran.*

This line did contain two discrepancies: His year of immigration was listed as 1864 instead of 1863 and "No" to being naturalized although he had been.[122]

To confirm this was our Buck Gratrix, I searched for information on each man above and below Buck's line, number 86. Jacob Brady's name was listed above Buck's on line 85 and George Manning's below Buck's on line 87.

Like Buck's, the personal information for both men matched the information written on the line *above* the line with their name.

Jacob Brady's information, including he had been born in Russia to Russian-born parents, was verified through the 1920 and 1940 censuses and his listing on the US Government's roster for a soldier residing in a National Home.

George Manning's information shown on Buck's line, including he was 46 years old, born in Massachusetts to Massachusetts-born parents, was verified by the 1920 census and by his listing for the same government roster for soldiers.[123]

On January 27, 1932, Buck died in the Soldier's Home of cerebral hemorrhage with a contributory cause of "Tuberculosis, chr. Act. Adv." (suspected to mean Tuberculosis. Chronic. Active. Advanced.). The duration of his illness was 10 years and 8 months. His date of birth was listed as Unknown, aged "About 86" years. His parents' names and birthplaces were listed as "Unknown."[124]

Buck was buried in the Los Angeles National Cemetery on January 29, 1932, in Section 74, Row A, Site 9.[125]

Also spelled Garatrix.

William B. Gratrix's headstone in the
Los Angeles National Cemetery,
Company B, 21st New York Cavalry.
–Courtesy of Wellington1, Findagrave.com

Harris, William H.
1859–September 17, 1910

William was a stockman killed by Bascom Skaggs "near Atlantic on September 17th, 1910."

After the murder, Skaggs turned himself in to Sheriff Stough and confessed. He killed him because William refused to allow sheep to be moved past his ranch in Pacific Springs, south of Atlantic City.

William and his homestead were described as:

It's a big sheep outfit, one of that Oregon slough or Harris slough. So, a man was in there and homesteaded. I guess he had a six-forty [adjoining acres totaling one square mile]—a big man. Bill Harris. So they rode in there and killed him, and Doc, his brother came and took it.[126]

The coroner and the sheriff found William "at the stable on his ranch and that several bullets had penetrated the body."[127]

The murder trial for 19-year-old Skaggs began with an empaneled jury in May 1911. Many of the jurymen were disqualified for having formed opinions given from a previous trial. (I can't locate news of the original November trial.)

"The court ordered fifty additional jurors drawn from within the five mile limit and directed the sheriff to summon them for 2 o'clock this afternoon."[128]

On May 25, despite a claim of self-defense Skaggs was found guilty of murder in the second degree for William's death. He received a sentence of 21 to 30 years.[129]

William's death certificate included his year of birth, 1859, and he was aged 51. He was a married stockman.

Oddly, the certificate did not include a date of death. On the section for "The Cause of Death" was a handwritten note "Killed 3-38 Bullets." I suspect the "3-38" referred to three bullets from a .38 rather than the 3-38 meant the number range of the "several" bullets that had "penetrated the body."[130]

Thanks to the information on his newly found death certificate, William's entry was moved from chapter 9, *Burial Sites Unknown,* and is placed here.

On September 20, 1910, William was buried in Lander's Mount Hope Cemetery, Block FOE, Lot 12F, Space 4.[131]

Side note: On October 9, 1914, Skaggs made a daring escape a few hundred yards from the State Penitentiary in Rawlins by freeing himself of his handcuffs. He stole a fine horse, and he was shot at by at least 30 shots by Sheriff McCourt and his deputy. They believe he was hit. Another article detailed how four deputies were closing in him, though they believed he was being aided by friends. The outlook for Skaggs' capture was "not favorable."[132]

Form V. S. No. 12

PLACE OF DEATH

County of _Fremont_

Town of _On Sweetwater_   Registration District No.

or

City of _____   No. _____   St. _____

[If death occurs away from USUAL RESIDENCE give facts called for under "Special Information"]

FULL NAME _William H. Harris_

STATE OF WYOMING
BUREAU OF VITAL STATISTICS
CERTIFICATE OF DEATH

File No. _1910_

Registered No. _____

[If death occurred in a Hospital or Institution, give its NAME instead of street and number]

N. B.—Every item of information should be carefully supplied. AGE should be stated EXACTLY. PHYSICIANS should state whole CAUSE OF DEATH in plain terms, that it may be properly classified. The "Special Information" for persons dying away from home should be given in every instance.

MARGIN RESERVED FOR BINDING

WRITE PLAINLY, WITH UNFADING INK—THIS IS A PERMANENT RECORD

PERSONAL AND STATISTICAL PARTICULARS

SEX _Male_   COLOR _White_

DATE OF BIRTH _1859_
(Month)   (Day)   (Year)

AGE _51_
_____ years, _____ months, _____ days.

SINGLE, MARRIED, WIDOWED, OR DIVORCED _Married_

BIRTHPLACE (State or Country)

OCCUPATION _Stockman_

NAME OF FATHER

BIRTHPLACE OF FATHER (State or Country)

MAIDEN NAME OF MOTHER

BIRTHPLACE OF MOTHER (State or Country)

THE ABOVE STATED PERSONAL PARTICULARS ARE TRUE TO THE BEST OF MY KNOWLEDGE AND BELIEF

(Informant) _S. C. Harris_

(Address) _Riverton Wyo_

Filed _Sept 4 1910_   _W H Dickinson_
Registrar

MEDICAL CERTIFICATE OF DEATH

DATE OF DEATH _____ 19___
(Month)   (Day)   (Year)

I HEREBY CERTIFY, That I attended deceased from _____ 19___ to _____ 19___

that I last saw h_____ alive on _____ 19___

and that death occurred, on the date stated above, at _____

_____ M. The CAUSE OF DEATH was as follows:

Where contracted? _____ (Duration) _____

Contributory _____

Where contracted? _____ (Duration) _____

(Signed) _____ M. D.

_____ 19___ (Address) _____

SPECIAL INFORMATION only for Hospitals, Institutions, Transients, or Recent Residents

Former or Usual Residence _____   How long at Place of Death _____ ? Days

PLACE OF BURIAL OR REMOVAL   DATE OF BURIAL

Lander, Wyo.   _Sept 30th 1910_

UNDERTAKER   ADDRESS

O. L. Magelstang   _Lander, Wyo._

William H. Harris' death certificate. 1910.
–Courtesy of Wyoming State Archives

William H. Harris' grave does not have a marker, so a wreath stands in its place.

209

Irwin, Frank Green
September 14, 1852–April 1, 1870

Frank was born in Bellefonte, Center County, Pennsylvania. With physician-father James, mother Sarah, and sisters Gertrude and Monetta, Frank arrived in Atlantic City.[133]

At the time of the 1869 Wyoming territorial census, the Irwin family had located to Carter County. The census stated Frank was 16 years old and had an occupation of printer.

Frank was likely between 14–17 years old when this photo was taken.[134]

On March 31, 1870, at 8 a.m., while walking about a half-mile northeast of Atlantic City, Frank saw about eight Indians. He thought they were friendly.

Suddenly, they attacked. They shot at him with arrows and bullets, striking him in the right shoulder. He fell. His attackers beat him and stripped him.

They "fired three arrows into his body, two in his chest and one in his left arm." His attackers fled.

Frank Irwin, aged between 14 and 17 years old, ca. 1868–1870.
–Courtesy of Patricia Saltgaver and Lynn Zerbe

As Frank staggered toward Atlantic City, a Mr. Ward found him and carried him to town. Dr. Frank H. Harrison was able to remove the bullet and arrows.

> One of the arrows, which had struck him between the shoulders, in the back, had passed entirely through his body, and the spiked end of this arrow protruded from his breast.[135]

Frank died the next day.

His casket "was a home-made casket … and then they covered it over with tin and soldered all the tin together." The purpose of the soldered tin made breaking into the casket harder in case any Indians wanted to dig him up.[136]

In October 1887, after the death of his sister Gertrude, Frank was disinterred. Robert McAuley wrote (spelling is as printed):

> Seventeen years after the boy was buried I assisted Fin Burnett in and disinterring the body. The family had provided for his removal at some future date as the burial at Atlantic City was regarded as temporary.

The casket was heavy inch pine lumber and putty with white lead was placed around the edge of the box to a thickness of an eighth of an inch to make the lid air tight.

There was a four by six inch hole cut in the lid over the boy's face and glass puttied over it. ... A tinner by the name of Hoffman had hermetically sealed the casket in tin. The tin was somewhat rusted from the moisture of the body but in no place was it rusted through. The lid had been screwed down by large wood screws whose heads had been coutersunk and puttied over.

When we removed the tin from the casket the face of the boy was plainly visible through the glass. The skin was a pale creamy color, the eyebrows just as natural as the day he was buried and his hair was nicely parted and covered the whole top of his head. There was no sign that there had been a wound any place. His white socks were just as white as the day they were put on and without a stain anywhere. His clothing was perfectly sound. I took hold of his pants at the feet and Mr. Burnett his coat lapels and thus we carefully placed his body into the new casket.[137]

Frank was reinterred to the North Fork Masonic Cemetery, north of Lander on Lower North Fork Road, in the family plot. He lies in the same space with his sister Hannah Gertrude Stephenson.[138]

Also spelled middle initial of "C."

Note: One date of his death was incorrectly stated to have been March 28, 1870, in the *Fremont Clipper*.[139]

Frank is buried beside older sister Gertrude Irwin Stephenson in the North Fork Masonic Cemetery, north of Lander. The carving visible on top of the markers is their first name.

Many Conflicting Stories Have Been Told Regarding the Tragedy which Resulted in Death to

Young Frank Irwin

Who Was Shot by a Poisoned Arrow as He Ran For His Life when Captured by Sioux Indians

(By BOB McAULEY)

Since all of your correspondents regarding the death of Frank Irwin have been in error as to the number of wounds received by him at the hands of the Sioux, I am constrained to write giving the facts and some other interesting material not heretofore published.

Frank was captured by the Indians on the top of the dugway between Little and Big Atlantic gulches. This point is a good half mile to the nearest cabin on Beer Garden gulch at the upper end of French town, the eastern end of Atlantic City. Had the boy been shot and beaten over the head as some of the writers aver it would have been impossible for him to have walked the half mile back to town, one rather stiff grade to ascend out of Little Atlantic gulch.

The Indians stripped the boy of all his clothing and shot but one arrow into his side. The Indian that shot the boy evidently on his horse for the arrow struck just above the right hip bone at about a 45 degree angle penetrating down into the pelvis. The Indian had but lightly twanged his bow for the arrow had penetrated but about five inches cutting the intestines but not reaching the pelvic bone. There were no other wounds upon the boy whatsoever, the Indians evidently designing that he should die a painful, lingering death.

John T. Huff and my father both saw the boy before the arrow was removed and demonstrated to me exactly how and at what angle it had penetrated the body.

Another common error regarding the incident is that Dr. Irwin performed the operation on the boy. Dr. William C. Stephenson, his son-in-law, extracted the weapon, his father shrinking from the operation.

Seventeen years after the boy was buried I assisted Fin Burnett in disintering the body. The family had provided for his removal at some future date as the burial at Atlantic City was regarded as temporary.

The casket was heavy inch pine lumber and putty with white lead was placed around the edge of the box to a thickness of an eighth of an inch to make the lid air tight. There was a four by six inch hole cut in the lid over the boy's face and glass puttied over it. In addition to this a tinner by the name of Hoffman had hermetically sealed the casket in tin. The tin was somewhat rusted from the moisture of the body but in no place was it rusted through. The lid had been screwed down by large wood screws whose heads had been countersunk and puttied over.

When we removed the tin from the casket the face of the boy was plainly visible through the glass. The skin was a pale creamy color, the eyebrows just as natural as the day he was buried and his hair was nicely parted and covered the whole top of his head. There was no sign that there had been a wound any place. His white socks were just as white as the day they were put on and without a stain anywhere. His clothing was perfectly sound. I took hold of his pants at the feet and Mr. Burnett his coat lapels and thus we carefully placed his body into the new casket.

The reason for removing the body at this time was the death of his sister whose last request was that she be buried beside that of her brother Frank. This sister was the first wife of Dr. Stephenson who died this month in Missouri. Instead of taking her body to Atlantic they removed Frank's to Lander and her request was fulfilled.

Others Killed in Same Raid

There were seven men lying dead in Atlantic the same day that Frank Irwin was killed. Two prospectors were killed on Big Atlantic gulch on the trail leading to Miner's Delight the same morning. Four buffalo hunters at St. Mary's station on the Sweetwater had met a tragic end at the hands of the Sioux.

The men killed on Big Atlantic were evidently eating their breakfast very early in the morning. They had a table made entirely out of Jack pine poles with the poles hewed on one side to make the level top. The table stood in the center of the room of a small log cabin with a fireplace in the back central end. Two bullets had struck the mantle piece stone and left plain lead marks showing the impact of the bullets on the stone just about the height of the men as they sat at the table. The Indians, of course, had surprised them without a sign of warning.

At this same place on Big Atlantic gulch Sid Davis and I experienced a strange hallucination. It is an unexplainable ghost story. I looked at Davis and Davis looked at me but we could never figure it out. But that ghost will have to wait for a future hearing.

Robert McAuley's remembrances and actions about the 1870 deaths of Frank Irwin and other men who met their terrible fate.

The article concludes with what may have been a paranormal occurrence.

–Courtesy of the Wyoming State Journal, April 26, 1933

Lamoreux, Richard
Unknown–Unknown

On a document compiled from the Wyoming 1870 Mortality Schedule, a handwritten note stated: "South edge of Harsh plot middle of fence Dick Larmaueraux sp."[140] Here is a scan of the segment from the paper:

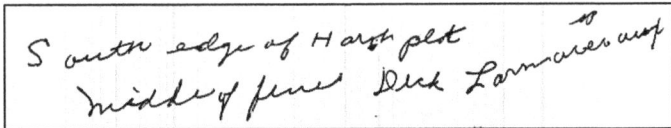

The only "Dick" I could find was the child of Lizzie and Jules Lamoureux. Richard was listed in the 1870 census as 5 years old and born in Wyoming. His "color" is "I" for Indian.[141]

Richard was born November 24, 1866, and died on June 27, 1953. He was buried in Lander's Mount Hope Cemetery on July 6, 1953, in Block IOOF, Lot 8K, Space 7.[142]

Richard's uncle Oliver is buried in Atlantic City. Refer to chapter 3, *Buried in Atlantic City, Specific Gravesite Unknown.*

It's unknown who wrote this note and for what reason. This entry is included here in case someone might one day discover the meaning of this message and solve this mystery.

For a riveting story about the Lamoureux family's arrival to the Atlantic area, see WyoHistory.org.[143]

Also spelled Lamoreau, Lamoreux, and Lamoureaux

Below: *Richard Lamoureux's headstone.*
Right: *Jules Lamoureux and his wife Lizzie Lamoureux in Lander's Mount Hope Cemetery.*

Mills, Harry E.
1881–August 22, 1931

Described as a pioneer, little is known about Harry.

His death had been initially investigated as a murder after his "shot riddled body was found in a forest near Atlantic City … after being paid at the Mary Ellen gold mine."[144]

The investigation determined he committed suicide by a gunshot to the head near Atlantic City. He was 50 years old. The coroner or undertaker released his body to James Carpenter.[145]

Harry's middle initial, "E.," came from the Atlantic City precinct poll books for the 1930 primary and general elections. For the primary, 49-year-old Harry served as election judge and voted as a Republican. For the general election he served as "Clerk of said Election."[146]

The 1930 census showed he was a boarder at Effie L. Worthen's place in Atlantic City, was 49 years old, single, was born in Iowa, his father was born in Virginia and his mother was born in Massachusetts, and was a carpenter in the industry of gold mine.[147]

Harry's Certificate of Death stated his death took place in the woods, Atlantic City, and by a "revolver shot in head; top of head taken off."

The certificate also stated he was 50 years old, incorrectly typed his birth year as 1861, and he died August 22, 1931.[148]

Harry Mills.
Date and location are unknown.
–Courtesy of the South Pass City
State Historic Site

His year of birth comes from his entry in the Mount Hope cemetery online database which states he was born in 1881. This year matches with his information listed in the 1930 census.

Harry was buried in Mount Hope cemetery in Lander in Block WOW, Lot 3C, Space 7.[149]

Harry Mills' grave does not have a marker, so a wreath stands in place of one.

Pelon, John
Circa 1832–February 2, 1913

John was an early pioneer to the Mountain West. He was born in Canada to French parents. When only 13 years old, he immigrated to the US.

Later, he was one of the pioneers of Colorado's Pike's Peak gold boom period, about 1858–59.[150]

When the Civil War broke out, in August 1862 John enlisted in Company A, 2nd Colorado Cavalry, as a private. When the war was over, in November 1865 he was discharged and "he returned to private life."[151]

News of the 1867 gold rush in the South Pass region "attracted him at French town as the colony was called, it was situated at the eastern side of Atlantic City." He worked "teaming."

He's most known in this region for a terrible day on June 17, 1870, with fellow pioneer Oliver Lamoureux. While south of Atlantic City, both men were attacked by Indians. Oliver was shot and fell off his horse against John, who dismounted, and laid the dead man on the ground. John continued to fight, then he retreated into willows. He hid for hours while the Indians searched for him.

At dark, he escaped and walked to Atlantic City. He "gave the news, and the mines went out and secured the body of his partner." Another article published in 1887 and reprinted in 1928 about this incident stated troops from Troop B, 2nd US Cavalry retrieved Oliver's body for interment in Atlantic City. This article incorrectly stated this occurred in 1871 and spelled John's name as Pelong.[152]

A segment of the transcription of John Pelon's Lease Agreement with John C. Hickey, Trustee, for the Wyoming Syndicate to lease 200 acres. This portion depicts John Pelon signed the agreement with his "X."
–Courtesy of the Fremont County Clerk's Office, Land Recording Office

The 1870 census for South Pass City stated John was 36 years old, he was a freighter, owned $2,000 worth of goods, born in Canada to parents of foreign birth, and was a US citizen.[153]

On July 22, 1890, John was granted a 170-acre homestead. The Land Office in Evanston recorded the document which was signed by President Benjamin Harrison.[154]

On January 5, 1906, he leased 200 acres from a syndicate. He was to search for oil and was paid $50 a year for every gas well found. The county transcriber noted John had signed the original document with his mark, an "X."[155]

The 1910 census showed John lived in the district of Beebe. He was 82 years old, single, immigrated in 1857, and was a naturalized citizen. Under the column heading of "Trade or profession ..." was "Own Money."[156]

John continued his mining life until the mines began to close. He moved to Lander Valley. Later he sold this place and moved to Skull Gulch (or Creek). Later, he sold the stock and house and moved in with Edward Stelzner.

He was a member of the McCoy Post of the Grand Army of the Republic, a veterans organization which began after the Civil War.

After his death on February 2, on the 4th he was "followed by his comrades in arms he was borne to his last resting place in the Odd Fellows cemetery."[157]

John was buried in Lander's Mount Hope Cemetery, Block IOOF, Lot 7F, Space 5.[158]

Also spelled Pelong.

Note: John Pelon's obituary on the front page of the *Wind River Mountaineer* on February 12, Vol. 28, No. 33, had an incorrect publication year of *1912*. An earlier obituary was published in the *Wyoming State Journal* on February 7, 1913, Vol. 31, No. 23, on the first page.

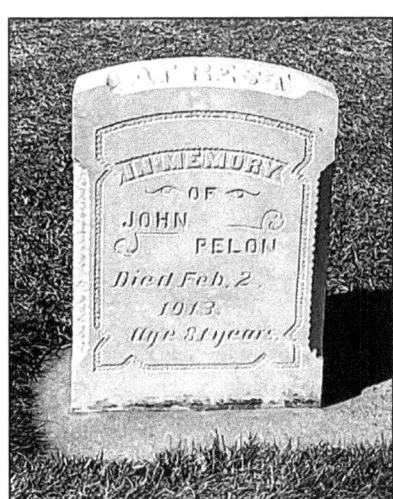

John Pelon's gravestone:
Face: *In Memory of John Pelon. Died February 2, 1913. Age 81 years.*
Top: *At Rest.*

Sypes, Charles L.
Circa 1866–March 2, 1936

Charles was a busy man. He was in charge of a mining companies including the Christina Lake and Dexter mining companies, and he served as postmaster. He had been a jeweler in Lander and a candymaker. He owned cows and sold their milk.

He was born in Buffalo, New York.

In Atlantic City, he lived in a huge house with two stories with six bedrooms and two bathrooms. He and wife Elizabeth would rent rooms.

Charles loved clocks.

When he was upset, he had a habit of saying, "Pshaw, dam," and would wring his hands.

While the Sypeses' house is now gone, the barn still exists. In the Sypeses' day, "they would have a dance, mostly square dancing and the Virginia Reel" in the barn.[159]

Charles was also a Mason and a member of the Wyoming Lodge #2.

The 1910 census stated he was 42 years old (which would give him a birth year of circa 1868. Information from Lander's Mount Hope Cemetery stated he died at age 70, which would be circa 1866). He had been married eight years, born in New York state as was his father with his mother born in Scotland, was a jeweler in a store, and owned his own home. Oddly, this was the only Atlantic City census where he or Elizabeth was listed. They're not in the 1900, 1920, or the 1930 censuses.[160]

In 1928 he also served as caretaker for the Timba-Bah Mining Company.[161]

Charles voted and acted as election clerk in the May 10, 1921, special election, and he was the second person to cast a vote. He was the 15th voter in the August 17, 1926, primary election and voted the Republican ticket. In the 1930 primary and general elections held on August 19 and November 4 respectively, he was the second and fourth voter to cast his ballots.[162]

After failing to return to Atlantic City from a trip to Lander on March 2, 1936. Searchers discovered his body the next day, five miles south of Lander on Ed Anesi's ranch.

The two men found:

His body slumped on a tire on which he had been working at the rear of his car. An investigation showed that the ignition switch of the car was on and the motor had apparently continued to run until the supply of gas was used up.

Town gossip has long asserted Charles took his own life by carbon monoxide poisoning because he was said to be in great debt.

A newspaper article described the scene. "Dr. Wilmoth and the entire group was satisfied that the case was one of accidental death."[163]

I could find no official notice of the inquest's findings. Charles' death certificate officially stated "Carbon Monoxide poisoning from automobile exhaust. Accidental."

The certificate stated the manner of injury was "Working in closed garage with auto running. Nature of injury Asphyxiation by CO."[164]

Fine Gold devotes chapter 10 to Charles and Elizabeth Sypes.[165]

Charles' funeral was held in Lander's Christian Scientist Church. From there, Charles was buried in Mount Hope Cemetery on March 5, 1936, Block FOE, Lot 7D, Space 1.[166]

*Charles Sypes' grave has no marker,
so a wreath stands in its stead.*

Yarnell, Mary Ellen Ward
December 30, 1856–July 16, 1910

When Mary arrived to this region from Glasgow, Scotland, she was a Wyoming pioneer and became a 40-year county resident.

On November 29, 1872, Mary and Nelson Yarnell were issued a marriage license.[167] They were married six years later on December 19, 1878.

The 1880 Wyoming census for Iahies Fork, County of Sweetwater, listed Ellen as 23 years old, wife, and her occupation was keeping house. Her place of birth was Scotland and she was born to Irish parents. In the line above hers was listed Nelson Yarnall [*sic*], 32 years old, occupation of farmer. His place of birth was Texas to parents born in Missouri. I cannot locate Iahies Fork.

Below Mary was listed William Ward, 17 years old, relationship was "Bro-in-law," also a farmer, born in England to Irish parents. William would be Mary's brother, brother-in-law to Head of Household Nelson.[168]

She died of heart trouble on July 16, 1910, in the home of her son, Silas, in Atlantic City. She was 53 years old.

At her death, Mary left husband Nelson, a son, and seven daughters.[169]

Oddly, her death certificate was nearly blank. It stated her place of death was in South Pass, which perhaps this meant this area. The informant for the certificate was notable H. G. Nickerson.[170]

Mary was buried in Lander's Mount Hope Cemetery in Block IOOF, Lot 11EX, Space 2. Nelson joined her in death in 1922 and lies beside her.[171]

Note: Before June 1878, marriage entries were handwritten in Sweetwater County's marriage ledger. Afterward, the County used printed certificates. In the scanned file of the marriage ledger, the certificates appear to have been glued in place and the Yarnells' certificate was covered by another certificate. Thanks to Wyoming State Archives' Carl Hallberg, we can see the Yarnells' beautiful Certificate of Marriage.[172]

Also spelled Yarnall.

Mary Ellen Ward and Nelson Yarnell's marriage certificate, December 19, 1878
–Courtesy of the Wyoming State Archives with thanks to Carl Hallberg

Mary Yarnell's death certificate, July 21, 1910 –Courtesy of the Wyoming State Archives

NINE

Burial Sites Unknown

For all the newspaper articles, death announcements, and obituaries, some did not include where the individuals were buried. It's easy to believe these people were buried in Atlantic City and possibly are.

The burial places for many of our people cannot be confirmed despite walking cemeteries, studying gravestones, and hoping the cemetery records are wrong; speaking with distant relatives and sextons; reviewing government documents, and burial listings; and prowling search engines, genealogy websites, and myriad old newspaper sites.

For the people included here, I cannot confirm where they are buried, whether it be in Atlantic City, in Wyoming, or elsewhere in the country.

While the final resting places are unknown for some of our people, we know their story, and we honor them.

Caution: Be wary of historical claims on the internet. Some posters claim a person is buried in a particular cemetery or lists the person's information, yet much of information may be erroneous. Verify these claims.

I've made phone calls to cemetery offices to confirm the specific burial site of a deceased person claimed by a poster to be in that specific cemetery only to have a voice at the other end state, "He's not here."

In-person requests for information from cemetery office personnel, such as from the helpful and kind crew in Lander's Mount Hope cemetery, result in discovering the person was not buried there.

To those posters I supplied whatever I have and know about this person, such as a newspaper article or information from the family's history. I requested the poster's source to compare with what I know or suspect in order to ensure the facts in this book are correct.

None supplied their source and a few have even caused nasty encounters. The deceased's information posted on the website is neither corrected nor verified to be correct.

Anderson, John, G.

Unknown–September 28, 1869

John was a blacksmith hauling lime when he was killed by Indians near Miner's Delight on September 28, 1869. He was 24 years old.[1]

He was born in Sweden.[2]

The 1870 and 1871 tax rolls indicated Atlantic City's "Estate of John Anderson" included Lot 69, valued at $45, and Lot 67, also valued at $45.[3]

It's possible he is buried at the Miner's Delight (also known as Hamilton City) Cemetery, according to Jean Mathisen Haugen.[4]

He is also listed on the US Federal Census Mortality Schedules Index, 1850-1880, though the document stated his year of death is 1870.[5]

Bennington, William B.

Circa 1827–circa March 31, 1870

William was a miner who was killed by Indians on March 31, 1870, "and found lying in Smith's Gulch, three miles northeast of Atlantic."[6]

The coroner's inquest was detailed in the *South Pass News*, where the deceased's initials were spelled "W. S."

John Powers, a friend of William, was called by the coroner's jury. He identified William's body, stated William was 43 year old on New Year's Eve, and William was formerly from Illinois.

A Mr. Perkins also testified he found William

lying in Smith's Gulch; saw a gunshot wound in the neck, cutting the jugular vein; saw signs of Indians in the vicinity, and saw about forty Indians retreating.

A Mr. H. Ware testified and corroborated Perkins' statement.

A commentary on the aftermath of the large number of murders is described in the *South Pass News*. Here, William's initials were listed as "W. C."

The inquest concluded on April 3, 1870.[7]

Also spelled W. C. and W. S.

Blewett, Charles "Charley"
July 1865–ca. November 20, 1917

Charley was often on the move. The first information found about him was from 1888 when he left the US to return to England a few years after his initial arrival in 1886. He soon returned to the US on April 9. The return ship was the *Etruria*. The ship departed Liverpool, England, stopped at Queenstown, Ireland, then arrived at the port of New York, New York.

He made his way to Cripple Creek, Colorado, to mine for silver. There, he met and befriended James Cassie, who would also become a beloved member of Atlantic City. As the price of silver dropped, in 1905 he and Jimmie made their way to Atlantic City.[8]

The 1900 census for Atlantic City stated Charley was born July 1865, was 34 years old, from England and immigrated in 1886, had been in country for 14 years, was not a naturalized US citizen, and was a quartz miner.

In 1906 Charley returned yet again to England, and then came back to the US on April 7. He was listed as single, aged 40, birth date about 1866, last known residence was the US, and with a final destination of Rock Springs, Wyoming.[9]

The Atlantic City 1910 census stated Charles was a boarder at the Carpenter Hotel, was 44 years old, from England and immigrated in 1887, and was a quartz miner. The typed version of the handwritten census included a birth year of 1866.[10]

Charley's ownerships of myriad properties included three Anchor claims near Meadow Gulch (five miles northeast of Atlantic City, north of Miners Delight), a mine deed to the Mars Loade [*sic*]and Penzance Fractions, Affidavit of Work for the Lottie Collins Lode, and the Carissa Saloon in South Pass City.[11]

Charles Blewett in South Pass City. Undated.
–Courtesy of the Betty Carpenter Pfaff Collection, South Pass City State Historic Site

Earlier, in 1904 Charles, along with Charles E. Bryson, had completed the payment for the Mars and Mars Jr. Penzance lode claim patent on July 11. On April 7, 1910, Charles and Bryson completed the purchase of 40.42 acres in a land patent for the Mars Penzance Lode. The Record of Patents was signed by US President William Taft on April 7, 1910.

In 1914 Charley traveled to Vancouver, British Columbia, intending to spend a year there because of being "restless." He soon returned in mid-July 1914, and he "came back happy again to be in Wyoming." He stated

> Fremont county is good enough for him. He found that part of Canada full of real estate grafters of the most ferocious kind, and was glad to get out of the country with enough clothes to cover his back.

Another newspaper article stated he "is now night bartender. ... Charley has a host of friends in this country, especially in the mining district, who will be glad to learn he has located in Lander."[12]

He played the concertina (a small accordion or "squeeze box") and would go to South Pass City to play for dances. *Fine Gold* includes a photograph of Charles.

This traveling man's death is another example of the danger of our extreme weather. Charley's body was found frozen between Atlantic City and Lewiston, 12 miles to the east. "On one of these trips [to South Pass City] he froze to death," though the location of his death was between Atlantic City and Lewiston.[13]

The date of his death shown above is November 20, the day his body was found.

> He had been dead for some time. ... He had been at Atlantic several days ago for his mail and nothing was seen of him afterward until his body was found.[14]

No mention of his burial location has been found, though it's likely in Atlantic City.

The tragic circumstances of Charles Blewett's death and the discovery of his body.
–Courtesy of the *Wyoming State Journal*, November 30, 1917

> • • • • • • • • • •
> • ATLANTIC AND SOUTH PASS •
> • • • • • • • • • •
> Charles Blewett was frozen to death early last wck at a point between Atlantic and Lewiston. He had been out for the mail to Atlantic. He started for home in the evening with a quart of whiskey in his pocket. He was not found for several days afterwards. Tracks in the sow indicated that he had been walking in a circle. Only a small amount of whiskey was left in the quart bottle. Mr. Blewett had resided here for number of years where he had been interested in mining and had prospected over the district.

Brother, Doris, R.
Unknown–Unknown

This inscription was handwritten on the bottom of an undated paper titled "Fremont County, Defunct Cemeteries" compiled by an unknown person.[15]

The inscription may read "Doris R. Brother Shot by Indians." This phrase could also be read as "Doris R. Shot by Brother Adrian," but this is unlikely.

Searching Lander's Mount Hope cemetery's search engine, online newspapers and historical research sites, Ancestry.com, and Familysearch.org revealed no information.

This document describing defunct cemeteries had three handwritten notes of deaths on the front page. While only one annotation resulted in the discovery of the person and his story, each is included in this book in case more information may come to light.

Scanned segment from a report of the handwritten note. –Courtesy of the Mount Hope Cemetery Office, City of Lander

Crimmins, Cornelius
Unknown–September 7, 1870

Crimmins was playing billiards in Charles Collins' Atlantic City billiard hall on the morning of September 7, 1870.

Without warning, Crimmins assaulted the notorious Frank D. McGovern. Bystanders jumped in to separate the two.

Again, without warning Crimmins attacked McGovern, knocked him to the ground, and kicked him.

McGovern obtained a pistol and tried to leave with a warning to Crimmins he "was now armed."

Crimmins

> drew and pulled trigger upon Mr. McG. who then also drew and both fired; Mr. Crimmins receiving a bullet in the forehead.

McGovern took off for South Pass City and turned himself in to the sheriff. Crimmins survived for several hours but died.

After an examination of the situation, Judge Wiswell fully acquitted McGovern for self-defense.

The altercation was said to have occurred because Crimmins had earlier filed a lawsuit against a Bill Smith. The jury decided against Crimmins.

McGovern had been a member of this jury.

On September 17, 1870, Crimmins was declared intestate and James Leighton was assigned as his estate administrator. Leighton was a notable Atlantic City 25-year-old wholesale grocer from Iowa who owned $6,000 worth of real and personal estates.[16]

Note: Frank D. McGovern's reputation was caused by his history of killing.

Eight years after the above incident, an 1878 *Laramie Weekly Sentinel* article detailed the "terror of the Sweetwater mining country" and McGovern's latest violence.

This article incorrectly stated the above incident occurred at Miner's Delight and was from a game of cards.

For once, this latest altercation had a different outcome.

Another man got the better of McGovern by shooting him in both thighs. The injuries were deemed "dangerous," but the shooter was "justified in using his pistol is the universal opinion of the best citizens here."[17]

Davis, Harden "Pardon"
December 18, 1827–May 24, 1870

Pardon was born on December 18, 1827, in Hornellsville, Steuben County, New York, to Mercy Davis and Jeremiah R. Davis. His family lived in Wisconsin and they returned there at some point.[18]

The 1850 census for Berlin, County of Marquette, Wisconsin, listed Harden Davis as 22 years old, a farmer like his father, and was born in New York.[19]

He had a most fascinating personal history. When he was about 27 years old, Pardon traveled to Louisiana in hopes of making his fortune.

In 1854, as he prepared to return home to Wisconsin, he was arrested for the heinous crime of giving food and clothing to escaped and abused slaves. With their backs lacerated and their feet bleeding, they had begged him for help.

To force the suffering slaves to confess Pardon had helped them, the slave catcher set his dogs on the wounded slaves who had already endured nightly whippings at the hands of the overseer.

He was arrested, clapped in irons, and paraded through the streets of town while townspeople screamed to hang him or give him a thousand lashes. He was tried, found guilty, and sentenced to 20 years in the Louisiana state penitentiary.

His people and church members in Wisconsin rallied on his behalf and solicited elected representatives and church officials for help. Pardon's brother traveled to Louisiana to try to free him.

When his brother's attempt failed, their father Jeremiah traveled to Louisiana to solicit support for his son's pardon. His attempts also failed when the outgoing governor refused to meet with him.

Jeremiah refused to give up. He finally achieved a meeting with the newly elected Governor Charles Wickliffe.

Governor Wickliffe made it clear to Jeremiah "aiding slaves to escape from their masters, they considered the most heinous of all crimes." The governor added, "Were it for murder, I could give you some encouragement."

Jeremiah still refused to give up. He came up with what he called "a real Yankee trick." He took this new story to the populace and quickly gained an outpouring of support. In a second meeting with the governor, Wickliffe was shocked at the overwhelming support. He signed the pardon.

Jeremiah wrote to his family of his success Pardon was free. "As to the fraudulent pleas, I never have published it, and never shall."[20]

The *Richland County Observer* in Wisconsin reported:

Pardon Davis formerly a resident of Milton ... has been pardoned out of the Louisiana Penitentiary, ... (eighteen months of which time he served) [1854–1856] ... for giving food and money to some Fugitive Slaves who appealed to him for relief.[21]

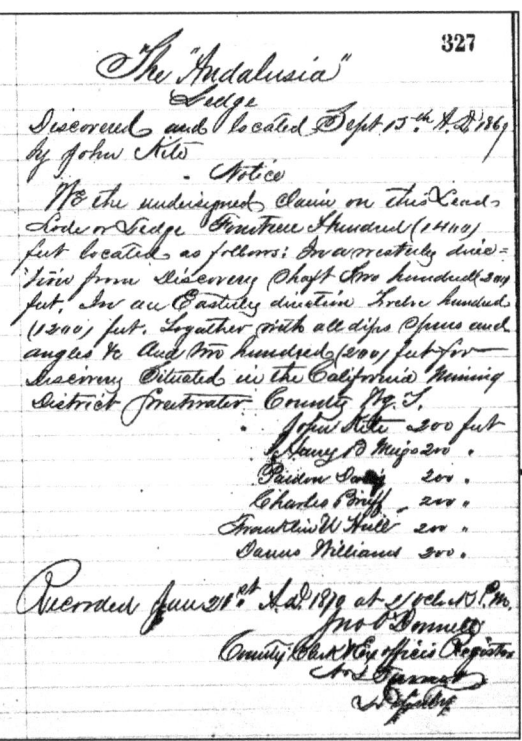

Pardon Davis and partners claim the Andalusia Ledge in the California Mining District in 1869.
–Courtesy of the South Pass City State Historic Site

Pardon headed north to home. He traveled and spoke of his experiences during his time in the south. In the late 1860s, he took off for a new adventure. This time he headed west.

From May 28–July 30, 1869, Wyoming Territory conducted its first census, which listed "Pardon Davis" in Carter County. He was aged 41, a white male, and a miner. His length of residence in the US was 41 years, and had lived 15 months in the territory. This means he was in Wyoming Territory since 1868, a pioneer. The census listed his place of birth was New York, and he declared his intention to become a citizen.[22]

Soon after, he voted in the September 2, 1869, Atlantic City, Carter County, election as the 214th voter.[23]

In short order, he became successful. On July 16, 1869, Pardon went in with several partners to claim 1,400 feet of the Eventon Lode in the Shoshoni District of which Pardon owned 15% of the claim. A month later with nearly every one of the original partners, he also claimed another 1,600 feet of the Mary Germin Lode in the California district of which he owned 200 feet. Both claims were recorded on August 19, 1869.

On September 15, 1869, with several new partners Pardon claimed another 1,400 feet of a ledge and named it the Andalusia Ledge. Again, he owned 200 feet. This claim was recorded on June 21, 1870, a month after Pardon's death.[24]

He owned a mine and a property which neighbored George Logan's.

On the evening of May 23, 1870, upon his return home from doing business, Pardon was gunned down in front of his cabin. He died the next day. In his death notice, Pardon was described as a gold miner "assassinated" at age 42.[25]

At the news of Pardon's murder, the *Janesville Gazette* gave an account of the fateful time:

> At about half-past nine o'clock p. m., our village was thrown into confusion and excitement by one of the most bloody and cowardly assassinations on record. The victim of this horrible crime was Mr. Pardon Davis. He had gone up town early in the evening to transact some business. On his return, when within a few yards of his house, he was fired at twice by some concealed person or persons, the shot taking affect in the left shoulder and spine. ...
>
> We hastened out and met him in front of the cabins. The night being intensely dark the assassins easily made the escape. Dr. Harris was soon in attendance and extracted the ball, but Mr. Davis's suffering during the night was intense, and he expired at one o'clock p. m., on the 24th; was in his right mind up to the time of his death and wished to be remembered to his friends in Wisconsin. ... his remains interred in the cemetery at this place, will be removed to Milton, Wisconsin, for burial, as soon as practical. ...
>
> He had been engaged in mining pursuits the past few years, and was a very highly esteemed man. His energy and perseverance in developing this mining district has not been surpassed, he was extensively engaged in Placer Mining on Rock Creek at the time of his death.[26]

William H. H. Crandall, a visiting minister to Carter County, was given $4 for performing Pardon's funeral.[27]

Later, two men were individually arrested for his murder, but neither Thomas Cook nor Joseph Powers were found guilty.[28]

For an article for a local magazine, I researched and wrote:

> The search began to find his killer and the reason for his murder. The *Janesville Gazette,* Wisconsin, on June 4, announced his murder: "He had been engaged in mining pursuits the past few years, and was a very highly esteemed man. ... he was extensively engaged in Placer Mining on Rock Creek." County tax records indicate Pardon owned a blacksmith shop, four cabins, and other property.
>
> The day of his shooting [two hours after Pardon died], Edwin A. Slack filed a [$114.07] lien against Pardon for lumber.
>
> The next day, Louis Chartier filed a [$106.00 mechanics] lien against Pardon for materials for his house and blacksmith shop [175 feet east of the Wheeler, Hull & Co. mill].
>
> Despite these legal actions, suspicion fell to two other individuals. The day Pardon died, John Kile swore on oath to the Sweetwater County Probate

Judge Wiswell accusing Thomas Cook of the murder. The judge issued an arrest warrant. Cook was brought before the court and pled not guilty. On June 14, this action against Cook was dismissed.

Two days after Davis died, Timothy Clawson swore an oath with the judge accusing Joseph Powers of the murder. An arrest warrant was issued and Powers was brought before the court. After examining the evidence, on June 3, the complaint against Powers was withdrawn. No other suspects are known.[29]

In 2024 while re-reading the biography of *Finn Burnett, Frontiersman*, another pioneer to Atlantic City and included in this book, I was floored to read a passage which can only be about Pardon Davis. This passage confirmed my suspicions about Thomas Cook and Joseph Powers' involvement. The segment also accused a third man, Bob Wheeling, as the one who pulled the trigger.

Three years earlier in 1867, Finn fought in the brutal Hay Field fight against Indians at Fort C. F. Smith in southern Montana. Wheeling was also present and Finn witnessed Wheeling's cowardice during the battle. While it wasn't proven Wheeling murdered Pardon, it is reasonable to believe Wheeling would have been capable of killing a man in cold blood.

One small sense of satisfaction came from the knowledge the locals condemned and harassed Cook and Powers to the point they fled the country, though they did carry off a great sum of gold.[30]

Note #1: Harden is his first name per the 1850 US census in Berlin, Wisconsin, and in the 1870 Mortality Schedule for Milton, Wisconsin. I suspect after the "Pardon Davis" crusade and his 1856 pardon the nickname stuck. He voted and signed contracts as Pardon. Even his inquest and hometown newspaper referred to him as Pardon Davis.[31]

Note #2: In 2016 I communicated with Pardon's great-great-great-grandniece. She wrote "Others in his immediate family were buried in the Milton Cemetery, so if he was removed, that is where I would expect to find him."[32]

The exhaustive search included calling the Milton cemetery where his parents and siblings are buried, other area cemeteries to review original records, genealogical sites, and old newspaper sites. He's not with his family. I believe he's still in Atlantic City and likely in the East Cemetery.

Note #3: My goal of getting my hands on Pardon's pardon documents lasted ten years. I wanted to know Jeremiah's "real Yankee trick." In 2024 a museum archivist and a private researcher searched the boxes which held Governor Wickliffe's pardon papers in the Louisiana Historical Center. Neither found documents with his name. Many of the documents were in poor condition.

Jeremiah's brave and determined effort to save his son with his "real Yankee trick" remains his secret.

Davis, Harriet
Circa 1836–December 21, 1887

Little is known of this early pioneer to the Wyoming Territory.

From the 1869 Wyoming territorial census, Harriet was 33 years old, the "occupation" column had a line through it, and she'd lived in the US for 16 years. She had newly arrived in the territory two months earlier. Her place of birth was Canada, and she declared her intentions to become a citizen.

Additionally, the census included who would be her two sons. Charles A. Davis was 15 years old, had lived his life in the US, had arrived with his mother two months earlier, and was born in Wisconsin. Sidney Davis was eight months old, born in Colorado, and of course arrived in the territory with his mother.[33]

The next year's US census in 1870 Harriet was listed in Atlantic City, and this time her husband Sidney was with them. Sidney was 42 years old, a brick mason, born in Canada, and was a citizen.

In the one year between censuses, Harriet had aged to 39 years old, her occupation was "keeping house," and she was not a citizen.

Son Charles was 17 years old and his occupation was already a miner. Son Sidney was one year old.[34]

In Atlantic City's 1880 census, husband Sidney and son Charles were not listed. Harriett [sic] was listed as 38 years old, still married, and an occupation of "house keeping." Son Sidney was 11 years old, and was listed as "at home." A third son, Samuel, was 9 years old, and was born in Wyoming.[35]

On March 13, 1880, Harriet B. Davis purchased 160 acres in section 4, Township 149, Range 52.[36] I could not locate this site.

Harriet remained in Atlantic City until she died on December 21, 1887.[37]

Harriet Davis' notice of her death on December 21, 1887.
–Courtesy of the *Fremont Clipper*, December 31, 1887.
Fremont County Library, Lander. From microfilm.

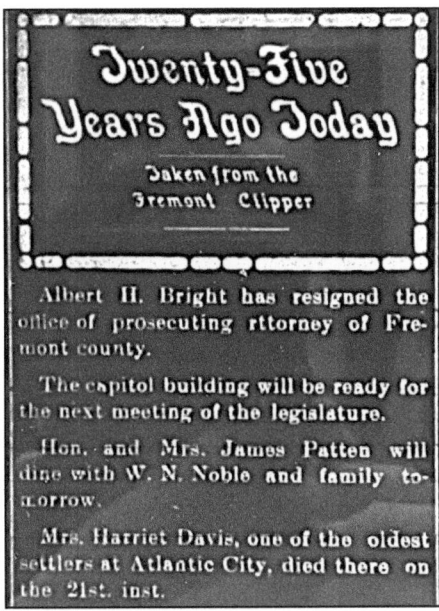

Mrs. Harriet Davis, one of the oldest settlers at Atlantic City, died there on the 21st. inst.

An article remembering Harriet Davis on the 25th anniversary of her 1887 death. –Courtesy of the *Wyoming State Journal*, January 3, 1913. Fremont County Library, Lander. From microfilm.

Twenty-Five
Years Ago Today

Taken from the
Fremont Clipper

Albert H. Bright has resigned the office of prosecuting attorney of Fremont county.

The capitol building will be ready for the next meeting of the legislature.

Hon. and Mrs. James Patten will dine with W. N. Noble and family tomorrow.

Mrs. Harriet Davis, one of the oldest settlers at Atlantic City, died there on the 21st. inst.

The photo at the top of this page was a segment of the bottom remembrance column printed in 1913. This serves as an admonishment to those who find the easily found top snippet on the internet, assume her death occurred in 1912, and pass on the incorrect information to internet websites.[38]

Tip: The *inst.* stands for "instant" which means "of the present month" in publishing terms. *Ult.* or *ultimo* in a newspaper article is Latin which means "the previous month."

Knowing this, for a death notice to include *inst.* in a published article on the 3rd of the month for a death that occurred the month prior makes no sense. The researcher would know something isn't right and must research further.

Two trips to Lander and hours scanning the microfiche resulted in the truth.

The remembrance article had simply copied a portion of the text from her original death notice (opposite page).

Fosburg, Eugene
Unknown–circa March 31, 1870

Eugene was a miner during a terrible year when several miners were killed by Indians. He became a victim on or about March 31, 1870, at St. Mary's stage station, about 16 miles east of Atlantic City on the Sweetwater River.[39]

The coroner's inquest and jury were held in Atlantic City on April 3.

His murder was detailed in the *South Pass News* where his last name was spelled "Fosbury."

> Whereas, on the 31st of March, 1870, … Eugene Fosberry at St. Mary's on Sweetwater, were surprised and murdered in the most cold-blooded and brutal manner.

Eugene had been shot by a gun once and five times with arrows.

Very little is known about him. A commentary on the aftermath of the massacres are described in the *South Pass News* on the front page."[40]

Also spelled Fosbury, Fasberry, and Fosberry.

Jolly, Levi M.
Unknown–January 17, 1905

Despite it being mid-winter, on January 10, 1905, Levi and two fellow quartz miners, Harry Hall and Lawrence Flynn, left Encampment, Wyoming, to look for mining work.

They chose to walk the roughly 144 miles to Point of Rocks.

Ten years earlier, Jolly had worked at the Mary Ellen mine south of Atlantic City and knew the area. He intended to return here and bring the other men.

Upon reaching Point of Rocks, they attempted to walk the 55 miles north through the Red Desert to Atlantic City.

He missed the road.

A days-long winter storm hit with temperatures plummeting as low as -47 °F (-44 °C).

The Red Desert offers little protection, but during the trek the men managed to warm up at the Bush ranch, Jared Williams' place, and the Giessler ranch.

The freezing men were discovered by Lawrence Giessler who had traveled to his ranch to check on some stock. He rescued the suffering men and brought them to Atlantic City.

Levi died the night of January 17. The other two men were expected to recover unless they succumbed to blood poisoning or pneumonia.

The newspaper article listed no burial information for Jolly.

To make such a trek in mid-winter in the first place was foolhardy. What's even more shocking is this decision was not his first time to make it.

Atlantic City old-timers recalled an incident from ten years earlier after the Mary Ellen mine had closed in January. That time, Jolly, Welsey Westfall, and a third man headed south for Point of Rocks.

While they were in the Red Desert, a winter storm hit. This time they found Giessler's camp. The next day they met a Doc Harris who furnished them with horses and helped them onward.

The old-timers said the men had

reached Point of Rocks in about a week, more dead than alive, suffering untold agonies from numerous frost-bites. ... It seems strange that the man should attempt this same trip, in the dead of winter, and in the face of such a terrible storm.[41]

Kellog, Alanson
Unknown–March 1870

Alanson was a miner killed by Indians in March of the worst year for Indian violence, 1870, at St. Mary's stage station. This former pony express station on the Sweetwater River was about 16 miles east of Atlantic City.

The *South Pass News* detailed the coroner's inquest on April 3. H. M. Taylor was called to testify. He stated Alanson had been "gun-shot" four times, and he was Canadian by birth.

Soon, resolutions by the town members were adopted to organize a company of men to protect life and property after the aftermath of the regional killings of 26 men this summer.[42]

Also spelled Kellogg and Anson B.

Lathan, Charles
Unknown–September 28, 1869

Charles was "killed while chopping wood at the Mammoth quartz mill but half a mile distant from Atlantic City."[43]

No other information on him can be found.

Also spelled Latham

Lewellyn, Maurice "Casey"
June 1860–March 21, 1918

Maurice was a highly regarded man in this area. He was one of the owners of the Mary Ellen mine, south of Atlantic City. After the Mary Ellen closed, he went on to work at the Carissa mine near South Pass City.

During a dance with the red-haired teacher Miss Dunkerd, Maurice asked her for every waltz. Each time, the violinist would play the song "Casey Would Waltz with a Strawberry Blonde."

The next day, child James Carpenter sang the song and mimicked Maurice waltzing around the room. The nickname stuck. For the rest of his life Maurice was called Casey.[44]

In 1896 "Lewellyn, Maurice" was included in a list posted by the Lander post office, Dead Letter Office, for unclaimed letters.[45]

In 1897 Casey was one of the miners present at the "Carriso" mine when William McCarroll was killed in a terrible explosion. He reported William had been killed. See William McCarroll in chapter 5.

Also known as Morris, he worked as the watchman for "a long period and does the assessment work every year."[46]

According to the 1900 census for Atlantic City, he was born in June 1860 and was 39 years old. His birthplace was Pennsylvania, his occupation was a quartz miner, and was single.

Maurice "Casey" Lewellyn holds the hand of Hazel Carpenter in front of the Carpenter Restaurant. Background: *Hazel's father, Clarence E. Carpenter, Sr. 1903.* —Courtesy of Betty Carpenter Pfaff

In the early 1900s, Casey asked engineer and friend Lou Penhoel to help complete his promise to John Marrin with enough Mary Ellen gold to make a watch case. They expected three ounces would work for a big watch. From a "free-showing gold quartz vein" and Casey doing the panning, they met his promise.[47]

His listing on Wyoming's "Compiled Census Index, 1860-1910" stated he was at Atlantic City in 1910, he was head of household with no family members, was 50 years old, and his place of birth was Pennsylvania. The complete 1910 census also listed him as single.[48]

In 1912 Casey leased the Mary Ellen mine to "engineer Smith of Denver, who will work the mine in a small way this winter."[49]

Fine Gold has an entire chapter, including photographs, devoted to Maurice.[50]

Maurice's death on March 21, 1918, was not reported in any newspaper I could locate. Afterward, the *Wyoming State Journal* printed several weekly legal notices about his estate.[51]

The only information about his death came from his death certificate. It stated he died of "Pullmonary [sic] tuberculosis." He had suffered from it for two years. Pneumonia contributed to his death.

His death certificate did not list his birthdate, but it stated he was 56 years old and born in Quakertown, Pennsylvania, to Welsh and English parents.

It also stated "Place of Burial or Removal" was "Lander I.O.O.F." and his date of burial was "3/22/1918." Lander's Mount Hope cemetery has a large Independent Order of Odd Fellows section.[52]

The cemetery's sexton made a great effort trying to locate him in the computer and the original records. He even checked books from other cemeteries. I walked the entire IOOF section and checked each marker. Maurice is not listed on the cemetery's online search engine.

A search of Riverton's cemetery listing and grounds of the defunct IOOF cemetery did not list him on its directory. His name was not engraved on any legible headstone—many looked melted from deterioration. Riverton's Mountain View Cemetery's on-site directory and online search engine did not list him.

One report discovered early in this project injected confusion because the report stated he was buried in the East Cemetery, he died July 1884, at age 38, and was buried "within gothic wooden fence now fallen down."[53]

There is no original source for this I could find. In 2021, a grave matching that description was confirmed to hold the remains of Casimer Melin. It's possible there was another grave that matched this description. If so, the distinguished wooden fence has decayed away.

Casey was a cherished member of this community. As such and with no confirmation from any cemetery records, despite what his death certificate stated I believe he is buried in the East Cemetery.

Also spelled Llewellyn, and also called Morris and spelled Morrice.

Logan, George
Circa 1838–May 1869

George's body and three other unidentified men killed by Indians were discovered by Indian scouts in May 1869 in the Wind River Valley. Their burial place was not specified.[54]

He owned the grocery store in Atlantic City.

George is listed in the 1869 Wyoming territorial census for Carter County. He was 31 years old, and his occupation was merchant. He was born in Canada, and he declared his intent to be a citizen. He had lived in the US for 21 years and had already spent 14 months in the territory. George was one of the first settlers in the early days of Atlantic City in 1868.[55]

His property, a grocery store, had been located next to Harden "Pardon" Davis' property, who is also included in this chapter.[56]

As he was a property and business owner here, it's possible his body was returned to Atlantic City.

McGuire, John
Unknown–circa March 31, 1870

John was included in the 1869 Wyoming territorial census for Carter County. He was listed as 21 years old, and his occupation was listed as cook. His length of time in the US was 12 years, and his residence in the territory had been 14 months. His place of birth was England, and he declared his intention to become a citizen.[57]

John was a miner killed by Indians on or about March 31, 1870, at St. Mary's stage station on the Sweetwater River, about 16 miles east of Atlantic City. His body had been mutilated.

He was one of 26 people in this region who were slain this terrible summer.[58]

H. M. Taylor testified at the coroner's inquest on April 3. He related he found John had been shot five times in the neck and face and with eight arrows "sticking in different parts of the body." Three scalps had been taken from his head and he had been stripped naked. Taylor supposed John's parents lived in Cheyenne.[59]

A commentary on the aftermath is described in the *South Pass News* on August 8, 1870. The Federal Census Mortality Schedules Index, 1850-1880, spelled his last name as "McQuire."[60]

Also spelled McQuire.

Othick, James H.
Circa 1845–March 31, 1870

Before leaving his home state of Illinois to head west, in 1864 James joined the fight in the Civil War. He entered service at 19 years old, and joined the 145th Illinois Infantry for 100 days.

His Service Entry Date was May 21, 1864; his Muster in Date was June 9. He was mustered out as a corporal on September 23, at Camp Butler, Illinois.[61]

Upon reaching the South Pass region, on June 25, 1868, James and six other men sold veins and the Thomas Cotter Ledge and the Ruralane Ledge in the Shoshoni Mining District to Thomas Bennett. James signed this quit claim before a notary public on July 3, 1868.[62]

Six months before his death in Wyoming Territory, E. A. Slack placed a lien against James' property on his lot northeast of Colfax and Washakie Alley on September 20, 1869.

The $30 lien on James' property was for lumber Slack had provided to James. "Although this was six months before Othick was killed by Indians near Miner's Delight, there is no record the bill was ever paid."[63]

James was one of many men killed by Indians in the terrible spring of 1870. He was 25 years old and was killed at Smith's Gulch, three miles northeast of Atlantic City.[64]

During the coroner's inquest, Frank Moore was sworn in and described how he found James dead the morning of April 4. Frank testified James

> was laying on his right side, and stripped of all his clothing except his shirt. A pick was driven in his bowels to the eye; three scalp locks have been taken from his head, and his body was pierced with six arrows and one gun-shot wound, also a pistol shot in his head.

Frank had known James for three years, and he testified James was a native of Carlyle, Illinois, and aged about 25 years. He left a mother, brother, and sister. His death came on March 31. His last name was spelled "Othic," and in the *Cheyenne Daily Leader* his name was spelled James "H. Athick."[65]

James' estate went to Probate Court on April 26, 1870, and he had died intestate. The Court appointed A. B. (illegible) as Administrator. His estate included a lot on Colfax Street in Lewiston which adjoined "Stillman's Old Residence." His estate included property in South Pass City, Lot 124 which was valued at $20 and referred to as a "vac. Lot" (believed to read "vacant lot").[66]

Also spelled Athick and Othic.

Raught, George H., Dr.
Unknown–July 23, 1888

Decades before arriving in Atlantic City, George had traveled from New York to Colorado during the Pike's Peak gold rush of 1857–58.

In 1867, he arrived in Wyoming.

A look-back article, "Early Days at Atlantic City" by Charles Bates in 1911, described his activities.

> Late in the fall of 1867 Dr. George H. Raught, Jack McTurk and one or two others found what afterward developed into the Buckeye mine. Winter was upon the boys. Money being short and grub on the same line, they determined to put off mining until the following spring. They held a conference and decided their best plan was to winter in the Big Horn country. So they hied themselves down to the head of the Big Horn canyon, where they found plenty of game, and as the doctor often informed me, they fared well. In the spring of 1868 they drifted back and went to work.[67]

In 1884, while George was in Utah, he sat on a jury for a polygamy trial.[68]

During this year, he filed a lawsuit against "Harry A. Holcomb ... for $75,723 in principal and interest of a debt." The outcome is unknown.[69]

In 1885 he was called to be in the jury pool for later service.[70]

After his return to Atlantic City the same year, on October 27 George signed an indenture to William Giessler and Frank Lenne for the "Black Eyed Susan Lode situated on what is known as the Cariboo Hill about ½ mile in a North-Westerly direction from Atlantic City."

On November 7 George signed an indenture to release the North Star Lode and the Hidden Treasure Lode to H. A. Van Praag and George W. Keel.[71]

He also owned several other local mines: Golconda Mine, Last Chance Mine, Cleaveland Mine, and the Buckeye mine.

George died at Atlantic City on July 23, 1888, of typhoid pneumonia.

Searches of old newspaper and genealogy sites revealed no other information including his death notice or where he was buried. I found this lack of information odd as he appeared to be a prominent man.[72]

Smith, Jennie S.
Circa 1842–May 1870

Jennie died in May 1870 of heart disease. She was only 28 years old. Jennie was a married housekeeper who died a month before the 1870 US census was taken. She was born in New York.

"Smith Jennie" was listed in the "List of Letters" notice in the *Cheyenne Daily Leader* as having mail "remaining in the Post Office at Cheyenne, Saturday, October 22d, 1870."[73]

Note: The 1870 Mortality Schedule compiled in 2015 incorrectly stated she was from Maryland. The error stems from the document titled "Cemetery Project, List of Graves and Possible Graves." This listing stated:

> Jennie Smith, 28 (Maryland), May [month of death], housekeeper, died of heart disease.

Another document titled "Fremont County, Defunct Cemeteries" by an unknown author correctly listed:

> Smith, Jennie S. (MD), 28, N.Y. [place of birth], May [month of death], Hsekpr [housekeeper], Heart Disease. Note: 'Md.' means married.[74]

Also spelled Jeannie.

Sostmann, Herman Henry
Circa 1860–February 20, 1891

In 1891, a barber in Atlantic City committed suicide. The *Fremont Clipper* article stated "He was buried the first of the week. ... The less said of the occurrence the better."

The *Cheyenne Daily Sun* stated he "has suicided by shoting [*sic*], at Atlantic, a mining camp."[75]

Little is known about Herman's history. There's an 1880 US census from St. Louis, Missouri, with a Herman Sostmann. He's 17 years old (which would mean a birth year circa 1863), he's a boarder, has an occupation as a barber, and is from Germany. This was the only online search item found. It's likely this man is our Herman.[76]

When Herman arrived in the region is unknown. In 1885, Fremont County recorded a Certificate of Marriage for Herman, who was 25 years old and living in Lander. He wed Miss Lizzie W. Richards. She was 21 years old and she also lived in Lander. They were married by renowned H. G. Nickerson.[77]

They were newly arrived to Atlantic City in 1890 when they opened a joint boarding house and barber shop.

Soon, Herman began making threats to kill Lizzie, jealousy was said to be the cause. The crisis escalated to the point Lizzie ran for her life out the door. A gunshot was heard. The bullet passed over her head.

The coroner's inquest convened the same day, February 20.

Mark R. Stratmoen intently studied this inquest for his book.

During the inquest Lizzie testified, "He had been cruel to me and threatened my life repeatedly."

One witness, G. A Zimmerman testified he heard two shots. He found Herman still alive, but Herman lived for only minutes.

The inquest's verdict stated Herman "killed himself with a .38 cal. Revolver ... whilst temporarily insane with suicidal intent."[78]

The belief was he intended to commit a murder-suicide.[79]

Herman was about 31 years old.

An ad for Herman Sostmann's barber skills in the Fremont Clipper, *January 7, 1888.*
–Courtesy of the Fremont County Library, Lander. From microfilm.

H. H. Sostmann, the physiognomical hair dresser, tonsorial artist, cranium manipulator, facial operator, capillary abridger and professor of crinicultural abscission and craniological tripsis is still at the old stand, ready and willing to give the dear people the benefit of his many accomplishments.

Certificate of Marriage for Herman Sostmann and Lizzie Richards, signed by H. G. Nickerson on October 20, 1885. –Courtesy of the Fremont County Clerk's Office

Note #1: The *Fremont Clipper* article stated Sostmann died "the day before the Father of his Country's birthday." George Washington's birthday and its holiday celebration was February 22. This would mean Herman died on February 21, which is incorrect. Perhaps this description was an attempt to wax poetic.

Note #2: Six months after Herman's death, Lizzie Sostmann remarried on August 16, 1891, to William Watt Ehelen in Lander.[80]

Also spelled Sostman and Soustmann.

Stambaugh, Charles B.
Circa 1845–May 4, 1870

Charles hailed from Lancaster, Fairfield County, in Ohio. In the 1850 US census, Charles lived with father Samuel and mother Susan. He was 5 years old with one sister, Ellen.

He was said to have been a nephew of General William T. Sherman. Both families lived in Lancaster, Ohio.

By the 1860 census mother Susan had been widowed. Charles was 15 years old and had three siblings ranging from 12 to 5 years old.[81]

In March 1864 at the age of 19, he enlisted as a private to fight in the Civil War. He joined the 11th Ohio Cavalry. He was released from service in May 1866 in Nebraska.

After his first Army service, he rejoined but this date is unknown.

Under First Lieutenant Charles Stambaugh, the 2nd Cavalry's Company B deployed to the South Pass area.

Charles engaged in an Arapaho Indian battle on May 4, 1870, not far from Miners Delight on Twin Creek Hill.[82]

They set up camp in Big Atlantic Gulch at a time when several raiding parties were in the vicinity, as yet unaware of the troops. When Arapahoes attacked the Jason Sherman Party on Twin Creek Hill, the troopers pursued them. Lieutenant Stambaugh, riding a fast horse, outstripped his men, was cut off and killed not far from the stream which bears his name. ...

Lieutenant Stambaugh, ... was shot dead from his horse, his body falling for a time into the hands of the Indians who robbed it of a watch, ring, his revolver and belt, the contents of his pockets, etc. They shot into his body several times, after which the company rallied and recovered the body.[83]

Charles was buried in Atlantic City with full military honors with six commissioned officers serving as pall bearers. Assisted by a full choir Reverend John C. Fitman conducted a graveside service. People "from the three mining camps turned out to honor the deceased officer."[84]

He must have been quickly exhumed as his body was transported to and was buried in a cemetery in Lancaster, Ohio, on May 15, Sunday, 1870. The newspaper article reported he was to be "interred in the Catholic burying ground, by the side of those of his father."[85]

On July 14, Charles' mother was awarded a pension from the Army.[86]

In honor of First Lieutenant Stambaugh, the Army renamed the camp near Miners Delight to Camp Stambaugh in August 1870.[87]

Note: An online grave search website listed he was buried in the St. Mary Catholic Cemetery in Ohio.

On February 21, 2024, I called this cemetery to find his plot, hoping to request a photograph of his headstone. The office clerk, Dawn, completed a search for him but they have no entry for him. Furthermore, the cemetery's website home page stated this cemetery was dedicated November 1, 1881, well after Charles' death.

I searched other Catholic and public cemeteries in the region. Hours spent on history-related websites revealed nothing.

Lastly, the US Government's National Cemetery Administration's Gravesite Locator revealed no result he was interred in a national cemetery.[88]

Also spelled Stambough and Stanbaugh

Walker, Lizzie
Unknown–March 6, 1898

Lizzie died on or about March 6, 1898. Her body was found near her home in Big Atlantic Gulch at the home she shared with W. H. Neff, a miner, for several years. Her head was in water pail and the water was frozen solid with ice.

The inquest on March 9 determined Neff had been in Lander for several days and found her upon his return. The inquest ruled she had suffered from "fits" (seizures) or experienced heart failure as she lugged pails of water from the spring and fell into the bucket.

Death came instantly as there was no indications of a struggle.

I could find no other information on her so I had no idea of her age. The discovery of this photograph informs us she was a young woman. With so little known about Lizzie it's gratifying to know she was a young woman enjoying a happy time with friends.

Lizzie's age, her birthplace, and burial place are unknown, though it's possible she's buried in Atlantic City.[89]

"Sept 1896 Day after wedding, Maud [Huff] Williams pouring, Babe [Nellie] Huff hat, Lizzie Walker [center], Marg Griffin, Henry Williams" was the title of the electronic file of this photograph.
–Courtesy of the Atlantic City Historical Society Collection, Wyoming State Archives

Accidental Death.

Coroner J. W. H. Schoo was called to Atlantic City last Wednesday to hold an inquest on the body of Lizzie Walker, who had been found dead at her home near that place Tuesday. From the evidence it seems that Mrs. Walker had gone to the spring and was returning with two pails of water. When about half way to the house she evidently sat down to rest, rising to go on she fell with her face in one of the pails and was found in that position frozen in the water.

Mrs. Walker was troubled with fits and it was probably one of these, or heart failure that caused her to fall, and death undoubtedly ensued instantly as there was no indications of a struggle.

Mr. Schoo summoned a jury who, after hearing the evidence returned the following

VERDICT:

Atlantic City, Wyo., March 9, 1898.

State of Wyoming,⎫ ss:
County of Fremont⎰

We the jurors summoned by the coroner to inquire into the cause of the death of Lizzie Walker, of Atlantic Gulch, do find that she came to her death on or about March 6, 1898, from falling into a bucket of water while suffering from heart failure or a fit, to the best of our belief.

C. E. Carpenter,
Foreman.
J. M. Dumphey,
John Godward.

J. W. H. Schoo, Coroner.

Coroner J. W. H. Schoo's inquest returned with a finding of Accidental for Lizzie Walker's death. This article referred to her as "Mrs."
—Courtesy of the *Wind River Mountaineer*, March 14, 1898

TEN

Cadaver Dogs

On June 7, 2016, at the East and West Cemeteries and adjacent areas, K. T. Irwin and her blue-eyed border collie Blue ran through their procedure for locating human remains. Their work was mesmerizing.

K. T. provided a wealth of information about this process. Cadaver dogs have the ability and the training to sniff out human remains in a variety of conditions, including underwater and cremated remains (also known as cremains).

These highly trained dogs do, however, have limitations. For example, they can't locate remains of infants whose bodies have decayed to the point there's nothing left. Other factors can influence whether the dog can scent the remains, such as how deeply the body was buried, whether the body was enclosed in a box and if it was sealed, and how large the person was. Weather conditions can also impact the dog's ability to detect scents and can tire the dog.[1]

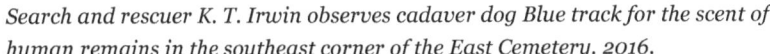

Search and rescuer K. T. Irwin observes cadaver dog Blue track for the scent of human remains in the southeast corner of the East Cemetery. 2016.

When a dog is trained to detect the scent of human remains, it's also trained to perform a move to alert the handler of the detection. K. T.'s dogs are trained to "down"—lay on their stomach.

According to her, these dogs don't have an on-off switch at a scent. They make a decision whether what they're smelling has enough of a human scent to convince the dog to down.

While the dog searches for a scent and downs, K. T. interprets the dog's actions. When Blue downs, depending upon the dog's actions and her knowledge and experience, she decides the legitimacy of the finding.

Confirmed Remains

For the East Cemetery's confirmed findings, K. T. recorded the site's Universal Transverse Mercator (UTM) coordinates, and I tied strips of yellow tape to the sagebrush at her direction to mark the spot. The coordinates were included in her final report.

The locations of confirmed remains are marked on the cemeteries' maps with a black star (pages 35 and 157). On color maps the star is green.

One surprise location for a confirmed finding occurred at the Carpenter family monument. See video *5 Search*, time stamp 05:00. The explanation for this surprise was a family member's cremains had been spread there. For more information see chapter 4, *East Cemetery, Marked Burials and Family Plots*.[2]

Unconfirmed Remains

During the searches there were occasions when Blue appeared to home in on *something*. He stopped, turned, sniffed, then resumed the search. K. T. explained he's making up his mind whether what he smells is enough for him to acknowledge the scent and down. It's possible there are remains at those sites, she said, but there wasn't enough scent for him to decide.

An example of Blue changing his mind occurred in the West Cemetery in the area of M12. Blue clearly lingers at a spot and even bends his legs to down, but at the last instant trots away. His actions were captured as shown in the photograph (opposite page) and on video *2 Search*, time stamp 3:50.[3]

The locations of unconfirmed remains are included on both maps with a white star. On color maps the star is yellow. The locations were not marked with tape nor were UTM coordinates taken. The map locations are approximate because the video couldn't capture the exact spots.

Another reason for including the location of unconfirmed remains on the maps is in case new information or technology surfaces which might confirm or refute remains.

Cadaver-seeking dog Blue changes his mind about scenting human remains while he and handler K. T. Irwin search for signs of human remains in the West Cemetery. 2016.

Note #1: Some portions of the searches were not recorded due to having to shut down the camera to replace batteries or SD cards.

Note #2: Special thanks to John Mionczynski for videographing the searches and for permitting these photographs from the recordings to be included in this book. Copies of these videos are held at the Atlantic City Historical Society's curator and the author. The video clips' titles listed in this book are the author's.

ELEVEN

Dowsing for Graves

Dowsing is controversial despite it having been practiced around the world for millennia. In modern times this activity is either wholeheartedly accepted or soundly rejected.

The earliest recorded "divination" was performed by Chinese Emperor Ta Yu (Da Yu) who was born in 2,205 BCE. Herodotus, the "father of history," wrote of dowsing around the fifth century. Since then it's been recorded in drawings and in texts throughout Europe, Asia, and Africa.

In the Middle Ages, the Catholic Church changed its attitude about dowsing. In 1362 Pope John XXII issued a bull against pendulum dowsing. In 1518 Martin Luther declared dowsing "broke the first commandment." The Church proclaimed dowsing as satanic, a sorcery, a sin, an evil.

Despite these edicts the practice continued, even among the clergy.

During the past 100 years scientists, including physicists and myriad "ologists," and other learned persons began earnest research and experiments.

Nobel Laureate Charles Richet declared in 1913: "We must accept dowsing as fact. It is useless to work up experiments merely to prove its existence. It exists. What is needed is its development."

Don Schooley dowses for a grave in the East Cemetery. 2016.

Knighted physicist William F. Barrett and fellow psychical researcher Theodore Besterman collected historical data and performed experiments and trials. Their conclusion in 1926 stated:

> The dowser, in our opinion, is a person endowed with a subconscious supernormal cognitive faculty, which, its nature being unknown, we call ... cryptesthesia. By means of this cryptesthesia knowledge of whatever object is searched for enters the dowser's subconscious and is revealed by means of an unconscious muscular reaction, ...
>
> All that is required is the discovery of some fruitful generalisation which will permit the orthodox scientist to incorporate cryptesthesia into the canon of accepted and indisputable scientific knowledge.

Ben G. Hester, an architect, studied dowsing for eight years. His summation in 1984 included a profound perspective:

> *There is supernormal intelligence involved in every type of dowsing.* ...
>
> The dowsing community is peopled with a majority who are learners, mediocre dowsers, and a few fakes. ... The dowsing societies are the first to admit it. ... They are endeavoring to correct it by teaching and self-discipline.
>
> The minority of *expert* dowsers are the ones through which a true picture of dowsing emerges.

Our three Wyoming *expert* dowsers have decades of dedicated practice and experience. They are trusted practitioners of this ancient knowledge.

Don Schooley has decades of experience as a county sexton. He knows cemeteries, burial practices, and how Mountain West graves change over time.

Ann Noble is an award-winning history writer with a master's degree in history and is a successful businesswoman.

Sam Drucker was an archeologist for the Bureau of Land Management with a master's degree in anthropology and was recognized by historical organizations.[1]

Ann Noble dowses for a grave in the East Cemetery. 2016.

Sam Drucker uses a rod to point to a grave he discovered in the West Cemetery. 2016.

Oft times called "witching," dowsing is usually associated with searching for water. Dowsers can also locate underground oil, coal, minerals (in the 1300s dowsing was initially used for locating minerals), buried power lines, buried bodies, human ashes, and can even provide medical diagnoses.[2]

In 2016 notable Wyoming historian Jonita Sommers introduced me to this new world and recommended three dowsers who dowse for graves. Within months of each other, Don Schooley, Ann Noble (twice), and Sam Drucker volunteered to travel for hours to this mountain town to locate our people.

If having the skill to find graves isn't enough, some dowsers have the practiced skill to determine the *sex* of the deceased. Don Schooley and Ann Noble have such an skill thanks to their decades of practice and experience.

In the East Cemetery Don and Ann discovered and sexed a combined 72 previously unknown graves. At each discovery, the grave was marked with a pink or blue pin flag marked with the dowser's unique code.

On the hill of the West Cemetery at what I had suspected was a grave, Don determined it was not but could not locate any other grave. Later, Ann discovered and sexed one grave as a male (M12) which was marked with a blue flag.

Sam Drucker, the final dowser whose sole undertaking was to scour the West Cemetery's massive hillside, discovered an astonishing 15 graves and confirmed Ann's finding. Sam didn't sex graves so his findings are marked with a white flag pinned to the ground. The white flag signals the sex is unknown.

Confirmed successes

One way to confirm the finding and the declared sex of the deceased is to exhume the grave and examine the body, which of course will not happen.

Ann Noble notes the edge of the grave she discovered in the East Cemetery. 2016.

Thanks to Don and Ann's efforts, here are a few confirmations of their findings in the East Cemetery.

One grave was an obvious burial because of the pile of fallen fence planks heaped on the site. Separately, each dowser determined the body was a male. Years later, on this pile of planks I recognized an original 1875 wooden marker. After verifying the identity of this person, Casimer Melin was definitely a man.

Another example came after the cadaver dog shockingly downed twice at the Carpenter family monument signifying human remains which were confirmed by handler K. T. Irwin. When Don arrived, I only told him the dog had downed on this spot. Don dowsed the site. When his rods indicated remains he pondered this. It made no sense there would be a burial there. He suspected placed ashes. He sexed the site and his rods registered them as a female.

I had earlier called the family matriarch and informed her the dog had downed at the monument. She said the ashes were of a female relative who had died out of state and they spread her ashes at the monument.

An unusual third situation arose which resulted in matching decisions between the dowsers. On the map for the East Cemetery (page 35) is grave M35. It's long and is placed on an angle.

Separately, both Don and Ann found this site and each remarked on its unusually long length. They sexed each end of the grave and both concluded two men overlapped in this space. They could not differentiate from one man to the other, so this grave is counted as one male on the map and in this book.

Note: Early in this process, the thought of grave diggers not noticing an earlier grave so near to where they were digging a new grave was unfathomable. How could they not know of the first man's grave?

Ann Noble sexes a grave in the West Cemetery. The rod had moved to the left, indicating this person was a female. 2016.

Now, comprehending the powerful effect of our weather and vegetation on our gravesites, I have no doubt when the second man was buried, the first grave was obscured and no longer detectible. The diggers dug and placed the second man where he overlapped the first man.

Full disclosure: In 2016, the sole difference in the 62 sex findings of Don and Ann took place in the West Cemetery. At the third known grave but of an unnamed child (F3), Don sexed the grave and determined the child was a female.

Later, Ann sexed the grave. I understood the child to be a male.

Of their 62 jointly dowsed and sexed graves, their findings matched but this one. My 2016 database and presentations disclosed this difference.

Before this book was finalized, I again floated through photographs of the West Cemetery. I came across a photograph (above) of Ann sexing *that* particular grave. By this time, I understood how to sex a grave and how to read the rod.

Her rod pointed left, indicating a female.

Horrified, I immediately emailed Ann and asked her to verify her finding based on this attached photograph as I was unsure of my information.

She responded and confirmed that the rod pointing left indicated a female.

Don and Ann had a 100% match in their individual sexing of 62 graves, a massive number ascertained under tough conditions. Their skill and dedication was a monumental achievement.

Preparation for dowsing

Before Don Schooley, Ann Noble, and Sam Drucker's arrival, I didn't know what to expect, but I knew to be ready for anything they might find or what could happen. They were all volunteers. There would be no expectation for a repeat

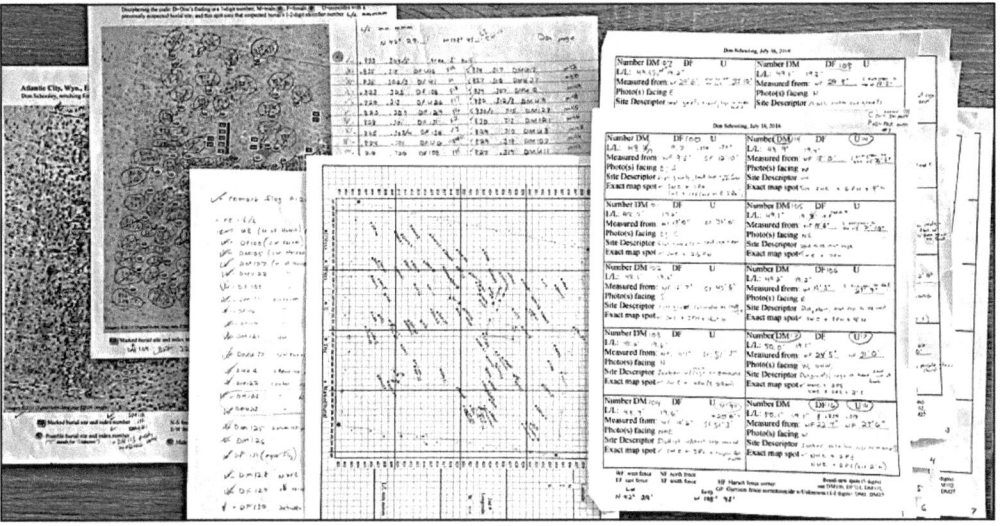

Above, left to right: *Satellite maps to annotate the discovered site, a listing of notes in the days following the dowsings, a graphed layout of the cemetery based on the Lat/Long coordinates, a listing of the graves' Lat/Long coordinates taken the day after the dowsing, and the worksheet to annotate the dowser's findings and comments during the search.*

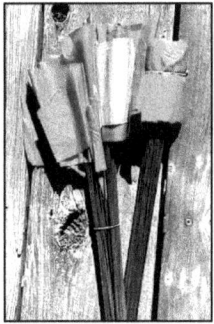

Right: *At the discovery of a grave, a pin flag was immediately marked with a permanent marker with its unique code and was placed at the head of the grave where the dowser directed.*

visit. Furthermore, in the large areas covered with vegetation, one discovered grave could easily be mistaken for another. The chance for errors in documentation and designating each gravesite was high.

To prevent an error, I assigned each dowser a unique code and a distinctive three-digit number which might resolve any possible question later.

I also developed a worksheet to distinguish between each finding:

- the dowser's and gravesite's unique code (D for Don and beginning with 100, A for Ann beginning with 200, and S for Sam beginning with 300. Examples: DM102, Don found Male number 2; AF220, Ann found Female number 20; SU314, Sam found Unsexed grave number 14)
- latitude and longitude coordinates taken at the grave's pin flag"
- measurements from two solid surfaces: a headstone, metal fence, or the wooden cemetery fence to the grave's pin flag. These measurements were for finding the location should the flag or stake be lost.
- photos of the site and listing the direction faced while taking the photo

- site descriptor: the vegetation and amount, the terrain, and any artifacts
- space to write comments from the dowser and any observations

Other documents and items included were:
- a printed satellite map to mark the placement of the grave at the time of discovery and with the site's unique code
- A graph of the graves' placement in the cemetery by its latitude and longitude to clarify their placement and to perceive any burial pattern
- bundles of pin flags of pink and blue and any other leftovers flags I had like yellow flags. Those yellow flags were handy for the odd burials such as the extra-long grave M35.

Most of the documentation could only be collected and finalized after the dowsers left. The complicated details were time-consuming and required several days to collect and confirm.

When the documentation was complete, simplified index numbers replaced the unique codes. In 2021 in the East Cemetery the pin flags were replaced with stakes painted red or blue (female or male) and with hand-painted index numbers.

Equipment

Centuries ago and even used today, a Y-shaped tree branch held with two hands would bend down to the earth in the presence of water.

More common today are metal L-shaped rods made from varying thicknesses of copper or myriad metals. Rods range from cut-up wire hangers all the way to hinged telescoping rods with ball bearings.

The metal rods are bent 90 degrees to form a handle about 3–5" long and with the main rod about 12–15" long.

Dowsing rods can be very small or large, light or heavy, but they all work.

How to dowse and find a grave

Ann said before she begins, she clears her mind, relaxes, and *listens.*

In each hand, loosely hold the handle of the rod so it can rotate without any interference. Elbows are relaxed by the waist. Some dowsers hold their arms straight out or far forward.

When I dowse, I keep the main rods parallel to each other and the tips slightly down to prevent the rods from crossing or separating incorrectly.

Furthermore, I focus on my hands to ensure I don't subconsciously turn my hands toward or away from each other and accidently cross or separate the rods. Be aware of the possibility of subconsciously causing a false indication. This is called the Ideomotor Phenomenon, named by William B. Carpenter in 1852. A person's subconscious can cause involuntary muscle movements which can cause the rods to inadvertently cross which can lead to a false reading.[3]

You do not need to assist the rods to move. They will move on their own.

Don Schooley sexes a grave in the tough terrain of the East Cemetery. His rod points to the right, so this grave is a male. 2016.

Walk north or south in a cemetery for the best chance to cross bodies at the longest side, since they're more commonly buried east-west.

Slowly take one step, pause, then take another step. If you walk over a grave, the rods will cross. Note the spot where the rods crossed.

Continue to slowly step and pause until the rods uncross, which indicates where the body or grave ends. Move to the other portion of the grave and repeat the process so you will have crossed all four sides of a suspected grave. Take note of the dimensions each time the rods cross and uncross.

These dimensions will determine the general size of the body or grave. One to three steps down the length of the grave may indicate the deceased is a baby or child. Four or more steps down the length of the grave may indicate an adult.

The Christian or western norm is the person is buried east-west, but you may also determine the person is buried north-south.

How to sex a grave

In researching dowsing, I learned there are differing methods to sex a grave.

Here is a description of the successful method used by Don and Ann. No matter how the body is laid in the grave, this method will give the correct sex.

Other methods can give a false reading if the body is placed in a grave backward," such as head to the east and feet to the west, rather than the norm, which is head to the west and feet to the east.

Don used very long metal L-shaped rods. He'd stick one main rod (the long portion) straight down into the grave, about where the head would be expected, and at enough depth for the rod to stand upright.

He bent over and held the second rod in his hand the standard way with the long rod horizontal. He held the handle directly above the vertical rod. The rods almost touched.

259

If the rod rotated clockwise, the body was a male; counterclockwise, the body was a female.

Ann's rods were telescoping rods, like a radio antenna. In use, the rods were hinged at the handle to form the traditional "L" shape.

To sex a grave, she straightened one rod at the hinge and then telescoped it down to around eight inches long.

She'd stick the straight rod's handle into the dirt about where the head would be, straight up. Her procedure was the same as Don's except the rod she held in her hand hovered about a foot above the tip of the rod stuck in the ground.

For anyone wanting to try dowsing, each person must practice to find which method works the best for them.

For a deeper knowledge of dowsing and its capabilities, pay a visit to the website for the American Society of Dowsers.[4]

Note #1: These 62 graves include the one grave of their original dowsing and sexing of who would be later identified as Casimer Melin (formerly known as M42, now Index #15) in the East Cemetery. This also includes the known but Unnamed grave of a child (F3) near Baby Williams in the West Cemetery.

The 62 graves do not include the 12 graves discovered by Ann Noble in the East Cemetery and the 15 graves found by Sam Drucker in the West Cemetery.

Note #2: The day after Don Schooley had worked so hard all day and found 60 graves, I was at the East Cemetery documenting his findings. When I was done for the day, I decided to make my first attempt at dowsing in a cemetery.

The row of Carpenters would be my first attempt.

On this day the wind was very strong out of the west.

I began just north of the Carpenter monument which had ashes placed there and planned to mimic Don's process. With a deep breath and my dowsing rods in position, I stepped in front of the monument.

My right rod, on its own, *turned into that strong wind*. It scared me so badly I fled the cemetery.

Note #3: In the early days of this research after Ann Noble had departed, I practiced dowsing for the second time ever in a cemetery in the West Cemetery.

My rods reacted to an unbeknownst grave. This suspected grave was later verified by Sam Drucker who was not aware of my finding. This grave is Unknown #1.

Notes

ABBREVIATIONS USED IN NOTES

AHC	American Heritage Center, University of Wyoming
ACHS	Atlantic City Historical Society
NARA	National Archives and Record Administration, Washington D.C.
SPCSHS	South Pass City State Historic Site
UW	University of Wyoming
WRM	*Wind River Mountaineer*
WSA	Wyoming State Archives
WSA and HD	Wyoming State Archives and Historical Department
WSGS	Wyoming State Geological Survey
WSJ	*Wyoming State Journal*

ILLUSTRATIONS:

Map, Territory of Wyoming. 1879. Courtesy of South Pass City State Historic Site.
Map, Plat, Township 29, Range 100. 1884. Courtesy of Wyoming State Archives.

CHAPTER 1: HOW THIS PROJECT STARTED AND HOW IT ENDED

[1] Boyd, Michael. Personal interview. Aug. 6-7, 2011. During his time with us, he was the director of the Royal Shakespeare Company. The following year, Queen Elizabeth II knighted him as an Honorary Fellow of the Royal Society of Edinburgh, HonFRSE, for his services to drama. Sadly, Sir Michael Boyd died Aug. 3, 2023.

[2] "Early History of Fremont County." H. G. Nickerson. (Written in 1886.) Quarterly Bulletin. Vol. 2. No. 1. *Annals of Wyoming*. State of Wyoming, Historical Department. Page 10.

[3] Trevor, Marjorie C. (1954). *History of Carter-Sweetwater County, Wyoming to 1875.* (Master's thesis, UW.) ProQuest Dissertations & Theses. Page 108-9.

[4] Beebe. Ruth. *Reminiscing Along the Sweetwater.* Boulder, Colorado. Johnson Publishing Co. 1973. Page 51; "Record of License Issued in." PDF "Sweetwater_records_roll_02-04-115_01." pdf pages 312 and 320. Original ledger had no page numbers. SPCSHS. Server. Note: Included in this ledger is the handwritten notation: "The above licenses were issued in Carter County under the laws of Dakota Territory and previous to the organization of Sweetwater County and copied into this Book by the undersigned by and order of the Board of County Commissioners. Dated March 1875. A. McIntosh, County Clerk." This notation is shown on pdf page 316.

[5] Pfaff, Betty Carpenter. Oral history by the ACHS, WSA and HD and/or the Wyoming State Historical Society. Jan. 24, 1984. Interviewer Philippina Halstead. Page 4. Transcription held at the SPCSHS.

[6] Freeburgh, Melvin. Oral History. ACHS. Interviewer David Geible. Jan. 28, 1984. Page 15. Transcript held at the SPCSHS. Accessed May 8, 2024; An online search of old newspapers yielded no information on when this earthquake took place that affected Hyde's Hall. In reviewing multiple oral histories, those who mentioned the earthquake could not recall the year; Golliher, Alma Williams. Oral history by the ACHS, WSA and HD and/or the Wyoming State Historical Society. June 30, 1984. Interviewer David Geible. Pages 21-22. Transcription held at the SPCSHS. Accessed March 8, 2024; Moerer, Lyle F. Wyoming State Historical Society. Dec. 8, 1983. Interviewer Philippina Halstead. Page 15. Transcription held at the SPCSHS. Accessed March 8, 2024; David Geible. Personal communication. July 9, 2020; John Mionczynski. Personal communication. Aug. 20, 2024; Lane, Jon, and Susan Layman. *South Pass City and the Sweetwater Mines.* Arcadia Publishing, 2012. Page 53.

7 Case, J. C., and Boyd, C.S., 1984. Preliminary Map of Earthquake Epicenters in Wyoming: Geological Survey of Wyoming [WSGS] Open File Report 84-13, scale 1:1,000,000. Accessed Sept. 1, 2024; Case, J. C., 1998. Basic Seismological Characterization for Fremont County and Surrounding Areas: WSGS Miscellaneous Publication, 13 p. Accessed Mar. 14, 2025; Wyoming Quakes 1871-2006. Water Resources Data System & State Climate Office. Water Resource Data System. www.wrds.uwyo.edu/wace/wace.html?LAY=Q. Accessed Sept. 1, 2024; Wyoming Earthquakes, 1921-1930. WSGS. Hazards Section. UW. www.wrds.uwyo.edu/wrds/wsgs/hazards/quakes/1921-1930.html. Accessed Sept. 1, 2024; Humphreys, W. J., 1924. Seismological reports for December 1923, in Henry, A. J., ed., Monthly Weather Review: US Department of Agriculture, Weather Bureau Monthly Weather Review, v. 51, no. 12, p. 676.; Wood, H. O., and Neumann, Frank (1931). Modified Mercalli Intensity Scale of 1931: Seismological Society of America Bulletin, v. 21, no. 4, p. 277-283, https://doi.org/10.1785/gicalBSSA0210040277. Accessed Sept. 1, 2024; Modified Mercalli Intensity Scale. US Geological Society. www.usgs.gov/media/images/modified-mercalli-intensity-scale. Accessed Mar. 14, 2025.

8 Massie, Michael A. *Teacher's Guide for That Gold Mine in the Sky*. 1985. The play was produced by KCWC-TV, Lander/Riverton, Wyo. Major funding was provided by a grant from the Wyoming Council for the Humanities and the National Endowment for the Humanities.

9 "Washington's Birthday Exercises at Atlantic," and "Atlantic City and South Pass Pointers." *WRM*. March 7, 1898. No. 25. Page 2.

10 Cook, Joseph. Oral History. ACHS. Interviewer Marjane Ambler. May, 24, 1984. Page 13. Transcript held at the SPCSHS. Accessed May 8, 2024; Pfaff, Betty Carpenter. Oral history by the ACHS, WSA and HD and/or the Wyoming State Historical Society. Jan. 24, 1984. Interviewer Philippina Halstead. Page 20. Transcription held at the SPCSHS. Accessed March 8, 2024; "Sweetwater_records_roll_02-04-115_01.pdf." pdf page 312. Scanned copy of "Record of License Issued in Sweetwater County, Wyoming Territory" ("issued in Carter County under the laws of Dakota Territory"). SPCSHS. Server. Accessed Dec. 17, 2019.

11 Redford, Robert. *The Outlaw Trail: A Journey Through Time*. New York: Grosset & Dunlap Publishers. 1978. Pages 55-58, 76-78.

12 Marrin, Laura Green. Aug. 7, 1987. Interviewer Michael A. Massie. Page 18; Fuller, Zoie Green. Jan. 4, 1984. Interviewer Philippina Halstead. Pages 16-17. Oral histories by the WSA and HD and/or the Wyoming State Historical Society. Transcriptions held at the SPCSHS. Accessed March 8, 2024; Lane, Jon, and Susan Layman. *South Pass City and the Sweetwater Mines*. Arcadia Publishing, 2012. Page 45; Trevor, Marjorie C. (1954). *History of Carter-Sweetwater County, Wyoming to 1875*. (Master's thesis, UW.) ProQuest Dissertations & Theses. Printed pages 75-76; pdf pages 83-84.

13 Pence, Mary Lou, and Lola M. Homsher. *Ghost Towns of Wyoming*. Pages 43-44. Hastings House. Jan. 1, 1956.

14 "Vandalism Deplored at Cemeteries of South Pass City, Atlantic City." *WSJ*. May 23, 1961. Vol. 74. No. 40 (the number 40 was lined out and "41" penciled in). Page 3.

15 Booth, Jacob. Oral history by the ACHS on Dec. 15, 1983. Interviewer Marjane Ambler. Pages 17-19. Transcription held at the SPCSHS. Accessed March 8, 2024.

16 Huseas, Marion McMillan. *Sweetwater Gold, Wyoming's Gold Rush 1867-1871*. Lander: Mortimore Publishing. 1991. Page 152 and footnotes 156n5 and 158n67. Robert Morris' letter to cousin Frankie, niece to Esther Hobart Morris. Letters are held in a private collection of Mrs. Rosamond (Edward C.) Day in San Rafael, California.

Chapter 2: From Government Lands to Private Property

1 "Louisiana Purchase, 1803. Florida Purchase, 1819." Library of Congress. Copyright by James McConnell. Chicago, Ill,: McConnell Map Co., (1919). Accessed June 17, 2024. https://lccn.loc.gov/2009581130; "Louisiana Purchase, 1803." Department of State. Office of the Historian. Accessed June 17, 2024. https://history.state.gov/milestones/1801-1829/louisiana-purchase.

2 OpenHistoricalMap. OpenHistoricalMap contributors. Edited May 7, 2024. Jeff Meyer. Accessed June 17, 2024. https://www.openhistoricalmap.org/.

3 "A Question of Boundaries." Library of Congress. Digital Collections. Article adapted from the essay "Louisiana, European Explorations and the Louisiana Purchase, a Special Presentation from the Geography and Map Division of the Library of Congress," n.d. www.loc.gov/collections/louisiana-european-explorations-and-the-louisiana-purchase/articles-and-essays/a-question-of-boundaries/. Accessed July 4, 2024.

4 "The Kansas -Nebraska Act," n.d. United States Senate. www.senate.gov/artandhistory/history/minute/Kansas_Nebraska_Act.htm. Accessed July 4, 2024.

5 "States in the Senate. North Dakota Timeline." United States Senate. www.senate.gov/states/ND/timeline.htm. Accessed July 4, 2024; OpenHistoricalMap. OpenHistoricalMap contributors. Edited May 7, 2024. Jeff Meyer. www.openhistoricalmap.org/. Accessed June 17, 2024.

6 "The Creation of the Territory of Idaho." March 1969. No. 264. Idaho State Historical Society. Idaho State Historical Society Reference Series. https://history.idaho.gov/wp-content/uploads/0264_The-Creation-of-the-Territory-of-Idaho.pdf. Accessed July 4, 2024.

7 Gray, David P. *Guide to North Dakota State Archives*. 1985. "Dakota Territory." State Historical Society of North Dakota. www.history.nd.gov/archives/stateagencies/dtrecords.html. Accessed July 4, 2024.

8 Blasi, Brigida. "The 'Peculiar Vibrations' of the Sweetwater County Seat." Nov. 14, 2024. *Discover History* blog. AHC, UW. https://ahcwyo.org/2022/11/14/the-peculiar-vibrations-of-the-sweetwater-county-seat/. Accessed July 4, 2024.

9 "Wyoming Organic Act." FindLaw Staff. Oct. 1, 2021. FindLaw. Accessed July 4, 2024. https://codes.findlaw.com/wy/wyoming-organic-act/wy-st-organic-act/; "WY-Wyoming." Timeline. US Senate. www.senate.gov/states/WY/ timeline.shtml. Accessed July 4, 2024.

10 AHC article: "Green River Was Not The Original County Seat of Sweetwater County." Nov. 26, 2022. Sweetwater County Historical Museum. This article refers an article by Brigida Blasi, "The 'Peculiar Vibrations' of the Sweetwater County Seat." Nov. 14, 2024. Discover History blog. AHC, UW. https://sweetwatermuseum.org/. Accessed July 4, 2022.

11 Gardner, Dudley. "Sweetwater County. "Nov. 8, 2014. WyoHistory.org. 2024. www.wyohistory.org/encyclopedia/sweetwater-county-wyoming. Accessed July 4, 2024.

12 "Wyoming History." State of Wyoming. www.wyo.gov/about-wyoming/wyoming-history. Accessed June 17 2024.

13 Howard, Robert West. *The South Pass Story*. G. P. Putnam's Sons. 1968. Page 115.

14 Potter, Lee Ann and Wynell Schamel. "The Homestead Act of 1862." *Social Education* 61, 6 (October 1997): 359-364. "The Homestead Act of 1862" adapted from this article. June 2, 2021. National Archives. https://www.archives.gov/education/lessons/homestead-act#background. Accessed March 26, 2024.

15 "Atlantic City." Historic American Buildings Survey. Office of Archeology and Historic Preservation, National Park Service. HABS No. WYO-60, HABS WYO, 7-ATCI, 1-. Page 2. Information provided by Carole Justice on Aug. 23, 2024; Trevor, Marjorie C. (1954). *History of Carter-Sweetwater County, Wyoming to 1875*. (Master's thesis, UW.) ProQuest Dissertations & Theses. Printed page 39; pdf page 47.

16 Claim. Wilbert B. Teters. Signed Nov. 10, 1884. Instrument No. 277 recorded Nov. 25, 1885. Quit Claim Record Book A. Pages 103-105. Fremont County Clerk's Office. Land Recording Office.

17 Indenture. Wilbert B. Teters to Emile Granier. Signed Nov. 22, 1884. Notarized on Nov. 24, 1884. Recorded Nov. 25, 1884. *Quit Claim Record Book A*. Pages 114-115. Fremont County Clerk's Office. Land Recording Office.

18 *Misc. Record A. Fremont County. 1884-1894*. Pages 3-4, 12-13, 18, 521. Fremont County Clerk, Land Recording Office.

19 "Warranty Deed Record No. 54." Teters Patented Mining Claim. The United States of America to Emile Granier. No. 115682. Jan. 28, 1889. Book 54. Page 373. Fremont County Clerk's Office. Land Recording Office. Copy by David Geible. March 23, 2024.

20 "Miscellaneous Deed Record, No. 2." Between Timba-Bah Mining Company and F. W. Thorne. Jan. 23, 1928. No. 116207. Recorded on March 30, 1928. Fremont County Clerk's Office. Land Recording Office. Copy by David Geible. March 23, 2024.

21 Quit Claim Deed. From Timba-Bah Mining Company to (Redacted). Dec. 28, 1998. Recorded May 19, 1999. No. 1200823. Fremont County Clerk's Office. Land Recording Office. Copy by David Geible. March 23, 2024.

22 "Warranty Deed Record No. 54." The United States of America to Emile Granier. No. 115683. Jan. 28, 1889. Warranty Deed Book 54. Page 375. Fremont County Clerk's Office. Land Recording Office. Copy by David Geible. March 23, 2024.

23 "Warranty Deed Record No. 54." The United States of America to Emile Granier. Jan. 28, 1889. No. 115683. Book 54. Page 375. Fremont County Clerk's Office. Land Recording Office. Copy by David Geible. March 23, 2024.

24 Quit Claim Deed. Timba-Bah Mining Company to (Redacted). May 8, 1978. Recorded May 19, 1978. Book 7. Page 949. Fremont County Clerk's Office. Land Recording Office. Copy by David Geible. March 23, 2024.

25 Private communication between David Geible and Richard Gist. There is no recorded conveyance of this transfer.

26 Quit Claim Deed. Timba-Bah Mining Company to (Redacted). July 31, 1968. Recorded Aug. 5, 1968. *Quit Claim Deeds Book 31*. Page 645; Quit Claim Deed. Timba-Bah Mining Company to (Redacted]. March 31, 1971. No. 803219. Filed on June 8, 1971, but lists no Quit Claim Deeds book. Fremont County Clerk's Office. Land Recording Office. Copies by David Geible. March 23, 2024.

27 Mechanics Lien." From William Glover. July 31, 1869. "sp_commerce_carter_co_1868_book _01_b." Carter County. PDF file. Pdf pages 8 and 444. Ledger pages 16-17 and 44-45. SPCSHS. Server. Accessed Dec. 17, 2019; Quit Claim. Rufus M. Ricketts to Emile Granier. Aug. 11, 1889. No. 3267. Quit Claim Book. Page 89. Fremont County Clerk's Office. Land Recording Office. April 11, 2022.

28 Linn, John. 1908. Townsend, Robert K., ed. *Atlantic City, Wyoming: Voices From a Powerful Place, 1868–2018, Voices From a Powerful Place*. Atlantic City, WY: Atlantic City Historical Society. 2017. Inside front cover; courtesy of the Betty Carpenter Pfaff Collection. 2017.

29 Gordon, Lisa Kaplan. "What is a Plat Map? A Survey That Can Tell You a Lot About Your Property. Aug. 3, 2022. Realtor.com. www.realtor.com/advice/buy/what-is-a-plat-map/. Accessed July 3, 2024.

30 Mann, Albert. Oral history by the ACHS, WSA and HD and/or the Wyoming State Historical Society. Sept. 11, 1983. Interviewer David Geible. Pages 11. Transcription held at the SPCSHS. Accessed March 8, 2024.

31 Moerer, Lyle F. Oral history by the Wyoming State Historical Society. Dec. 8, 1983. Interviewer Philippina Halstead. Page 3. Transcription held at the SPCSHS. Accessed March 8, 2024.

32 Reynolds, Rick. Timba-Bah Mining Company records. Email interview. May 20, 2024.

CHAPTER 3: BURIED IN ATLANTIC CITY, GRAVESITE UNKNOWN

1 Two newspaper articles state different Giessler brothers as the deputy sheriff. "Peculiar Killing Near Atlantic City" states William Giessler. "Killing at Seven Lakes" states Smith surrendered to Lawrence Geissler," who "immediately notified Sheriff Stough and Coroner Schoo." "Peculiar Killing." *WSJ*. No. 27. Feb. 26, 1909. Page 1. "Killing at Seven Lakes." *WRM*. Vol. 24. No. 16. Feb. 18, 1909. UW and Wyoming State Library. https://wyomingnewspapers.org. Accessed Sept. 29, 2015.

2 "Peculiar Killing." *WSJ*. No. 27. Feb. 26, 1909. Page 1. "Killing at Seven Lakes." *Wind River Mountaineer*. Vol. 24. No. 16. Feb. 18, 1909. UW and Wyoming State Library. https://wyomingnewspapers.org. Accessed Sept. 29, 2015.

3 "Criminal Cases Completed." *WSJ*. Vol. XXII. No. 39. May 21, 1909. Page 1; "District Court Proceedings for the Week." *WSJ*. Vol. XXII. No. 40. May 28, 1909. Page 1. UW and Wyoming State Library. https://wyomingnewspapers.org. Accessed Jan. 5, 2022.

4 "Fremont County, Defunct Cemeteries," n.d. Compiler of this document is unknown. Accessed Sept. 25, 2015. Mount Hope Cemetery Office. City of Lander.

5 *Deeds* book. Fremont County Courthouse. County Clerk. Land Recording Office. Pages 169-170.

6 1870 US Federal census. Silver Creek Township. County of Mills. Iowa. Line 17. Ancestry.com. https://ancestry.com. Accessed April 12, 2022; Find a Grave. https://findagrave.com. Accessed April 26, 2022.

7 "James. R. Boston." FamilySearch.org. www.familysearch.org/tree/person/details/L7PW-PDD. Accessed April 12, 2022.

8 "Andrew Jackson Boston." *Find A Grave*. www.findagrave.com/memorial/43305042/andrew-jackson-boston. Accessed April 26, 2022.

9 Wyoming Mortality Schedule ending June 1870. Compiled by members of the ACHS, n.d.; *Sweetwater Mines*. No. 36. August 1, 1868. Page 3. UW and Wyoming State Library. Accessed June 17, 2017.

10 Stratmoen, Mark R. *Mayhem and Mystery, Coroner Inquests in Fremont County 1885-1900*. Riverton, WY: Lenore Wyoming Publications, 2010. Pages 249-250.

11 "A Death at Atlantic City." *Clipper*. No. 38. May 19, 1899. Page 1. No. 38; May 19, 1899. Page 4. UW and Wyoming State Library. https://wyomingnewspapers.org. Accessed Nov. 19, 2015.

12 "Night Watchman Found Dead at Duncan Mine." *Pinedale Roundup*. Vol. 10. No. 8. Thursday, Nov. 20, 1913. Page 1. Information provided by Sharon Lass Field, October 15, 2021;

(continued): *Pine Bluffs Post.* Dec. 12, 1913. Vol. 6. No. 44. Page 2; "Wyoming News." *The Sheridan Post.* Nov. 28, 1913. No. 82. Page 8. UW and Wyoming State Library. https://wyomingnewspapers.org. Accessed Oct. 15, 2021.

13 "Mickel Kennedy." Certificate of Death. File No. 1913. Registered No. 1137. Received paper copy on Feb. 21, 2024, from WSA. Carl Hallberg.

14 Wyoming Mortality Schedule ending June 1870. Compiled by members of the ACHS, n.d.; US Federal Census Mortality Schedules Index, 1850-1800. Ancestry.com. www.ancestry.com. Accessed October 19, 2015.

15 "Establishing Wyoming Territory." WyoHistory.org. Project of the Wyoming Historical Society. https://www.wyohistory.org. Accessed March 7, 2024; 1869 census of Wyoming Territory. Lines 1421-1423. Original data from the WSA. Ancestry.com. www.ancestry.com. Accessed March 6, 2024.

16 1870 US Federal census. Atlantic City. County of Sweetwater. Enumerated June 10, 1870. Page 6. Lines 30 and 31. Ancestry.com. www.ancestry.com. Accessed Nov. 20, 2015. Digital images, citing NARA microfilm publication.

17 Williamson, Rosemary. "There are Times When Even Cowboys Must Cry." *WSJ.* July 1, 1982. Page B-1. Accessed Oct. 5, 2015.

18 SPCSHS. "Carter County, Book A of Deeds, p. 92 to End, Book B of Deeds through p. 89." The specific pdf page is 243. The original paper document is Book A of *Deeds*, page 556. Sweetwater County Historical Museum, Green River. Accessed December 17, 2019.

19 1870 US Federal census. Atlantic City. County of Sweetwater. Enumerated June 10, 1870. Page 6. Lines 11-19. Ancestry.com. www.ancestry.com. Accessed Nov. 20, 2015.

20 "Early History of Fremont County." H. G. Nickerson. (Written in 1886.) Quarterly Bulletin. Vol. 2. No. 1. *Annals of Wyoming.* State of Wyoming, Historical Department. Page 4.

21 Murphy, John R. "Indian Raids of '69 and'70 on Settlers in Lander Valley Told by First Little Popo Agie Rancher." Originally printed in three installments in the *Fremont Clipper* on Oct. 8, Oct. 15, and Oct 22, 1887. Page 3. From microfilm. Located at Fremont County Library System, Lander branch, Wyo. Reprinted in one article in the *WSJ.* April 4, 1928. Vol. 44. No. 32. Pages 1 and 6.

22 McDermott, John D. *Dangerous Duty: A History of Frontier Forts in Fremont County, Wyoming.* The Fremont County Historic Preservation Commission. 1993. Page 102; ACHS members from oral histories, newspapers, letters, etc.; Boyack, A. R., Mrs., comp. "As told by Jules Farlow, Sr. about his Grandfather, Mr. Jules Lamoreaux." "Oregon Trail Trek No. Eight." *Annals of Wyoming.* April 1959. Vol. 31. No. 1. Wyoming State Historical Society. Page 87.

23 "Oregon Trail Trek No. Eight." *Annals of Wyoming.* April 1959. Vol. 31. No. 1. Page 87. WSA.

24 *WSJ.* No. 23, Feb. 7, 1913. Page 1; and August 18, 1997; page B-1. UW and Wyoming State Library. https://wyomingnewspapers.org. Accessed Oct. 6, 2015.

25 "Fremont County, Defunct Cemeteries," n.d. Unknown who compiled this document. Accessed Sept. 25, 2015. Mount Hope Cemetery Office. City of Lander.

26 Haugen, Jean Mathisen. "A Grave Project—Cataloging Cemeteries." *WSJ.* August 18, 1997. Page B-1.

27 *Pinedale Roundup.* Vol. 1. No. 23. Thursday, Feb. 9, 1905. Page 1. Paper copy and information provided by Sharon Lass Field, October 15, 2021.

Chapter 4: East Cemetery, Marked Burials and Family Plots

1 "Local Matters" and "Died." *Sweetwater Mines.* Aug. 1, 1868. Page 3. UW and Wyoming State Library. Accessed Dec. 4, 2016.

2 "Obituary." *WRM.* Feb. 24, 1911. Vol. 26. No. 17. Page 1. UW and Wyoming State Library. Accessed Sept. 29, 2015.

3 *Record Book for Atlantic City.* Burials. Pages 114-115. St. Andrew's Episcopal Church.

4 Sommers, Jonita. Williams Family History, 2002. Unpublished manuscript. Subsection "Jared." Accessed April 22, 2016.

5 Tschirgi, Loretta. Personal communication. Aug. 30, 2024; Google, n.d. Google Maps. Imagery @2024. Maxar Technologies, Map data @2024. https://www.google.com/. Accessed Aug. 30, 2024.

6 Layman, Susan and David. Personal tour. Sept. 16, 2024.

7 "Gold Prospector Joe Barbett Dies." *WSJ.* June 2, 1960. Page 10.

8 Hallberg, Carl. WSA. "Re: Joseph Barbett's Death Certificate." Received by author. Email Interview. Oct. 26, 2015.

9 Pfaff, Betty Carpenter. *Changes.* Privately published. 2018. Page 69.

[10] 1910 US Federal Census. Atlantic City. Precinct 12. Sheet 7. Line 9; 1930 US Federal Census. Election District 11. Line 7; 1940 US Federal Census. Population Schedule. Atlantic City Village. Election District 15. Sheet 1A. Line 1. Ancestry.com. https://ancestry.com. Accessed Nov. 20, 2015. Digital images, citing NARA microfilm publication.

[11] "The South Pass Gold Discoveries, 1842-1869." *WRM*. Vol. X. No. 2. Page 11. Fremont County Pioneer Museum. Accessed March 18, 2024.

[12] Sherlock, James L. Oral history, Part 1, by the ACHS, WSA and HD and/or the Wyoming State Historical Society. July 11, 1984. Interviewer Marjane Ambler. Page 14. Transcription held at the SPCSHS. Accessed March 8, 2024.

[13] Booth, Jacob. Oral history by the ACHS, WSA and HD and/or the Wyoming State Historical Society. Dec. 15, 1983. Interviewer Marjane Ambler. Pages 20-21. Transcription held at the SPCSHS. Accessed March 8, 2024.

[14] "Poll Book." Aug. 17, 1926. Primary Election. Election District No. 12. Polling Precinct No. 1. Line 11; "Poll Book of a Primary Election Held August 19, 1930." Atlantic City. Election District No. 11. Polling Precinct No. 1. Line 19; "Registration Poll Book and Official Return of a General Election Held November 4, 1930." Election District No. 11. Polling Precinct No. 1. Line 5. Fremont County Elections Office. Accessed Aug. 2, 2019.

[15] Fuller, Zoie Green. Oral history by the ACHS, WSA and HD and/or the Wyoming State Historical Society. Jan. 4, 1984. Interviewer Philippina Halstead. Pages 31-32. Transcription held at the SPCSHS. Accessed March 8, 2024; Current locals did not know the meaning of the term "lily bend." Online searches revealed nothing.

[16] Roe, Clarence. Oral history by the ACHS, WSA and HD and/or the Wyoming State Historical Society. Jan. 28, 1984. Interviewer Marjane Ambler. Page 6. Transcription held at the SPCSHS. Accessed March 8, 2024.

[17] Booth, Aurlein. Oral History. OH-0967A. Side 1. December 6, 1983. Oral history by the ACHS, WSA and HD and/or the Wyoming State Historical Society. WSA. http://spcrphotocollection.wyo.gov. Accessed June 17, 2021. Transcription held at the SPCSHS. Page 3. Accessed March 8, 2024.

[18] Booth, Aurlein. Oral history by the ACHS, WSA and HD and/or the Wyoming State Historical Society. Dec. 16, 1983. Interviewer Marjane Ambler. Page 3. Transcription held at the SPCSHS. Accessed March 8, 2024.

[19] Pfaff, Betty Carpenter. *Fine Gold*. Private printing. 1998. Chap. 2, page 1; *Changes*. 2018. Private printing. Page 83; *Atlantic City Nuggets*. Private Printing. 1978. Page 46.

[20] Pfaff, Betty Carpenter. Anne Carpenter Robinson's death and ashes placed. Two telephone Interviews; Pfaff, Betty Carpenter. Carpenter Family History, n.d. June 26, 2016.

[21] "Mrs. Nellie Carpenter." *WSJ*. August 20, 1930. Page 8; Pfaff, Betty Carpenter. Carpenter family history, n.d. Unpublished manuscript; *Record Book for Atlantic City*. Burials. Pages 114-115. Line 7. St. Andrew's Episcopal Church.

[22] Pfaff, Betty Carpenter. *Changes*. Private printing. 2018. Page 105.

[23] Pfaff, Betty Carpenter. *Fine Gold*. Private printing. 1998. Chap. 43. Pages 3-4.

[24] Golliher, Alma Williams. Oral history by the ACHS, WSA and HD and/or the Wyoming State Historical Society. June 30, 1984. Interviewer David Geible. Pages 4 and 15. Transcription held at the SPCSHS. Accessed March 8, 2024; Sommers, Jonita. Personal interview. April 22, 2016; Pfaff, Betty Carpenter. *Fine Gold*. Private printing. 1998. Chap. 27. Page 5.

[25] *Record Book for Atlantic City*. Confirmations. Pages 102-3. Line 7. St. Andrew's Episcopal Church.

[26] Pfaff, Betty Carpenter. *Changes*. Private printing. 2018. Pages 111-112.

[27] 1900 US Federal Census. Atlantic Precinct. Sheet A83. Enumeration District No. 29. Line 45; 1910 US Federal Census. Atlantic City. Precinct 12. Sheet 7A. Line 14; 1920 US Census; Atlantic City, Election District #14. Enumeration District No. 57. Sheet 10B. Line 64; 1930 US Federal Census. Atlantic City. Election District #11. Enumeration District No. 7-13. Sheet No. 1A. Line 20. Ancestry.com. http://www.ancestry.com. Accessed Nov. 20, 2015. Digital images, citing NARA microfilm publication.

[28] *Abstract Mining Claims, Book F* (book with the spine cover torn off). Page 13. Fremont County Courthouse. County Clerk. Land Recording Office. Lander, Wyo. Accessed April 6, 2022; "The Atlantic Gold District, Fremont County, Wyoming." Arthur C. Spencer. Pages 9–45. The map showing her mine is immediately after page 22. "No. 73. Philistine." *The Atlantic Gold District and the North Laramie Mountains; Fremont, Converse, and Albany Counties.* (continued) *Wyoming*. Bulletin 626. Papers by Arthur C. Spencer. Dept. of the Interior. United States Geological Survey. Washington Government Printing Office. 1916.

[29] Pfaff, Betty Carpenter. *Fine Gold*. Private printing. 1998; *Changes*. Private printing. 2018.

30 Index Card. File No. 1930. Certificate No. 1280. Wyoming, US Death Records, 1909-1971. WSA. *Ancestry.com*. https://ancestry.com. Accessed April 29, 2024.

31 "Carpenter Hotel Historic District." NAID: 73730350. Reference No. 12001054. National Park Service. National Register of Historic Places. Accessed Feb. 27, 2024. https://catalog.archives.gov/id/73730350; "St. Andrew's Episcopal Church." Reference No. 100009595. National Park Service. National Register of Historic Places. www.nps.gov/subjects/nationalregister/database-research.htm#table. Accessed Feb. 27, 2024.

32 *WSJ*, No. 39; May 16, 1961. Page 1; Pfaff, Betty Carpenter. Carpenter family history, n.d.; *Record Book for Atlantic City*. Burials. Pages 114-115. Line 8. St. Andrew's Episcopal Church.

33 *Record Book for Atlantic City*. Confirmations. Pages 102-103. Line 8. St. Andrew's Episcopal Church; Pfaff, Betty Carpenter. Oral history by the ACHS, WSA and HD and/or the Wyoming State Historical Society. Jan. 24, 1984. Interviewer Philippina Halstead. Page 14. Transcription held at the SPCSHS. Accessed March 8, 2024.

34 Pfaff, Betty Carpenter. Oral history by the ACHS, WSA and HD and/or the Wyoming State Historical Society. Jan. 24, 1984. Interviewer Philippina Halstead. Page 6. Transcription held at the SPCSHS. Accessed March 8, 2024.

35 Fuller, Zoie Green. Oral history by the ACHS, WSA and HD and/or the Wyoming State Historical Society. Jan. 4, 1984. Interviewer Philippina Halstead. Page 25. Transcription held at the SPCSHS. Accessed March 8, 2024.

36 Pfaff, Betty Carpenter. Oral history by the ACHS, WSA and HD and/or the Wyoming State Historical Society. Jan. 24, 1984. Interviewer Philippina Halstead. Pages 15-16. Transcription held at the SPCSHS. Accessed March 8, 2024.

37 Parker, Pearl, and Frank Hugh Tatro. Oral history by the ACHS, WSA and HD and/or the Wyoming State Historical Society. May 16, 1984. Interviewer David Geible. Page 5. Transcription held at the SPCSHS. Accessed March 8, 2024.

38 Roe, Clarence. Oral history by the ACHS, WSA and HD and/or the Wyoming State Historical Society. Jan. 28, 1984. Interviewer Marjane Ambler. Page 3. Transcription held at the SPCSHS. Accessed March 8, 2024.

39 Pfaff, Betty Carpenter. *Fine Gold*. Private printing. 1998; *Changes*. Private printing. 2018.

40 "Registration and Poll Book." Special Election. May 10, 1921. Atlantic City. Election District No. 14. Polling Precinct 1. Line 7; "Poll Book." Primary Election. Aug. 17, 1926. Atlantic City. Election District No. 12. Polling Precinct No. 1. Line 20. "Registration Poll Book and Official Return of a General Election Held November 4, 1930." Election District No. 11. Polling Precinct No. 1. Line 30. Fremont County Elections Office. Accessed Aug. 2, 2019.

41 1900 US Federal Census. Atlantic Precinct. Sheet A83. Enumeration District No. 29. Line 46; 1910 US Federal Census. Atlantic City. Precinct 12.Sheet 7A. Line 15; 1920 US Census; Atlantic City, Election District #14. Enumeration District No. 57. Sheet 10B. Line 65. The 1930 US Federal Census. Atlantic City, Election District #11. Enumeration District No. 7-13. Sheet No. 1A. Line 21; 1940 Federal US Census. Atlantic City-Village. Election District No. 15. Sheet 1A. Line 25. Ancestry.com. www.ancestry.com. Accessed Nov. 20, 2015. Digital images, citing NARA microfilm publication.

42 Fuller, Zoie Green. Oral history by the ACHS, WSA and HD and/or the Wyoming State Historical Society. Jan. 4, 1984. Interviewer Philippina Halstead. Pages 24-25. Transcription held at the SPCSHS. Accessed March 8, 2024; Roe, Clarence. Oral history by the ACHS, WSA and HD and/or the Wyoming State Historical Society. Jan. 28, 1984. Interviewer Marjane Ambler. Pages 3-4. Transcription held at the SPCSHS. Accessed March 8, 2024.

43 Death certificate. 1961. State File No. 895. WSA. Ancestry.com. https://ancestry.com. Accessed April 29, 2024.

44 Pfaff, Betty Carpenter. Woman found in grave. June 26, 2016. Telephone interview; Carpenter, James Wallace. Sept. 30, 2016. Woman found in Miss Ellen's grave. Personal interview.

45 "Carpenter Hotel Historic District." NAID: 73730350. Reference No. 12001054. National Register of Historic Places. https://catalog.archives.gov/ id/73730350. Accessed Feb. 27, 2024.; "St. Andrew's Episcopal Church." Reference No. 100009595. National Park Service. National Register of Historic Places. www.nps.gov/subjects/nationalregister/database-research.htm#table. Accessed Feb. 27, 2024.

46 Pfaff, Betty Carpenter. Carpenter family history n.d.; *The WSJ*. No. 25. Feb. 17, 1911. Page 1. UW and Wyoming State Library. https://wyomingnewspapers.org. Accessed Dec. 15, 2016; Pfaff, Betty Carpenter. *Fine Gold*. Private printing. 1998. Chap. 17. Page 3.

47 Private letter from A. J. Schepp (Dr. Schepp's child) to Mrs. Charlotte Dehnert dated April 4, 1967. Paper copy from Charlotte Dehnert.

[48] Photo on pages 50 and 237: Betty Carpenter Pfaff identified Maurice Lewellyn in *Fine Gold*. Private printing. 1998. Chap. 29, page 1; A scanned copy of the photo with Clarence E. Carpenter, Sr. has a handwritten annotation on the back: "1st Carpenter Hotel, Clarence Emmett Carpenter I, Hazel Carpenter, Hi Shears, Bud Carpenter, Probably 1902. B. Pfaff." *Wind River Mountaineer*. No. 17. February 24, 1911. Page 1. UW and Wyoming State Library. https://wyomingnewspapers.org. Accessed Sept. 29, 2015; *Record Book for Atlantic City*. Burials. Pages 114-115. Line 1. St. Andrew's Episcopal Church.

[49] 1900 US Federal Census. Atlantic Precinct. Sheet A83. Enumeration District No. 29. Line 51; 1910 US Federal Census. Atlantic City. Precinct 12. Sheet 7A. Line 10. Ancestry.com. www.ancestry.com. Accessed Nov. 20, 2015. Digital images, citing NARA microfilm publication.

[50] 1900 US Federal Census. Atlantic Precinct. Sheet A83. Enumeration District No. 29. Line 48; 1910 US Federal Census. Atlantic City. Precinct 12. Sheet 7A. Line 17. Ancestry.com. www.ancestry.com. Accessed Nov. 20, 2015. Digital images, citing NARA microfilm publication.

[51] *Soldiers Discharge Record, Book A. Fremont County, 12-19-17 – 1-30-30*. Page 88. Fremont County Courthouse. County Clerk. Land Recording Office. Accessed April 11, 2022; 1930 US Federal Census. Election District 11. Enumeration District 7-13. Sheet 1A. Line 14. Ancestry.com. www.ancestry.com. Accessed Nov. 20, 2015. Digital images, citing NARA microfilm publication.

[52] 1920 Federal US Census. Atlantic City. Election District No. 14. Sheet 10B. Line 66; 1930 US Federal Census. Atlantic City. Election District No. 11. Sheet 1A. Line 4; 1940 US Federal Census. Atlantic City Village. Election District 15. Sheet 1A. Line 32. Ancestry.com. www.ancestry.com. Accessed Nov. 20, 2015. Digital images, citing NARA microfilm publication.

[53] "Poll Book." Aug. 17, 1926. Primary Election. Election District No. 12. Polling Precinct No. 1. Line 1; "Registration Poll Book and Official Return of a General Election Held November 4, 1930." Election District No. 11. Polling Precinct No. 1. Line 19. Fremont County Elections Office. Accessed Aug. 2, 2019.

[54] *Poll Book and Official Return*. "List of Absent Voter Ballot Envelopes." Atlantic City. Aug. 21, Nov. 6, 1962. Election District No. 15. Polling Precinct No. 1. Fremont County Elections Office. Accessed Aug. 26, 2024; "Carpenters, 1938." The original photo is in SPCSHS. Betty Carpenter Pfaff Collection. Top drawer, folder labeled "Misc, & Photos." Accessed August 22, 2022.

[55] Death certificate. 1968. State File No. 0377. WSA. Ancestry.com. https://ancestry.com. Accessed April 29, 2024.

[56] *WSJ*, February 12, 1968. Page 1; Pfaff, Betty Carpenter. Carpenter family history, n.d.; Pfaff, Betty Carpenter. Private printings. *Atlantic City Nuggets*. 1978, *Fine Gold*, 1998, and *Changes*, 2018.

[57] "Water Right of John Garrison." July 13, 1897. Book "Misc. Records. Vol. B. 11-5-1894 – 7-24-1906." Page 167. Fremont County Clerk, Land Recording Office.

[58] 1900 US Federal Census. South Pass City. Enumeration District No. 29. Page A85. Sheet No. 3. Lines 9 and 10. Database with images. FamilySearch.org. https://FamilySearch.org: 31 December 2023. Citing NARA microfilm publication T9. Washington, D.C.: NARA, n.d. Accessed Feb. 21, 2024.

[59] The *Miner*. March 28, 1913. Page 6. pluto.wyo.gov/awweb (now a defunct site). Accessed Nov. 18, 2024; 1910 US Federal Census. South Pass City. Precinct 13. Enumeration District 65. Sheet No. 6B. Lines 68 and 69. Family Search. https://familysearch.org. Accessed May 8, 2022.

[60] *WRM*. Vol. 27. No. 22. March 29, 1912. Page 4. UW and Wyoming State Library. Accessed April 19, 2023; Caption: The *Miner*. Vol. 6. No. 52. March 28, 1913. Wyoming Digital Newspaper Collection. UW and Wyoming State Library. https://wyomingnewspapers.org. Accessed March 16, 2024.

[61] *WRM*. Vol. 28. No. 40. March 28, 1913. Page 1. Wyoming Digital Newspaper Collection. UW and Wyoming State Library. https://wyomingnewspapers.org. Accessed March 16, 2024.

[62] "Notice of Forfeiture." *WSJ*. April 5, 1918. Vol. 35. No. 25. Page 2. Microfilm. Lander Library.

[63] Marriage license. John C. Garrison and Rose Simmons. *Marriage Record*, book C. Page 15. Fremont County Clerk, Land Recording Office.

[64] Sherlock, James. L. *South Pass and Its Tales*. Private printing. Lander, Wyo. 1978. Page 23; *WSJ*. December 27, 1949. Page 1.

[65] Pfaff, Betty Carpenter. *Fine Gold*. Private printing. 1998. Chap. 22. Page 6.

[66] *Record Book for Atlantic City*. Marriages. Page 132. St. Andrew's Episcopal Church; Marriage License. Marriage Records. Book C. March 18, 1908-Nov. 4 1914. Page 272. Feb. 7, 1912. Fremont County Clerks' Office. Land Recording Office.

67 Guenther, Todd. "Harsch Notes." Oct. 2, 1991. Information from interviews with Louise Connell York, Tom Connell, Martha Connell Williamson, and Myra Connell. Handwritten annotation of "Conne-13-T." Page 4. SPCSHS. Filing cabinet, folder titled "Connell, M. Emmett." Accessed on May 8, 2024.

68 Pfaff, Betty Carpenter. *Changes*. Private printing. 2018. Page 57.

69 "Poll Book and Official Registration of a General Election Held November 6, 1928." Election District No. 11. Polling Precinct No. 1. Oath of Judges and Clerks of Election, page 1. Fremont County Elections Office. Accessed Aug. 2, 2019.

70 "Registration and Poll Book." Special Election. May 10, 1921. Atlantic City. Election District No. 14. Polling Precinct 1. Line 8; "Poll Book." Aug. 17, 1926. Primary Election. Election District No. 12. Polling Precinct No. 1. Line 2; "Poll Book of a Primary Election Held August 19, 1930." Atlantic City. Election District No. 11. Polling Precinct No. 1. Line 4; "Registration Poll Book and Official Return of a General Election Held November 4, 1930." Election District No. 11. Polling Precinct No. 1. Line 7. Fremont County Elections Office. Accessed Aug. 2, 2019.

71 1910 US Federal Census. South Pass City. Enumeration District No. 65. Election District No. 4. Precinct 13. Line 5. Database with images. FamilySearch. https://FamilySearch.org : 31 December 2023. Accessed Feb. 21, 2024. Citing NARA microfilm publication T9. Washington, D.C.: NARA, n.d.

72 1920 US Federal Census. Atlantic City, Election District #14. Sheet No. 10B. Line 89; 1930 US Federal Census. Atlantic City. Election District #11. Sheet 1A. Line 29; 1940 US Federal Census. Atlantic City Village, Election District 15. Sheet No. 1A. Line 16. Ancestry.com. www.ancestry.com. Accessed Nov. 21, 2015. Digital images, NARA microfilm publication.

73 Death certificate. Peter Gustafsen. 1949. State File No. 2257. WSA. Ancestry.com. https://ancestry.com. Accessed April 29, 2024.

74 *WRM*. August 29, 1899. Page 3. pluto.wyo.gov (now defunct). Accessed Oct. 7, 2015.

75 1870 US Federal Census. Hermit Gulch. County of Sweetwater. Sheet (stamped) 485. Page No. 1. Lines 2 and 3. Database with images. FamilySearch. Accessed Feb. 21, 2024. https://FamilySearch.org: 31 December 2023. Citing NARA microfilm publication T9. Washington, D.C.: NARA, n.d.

76 Guenther, Todd. "Harsch Notes." Oct. 2, 1991. Information from interviews with Louise Connell York, Tom Connell, Martha Connell Williamson, and Myra Connell. Handwritten annotation of "Conne-13-T." Page 1. SPCSHS. Filing cabinet, folder titled "Connell, M. Emmett." Accessed on May 8, 2024.

77 Connell, M. "Family Chronicle," n.d. Electronic copy. SPCSHS server. Page 4. Accessed Aug. 22, 2022; Connell, M. "Family Chronicle," n.d. Paper copy. Handwritten "Given by" with arrow to "M. Connell" "B. Pfaff. South Pass. June 96. "Fremont County Pioneer Museum. Cabinet A1, Box 3. Folder: "Harsch." Note: The document's first three pages are missing. I suspect this document was researched and written by Myra Connell, who was married to Thomas Connell. Thomas' parents were Katherine Harsch and Michael Emmett Connell, making Myra as Elizabeth and Philip Harsch's granddaughter-in-law. My suspicion that this was written by Myra is based on a paper document titled "Harsch Notes" written by historian Todd Guenther on Oct. 2, 1991. SPCSHS filing cabinet, folder "Connell, M. Emmett," accessed on May 8, 2024. The paper has a hand-written notation of "Conne-13-T." Mr. Guenther indicated that the family information based on the research by Myra Connell had been accepted. Additionally, Myra Connell wrote a published article, "Here lies … A history of Old Graves in Fremont County," in the *WSJ*, Dec. 15, 1980, Page B-1.

78 *United States, Western States Marriage Index*. Volume 1, page 12. FamilySearch.org. Oct. 19, 2018; http://genealogytrails.com/wyo/fremont/marriages.html. Accessed Feb. 13 and March 5, 2022.

79 "William Henry Harsch." *WSJ*. May 9, 1928. Page 6.

80 1880 US Federal Census. Atlantic City. County of Sweetwater. Sheet No. (stamped) 299. Page No. (penned) 5. Lines 22-27. Digital images. Ancestry.com. www.ancestry.com. Accessed Nov. 20, 2015. Digital images, citing NARA microfilm publication; Pfaff, Betty Carpenter. *Fine Gold*. Chap. 22, pages 2-4. Private printing. 1998.

81 Poll Books. Sweetwater County Historical Museum. Green River, Wyo. Accessed Jan. 11, 2017.

82 Connell, Myra. "Here Lies … A History of Old Graves in Fremont County." *WSJ*. Dec. 15, 1980. Page B-1.

83 "Elizabeth Hesse vs Frederick Hesse." Divorce. Civil Appearance Docket 1. Page 203. Sweetwater County Deputy Clerk of Court Donna Sue Ratliff and WSA Carl Hallberg. Personal communications. Various dates in June 2024.

84 Indexes, Books 1-3, 1871-1896. District Court, Third District. Digital Collection. State of Utah Archives. Accessed Oct. 7, 2024. https://images.archives.utah.gov/digital/collection/3243/.

[85] Connell, M. "Family Chronicle," n.d. Electronic copy. SPCSHS server. Pages 11, 12. Accessed Aug. 22, 2022. Note: See the "Note" in endnote 269n77.

[86] 1880 Federal US Census. Atlantic City, Sweetwater County. Sheet (stamped) 299. Page 5. Line 27; 1900 US Federal Census. Atlantic Precinct. Sheet (stamped) B. Sheet No. 1, Line 54; 1910 US Federal Census. Precinct 12. Atlantic City. Sheet No. 7. Line 37; 1920 US Federal Census. Atlantic City, Election District #14. Enumeration District 57. Sheet No. 10B. Line 91. Digital images. Ancestry.com. www.ancestry.com. Accessed Nov. 15, 2015. Digital images, citing NARA microfilm publication.

[87] Cook Joseph. Oral History. ACHS. Interviewer: Marjane Ambler. May, 24, 1984. Pages 7-9. Transcript held at the SPCSHS. Accessed May 8, 2024.

[88] "Poll Book." Aug. 17, 1926. Primary Election. Election District No. 12. Polling Precinct No. 1. Line 17. Fremont County Elections Office. Accessed Aug. 2, 2019.

[89] Pfaff, Betty Carpenter. Oral history by the ACHS, WSA and HD and/or the Wyoming State Historical Society. Jan. 24, 1984. Interviewer Philippina Halstead. Page 6. Transcription held at the SPCSHS. Accessed March 8, 2024.

[90] "Henry Harsh [sic] Passes." WSJ. May 2, 1928. Page 3; "William Henry Harsch." WSJ. May 9, 1928. Page 6; WSJ. April 28, 1928. Page 8; Pfaff, Betty Carpenter. Fine Gold. Private printing. 1998. Chap. 22, pages 4-5; Hallberg, Carl, WSA. Received by Barbara Townsend. Email Interview. October 26, 2015.

[91] WSJ. May 9, 1928. Page 6.

[92] Photograph of printed certificate by Barbara Townsend, Aug. 22, 2022. The document was a copy with an original stamp on the back by the WSA, File No. 1928, registered No. 771. Betty Carpenter Pfaff Collection. SPCSHS. Second drawer from the top, in the folder labeled "Harsch." Accessed August 22, 2022; Death certificate. 1928. State File No. 771. WSA. Ancestry.com. www.ancestry.com. Accessed April 29, 2024; Death card. File No. 1928. Certificate No. 771. Wyoming, US, State and County Death Records, 1896-1971. WSA. Ancestry.com. Accessed May 25, 2024. www.ancestry.com; Fremont County Coroner Erin Evie and staff. Personal interview. Fremont County Coroner's Office, Riverton. June 14, 2024.

[93] "Philip Harsch." WRM. July 11, 1913. Page 1. Accessed Oct. 26, 2014; "Death of Old Pioneer of Atlantic Mining District." The WSJ. July 11, 1913. Vol. 31. No. 18. Page 1. UW and Wyoming State Library. https://wyomingnewspapers.org. Accessed Oct. 7, 2015; Record Book for Atlantic City. Burials. Pages 114-115. Line 3. St. Andrew's Episcopal Church. Accessed Nov. 16, 2015.

[94] Connell, M. "Family Chronicle," n.d. Electronic copy. SPCSHS server. Page 5. Accessed Aug. 22, 2022; "Wilson's Creek," n.d. American Battlefield Trust. 2024. www.battlefields.org/learn/civil-war/battles/wilsons-creek. Accessed July 28, 2024; Jan. 30, 2020. US Department of the Interior, National Park Service. www.nps.gov/wicr/index.htm. Accessed June 3, 2024.

[95] Pfaff, Betty Carpenter. Fine Gold. Private printing. 1998. Chap. 22, page 4; Connell, M. "Family Chronicle," n.d. Electronic copy. SPCSHS server. Page 5. Accessed Aug. 22, 2022. Note: See the "Note" in endnote 269n77; "Antietam." Dec. 7, 2023. US Department of the Interior, National Park Service. www.nps.gov/anti/index.htm. Accessed June 3, 2024; www.battlefields.org/. Accessed June 3, 2024.

[96] 1890 Veterans' Schedule. Special Schedule-Surviving Soldiers, Sailors, and Marines, and Widows. Page 3. Line 33. Ancestry.com. www.ancestry.com. Accessed Dec. 9, 2015. Digital images, citing NARA microfilm publication; Guenther, Todd. "Harsch Notes." Oct. 2, 1991. Information from interviews with Louise Connell York, Tom Connell, Martha Connell Williamson, and Myra Connell. Handwritten annotation of "Conne-13-T." Page 2. SPCSHS. Folder titled "Connell, M. Emmett."; Connell, M. "Family Chronicle," n.d. Electronic copy. SPCSHS server. Pages 6, 8. Accessed Aug. 22, 2022. Note: See the "Note" in endnote 269n77.

[97] "Death of Old Pioneer of Atlantic Mining District." The WSJ. July 11, 1913. Vol. 31. No. 18. Page 1. UW and Wyoming State Library. https://wyomingnewspapers.org. Accessed Oct. 7, 2015.

[98] C. G. Coutant. The History of Wyoming: From the Earliest Known Discoveries, In Three Volumes. Chaplin, Spafford & Mathison, 1899. Page 656; United States, Western States Marriage Index. Volume 1. Page 12. Oct. 19, 2018. FamilySearch. https://familysearch.org. Accessed March 5, 2022; Pfaff, Betty Carpenter. Changes. Private printing. 2018. Page 57; Guenther, Todd. "Harsch Notes." Oct. 2, 1991. Information from interviews with Louise Connell York, Tom Connell, Martha Connell Williamson, and Myra Connell. Handwritten annotation of "Conne-13-T." Page 2. SPCSHS. Filing cabinet, folder titled "Connell, M. Emmett." Accessed on May 8, 2024; Connell, M. "Family Chronicle," n.d. Electronic copy. SPCSHS server. Pages 7-8. Accessed Aug. 22, 2022. Note: See the "Note" in endnote 269n77.

99 "Poll list." Sept. 2, 1869. Atlantic City. Carter County. Page 3. Line 166. Paper and electronic copies. Carl Hallberg. WSA. Aug. 22, 2022.]

100 1870 US Federal Census. South Pass City. Page opposite (stamped) page 505. Line 33. Database with images. FamilySearch. https://FamilySearch.org : 31 December 2023. Accessed Feb. 21, 2024. Citing NARA microfilm publication T9. Washington, D.C.: NARA, n.d.

101 Guenther, Todd. "Harsch Notes." Oct. 2, 1991. Information from interviews with Louise Connell York, Tom Connell, Martha Connell Williamson, and Myra Connell. Handwritten annotation of "Conne-13-T." Page 1. SPCSHS. Filing cabinet, folder titled "Connell, M. Emmett." Accessed on May 8, 2024; "Sweetwater County Marriage Index, Reverse L to End, Book 1&2 or A&B, Book 3 or C through p.43." Pdf page 174. Ledger page 12. SPCSHS. Server. Accessed Dec. 17, 2019.

102 Handwritten cards. 1869, 1872, and 1874 Carter County tax rolls. SPCSHS. Sweetwater County. Accessed Oct. 31, 2016.

103 "Poll Book." Atlantic City. Sweetwater County. Nov. 2, 1880. Line 15; "Poll Book. Atlantic City. Sweetwater County. June 14, 1881. Line 6; "Oath of Judges and Clerks of Election." Atlantic City. Sweetwater County. June 14, 1881. Sweetwater County Historical Museum. Accessed Jan. 11, 2017.

104 1880 US Federal Census. Atlantic City. Sweetwater County. Sheet (stamped) 5. Page No. (penned) 5. Line 21; . 1900 US Federal Census. Atlantic Precinct. Sheet (stamped) B. Sheet No. (penned) 1. Line 53; 1910 US Federal Census; Precinct 12. Atlantic City. Enumeration District No. 66. Sheet No. 7. Line 36; Ancestry.com. www.ancestry.com. Accessed Nov. 15, 2015. Digital images, citing NARA microfilm publication.

105 "Philip Harsch." WRM. July 11, 1913. Vol 28. No. 34. Page 1. UW and Wyoming State Library. Accessed Oct. 25, 2014.

106 Photograph and caption: Scanned and photographed by author. Undated. Original photo located SPCSHS. Betty Carpenter Pfaff Collection. Top drawer, in the folder labeled "Misc, & Photos." Accessed August 22, 2022; Pfaff, Betty Carpenter. Fine Gold. Privately published. 1978.

107 Manifest. July 3, 1856. Page 5. Line 230. New York, US, Arriving Passenger and Crew Lists, 1820-1957 for Alwin Heyroth. NARA images, 1820-1897. Microfilm Serial or NAID: M237, RG Title: Records of the US Customs Service; RG:36. Reel: 164. Online film viewer, page 47. FamilySearch. www.familysearch.org. Accessed June 30, 2024.

108 1870 US Federal Census. Atlantic City. County of Sweetwater. Page No. (penned) 2. Line 11 and 12. Digital images. Ancestry.com. www.ancestry.com. Accessed Nov. 20, 2015. Digital images, citing NARA microfilm publication.

109 "Licenses." Electronic file "Sweetwater_records_roll_02-04-115_01." SPCSHS. Server. Pdf page 315. Accessed Dec. 17, 2019. The first visible license for a saloon keeper was Blatcheley and Coles, May 1869.

110 "Record of [Liquor] License Issued in 1870-1873." Sweetwater County Licenses. Paper copies. SPCSHS. Accessed Oct. 27, 2016.

111 "Licenses." Electronic file "Sweetwater_records_roll_02-04-115_02." SPCSHS. Server. Pdf pages 1-27. Accessed Dec. 17, 2019.

112 "Poll Book." Nov. 2, 1880. Atlantic City. Sweetwater County. Line 31; "Oath of Judges and Clerks of Election." Atlantic City Precinct. Sweetwater County; "Poll Book." Atlantic City Precinct. Sweetwater County. June 14, 1881. Line 7. Sweetwater County Historical Museum. Accessed Jan. 11, 2017.

113 Sweetwater County Deeds, Book D. Pages 130-133. Pages 80-81. Page 205-206. Paper copies; Sweetwater County Licenses. SPCSHS. Accessed Oct. 27, 2016; 1880 US Census for Atlantic City. 1880 US Federal Census. Atlantic City. County of Sweetwater. Page No. (penned) 6. (continued) Line 20. Digital images. Ancestry.com. www.ancestry.com. Accessed Nov. 15, 2015. Digital images, citing NARA microfilm publication.

114 Handwritten 4x6-inch cards of tax assessments from 1870–1873, Justice of the Peace dockets. SPCSHS. "Fremont County Court Proceedings from South Pass City and Atlantic City; 1884-1912." Carter County tax records held in Sweetwater County. Accessed Dec. 3, 2016.

115 Connell, Myra. "Here Lies ... A History of Old Graves in Fremont County." WSJ. Dec. 15, 1980. Page B-1 An Inventory of Wyoming Cemeteries." [Preliminary]. May 21, 1968. Daniel Y. Meschter papers. Collection 1974, Box #7. Atlantic City section. Page 2. AHC, UW. Accessed May 12, 2024; Cheyenne Daily Sun. No. 139. August 15, 1884. Page 3. UW and Wyoming State Library. https://wyomingnewspapers.org. Accessed Nov. 19, 2015.

116 The Anthony building was constructed by J. W. Anthony, date unknown. This stone structure was also known as (Robert) McAuley's Store, and later was a saloon. The structure is

(continued) commonly known as Hyde's Hall. Originally a two-store structure, an earthquake in possibly 1923 forced the removal of that second story. Sources: "South Pass Mining District." *Wyoming Tales and Trails*. Atlantic City. http://www.wyomingtalesandtrails.com/atlanticcity.html. Accessed March 17, 2024; Fremont County Pioneer Museum. Folder "Atlantic City." Accessed Nov. 15, 2016; Cook Joseph. Oral History by the ACHS, WSA and HD and/or the Wyoming State Historical Society. Interviewer: Marjane Ambler. May, 24, 1984. Page 4. Transcript held at the SPCSHS. Accessed May 8, 2024.

[117] Hart, Sheila. "Ledger Found at Ghost Town of Atlantic City Give a Glimpse of Life and Death at South Pass." *WSJ*. Vol 70. No. 53. Page 7.

[118] *WSJ*. Feb. 4, 1954. Vol. 67. No. 10. Page 1. Accessed Feb 8, 2016. Located at Fremont County Library System, Lander branch, Wyo.; "Record Book for Atlantic City." Baptisms. Pages 60-61. Line 16. St. Andrew's Episcopal Church. Accessed Feb. 8, 2016; Connell, M. "Family Chronicle," n.d. Electronic copy. SPCSHS server. Pages 12, 13. Accessed Aug. 22, 2022. Note: See the "Note" in endnote 269n77. Additionally, Myra Connell wrote a published article, "Here lies ... A history of Old Graves in Fremont County," in the *WSJ*. Dec. 15, 1980. Page B-1.

[119] *Marriage Record Book A 1884-1904*. Index page "H." Certificate. Page 355. Fremont County Courthouse. County Clerk. Land Recording Office. Lander, Wyo. Accessed Jan. 16, 2017.

[120] *Progressive Men of the State of Wyoming*. Chicago, Illinois.: A.W. Bowen & Co. 1903. Pages 573-74. Library of Congress. Images 639 and 640. Control #: a15002727. OCLC 6398383. https://lccn.loc.gov/a15002727; 1900 US Federal Census. Atlantic Precinct. Sheet (stamped) B. Sheet No. 1, Line 9. Ancestry.com. www.ancestry.com. Accessed Nov. 21, 2015. Digital images, citing NARA microfilm publication.

[121] "Remittance man." *Random House Compact Unabridged Dictionary*. Special 2nd Edition. Random House, 1996; *Oxford Reference*. Oxford University Press. PubFactory. 2024. www.oxfordreference.com; 1900 US Federal Census. Atlantic Precinct. Sheet (stamped) B. Sheet No. 1, Lines 9-10. Ancestry.com. www.ancestry.com. Digital images, citing NARA microfilm publication.

[122] US, Appointments of US Postmasters, 1832-1971. 1900. Page 488. NARA. Record Group No. 28. Series M841. Roll No. 145; US Register of Civil, Military, and Naval Services, 1863-1959. July 1901. Vol. 2. Page 420.; July 1, 1903. Page 417. Oregon State Library, Salem, Oregon. Ancestry.com. www.ancestry.com. Accessed May 13, 2024; Pfaff, Betty Carpenter. *Fine Gold*. Privately Published. 1998. Chap. 22. Pages 5-6; *Atlantic City Nuggets*. 1978. Page 67; Guenther, Todd. "Harsch Notes." Oct. 2, 1991. Information from interviews with Louise Connell York, Tom Connell, Martha Connell Williamson, and Myra Connell. Handwritten annotation of "Conne-13-T." Page 4. SPCSHS. Filing cabinet, folder titled "Connell, M. Emmett."; Fuller, Zoie Green. Oral history by the ACHS, WSA and HD and/or the Wyoming State Historical Society. Jan. 4, 1984. Interviewer Philippina Halstead. Page 25. Transcription held at the SPCSHS.

[123] "England & Wales, National Probate Calendar (Index of Wills and Administrations), 1858-1995." Paper document held at SPCSHS. Folder "Hunt, RC." Document credits Ancestry.com.

[124] Pfaff, Betty Carpenter. *Fine Gold*. 1998. Chap. 22. Pages 5-6. *Atlantic City Nuggets*. Page 67. 1978. Private printings; *WSJ*. Feb. 4, 1954. Vol. 67. No. 10. Page 1.

[125] 1910 US Federal Census. County of Fremont. De Pass. Enumeration District No. 57. Election Precinct No. 35. Sheet No. 6B. Lines 69–75. Ancestry.com. www.ancestry.com. Accessed May 20, 2024. Digital images, citing NARA microfilm publication.

[126] 1920 US Federal Census. Atlantic City, Election District #14. Enumeration District 57. Sheet No. 10B. Line 92. Ancestry.com. www.ancestry.com. Accessed Nov. 21, 2015. Digital images, citing NARA microfilm publication.

[127] "Registration and Poll Book." Special Election. Atlantic City. Election District No. 14. Polling Precinct 1. Line 5; "Poll Book." Primary Election. Atlantic City. Election District No. 12. Polling Precinct No. 1. Line 13. "Registration Poll Book and Official Return of a General Election Held November 4, 1930." Election District No. 11. Polling Precinct No. 1. Lines 2-3. Fremont County Elections Office. Accessed Aug. 2, 2019.

[128] 1900 US Federal Census. Atlantic Precinct. Sheet (stamped) B. Sheet No. 1, Line 10; 1920 US Federal Census. Atlantic City, Election District #14. Enumeration District 57. Sheet No. 10B. Line 92; 1930 US Federal Census. Election District 11. Atlantic City, Election District #11, Enumeration District No. 7-13. Sheet No. 1A. Line 31; 1940 Federal Census. Atlantic City Village. Election District 15. E.D. No. 7-14. Sheet No. 1A. Line 18; 1950 US Federal Census. Election District

No. 7-25. Sheet No. 2. Digital images. Line 6. Ancestry.com. www.ancestry.com. Accessed Nov. 21, 2015. Digital images, citing NARA microfilm publication.

129 Pfaff, Betty Carpenter. *Atlantic City Nuggets*. Private printing. 1978. Page 66; *Fine Gold*. Private printing. 1998.

130 "Fremont County, Defunct Cemeteries," n.d. Unknown compiler. Accessed Sept. 25, 2015. Mount Hope Cemetery. City of Lander; Meschter, Daniel Y. "An Inventory of Wyoming Cemeteries." [Preliminary]. May 21, 1968. Daniel Y. Meschter papers. Collection 1974, Box #7. Atlantic City section. Page 2. AHC, UW. Accessed May 12, 2024. Note: I cannot locate a final report.

131 "New Orleans, Passenger Lists, 1813-1963." Digital images. Ancestry.com. www.ancestry.com. Accessed July 26, 2016. Digital images, citing NARA microfilm publication.

132 "Civil War Draft Records, 1863-1865." No page numbers. Digital images. Ancestry.com. www.ancestry.com. Accessed July 27, 2016. Digital images, NARA microfilm publication; "List of Letters." *Cheyenne Leader*; No. 108; January 25, 1868; Pages 3, 15. UW and Wyoming State Library. 2023. https://wyomingnewspapers.org. Accessed July 28, 2016; Huseas, Marion McMillan. *Sweetwater Gold, Wyoming's Gold Rush 1867-1871*. Lander: Mortimore Publishing. 1991. Page 15; *The Wyoming Weekly Leader*. May 1, 1869. Page 7. UW and Wyoming State Library. Accessed April 10, 2024; "Nickerson, Early History of Fremont County." Handwritten card. SPCSHS. Undated green index card. Accessed Dec. 3, 2016; "Poll List." Atlantic City. Carter County. Territory of Wyoming. Sept. 2, 1869. Line 108. Paper and electronic copies. Carl Hallberg. WSA. Aug. 22, 2022.

133 1870 US Federal Census. County of Sweetwater. Atlantic City. Sheet No. (stamped) 460. Page 6. Line 20; Digital images. Ancestry.com. www.ancestry.com. Accessed Nov. 20, 2015. Digital images, citing NARA microfilm publication.

134 *South Pass News*. No. 52. August 31, 1871. Page 4. UW and Wyoming State Library. https://wyomingnewspapers.org. Accessed July 28, 2016.

135 "Marriage Books, Book 1." Page 2. Sweetwater County Historical Museum. Accessed Aug. 13, 2021; *South Pass News*. No. 52. August 31, 1871. Page 4. UW and Wyoming State Library. https://wyomingnewspapers.org. Accessed July 28, 2016.

136 Poll results. Atlantic City. 1871. Territory of Wyoming. Paper and electronic copies. Carl Hallberg. WSA. Aug. 25, 2021.

137 Handwritten on a cream index card #24; handwritten on an gray index card; handwritten on a gray index card, #36 on back. Accessed Oct. 12, 2016. SPCSHS; *Daily Independent*. August 18, 1874. No. 200. Page 3, and in September 1, 1874. No. 212. Page 3. UW and Wyoming State Library. https://wyomingnewspapers.org. Accessed July 28, 2016.

138 Hallberg, Carl, WSA. Personal communication. Aug. 17, 2021; Hamilton, Alicia. Personal communication. Sept. 30, 2021.

139 "Allene Moffitt's Teeny Tales." Allene Moffitt. *The Fayetteville Observer*. November 19, 1972. Pages 2E and 8E; Akers, Marshall. "1971-72 Episode Guide." *To Tell The Truth on the Web*. Line 0962. Georgina Newman. June 8, 2015. www.ttttontheweb.com/ttt69s3guide.html. Accessed July 28, 2024; "To Tell The Truth #0962." Episode 0962 video. BillCullenNet. *YouTube*. www.youtube.com/@BillCullenNet. www.youtube.com/watch?v=u23PDi_eAVk. Accessed July 28, 2024; Genealogic Form. Georgina D. Newman, n.d. Gaylin Carpenter. Accessed Oct. 23, 2012.

140 *The Denver Post*. "Empire Magazine." April 20, 1972. Page 54.

141 *Congressional Record, Proceedings and Debates of the 92d Congress, First Session*. Sept. 29, 1971. S15307. Ed Christopherson.

142 *Poll Book and Official Return*. Atlantic City. Aug. 18, 1964 – Nov. 7, 1878. Election District No. 15 (Aug. 21, 1962 – Nov. 2, 1965) or 24 (Aug. 20, 1968 – Nov. 7, 1978). Polling Precinct No. 1. Fremont County Elections Office.

143 Ruebelmann, Lorna. Personal conversation. August 26, 2017, and June 22, 2024.

144 Justice, Carole. Personal conversation. July 30, 2024.

145 *WSJ*. Sept. 9, 1998. Page B-4.

146 "Newman Estate Gift Will Fund Scholarships." *Casper Star-Tribune*. Ernie Over, editor. Sept 10, 1998. Page A-2; "Georgina Dewey Newman." *Casper Star-Tribune*. Sept. 10, 1998.

147 *High Performance Pontiac*, Vol. 27. No. 12. (December 2006). Pages 12-13.

148 Tyler, Carolyn B. "Wide-Tracking Man Follows Pioneer Tracks to His Miner's Delight." *Riverton Ranger*. Dec. 4, 1968. Section 2. Page 1.

149 *The Denver Post*. "Empire Magazine." April 20, 1972. Page 54.

150 Congressional Record, Proceedings and Debates of the 92d Congress, First Session. Sept. 29, 1971. S15307. Ed Christopherson.

151 *Poll Book and Official Return*. Atlantic City. Aug. 18, 1964 – Nov. 7, 1878. Election District No. 15 (Aug. 21, 1962 – Nov. 2, 1965) or 24 (Aug. 20, 1968 – Nov. 7, 1978). Polling Precinct No. 1. Fremont County Elections Office.

152 "Paul E. Newman." *New York Times*. May 14, 1986. http://www.nytimes.com/1986/05/14/obituaries/paul-e-newman.html. Accessed Dec. 15, 2016.

153 *WSJ*. December 15, 1980. Page B-1.

154 "An Inventory of Wyoming Cemeteries." [Preliminary]. May 21, 1968. Daniel Y. papers. Collection 1974, Box #7. Atlantic City section. Page 2. AHC, UW.

155 Pfaff, Betty Carpenter. *Atlantic City Nuggets*. Story told by James Carpenter. Private printing. 2018. Pages 71-73. Note: The 1870 census was conducted a month after Stambaugh was killed. If he left a widow, I have found no information of her.

156 The *Miner*. Vol. 4. No. 15. July 15, 1910. Page 6. UW and Wyoming State Library. https://wyomingnewspapers.org. Accessed April 19, 2023.

157 1900 US Federal Census. Atlantic Precinct. Enumeration District No. 29. Page A 83. Sheet No. (penned) 1. Line 47. Digital images. Ancestry.com. www.ancestry.com. Accessed April 1, 2022. Digital images, citing NARA microfilm publication; *Record Book for Atlantic City*. Baptisms. Pages 66-67. Line 39. St. Andrew's Episcopal Church. Accessed March 15, 2019.

158 Pfaff, Betty Carpenter. *Changes*. Private printing. 2018. Pages 116 and 120.

159 1950 US Federal Census. Atlantic City. Election District 7-25. Sheet No. (penned) 2. Line 16. Digital images. Ancestry.com. www.ancestry.com. Accessed April 1, 2022. Digital images, citing NARA microfilm publication.

160 Pfaff, Betty Carpenter. Carpenter Family History, n.d.

161 Pfaff, Betty Carpenter. Anne Robinson's cremains, Ellen Carpenter's gravesite. June 26, 2016. Two telephone conversations; Carpenter Family History, n.d. Accessed July 25, 2016.

162 *WRM*. No. 46. Sept. 26, 1919. Page 8. UW and Wyoming State Library. https://wyomingnewspapers.org. Accessed Jan. 22, 2020; "Early Reorganization Minutes, 1862-1871, Book A," pp. 135, 305; "Membership of The Church of Jesus Christ of Latter-day Saints, 1830-1848." Early Members of the Reorganized Church of Jesus Christ of Latter-day Saints. Ancestry.com. www.ancestry.com. Accessed May 5, 2024.

163 Golliher, Alma Williams. 1977. Oral history (a series). Interviewed by Rosemary Williamson. Pages 11-13. Transcription held at SPCSHS; Sommers, Jonita. *Williams Family History*. 2020. Unpublished manuscript. Possibly chap. 3. Accessed April 22, 2016.

164 Pfaff, Betty Carpenter. *Atlantic City Nuggets*. Private Printing. 1978. Page 114.

165 *Lander Clipper, WSJ*. Vol. 22, No. 33. April 9, 1909. Page 4. UW and Wyoming State Library. https://wyomingnewspapers.org. Accessed April 19, 2023; Serial Patent. Issue Date: 3/3/1910. Document No. 01019. BLM Serial No. WYE 0001019. Authority: May 20, 1862: Homestead EntryOriginal (12 Stat. 392). Accession No. 115086. US Dept of the Interior. BLM. https://glorecords.blm.gov. Accessed May 5, 2024.

166 1910 US Census. Big Sandy Town. Enumeration District No. 61. Election District No. 5. Sheet No. 1A. Lines 20 and 33-40. NARA Records. FamilySearch. www.familysearch.org. Accessed May 5, 2024.

167 "10, Two Children and Adult Man Standing in Front of Log Building." Page 2. Golliher Photograph Collection. SPCSHS. Server "SPC2019" folder, subfolder "South Pass museum," subfolder "Documentation of Aunt Almas photos." Accessed Aug. 22, 2022.

168 Sommers, Jonita. *Williams Family History*. 2020. Unpublished manuscript. Chap. 4, page 6. Accessed April 22, 2016.

169 Sommers, Jonita. The Williams Family history. Personal Interview by author. April 22, 2016.

Chapter 5: East Cemetery, People Buried Here, Gravesite Unknown

1 Photo: SPCSHS. "SPC Data Files", "Public" and "Research" folders, subfolder "Uncle Always, Alwes." Donated by Betty Carpenter Pfaff. Accessed August 22, 2022; Handwritten on a photograph. Paper copy. SPCSHS. Accessed Oct. 12, 2016.

2 1910 US Federal Census. Fremont County, WY. Atlantic City. Precinct 12. Page 2, line 52. Digital image. Ancestry.com. www.ancestry.com. Accessed Nov. 20, 2015. Digital images, citing NARA microfilm publication.

3 "Perished in Snowstorm." *WSJ*. No. 26; April 25, 1919, page 1. UW and Wyoming State Library. https://wyomingnewspapers.org. Accessed April 19, 2023.

4 Betty Carpenter Pfaff. *Fine Gold*. Private printing. 1998.

5 *Record Book for Atlantic City*. Burials, pages 114-115, line 6. St. Andrew's Episcopal Church. Atlantic City, Wyo. Accessed Nov. 16, 2015.

6 Notes of an interview by Todd Guenther with Hilda (Anderson) Gordon on July 25, 1992. SPCSHS. Server's "Public" folder, subfolder "Research," subfolder "Anderson." Accessed August 22, 2022.

7 *Marriage Record Book A: Index*. Pages 1, 351. Fremont County Courthouse. County Clerk's Office. Land Recording Office. Accessed Oct. 19, 2015.

8 1900 US Federal Census. Lewiston, Wyo. District 29. Sheet 5. Line 21. Accessed Nov. 20, 2015; 1910 US Federal Census. Lewiston, Wyo. Enumeration District 66. Page (illegible), line 55. Digital images. Ancestry.com. www.ancestry.com. Accessed Dec. 12, 2015. Digital images, citing NARA microfilm publication.

9 *Record Book for Atlantic City*. Burials, pages 114-115, line 5. St. Andrew's Episcopal Church. Atlantic City, Wyo. Accessed Nov. 16, 2015.

10 Death certificate, James Frederick Anderson. State of Wyoming. Bureau of Vital Statistics Certificate of Death. File No. 1916. Registered No. 558. WSA. Ancestry.com. https://ancestry.com. Accessed March 30, 2024.

11 Martha Walrath, great-granddaughter. Telephone interview. Aug. 25, 2022. Email interview. Aug. 30, 2022. Printed with her permission granted on Aug. 30, 2022.

12 *WSJ*; No. 1. October 6, 1916, page 5. UW and Wyoming State Library. https://wyomingnewspapers.org. Accessed Nov. 15, 2015.

13 Photo courtesy: SPCSHS. Server "Public" folder, subfolder "Research," subfolder "Anderson." Photo entitled "James Anderson, according to Martha Walrath descendant." Artist and donor information pending. Accessed August 22, 2022.

14 *WSJ*. No. 34. May 19, 1916. Page 4. UW and Wyoming State Library. Accessed Nov. 13, 2015. https://wyomingnewspapers.org; 1900 US Federal Census. Lewiston, Wyo. District 29. Sheet 5. Line 22; Digital images. Ancestry.com. www.ancestry.com. Accessed Nov. 20, 2015. Digital images, citing NARA microfilm publication.

15 *Marriage Record Book A: Index*. Pages 1, 351. Fremont County Courthouse. County Clerk. Land Recording Office. Lander, Wyo. Accessed Oct. 19, 2015.

16 1910 US Federal Census. Lewiston, Wyo. Precinct 14. Enumeration District 66. Page 2, line 56. Digital images. Ancestry.com. https://ancestry.com. Accessed Dec. 12, 2015. Digital images, citing NARA microfilm publication.

17 *WSJ*, No. 34. May 19, 1916, page 4. UW and Wyoming State Library. https://wyomingnewspapers.org. Accessed Nov. 13, 2015.

18 *WRM*. May 19, 1916. Vol. 32. No. 27. Page 1. UW and Wyoming State Library. https://wyomingnewspapers.org. Accessed May 10, 2024.

19 *Record Book for Atlantic City*. Burials. Pages 114-115, line 4. St. Andrew's Episcopal Church. Atlantic City, Wyo. Accessed Nov. 16, 2015.

20 M. Walrath, great-granddaughter. Personal communications. Aug. 25, 2022. This information is printed with her permission on Aug. 30, 2022; M. Walrath, great-granddaughter. Personal communications. Feb. 5, 2025.

21 Death certificate, Martha B. Anderson. State of Wyoming. Bureau of Vital Statistics Certificate of Death. File No. 1916. Registered. No. 384. WSA. Ancestry.com. www.ancestry.com. Accessed Mar. 29, 2024.

22 "Cirrhosis." Sumera Ilyas. Feb. 11, 2023. Mayo Clinic. Accessed Mar. 30, 2024. www.mayoclinic.org/; "Liver Disease in Pregnancy." Sharma V. Anuj and John Savio. June 12, 2023. National Institute of Health. National Library of Medicine. Accessed Mar. 30, (continued) 2024. www.ncbi.nlm.nih.gov/; "Chronic Liver Disease/Cirrhosis." 2024. Johns Hopkins Medicine. www.hopkinsmedicine.org. Accessed Mar. 30, 2024.

23 "Willow Bark." Reviewed June 12, 2023. *MedlinePlus*. Bethesda (MD): National Library of Medicine (US). https://medlineplus.gov/druginfo/natural/955.html. Accessed July 30, 2024.

24 Fremont County Coroner Erin Evie, Tony Simmers, and Kirsten Kenny. Personal interview. June 14, 2024; "What is HELLP Syndrome?" Preeclampsia Foundation. July 5, 2023. https://www.preeclampsia.org/hellp-syndrome. Accessed June 14, 2024; Bhat KJ, Shovkat R, Samoon HJ. "Postpartum Acute Liver Dysfunction: A Case of Acute Fatty Liver of Pregnancy Developing Massive Intrahepatic Calcification." Gastroenterology Res. 2015 Dec;8(6):313-315. DOI: 10.14740/gr693w. Epub 2015 Dec 31. PMID: 27785315; PMCID: PMC5051032. Accessed June 14, 2024.

25 *WSJ*; No. 1; October 6, 1916, page 5. UW and Wyoming State Library. https://wyomingnewspapers.org. Accessed Nov. 15, 2015; M. Walrath, great-granddaughter. Personal communications. Feb. 5, 2025.

26 Information from Chuck Emerson, re letter from relatives; Philippina Halstead's report to the ACHS on August 25, 2007; *Record Book for Atlantic City*. Burials, pages 114-115, line 4. St. Andrew's Episcopal Church. Accessed Nov. 16, 2015.

27 "Died." *WRM*. Aug. 3, 1898. Vol. XI. No. 46. Page 3.

28 Pfaff, Betty Carpenter. *Fine Gold*. Private printing. 1998. Chap. 22, page 4; *Lander Clipper*. No. 44. July 3, 1903. Page 4. UW and Wyoming State Library. Accessed April 19, 2023.

29 "A Distressing Accident." *Lander Clipper*. No. 44. July 3, 1903. Page 4; No. 45. July 10, 1903. Page 4. UW and Wyoming State Library. Accessed April 19, 2023; "Laid to Rest." *The Clipper*. July 10, 1903. Vol. 16. No. 45. Page 4. UW and Wyoming State Library. Accessed Aug. 28, 2015.

30 1900 US Federal Census. Atlantic Precinct. Sheet 1. Line 20. Digital images. Ancestry.com. https://ancestry.com. Accessed April 28, 2022. Digital images, citing NARA microfilm publication. Mionczynski, John. Personal communication. Aug. 15, 2024.

31 "Early Atlantic City Settler Succumbs." *Lander Evening Post*. No. 302. Dec. 28, 1939, page 1.

32 Compiled from ACHS members from oral histories, newspapers, letters, etc.; "Charles Jackson." Certificate of Death. File No. 1939. Registered No. 2130. Local Registrar's No. 6. Received mailed paper copy. WSA. Carl Hallberg. Feb. 21, 2024.

33 Pfaff, Betty Carpenter. *Atlantic City Nuggets*. Privately published. 1978. Pages 19, 92.

34 "Notice of Rights to Water." Misc Records. Vol. B. 11-5-1894 - 7-24-1906. Dated April 23, 1904. Page 416. Recorded on April 26, 1904. Fremont County Clerk's Office. Land Recording Office.

35 1900 US Federal Census. Lewiston Precinct. Enumeration District 29, Sheet no. 5. Printed Page A87. line 7; 1910 US Federal Census. Enumeration District 66. Sheet number illegible. Precinct 14, Lewiston. Page 2, line 63; 1920 US Federal Census. Atlantic City. Election District 14. Enumeration District 567. Sheet No. penned 10. Line 50; 1930 US Federal Census. Atlantic City. Election District 11. Enumeration District 7-13. Printed page 232. Line 48. Ancestry.com. www.ancestry.com. Accessed Nov. 20, 2015. Digital images, citing NARA microfilm publication. Note: The 1920 Census sheets had "Lander Town" written in but on each page it was struck out with a pen stroke.

36 "Poll Book of a Primary Election Held August 19, 1930." Atlantic City. Election District No. 11. Polling Precinct No. 1. Line 3; "Registration Poll Book and Official Return of a General Election Held November 4, 1930." Election District No. 11. Polling Precinct No. 1. Line 2. Fremont County Elections Office. Accessed Aug. 2, 2019.

37 Pfaff, Betty Carpenter. *Atlantic City Nuggets*. Privately published. 1978. Page 95; *Field Notes and Reports Mineral Surveys*. Volume 17. 1893-1906. Claimant Wallace Grosvenor. "Survey approved Dec. 10, 1906." Printed page 5. Field Notes. Handwritten page number 665. Bureau of Land Management. www.wy.blm.gov/cadastral/countyplats/fremont/fieldnotes/t30nr98w_rptfreesilver.pdf. Accessed July 30, 2024.

38 Betty Carpenter Pfaff. *Changes*. Page 3. Private printing. 2018; *Fine Gold*. Chap. 9. Private printing. 1998.

39 "Early Atlantic City Settler Succumbs." *Lander Evening Post*. Dec. 28, 1939. Vol. XXI. No. 302. Page 1.

40 "An Inventory of Wyoming Cemeteries." [Preliminary]. May 21, 1968. Daniel Y. Meschter papers. Collection 1974, Box #7. Atlantic City section. Page 2. AHC, UW. Accessed May 12, 2024. Note: I cannot locate a final report.

41 Find a Grave. www.findagrave.com/cgi-bin/fg.cgi?page=gr&GRid=43180945 &ref= acomon. Accessed October 19, 2015; *Vernal Express*. December 9, 1897. Image courtesy of the J. Willard Library, Utah Digital Newspapers. https://digitalnewspapers.org/newspaper/?paper=Vernal+Express. Accessed April 12, 2023; *WRM*, No. 12; December 6, 1897, page 2. UW and Wyoming State Library. Accessed Oct. 7, 2015. https://wyomingnewspapers.org. Accessed July 28, 2016.

42 *Lander Clipper*. No. 14, December 3, 1897. page 1. UW and Wyoming State Library. https://wyomingnewspapers.org. Accessed Oct. 7, 2015; ACHS members from oral histories, newspapers, letters, etc.; *Vernal Express*. Utah. Dec. 9, 1897. Page 4. Image courtesy of the J. Willard Library, Utah Digital Newspapers. https://digitalnewspapers.org/newspaper/ ?paper=Vernal+Express. Accessed April 12, 2023.

43 *Mayhem, and Mystery, Coroner Inquests in Fremont County 1885-1900*. Mark R. Stratmoen. Lenore Wyoming Publications, Riverton, WY. 2010. Pages 237-238.

44 Stratmoen, Mark. Personal communications. Various times, Nov. 16-20, 2015.

45 Mann, Albert. Oral history by the ACHS, WSA and HD and/or the Wyoming State Historical Society. Sept. 11, 1983. Interviewer David Geible. Pages 20. Transcription held at the SPCSHS. Accessed March 8, 2024.
46 *WRM.* Vol. 11. No. 11. November 29, 1897. Page 2. UW and Wyoming State Library. https://wyomingnewspapers.org. Accessed Oct. 19, 2015.
47 ACHS members from oral histories, newspapers, letters, etc.; Find a Grave. Accessed Oct. 19, 2015. http://www.findagrave.com; *Vernal Express* (Utah), December 9, 1897. Page 4. Image courtesy of the J. Willard Library, Utah Digital Newspapers. https://digitalnewspapers.org/newspaper/?paper=Vernal+Express. Accessed April 12 2023.
48 *WRM.* No. 12. December 6, 1897. Page 2. UW and Wyoming State Library. https://wyomingnewspapers.org. Accessed July 28, 2016; Jail Record, pages 28-29, number 237. Fremont County Pioneer Museum. Accessed July 26, 2016.

CHAPTER 6: EAST CEMETERY, DOWSED GRAVES OF UNKNOWN PERSONS

1 The East Cemetery now has 71 staked graves. In 2021, the site formerly known as M42 was identified as Casimer Melin.
2 Myriad photographs by unknown photographer(s). 1950s. Courtesy of the Henderson Collection, SPCSHS collections, and Legacy of the Plains Museum, Nebraska. Accessed May 8, 2024.

CHAPTER 7: WEST CEMETERY BURIALS

1 "ACHS Cemeteries Project; List of Graves and Possible Graves," n.d. Copy of the report received from Jean Mathisen Haugen in her home. Nov. 13, 2015.
2 Mionczynski, John. Personal conversation. March 3 and April 9, 2024.
3 Photograph. "The Lone Graves, Killed By Indians, Atlantic City, Wyo." W.B.D. and Annette B. Gray Papers Collection. AHC and the UW. Accession Number: 1053; Box 6, Folder 11.
4 Pfaff, Betty Carpenter. Telephone interview. Aug. 16, 2022.
5 Booth, Jacob. Oral history by the ACHS on Dec. 15, 1983, by Marjane Ambler. Pages 20-21. Transcription held at the SPCSHS. Accessed March 8, 2024.
6 "Personal." *WRM.* Feb. 21, 1898. O.S. Vol. XI. No. 23. Page 2. UW and Wyoming State Library. https://wyomingnewspapers.org. Accessed April 19, 2024.
7 "An Inventory of Wyoming Cemeteries." [Preliminary]. May 21, 1968. Daniel Y. Meschter papers. Collection 1974, Box #7. Atlantic City section. Page 1. AHC, UW. Accessed May 12, 2024; "Fremont County, Defunct Cemeteries," n.d. Unknown who compiled this document. Accessed Sept. 25, 2015. Mount Hope Cemetery. City of Lander.
8 "Pioneer Cemetery and Grave Inventory Form." The form is dated "Nov 1970," but lower on the page references a 1980 WSJ article. This form may have been compiled by Daniel Y. Meschter, but one attached and undated document from an unknown person stated "This cemetery was visited by Daniel Y. Meschter in 1970" even though in his preliminary report stated he visited here in 1968. Note: I have not been able to locate a final report. This attached document also listed a newspaper article published in 1982. Copy of this form and all attachments provided by Jean Mathisen Haugen. Nov. 13, 2015.
9 Pence, Mary Lou, and Lola M. Homsher. *Ghost Towns of Wyoming*. Hastings House, New York, 1956. Page 44.
10 Tax Assessment Roll. 1870. Handwritten card. SPCSHS. Take from the 1870 Carter County tax rolls located in Sweetwater County. Dec. 3, 2016.
11 "Died." *Daily Inter-Ocean*. Illinois. May 7, 1874. Page 8. University of Illinois Urbana-Champaign library. Accessed Jan. 21, 2015.
12 Williamson, Rosemary. "There are Time When Even Cowboys Must Cry." *WSJ*. July 1, 1982. Page B-1. Accessed Oct. 5, 2015.
13 Sommers, Jonita. *Williams Family History.* 2020. Unpublished manuscript. Page 13. Accessed April 22, 2016.
14 Attached to this document was another document entitled "Fremont County, Atlantic City #1 Cemetery," n.d. Paper copy received from Jean Mathisen Haugen. Nov. 13, 2015.
15 Williams, Emmett. *Williams Family History in Pictures by Emmett Williams.* December 2000. Unpublished manuscript. Page 58. Accessed April 22, 2016.
16 Sommers, Jonita. Re: Williams' family history. Personal conversation. April 22, 2016.

[17] The *Wyoming Mortality Schedule* lists ending in June 1870. Compiled by the ACHS. Sept. 26, 2015. Accessed October 9, 2015; Williamson, Rosemary. "There Are Times When Even Cowboys Must Cry." *WSJ*. July 1, 1982. Page B-1.
[18] Williamson, Rosemary. "There are Times When Even Cowboys Must Cry." *WSJ*. July 1, 1982. Page B-1.
[19] ibid.

CHAPTER 8: BURIED OUTSIDE ATLANTIC CITY

[1] 1969 Wyoming Territorial Census. Carter County. Line 1511. WSA. Ancestry.com. www.ancestry.com. Accessed June 16, 2024.
[2] Herman Barghafer. US Civil War Soldiers, 1861-1865. Film No. M390. Roll 2. Ancestry.com. www.ancestry.com. Accessed May 12, 2024; Baarghhafer, Herman. US Civil War Pension Index. NARA. 1861-1934. NAI No. 563268. Record Group Title: Records of the Department of Veterans Affair, 1773-2007. Record Group No. 15. Series No. T288. Roll 15. Ancestry.com. www.ancestry.com. Accessed May 12, 2024; US Veterans Administration Master Index, 1917-1940. NAI 76193916. Record Group 15. Records of the Department of Veterans Affairs, 1773-2007. National Archives at St. Louis, Missouri. Ancestry.com. www.ancestry.com. Accessed June 16, 2024.
[3] 1870 US Federal Census. Rock Creek Gulch. Line 28. Printed page 491. Database with images. FamilySearch. https://familysearch.org: 31 December 2023. Accessed Feb. 21, 2024. Citing NARA microfilm publication T9. Washington, D.C.: NARA, n.d.
[4] 1880 US Census. Sweetwater County. Near Shushownee [*sic*] and Bannock Indian Agency. Line 8. Page (written) No. 18. Enumeration District: 012. Roll 1454. Page 319b. Ancestry.com. www.ancestry.com. Accessed June 16, 2024.
[5] 1900 US Census. Fremont County. Lewiston Precinct. Line 10. Page No. A87. Sheet No. 5. Enumeration District: 29. Roll No. 1826. Page 5. Ancestry.com. www.ancestry.com. Accessed June 16, 2024.
[6] Accession No. MV-0776-196. Application No. 2257. Final Certificate No. 801. May 21, 1908. US Government Land Office. BLM. https://glorecords.blm.gov. Accessed May 12, 2024.
[7] Killed by Lightning." The *Miner*. June 2, 1916. Vol. X. No. 9. Page. 1; Barrghoffer, Herman (Harry Burk). Death Record. May 16, 1916. Certificate No. 517. WSA. Wyoming Marriage, Death, and Divorce Indices. Ancestry.com. www.ancestry.com. Accessed May 12, 2024.
[8] Killed by Lightning." The *Miner*. June 2, 1916. Vol. X. No. 9. Page. 1; Cook, Joseph. Oral History. ACHS. Interviewer: Marjane Ambler. May, 24, 1984. Pages 15-16. Transcript held at the SPCSHS. Accessed May 8, 2024.
[9] "Names of G.A.R. Veterans Buried in the Lander Cemetery." Herman Berghafer (Harry Burk). Line 29. July 27, 1992. Original document. Catalog No. 988.518.1. Fremont County Pioneer Museum. Accessed June 6, 2024; Barghofer, Herman. Mount Hope Cemetery. City of Lander, Wyo. Map data @2024 Imagery @2024 Airbus, CNES / Maxar Technologies, USDA/ FPAC/GEO. https://burialsearch.com/ecims#/s/145/Mount_Hope_Cemetery/1728. Accessed May 12, 2024.
[10] 1900 US Federal Census. South Pass Precinct. Enumeration District No. 29. Lines 57 and 58; 1910 US Federal Census. South Pass City. Enumeration District No. 65. Election District No. 4. Precinct 13. Line 41. Database with images. FamilySearch. https://familysearch.org : 31 December 2023. Accessed Feb. 21, 2024. Citing NARA microfilm publication T9. Washington, D.C.: NARA, n.d. Database with images. FamilySearch. https://familysearch.org: 31 December 2023. Accessed Feb. 21, 2024. Citing NARA microfilm publication T9. Washington, D.C.: NARA; Lane, Jon. Frank Barrett's burial place question. Email interview. Jan. 6, 2023.
[11] Sherlock, James L. *South Pass City and Its Tales*. Private Printing. 1978. Page 30; Sherlock, James L. Oral History by the ACHS, WSA and HD and/or the Wyoming State Historical Society. Interviewer Michael A. Massie. Dec. 10, 1986. Tape 3. Page 1. Transcript held at the SPCSHS. Accessed May 8, 2024.
[12] Information and photograph of the death notice, *WSJ*. Vol. IXL. No. 16. April 18, 1924. Page 1. Article supplied by Jon Lane. SPCSHS. Jan. 6, 2023; Sherlock, James L. Dec. 10, 1986. Tape 3. Oral History by the ACHS, WSA and HD and/or Wyoming State Historical Society. Interviewer Michael A. Massie. Page 1. Transcript held at the SPCSHS. Accessed May 8, 2024.
[13] Sherlock, James L. *South Pass City and Its Tales*. Private Printing. 1978. Page 30.
[14] "Joseph Basco." *WSJ*. March 30, 1939. Vol. 52. No. 31. Page 8.
[15] Handwritten tan-green index card. SPCSHS. Accessed Oct. 21, 2016. Original source unknown.
[16] "Friend of Joe Basco Tells of His Life." Peter Sherlock. *WSJ*. April 6, 1939. Vol. 52. No. 32. Page 2.

17 "Joseph Basco." *WSJ*. March 30, 1939. Paper copy of page, marked "Bascj-2-T." Folder "Basco, Joseph." SPCSHS. Accessed March 8, 2024; "Friend of Joe Basco Tells of His Life." Told by Peter Sherlock. *WSJ*. April 6, 1939. Vol. 52. No. 32. Page 2.

18 Pfaff, Betty Carpenter. *Fine Gold*. Private Printing. 1998. Chap. 6. Page 3; Mann, Albert. Oral history by the ACHS, WSA and HD and/or the Wyoming State Historical Society. Sept. 11, 1983. Interviewer David Geible. Page 24. Transcription held at the SPCSHS. Accessed March 8, 2024.

19 Sherlock, James L. Oral history, Part 2. Tape 2. ACHS, WSA and HD and/or the Wyoming State Historical Society. Nov. 15, 1985. Interviewer Michael A. Massie. Page 11. Transcription held at the SPCSHS. Accessed March 8, 2024.

20 Sherlock, James L. Oral history, Part 3. Tape 5. Mar. 31, 1987. ACHS, WSA and HD and/or the Wyoming State Historical Society. Dec 10, 1986, and Mar. 31, 1986. Interviewer Michael A. Massie. Page 7. Transcription held at the SPCSHS. Accessed March 8, 2024.

21 1930 US Federal Census. Atlantic City. County of Fremont. Election District 11. Enumeration District No. 7-13. Line 46. Digital images. Ancestry.com. www.ancestry.com. Accessed Nov. 20, 2015; "Poll Book of a Primary Election Held August 19, 1930." South Pass City. Election District No. 11. Polling Precinct No. 2. Line 9. "Registration Poll Book and Official Return of a General Election Held November 4, 1930." Election District No. 11. Election District No. 11. Polling Precinct No. 2. Line 23. Fremont County Elections Office. Accessed Aug. 2, 2019.

22 "Registration and Poll Book." Polling Precinct No. 2. Nov. 6, 1928. Line 5. Fremont County Elections Office. Accessed Aug. 2, 2019. Note: The location in the poll book was blank. Since many of the voters were of the Sherlock family, I believe this had taken place in South Pass City.

23 Betty Carpenter Pfaff. *Fine Gold*. Private printing. 1998. Chap. 51.

24 "Joseph Basco." *WSJ*. March 30, 1939. Paper copy of page, marked "Bascj-2-T." Folder "Basco, Joseph." SPCSHS. Accessed March 8, 2024

25 Certificate of Death. State of Wyoming. Bureau Vital Statistics. File No. 1939. Registered No. 438. Ancestry.com. https://ancestry.com. Accessed April 29, 2024.

26 Mount Hope Cemetery. Lander, Wyo. Maxar Technologies, USDA/FPAC/GEO. Map data 2022. Accessed April 28, 2022. https://burialsearch.com/ecims#/s/145/ Mount_Hope_Cemetery/7015.

27 Reviewing 1870 censuses in multiple areas, I can find no trace of "Mrs. Stewart."

28 "Married Records." Genealogy Trails History Group. Fremont County, Wyoming. Genealogy and History. Genealogytrails.com. https://genealogytrails.com/ wyo/fremont/marriages.html. Accessed Feb. 29, 2024; Certification of Marriage. Fincelius Burnett and Eliza Ann McCarty by Judge F. W. Wiswell. March 2, 1870. Ledger "Probate Court, H. A. Thompson." Pdf page 366. Ledger page 511. "sp_commerce_carter_co_1868_book_11.pdf." Accessed Sept 4, 2024.

29 David, Robert Beebe. *Finn Burnett, Frontiersman*. Mechanicsburg: Stackpole Books. 2003. Pages 235-256; "Enrollment Form, Wyoming Pioneers." WSA, Digital Collections. WPA Federal Writers Project. WPA Bio 121. Creator: Beryl M. Thompson. Cheyenne, Wyo. Feb. 24, 1939. Accessed April 10, 2024; Notes: Eliza's date of birth came from this Pioneer Enrollment document. Sources of Eliza's parents' name range from names-not-mentioned in Robert Beebe David's book, to mother's name not mentioned and father named Michael McCarty (McCarthy) on the "Enrollment Form, Wyoming Pioneers," to mother and father named on Ancestry.com.

30 Sherlock. James L. *South Pass and Its Tales*. Privately published. 1978. Page 92.

31 1870 US Federal Census. Atlantic City. County of Sweetwater. Sheet No. 457. Page No. 1. Lines 7 and 8. Digital images. Ancestry.com. www.ancestry.com. Accessed Nov. 20, 2015. Digital images, citing NARA microfilm publication.

32 "Enrollment Form, Wyoming Pioneers." WSA, Digital Collections. WPA Federal Writers Project. WPA Bio 121. Creator: Beryl M. Thompson. Cheyenne, Wyo. Feb. 24, 1939.

33 1880 US Federal Census. Big Popo Agie Valley. County of Sweetwater. Enumeration District No. 11. Sheet 306. Page 18. Lines 10-16. Digital images. Ancestry.com. www.ancestry.com. Accessed Feb. 29, 2024. Digital images, citing NARA microfilm publication.

34 David, Robert Beebe. *Finn Burnett, Frontiersman*. Mechanicsburg: Stackpole Books. 2003. Pages 223-256.

35 "Mrs. Eliza Ann Burnett Dies at San Joaquin." *The Fresno Morning Republican*. Fresno, Cal. June 7, 1924. Page 11. Newspapers.com. www.newspapers.com/article/the-fresno-morning-republican-obituary-f/55004008. Accessed March 1, 2024.

36 Funeral Home Record. Halsted and Company. San Diego. No. B-1283. No. 10. "California, US San Francisco Funeral Home Records, 1895-1985." Microfilm Publication, 1129 rolls.

(continued) Ancestry.com. Accessed Feb. 29, 2024; "Eliza Ann McCarty Burnett." Memorial ID: 75891823. Find a Grave.com. Accessed Feb. 29, 2024. www.findagrave.com/memorial/75891823/.

[37] 1850 US Federal Census. Canton. County of Lewis. Missouri. District No. 48. Page No. (penned) 82. Ancestry.com. www.ancestry.com. Accessed Feb. 29, 2024.

[38] "Burnett, F. G." Soldier Details. US Department of the Interior. National Park Service. www.nps.gov/civilwar/search-soldiers-detail.htm?soldierId=31EE3989-DC7A-DF11-BF36 -B8AC6F5D926A. Accessed June 27, 2024; "Fincelius G. Burnett." *Progressive Men of The State of Wyoming*. A. W. Bowen & Co., 1903. Pages 765-66.

[39] David, Robert Beebe. *Finn Burnett, Frontiersman*. Mechanicsburg: Stackpole Books. 2003. Pages 17-20.

[40] "Fincelius G. Burnett." *Progressive Men of The State of Wyoming*. A. W. Bowen & Co., 1903. Pages 765-66.

[41] I cannot locate Hallsville, not even a mention of it, in Carter County maps or current maps. It's likely this was short-lived settlement or later the name was changed; 1869 Wyoming Territory Census. Hallsville & Vicinity. Carter County, Wyoming. Line 54. Ancestry.com. https://www.ancestry.com. Accessed Feb. 29, 2024.

[42] "Married Records." Genealogy Trails History Group. Fremont County, Wyoming. Genealogy and History. Genealogytrails.com. Accessed Feb. 29, 2024. https://genealogytrails.com/ wyo/fremont/marriages.html; Certification of Marriage. Fincelius Burnett and Eliza Ann McCarty by Judge F. W. Wiswell. March 2, 1870. Ledger "Probate Court, H. A. Thompson." Pdf page 366. Ledger page 511. "sp_commerce_carter_co_1868_book_11.pdf." Accessed Sept 4, 2024.

[43] 1870 US Federal Census. Atlantic City. County of Sweetwater. Sheet No. 457. Page No. 1. Lines 7 and 8. Digital images. Ancestry.com. www.ancestry.com. Accessed Nov. 20, 2015. Digital images, citing NARA microfilm publication.

[44] 1880 US Federal Census. Big Popo Agie Valley. County of Sweetwater. Enumeration District No. 11. Sheet 306. Page 18. Lines 10-16. Digital images. *Ancestry.com*. www.ancestry.com. Accessed Feb. 29, 2024. Digital images, citing NARA microfilm publication.

[45] David, Robert Beebe. *Finn Burnett, Frontiersman*. Mechanicsburg: Stackpole Books. 2003. Pages 223-256; "Enrollment Form, Wyoming Pioneers." Electronic file. WSA, Digital Collections. WPA Federal Writers Project. WPA Bio 121. Creator: Beryl M. Thompson. Cheyenne, Wyo. Feb. 24, 1939. Accessed April 10, 2024.

[46] "Evanston as Convention City Makes Hit With Visitors." *Wyoming Press*. July 16, 1927. Vol. 29. Page 1. UW and Wyoming State Library. Access March 1, 2024. https://wyomingnewspapers.org; "Enrollment Form, Wyoming Pioneers." WSA, Digital Collections. WPA Federal Writers Project. WPA Bio 121. Creator: Beryl M. Thompson. Cheyenne, Wyo. Feb. 24, 1939. Accessed April 10, 2024.

[47] "Enrollment Form, Wyoming Pioneers." WSA, Digital Collections. WPA Federal Writers Project. WPA Bio 121. Creator: Beryl M. Thompson. Cheyenne, Wyo. Feb. 24, 1939. Access April 10, 2024.

[48] Funeral Home Record. Halsted and Company. San Diego. No. B-1283. No. 10. "California, US San Francisco Funeral Home Records, 1895-1985." Microfilm Publication, 1129 rolls. Ancestry.com. Accessed Feb. 29, 2024; "Fincelius G. Burnett." Memorial ID: 242393150. Findagrave.com. Accessed Feb. 29, 2024. Find a Grave. https://www.findagrave.com/ memorial/242393150/fincelius-g-burnett; Photo of Headstone. Cypress Lawn Memorial Park. Designed & Produced by MKJ Marketing. https://cemetery360.com/player/ ?lat=37.6756916651745&long=-122.451318552209. Accessed March 1, 2024.

[49] Pfaff, Betty Carpenter. *Changes*. Private printing. 2018. Page 69.

[50] 1900 US Federal Census. Victor Town. County of Teller. Precinct 35. Colorado. Enumeration District No. 134. Page (stamped) 260 A. Sheet No. 12. Line No. 40. Digital images. Ancestry.com. www.ancestry.com. Accessed Feb. 26, 2024. Digital images, citing NARA microfilm publication, T623, 1854 rolls.

[51] "Colorado, US, State and Federal Naturalization Records, 1868-1990." Naturalization Card File Index, Buckingham, John P-Corsberg, Carl G, Ca 1880-1906. Ancestry.com. www.ancestry.com. Accessed Feb. 26, 2024. Digital images, citing National Archives at Denver, Broomfield, Colorado. NARA microfilm publication, NAI No. 1307044. Record Group No. 85.

[52] Pfaff, Betty Carpenter. *Fine Gold*. 1998. Private printing. Chap. 50. Page 1. ———; *Changes*. 2018. Private printing. Page 108.

53 1910 US Federal Census. Atlantic City ("Lander Town" had been written in but a pen stroke crossed through it), Election District No. 4. Precinct 12. Fremont County. Enumeration District 65. Sheet No. 7A. Line 23. Digital images. Ancestry.com. www.ancestry.com. Accessed Nov. 20, 2015. Digital images, citing NARA microfilm publication.

54 Freeburgh, Melvin. Oral History by the ACHS, WSA and HD and/or the Wyoming State Historical Society. Interviewer David Geible. Jan. 28, 1984. Page 4. Transcript held at the SPCSHS. Accessed May 8, 2024.

55 Freeburgh, Melvin. Oral History by the ACHS, WSA and HD and/or the Wyoming State Historical Society. Interviewer David Geible. Jan. 28, 1984. Pages 5 and 6. Transcript held at the SPCSHS. Accessed May 8, 2024; Pfaff, Betty Carpenter. *Fine Gold*. Private Printing. 1998. Chap. 50. Page 2.

56 "Development is the Order of the Day." The *Miner*. July 15, 1910. Vol. 04. No. 15. Pages 1, 6. UW and Wyoming State Library. https://wyomingnewspapers.org. Accessed Feb. 26, 2024.

57 Klover, George W. Oral history by the ACHS, WSA and HD and/or the Wyoming State Historical Society. Sept. 4, 1983. Interviewer David Geible. Pages 8-9. Transcription held at the SPCSHS. Accessed March 8, 2024; Pfaff, Betty Carpenter. Oral history by the ACHS, WSA and HD and/or the Wyoming State Historical Society. Jan. 24, 1984. Interviewer Philippina Halstead. Page 19. Transcription held at the SPCSHS. Accessed March 8, 2024.

58 Roe, Clarence. Oral history by the ACHS, WSA and HD and/or the Wyoming State Historical Society. Jan. 28, 1984. Interviewer Marjane Ambler. Page 16. Transcription held at the SPCSHS. Accessed March 8, 2024.

59 "Of Local Interest." *WSJ*. Sept. 19, 1913. Vol. 31. No. 28. Page 1. UW and Wyoming State Library. https://wyomingnewspapers.org. Accessed Feb. 26, 2024.

60 "Explosives Licenses." The *Riverton Review*. May 7, 1918. Vol. 11. No. 47. Page 1. UW and Wyoming State Library. https://wyomingnewspapers.org. Accessed Feb. 26, 2024.

61 Pfaff, Betty Carpenter. *Atlantic City Nuggets*. Privately published. 1998. Page. 112.

62 *Abstract Mining Claims, Book F* (book with the spine cover torn off). Page 13. Fremont County Courthouse. County Clerk. Land Recording Office. Lander, Wyo. Accessed April 6, 2022; "The Atlantic Gold District, Fremont County, Wyoming." Arthur C. Spencer. Pages 9–45. The map showing her mine is immediately after page 22. "No. 40. Britannia." *The Atlantic Gold District and the North Laramie Mountains; Fremont, Converse, and Albany Counties. Wyoming*. Bulletin 626. Papers by Arthur C. Spencer. Dept. of the Interior. United States Geological Survey. Washington Government Printing Office. 1916.

63 Fuller, Zoie Green. Oral history by the ACHS, WSA and HD and/or the Wyoming State Historical Society. Jan. 4, 1984. Interviewer Philippina Halstead. Page 3. Transcription held at the SPCSHS. Accessed March 8, 2024.

64 1920 US Federal Census. Atlantic City. Election District 14. Enumeration District 15. Sheet No. 10B. Line 73; 1930 US Federal Census. County of Fremont. Election District 11. Enumeration 7-13. Sheet No. 1A, 232. Line 12. 1950 US Federal Census. Enumeration District 7-25. Line 10. Digital images. Ancestry.com. www.ancestry.com. Accessed Nov. 20, 2015. Digital images, citing NARA microfilm publication.

65 "Registration and Poll Book." Special Election. May 10, 1921. Atlantic City. Election District No. 14. Polling Precinct 1. Line 9; "Poll Book." Aug. 17, 1926. Primary Election. Election District No. 12. Polling Precinct No. 1. Line 6; "Poll Book of a Primary Election Held August 19, 1930." Atlantic City. Election District No. 11. Polling Precinct No. 1. Line 23; "Registration Poll Book and Official Return of a General Election Held November 4, 1930." Election District No. 11. Polling Precinct No. 1. Line 16. Fremont County Elections Office. Accessed Aug. 2, 2019.

66 James Wallace Carpenter. Oral History by the ACHS, WSA and HD and/or the Wyoming State Historical Society. Jan. 23, 1984. Interviewer Philippina Halstead. Page 13. Transcription held at the SPCSHS. Accessed March 8, 2024.

67 "Certificate of Death." James Cassie. Registration District No. 7097. Registrar's No. 10099. State of California—Department of Health. Received the certificate courtesy of the Antelope Valley Genealogical Society. Feb. 26, 2024; "James Cassie." Memorial ID 12793240. Find a Grave. www.findagrave.com. Accessed Feb. 26, 2024.

68 Pfaff, Betty Carpenter. *Fine Gold*. Private Printing. 1998. Chap. 50. Pages 2-4.

69 1850 US Federal Census. Conneaut Town. County of Crawford. Pennsylvania. Lines 5-8. Digital images by NARA. Ancestry.com. www.ancestry.com. Accessed April 28, 2024.

70 *WSJ*. Oct. 6, 1922. Vol. XXXIX (39). No. 40. Page 1. Lander Library. Accessed April 30, 2024.

71 Nottage, Emma Cheney. "Ervin Franklin Cheney," n.d. Typed E. F. Cheney history. Page 2. Folder "Cheney, E. F." Collections Department. Fremont County Pioneer Museum. Accessed June 5, 2024.

72 "The Battle of Malvern Hill." US Department of the Interior. National Park Service. Accessed April 29, 2024. www.nps.gov; "Malvern Hill." American Battlefield Trust. Accessed April 29, 2024. www.battlefields.org/learn/civil-war/battles/malvern-hill; Coutant, C. G. *History of Wyoming: From the Earliest Known Discoveries. In Three Volumes.* Chaplin, Spafford & Mathison, 1899. Page 673; 1890 Veterans' Schedule. *Special Schedule-Surviving Soldiers, Sailors, and Marines, and Widows.* Page 3. Line 16. Ancestry.com. www.ancestry.com. Accessed Dec. 9, 2015. Digital images, citing NARA microfilm publication; Nottage, Emma 72 Cheney. "Ervin Franklin Cheney," n.d. Typed E. F. Cheney history. Pages 1 and 2. Folder "Cheney, E. F." Collections Department. Fremont County Pioneer Museum. Accessed June 5, 2024; Baker, J. C., General. Letter to Mr. William F. McAleenan, Director of Fremont County Pioneer Museum. Mar. 18, 1971. Folder "Cheney." M-800, A26 Box 2. Fremont County Pioneer Museum; 1890 "Special Schedule-Surviving Soldiers, Sailors, and Marines, and Widows, etc." Line 16. National Archives at Washington D.C. Series No. M123. Record Group No. 15. Ancestry.com. https://ancestry.com. Accessed April 28, 2024.

73 "Elnathan Sanderson "Nathan" Cheney. Memorial ID# 21599699. Find a Grave. www.findagrave.com. Accessed April 28, 2024; "Notice to Creditors." *WSJ.* Oct. 25, 1918. Vol. 35. No. 52. Page 2. Elnathan acted as executor to Sylvia Amira Mikkelson.

74 1869 Wyoming Territory Census. "Establishing Wyoming Territory." WyomingHistory.org, Wyoming Historical Society. Original data from WSA. Line 1,115. Ancestry.com. www.ancestry.com. Accessed March 7, 2024.

75 "Poll List." Atlantic City. Carter County. Territory of Wyoming. Sept. 2, 1869. Page 3. Line 187. Paper and electronic copies. Carl Hallberg. WSA. Aug. 22, 2022.

76 Coutant, C. G. *The History of Wyoming: From the Earliest Known Discoveries, In Three Volumes.* Chaplin, Spafford & Mathison, 1899. Page 662, 673; Koch, Hugo. "True Tales of the Old Timers, The Cow War." *Lander Eagle* and *Riverton News.* March 17, 1911. Vol. 1. No. 9. UW and Wyoming State Library. https://wyomingnewspapers.org. Accessed May 27, 2024.

77 1870 US Federal Census. Atlantic City. County of Sweetwater. Page 21. Line 21. Digital images. Ancestry.com. www.ancestry.com. Accessed Nov. 20, 2015.

78 Spurlock, Barbara. "Ervin Franklin Cheney. Skill, courage helped dreams come true." *WSJ.* Pioneer Days Edition. July 3, 1985. Page F-2; Mable Cheney Moudy's account, likely relayed by E. F. Cheney himself, is included in her document "Supplement to my Sister Emma's [Emma Cheney Nottage] History of Our Father's Life, Plus Other History in Wyoming," n.d. Page 4; Emma Cheney Nottage's paper entitled "Ervin Franklin Cheney," n.d. Copies of both documents are located in the Fremont County Pioneer Museum, Collection Department. Accessed June 11, 2024; Nottage, Emma Cheney. "Ervin Franklin Cheney," n.d. Page 5. Folder "Cheney, E. F." Collections Department. Fremont County Pioneer Museum. Accessed June 5, 2024; Trevor, Marjorie C. (1954). *History of Carter-Sweetwater County, Wyoming to 1875.* [Master's thesis, UW.] ProQuest Dissertations & Theses. Printed pages 73-4; pdf pages 81-82.

80 Poll Books. 1869, 1871, 1872 poll books. Sweetwater County Historical Museum. Green River, Wyo. Accessed Jan. 11, 2017; Poll results. Atlantic City. 1871. Territory of Wyoming. Paper and electronic copies. Carl Hallberg. WSA. Aug. 25, 2021; Poll Book of a Primary Election Held August 19, 1930." Atlantic City. Election District No. 11. Polling Precinct No. 1. Line 5. "Registration Poll Book and Official Return of a General Election Held November 4, 1930. Election District No. 11. Polling Precinct No. 1. Line 9. Fremont County Elections Office. Accessed Aug. 2, 2019; Beach, Cora M. "Mrs. Ervin F. Cheney." *Women of Wyoming.* Vol. I. S. E. Boyer & Company, 1927. Pages 148-50.

81 "Details for Marriage ID#265789. Western States Marriage Record Index. BYU-Idaho Special Collections. David O. McKay Library, Idaho. https://abish.byui.edu. Accessed April 28, 2024.

82 Nottage, Emma Cheney. "Ervin Franklin Cheney," n.d. Typed E. F. Cheney history. Page 6. Folder "Cheney, E. F."; Moudy, Mable Wyoming Cheney. "Supplement to my Sister Emma's History of our Father's Life, Plus Other History in Wyoming," n.d. Three-ring Binder. Collections Department. Fremont County Pioneer Museum. Accessed June 5, 2024.

83 1910 US Federal Census. Beebe. County of Fremont. Precinct 20. Election District No. 4. Enumeration District No. 64. Sheet No. 9B. Lines 73 and 74. Digital images. Ancestry.com. www.ancestry.com. Accessed April 28, 2024.

84 "Death of Mr. Cheney." WSJ. *WSJ.* Oct. 6, 1922. Vol. XXXIX (39). No. 40. Page 1. Lander Library. Accessed April 30, 2024.

85 "Certificate of Death." Ervin Franklin Cheney. State of Wyoming. Bureau of Vital Statistics. File No. 1922. Registered No. 1455. Ancestry.com. www.ancestry.com. Accessed April 28, '2024; Mount Hope Cemetery. City of Lander. Mount Hope Cemetery. City of Lander, Wyo. Map data @2024 Imagery @2024 Airbus, CNES / Maxar Technologies, USDA/FPAC/GEO. Accessed April 22, '2024. https://burialsearch.com/ecims#/s/145/Mount_Hope _Cemetery/1947, 1992.

86 Burial Search, Mount Hope Cemetery. City of Lander, Wyo. Map data 2022. https://burialsearch.com/ecims#/s/145/Mount_Hope_Cemetery/6518. Accessed April 10, 2022.

87 *WSJ*. Vol. XXXVI, No. 34. June 20, 1919. Page 6.

88 Certificate of Death. State of Wyoming. Bureau Vital Statistics. File No. 1919. Registered No. 1113. *Ancestry.com*. https://ancestry.com. Accessed April 29, 2024.

89 Pfaff, Betty Carpenter. *Changes*. Private printing. 2018. Page 56.

90 *Benson-Coolidge Funeral Records, 1918-1947*. Fremont County Library System, Riverton branch. GEN 929.1 BENSON. Accessed Aug. 2, 2019; Betty Carpenter Pfaff. *Fine Gold*. Privately published. Chap. 6. Page 5.

91 Pfaff, Betty Carpenter. *Fine Gold*. Private printing. 1998. Chap. 6; *Changes*. Private printing. 2018. Page 49. Referenced article is not known.

92 1900 US Federal Census. Atlantic Precinct. Enumeration District No. 29. Page A83. Lines 24 and 25; 1910 US Federal Census. Atlantic City. Precinct 12. Enumeration District No. 65. Sheet No. 7A. Lines 33 and 34. 1920 US Federal Census. (Lander Town had been written in but lined out.) Election District #14. Enumeration District No. 57. Sheet No. 11A; 1930 US Federal Census. Election District 11. Enumeration District No. 7-13. Sheet No. 1A. Lines 13-15. Database with images. FamilySearch. https://FamilySearch.org: 31 December 2023. Accessed Feb. 21, 2024. Citing NARA microfilm publication T9. Washington, D.C.: NARA, n.d.

93 "Certificate of Death." State of Wyoming. Bureau Vital Statistics. File No. 1935. Registered No. 2177. Ancestry.com. https://ancestry.com. Accessed April 29, 2024; Pfaff, Betty Carpenter. *Changes*. Privately published. 2018. Page 60.

94 Burial Search, Mount Hope Cemetery. City of Lander, Wyo. Map data 2022. Accessed April 10, 2022. https://burialsearch.com/ecims#/s/145/Mount_Hope_Cemetery/6418 (Emma) and /6520 (Lawrence); Photo of the Giesslers and Edna and Dorothy Dohm Giessler, circa 1925: SPCSHS. Server "Public" folder, subfolder SPC2019, subfolder "Gaylin Carpenter 1-20-2017." Photos entitled "Giesslers_0001" and Giesslers_0002." Donated by Gaylin Carpenter. Accessed August 22, 2022.

95 "Atlantic City Mercantile." NAID: 73730344. Reference No. 85000869. National Register of Historic Places. https://catalog.archives.gov/id/73730344. Accessed Feb. 27, 2024.

96 1880 Wyoming Territory Census. Beaver. Sweetwater County. Enumeration District 11. Page 599 (written). Line No. 10. Image Group 004244782. Image 611; 1880 Wyoming Territory Census. Willow Creek. Sweetwater County. Enumeration District 11. Page 303A. Line 10. Image Group 004244782. Image Group 004244782. Image 614; for both censuses Enumerator H.G. Nickerson. *FamilySearch*. www.familysearch.org. Accessed June 8, 2024.

97 Mann, Albert. Oral history by the ACHS, WSA and HD and/or the Wyoming State Historical Society. Sept. 11, 1983. Interviewer David Geible. Page 24. Transcription held at the SPCSHS. Accessed March 8, 2024.

98 Moerer, Lyle F. Wyoming State Historical Society. Dec. 8, 1983. Interviewer Philippina Halstead. Pages 1, 4, 5-6. Transcription held at the SPCSHS. Accessed March 8, 2024.

99 Marrin, Laura Green. Oral history by the WSA and HD and/or the Wyoming State Historical Society. Aug. 7, 1987. Interviewer Michael A. Massie. Page 13. Transcription held at the SPCSHS. Accessed March 8, 2024.

100 "Poll Book." South Pass City precinct. Nov. 2, 1880. Line 10. Sweetwater County Historical Museum. Accessed Jan. 11, 2017; "Poll Book." Aug. 17, 1926. Primary Election. Election District No. 12. Polling Precinct No. 1. Line 8. Fremont County Elections Office. Accessed Aug. 2, 2019.

101 Pfaff, Betty Carpenter. *Changes*. Privately published. 2018. Page 57.

102 "Certificate of Death." Lawrence Giessler. State of Wyoming. Bureau Vital Statistics. File No. 1929. Registered No. 946. Ancestry.com. https://ancestry.com. Accessed April 29, 2024.

103 *Benson-Coolidge Funeral Records*. Riverton branch of Fremont County Library. GEN 929.1 BENSON 1918-1947; Pfaff, Betty Carpenter. *Fine Gold*. Privately published. 1998. Chap. 6. *Atlantic City Nuggets*. Pages 26-27, 30. Privately published. 1978. Chap. 6; "Certificate of Death." State of Wyoming. Bureau Vital Statistics. File No. 1929. Registered No. 946.

(continued) Ancestry.com. https://ancestry.com. Accessed April 29, 2024; *Shoshoni Enterprise*, No. 6, June 21, 1929, page 4. UW and Wyoming State Library. https://wyomingnewspapers.org. Accessed Aug. 28, 2015; Mount Hope Cemetery. City of Lander, Wyo. Map data @2024 Imagery @2024 Airbus, CNES / Maxar Technologies, USDA/FPAC/GEO. Accessed Feb. 22, 2024. https://burialsearch.com/ecims#/s/145/Mount_Hope_Cemetery/6520.

104 "Certificate of Death." Lawrence Giessler. State of Wyoming. Bureau Vital Statistics. File No. 1929. Registered No. 946. Ancestry.com. https://ancestry.com. Accessed April 29, 2024.

105 1880 Wyoming Territory Census. Willow Creek. Sweetwater County. Enumeration District 11. Page 303A. Line 10. Enumerator H.G. Nickerson. Image Group 004244782. Image Group 004244782. Image 614. FamilySearch. www.familysearch.org. Accessed June 8, 2024.

106 "Death Certificate." William Giessler. File No. 1916. Registered No. 1256 (The stamped No. 2394 had been lined out with red ink). State of Wyoming. Bureau of Vital Statistics. WSA. Ancestry.com. www.ancestry.com. Accessed June 8, 2024.

107 Meier, Michael T. "Civil War Draft Records: Exemptions and Enrollments." *Prologue Magazine*. Winter 1994. Vol. 26. No. 4. National Archives. www.archives.gov/publications/prologue/1994/winter/civil-war-draft-records.html. Accessed June 28, 2024.

108 New York, U.S., Civil War Muster Roll Abstracts, 1861-1900 for William B. Gratrix. Box #: 572. Page 857. Microfilm, 1185 rolls. New York State Archives. Ancestry.com. Accessed Dec. 7, 2024. Note: this form stated William Gratrix left the Army on May 30, 1865.

109 Golliher, Alma Williams. Oral history by the ACHS, WSA and HD and/or the Wyoming State Historical Society. June 30, 1984. Interviewer David Geible. Page 1. Transcription held at the SPCSHS. Accessed March 8, 2024.

110 1890 Veterans Schedule. "Special Schedule.—Surviving Soldiers, Sailors, and Marines, and Widows, etc. S.D.: of Wyo.; E.D.: 14; Minor Civil Division: Wyoming." Page 3. Line 35. Accessed Dec. 9, 2015; US, "Civil War Pension Index: General Index to Pension Files, 1861-1934." NARA. NAIA No. 563268. Record Group No.: 15. Series No. T288. Roll, 183. Accessed Feb 28, 2024. Ancestry.com. www.ancestry.com. Digital images, NARA microfilm publication.

111 Mionczynski, John. Gratrix's cabin. Personal interview March 3, 2024; Photograph: A man possibly named Richards stands at the Quaking Aspen Hut Crossing Cabin. 1943. Photographer: Walter Marsh. Fremont County Pioneer Museum. Accessed May 7, 2024.

112 Golliher, Alma Williams. Oral history (a series). Interviewer Rosemary Williamson. 1977. Page 6. Transcription held at the SPCSHS. Accessed March 8, 2024.

113 "The South Pass Gold Discoveries, 1842-1869." *WRM*. Vol. X. No. 2. Page 21. Fremont County Pioneer Museum; Photo: Quaking Aspen Hut Crossing Cabin. 1943. Photographer: Walter Marsh. Cabinet A1, Box 3. Catalog No. 980.52.36. Electronic file by Randy Wise, May 7, 2024. Fremont County Museums, Lander Pioneer Museum.

114 Preston, Donald A. "Unique Record Made by Wyoming Pioneer." July 7, 1917. Paper copy in black binder. St. Andrew's Episcopal Church. Accessed May 20, 2023.

115 Mionczynski, John. Shoshoni history and Gratrix's cabin and history. Personal interview. March 3 and Aug. 15, 2024; Photographed and included in this book with permission by Bonnie and Scott Robinson. Aug. 17, 2024.

116 Indenture. William B. Gratrix, et al, to Merritt Thompson. Signed Sept. 29, 1884. *Quit Claim Record Book A*. Pages 3-5. Fremont County Clerk's Office. Land Recording Office.

117 Pfaff, Betty Carpenter. *Fine Gold*. Privately published. 1998. Chap. 7; "Agreement." For transferring possession of the Britannia Gold Lode Mining Claim. Sept. 25, 1905. Folder "William 'Buck' Gratrix. Cabinet A1, Box 3. Fremont County Pioneer Museum. Accessed June 5, 2024.

118 "Grand Army of the Republic." Fremont County, Wyoming. Genealogy and History. Genealogy Trails Group. https://genealogytrails.com/wyo/fremont/gar.html. Accessed Oct. 14, 2020.

119 "Poll Book." Atlantic City. Sweetwater County. Nov. 2, 1880. Line 5; "Official Return"; Sweetwater County Historical Museum. Accessed Jan. 11, 2017.

120 "Poll Book." June 14, 1881. Miners Delight Precinct. Sweetwater County. Line 9. Sweetwater County Historical Museum. Accessed Jan. 11, 2017; "Tally List." Election. Miners Delight. June 14, 1881. Paper and electronic copies. Carl Hallberg. WSA. Accessed Aug. 22, 2022; "Local Overflow." *Lander Clipper, WSJ*. July 21, 1911. Vol. 29. No. 46. Page 3. UW and Wyoming State Library. https://wyomingnewspapers.org. Accessed May 27, 2024.

121 1870 US Federal Census. Rock Creek Gulch. County of Sweetwater. Line 8; 1880 US Federal Census. Atlantic City. County of Sweetwater. Sheet 209. Page 5. Line 7; 1900 US Federal Census. Atlantic Precinct. Sheet No. 1B. line 88.; 1910 US Federal Census. Atlantic City. Precinct 12. Enumeration District No. 65. Sheet No. 7A. Lines 8 and 9.

122 1920 US Federal Census. National Military Home. Malibu Township. County of Los Angeles, CA. Enumeration District: 486. Sheet No. 15B. Line 80. NARA microfilm publication T625, 2076 rolls; 1930 US Federal Census. Los Angeles, Cal. National Home Township. Pacific Branch National Military Home. Enumeration District 19-118. Sheet 34B. Lines 85-87. Digital images. Ancestry.com. www.ancestry.com. Accessed Feb. 28, 2024. Digital images, citing NARA microfilm publication.

123 1920 US Federal Census. County of Cook. Chicago City. Illinois. Enumeration District No. 888. Page 1B. Roll: T625_325. Jacob Brady. Line 80. Ancestry.com. Accessed Aug. 1, 2024; 1940 US Federal Census. Murray Judicial Township. Alameda, Cal. US Veterans Hospital No. 102. Enumeration District 1-69. Jacob Brodey. Line 37. Roll: m-t0627-00186. Page 5A. Ancestry.com. Accessed Aug. 1, 2024; Brodey, Jacob. National Homes for Disabled Volunteer Soldiers, 1866-1938. Series: M1749. Page 18905. Ancestry.com. Accessed Aug. 1, 2024; 1920 US Federal Census. County of Santa Barbara. City Santa Barbara 2nd Precinct, Cal. Enumeration District No. 87. Page 3A. Roll: T625_146. George Manning. Line 7. Ancestry.com. Accessed Aug. 1, 2024; Manning, George E. National Homes for Disabled Volunteer Soldiers, 1866-1938. Series: M1749. Page 25566. Ancestry.com. Accessed Aug. 1, 2024.

124 Standard Certificate of Death. "California, County Birth and Death Records, 1800-1994" FamilySearch (https://www.familysearch.org/ark:/61903/1:1:QG15-65L9: Sat Mar 09 00:54:48 UTC 2024), Entry for William B Gratrix, 27 January 1932. Accessed Aug. 1, 2024.

125 Nationwide Gravesite Locator. National Cemetery Administration. US Department of Veterans Affairs. https://www.cem.va.gov/nationwide-gravesite-locator/. Accessed May 7, 2024.

126 Mann, Albert. Oral history by the ACHS, WSA and HD and/or the Wyoming State Historical Society. Sept. 11, 1983. Interviewer David Geible. Page 8. Transcription held at the SPCSHS. Accessed March 8, 2024.

127 "William Harris Murdered." WRM. Sept. 23, 1910. Vol. 25. No. 47. Page 1. UW and Wyoming State Library. https://wyomingnewspapers.org. Accessed April 23, 2023.

128 WSJ. Vol. 29, No. 38. May 19, 1911. Page 1. UW and Wyoming State Library. https://wyomingnewspapers.org. Accessed April 19, 2023.

129 "Seven Convicted Receive Sentence." The Lander Eagle. June 16, 1911. Vol. 1, No. 22. Page 1. UW and Wyoming State Library. https://wyomingnewspapers.org. Accessed April 23, 2023.

130 Certificate of Death. William H. Harris. File No. 1910. Registered No. 1030. Received mailed paper copy on Feb. 21, 2024. WSA. Carl Hallberg; Electronic file, Ancestry.com. www.ancestry.com. Accessed Mar. 29, 2024.

131 Mount Hope Cemetery. City of Lander, Wyo. Map data @2024 Imagery @2024 Airbus, CNES/Maxar Technologies, USDA/FPAC/GEO. Accessed Feb. 22, 2024. https://burialsearch.comecims #/s/145/Mount_Hope_Cemetery/4917.

132 Bascom Skaggs Still at Large." The Kemmerer Republican. Oct. 9, 1914. Vol. 2. No. 7. Page 1. UW and Wyoming State Library. https://wyomingnewspapers.org. Accessed April 19, 2023.

133 1869 Wyoming Territory Census. Carter County. "Establishing Wyoming Territory." WyomingHistory.org. Wyoming Historical Society. Original data from WSA. Lines 1,099–1,103. Ancestry.com. https://ancestry.com. Accessed April 12, 2024.

134 Permissions to use Frank's photograph were given by family member Pat Saltgaver, Jan. 31, 2020, via Findagrave.com messaging system and by personal email; and Lynn Zerbe, January 27, 2020, through the Ancestry.com messaging system.

135 Dr. Francis Hastings Harrison had a practice on "C" Street in Atlantic City. Huseas, Marion McMillan. Sweetwater Gold: Wyoming's Gold Rush 1867-1871. Mortimore Publishing, 1991. Page 122; South Pass News. April 9, 1870, No. 56, August 31, 1870. No. 4. Page 2. UW and Wyoming State Library. Access Sep. 25, 2015; Cheyenne Daily Leader. April 4, 1870. Vol. III. No. 193. Page 1. Chronicling America: Historic American Newspapers. Library of Congress. Accessed April 18, 2023. https://chroniclingamerica.loc.gov/data/batches/wyu_diamondville_vero5/data/sn84022149/00514150096/1870040401/0433.pdf; Sherlock, James L. South Pass and Its Tales. Vantage Press. 1978. Page 127.

136 Golliher, Alma Williams. Oral history by the ACHS, WSA and HD and/or the Wyoming State Historical Society. June 30, 1984. Interviewer David Geible. Pages 21-22. Transcription held at the SPCSHS. Accessed March 8, 2024. Alma Golliher was born after Frank's murder, so it's likely this description and information was told to her by her pioneer parents, Maude Huff Williams and Henry Williams, who lived in Atlantic City at that time.

137 "Young Frank Irwin." WSJ. April 26, 1933. Vol. 46. No. 36. Page 3.

138 "Obituary." Below the obituary for sister Hannah Gertrude Stephenson, Frank Irwin's obituary was included. *Fremont Clipper.* Oct. 15, 1887. No. 8. Page 3. UW and Wyoming State Library. https://wyomingnewspapers.org. Accessed Sept. 27, 2015.

139 *Dangerous Duty; A History of Frontier Forts in Fremont County, Wyoming.* John D. McDermott. The Fremont County Historic Preservation Commission. 1993. Page 98; Murphy, John D. "Old Folks Interviewed." *Fremont Clipper.* October 8, 1887. No. 7, Page 3. Accessed Sept. 27, 2015; *Fremont Clipper.* Oct. 15, 1887. No. 8. Page 3. Accessed April 9, 2015. UW and Wyoming State Library. https://wyomingnewspapers.org; Wyoming Mortality Schedule ending June 1870.

140 "Fremont County, Defunct Cemeteries," n.d. Unknown who compiled this document. Accessed Sept. 25, 2015. Mount Hope Cemetery Office. City of Lander.

141 1870 US Federal Census. Atlantic City. County of Sweetwater. Page No. (stamped) 460. Page No. (penned) 6, line 14. Digital images. Ancestry.com. www.ancestry.com. Accessed Nov. 20, 2015. Digital images, citing NARA microfilm publication.

142 ACHS members from various oral histories, newspapers, letters, etc.; Burial Search, Mount Hope Cemetery. Lander, Wyo. Map data 2022. https://burialsearch.com/ecims#/s/145/Mount_Hope_Cemetery/218. Accessed April 10, 2022.

143 Hein, Rebecca. *Three Mixed-race Families and a Wagon Trail Attack: A Story of Frontier Survival.* Wyoming Historical Society. WyoHistory.org. www.wyohistory.org/essays/wagon-train-attack-story-frontier-survival. Accessed Nov. 11, 2015.

144 The *Pinedale Roundup*, September 10, 1931, page 7. UW and Wyoming State Library. https://wyomingnewspapers.org. Accessed Dec. 4, 2016.

145 *Wyoming, US Death Records, 1909-1960.* Ancestry.com. www.ancestry.com. Accessed April 28, 2022; "Cemetery Records Index," n.d. Fremont County Clerk. Accessed March 3, 2022.

146 "Poll Book of a Primary Election Held August 19, 1930." Atlantic City. Election District No. 11. Polling Precinct No. 1. Line 5. "Registration Poll Book and Official Return of a General Election Held November 4, 1930. Election District No. 11. Polling Precinct No. 1. Line 9. Fremont County Elections Office. Accessed Aug. 2, 2019.

147 1930 US Federal Census. Election District #11. Enumeration District No. 7-13. Sheet No. 1B. Line 55. Ancestry.com. www.ancestry.com. Accessed April 28, 2002. Digital images, citing NARA microfilm publication.

148 "Certificate of Death." Bureau Vital Statistics. State of Wyoming. File No. 1931. Registered No. 1337. WSA. Ancestry.com. www.ancestry.com. Accessed April 29, 2024.

149 Burial Search, Mount Hope Cemetery. Lander, Wyo. Map data 2022. https://burialsearch.com/ecims#/s/145/Mount_Hope_Cemetery/7810. Accessed Dec. 4, 2016.

150 "Colorado Gold Rush." Encyclopedia staff. Colorado Encyclopedia. Accessed June 28, 2024. https://coloradoencyclopedia.org/article/colorado-gold-rush#id-field-author. Adapted from Carl Abbott, Stephen J. Leonard, and Thomas J. Noel. *Colorado: A History of the Centennial State*, 5th ed. Boulder: University Press of Colorado, 2013; and Robert R. Crifasi. *A Land Made from Water.* Boulder: University Press of Colorado, 2015.

151 *Special Schedule-Surviving Soldiers, Sailors, and Marines, and Widows.* S.D. of Wyo.; E.D.: 14. Line 44. Ancestry.com. www.ancestry.com. Accessed April 28, 2024. Digital images, citing NARA microfilm publication.

152 "John Pelon Dead." *WRM.* Feb. 7, 1912 [sic, should have been 1913]. Vol. 28. No. 33. Page 1. UW and Wyoming State Library. https://wyomingnewspapers.org. Accessed March 30, 2024; Murphy, John R. "Indian Raids of '69 and'70 on Settlers in Lander Valley Told by First Little Popo Agie Rancher." Originally printed in three installments in the *Fremont Clipper.* Oct. 8, Oct. 15, Oct 22, 1887. Page 3. From microfilm. Reprinted in the *WSJ.* April 4, 1928. Vol. 44. No. 32. Pages 1 and 6.

153 1870 US Federal Census. South Pass City. County of Sweetwater. Line 6. Database with images. FamilySearch. https://FamilySearch.org: 31 December 2023. Accessed Feb. 21, 2024. Citing NARA microfilm publication T9. Washington, D.C.: NARA, n.d.

154 "Certificate of the Register of the Land Office at Evanston, Wyoming Territory." State Volume Patent. Accession No. WY0220___.07. John Pelon. Homestead Certificate No. 44. Application No 29. July 22, 1890. US Department of the Interior. Bureau of Land Management. Government Land Office. https://glorecords.blm.gov. Accessed March 31, 2024.

155 Lease Agreement. John Pelon to John C. Hickey, Trustee." Book *Miscellaneous Records, Vol. C.* Dated 5-5-[19]06 – 4-9-1908. No. 8568. Page 168-70. Signed Jan. 5, 1906. Filed on May 5, 1906. Fremont County Clerk's Office. Land Recording Office. Accessed April 3, 2024.

156 1910 US Federal Census. Beebe. County of Fremont. Precinct 20. Election District No. 4. Enumeration District No. 64. Sheet No. 9B. Line 67. Digital images. Ancestry.com. www.ancestry.com. Accessed April 28, 2024.

157 "John Pelon Dead." *WRM*. Dated Feb. 7, 1912 [sic, 1913]. Vol. 28. No. 33. Page 1; "John Pelon, Pioneer Passes Away Tuesday." *WSJ*. Feb. 7, 1913. Vol. 31. No. 23. Page 1. UW and Wyoming State Library. https://wyomingnewspapers.org. Access March 30, 2024.

158 Mount Hope Cemetery. City of Lander, Wyo. Map data @2024 Imagery @2024 Airbus, CNES/Maxar Technologies, USDA/FPAC/GEO. https://burialsearch.com/ecims#/s/145/Mount _Hope_Cemetery/2677. Accessed Mar. 30, 2024.

159 Klover, George W. Oral history by the ACHS, WSA and HD and/or the Wyoming State Historical Society. Sept. 4, 1983. Interviewer David Geible. Page 3. Transcription held at the SPCSHS. Accessed March 8, 2024.

160 1910 US Federal Census. Atlantic City. Precinct 12. Enumeration District No. 66. Sheet No. 7A. Lines 27 and 28. Digital images. Ancestry.com. www.ancestry.com. Accessed Nov. 20, 2015. Digital images, citing NARA microfilm publication.

161 Pfaff, Betty Carpenter. *Changes*. Privately published. 2018. Page 57; "Tim Bah-Bah Placer Claims Sold to Tacoma Men for Spring Dredging." *WSJ*. Vol. 40. No. 50. Page 1.

162 "Registration and Poll Book." Special Election. May 10, 1921. Atlantic City. Election District No. 14. Polling Precinct 1. Line 2; "Poll Book." Aug. 17, 1926. Primary Election. Election District No. 12. Polling Precinct No. 1. Line 15. "Poll Book of a Primary Election Held August 19, 1930." Atlantic City. Election District No. 11. Polling Precinct No. 1. Line 2; "Registration Poll Book and Official Return of a General Election Held November 4, 1930." Election District No. 11. Polling Precinct No. 1. Line 4. Fremont County Elections Office. Accessed Aug. 2, 2019.

163 "Charles Sypes Succumbed to Deadly Fumes While Repairing tire in a Garage at Country Ranch." *Lander Evening Post*. March 3, 1936. Vol. 18. No. 53. Page 1.

164 Certificate of Death. State of Wyoming. Bureau Vital Statistics. File No. 1936. Registered No. 474. Ancestry.com. https://ancestry.com. Accessed April 29, 2024.

165 Pfaff, Betty Carpenter. *Fine Gold*. Privately published. 1998.

166 "Funeral Service for Charles Sypes Here on Thursday." *Lander Evening Post*. March 4, 1936. Page 1; Mount Hope Cemetery. City of Lander, Wyo. Map data @2024 Imagery @2024 Airbus, CNES / Maxar Technologies, USDA/FPAC/GEO. Accessed Feb. 21, 2024. https://burialsearch.com/ecims#/s/145/Mount_Hope_Cemetery/4333.

167 "SW County Marriage Index, Reverse L to End, Book 1&2 or A&B, Book 3 or C through p43." Sweetwater County pdf file. Pdf page 165. Ledger pages not numbered. SPCSHS. Server. Accessed Dec. 17, 2019.

168 1880 Wyoming Territory Census. Iahies Fork. Sweetwater County. Lines 2-4. Enumeration District 12. Page 8 (written). Image 614. Image Group 004244782. FamilySearch. www.familysearch.org. Accessed June 8, 2024. This location cannot be found on a map.

169 *WSJ*. Vol. 23, No. 52. July 22, 1910. Page 1. UW and Wyoming State Library. https://wyomingnewspapers.org. Accessed April 19, 2023.

170 "Certificate of Death." State of Wyoming. Bureau Vital Statistics. File No. 1910. Registered No. 1019. Ancestry.com. https://ancestry.com. Accessed April 29, 2024.

171 The *Miner*. No. 17. July 29, 1910. Page 8; the *Wyoming Semi-Weekly Tribune*. July 29, 1910 No. 60. Page 3; Mount Hope Cemetery, Lander, Wyo., Burial Search. https://burialsearch.com/ecims#/s/145/Mount_Hope_Cemetery/2294. Accessed August 6, 2016.

171 "SW County Marriage Index, Reverse L to End, Book 1&2 or A&B, Book 3 or C through p.43." Pdf page 118. Ledger pages "W" and "Y," and "SW County Marriage Index, Direct and (continued) Reverse through K." Pdf page 266. Ledger page "Y." SPCSHS. Server. Accessed Dec. 17, 2019; Marriage Certificate. Nelson Yarnell, Mary Ellen Ward. Sweetwater County. Territory of Wyoming. Marriage book A. Page 37. Carl Hallberg. Received Oct. 21, 2024. Wyoming State Archives.

Chapter 9: Burials Sites Unknown

1 "The Indian Question." *The South Pass News*. April 9, 1870. No. 56. Page 1. UW and Wyoming State Library. https://wyomingnewspapers.org. Accessed July 25, 2016; McDermott, John D. *Dangerous Duty; A History of Frontier Forts in Fremont County, Wyoming*. The Fremont County Historic Preservation Commission. 1993. Page 98.

2 1870, Wyoming Mortality Schedule ending June 1870. Compiled by the ACHS. Accessed Sept. 26, 2015.

3 Handwritten cards. SPCSHS. 1870 and 1871 Carter County tax rolls located in Sweetwater County, Wyo. Accessed Oct. 31, 2016.

4 "Report on ACHS Cemetery follow-up meeting. July 26, 1997. Author unknown. Page 2. Copy presented by Jean Mathison Haugen. Nov. 13, 2015.

5 1870 Wyoming Mortality Schedule. Carter County. Page 1. US, Federal Census Mortality Schedules Index, 1850-1880. www.ancestry.com/search/collections/3530/?birth=_Carter+County&death=1870_wyoming-usa_53&count=50. Accessed March 7, 2024.

6 McDermott, John D. *Dangerous Duty: A History of Frontier Forts in Fremont County, Wyoming.* The Fremont County Historic Preservation Commission. 1993. Page 98; Wyoming Mortality Schedule ending June 1870. Accessed Oct. 9, 2015; "Coroner's Inquest." *The South Pass News.* August 8, 1870. No. 4. Page 2. UW and Wyoming State Library. https://wyomingnewspapers.org. Accessed July 25, 2016.

7 "Preamble and Resolution." *The South Pass News.* April 9, 1870. No. 56. Page 4; "Coroner's Inquest." August 8, 1870. No. 4. Page 2. UW and Wyoming State Library. https://wyomingnewspapers.org. Accessed July 25, 2016.

8 Pfaff, Betty Carpenter. *Fine Gold.* Private printing. 1998. Chap. 50. Page 1.

9 Lehi, UT, USA: Ancestry.com Operations, Inc., 2010. Year: *1888*; Arrival: *New York, New York, USA*; Microfilm Serial: *M237, 1820-1897*; Line: *22*; List Number: *421*; Year: 1906; Arrival: New York, New York, USA; Microfilm Serial: T715, 1897-1957; Line: 4; Page Number: 40. *New York, US, Arriving Passenger and Crew Lists (including Castle Garden and Ellis Island), 1820-1957.* Ancestry.com. https://ancestry.com. Accessed April 28, 2022.

10 Land Patent. Bureau of Land Management. http://glorecords.blm.gov; 1900 US Federal Census. Atlantic Precinct. Sheet (stamped) B. Line 82. 1910 US Federal Census. Atlantic City. Precinct 12. Enumeration District No. 65. Sheet No. 7. Line 24; Ancestry.com. www.ancestry.com. Accessed April 28, 2022. Digital images, citing NARA microfilm publication.

11 "Archive: Topical Files." Folder: Blewett (Blewc-T). Folder Document Inventory (Compiler: je). SPCSHS. Accessed March 8, 2024; "Miners' Delight." *Fremont Clipper.* March 29, 1895. Paper copy located in Charles Blewett's folder at SPCSHS. Accessed March 8, 2024.

12 *WSJ.* July 24, 1914, Vol. 32, No. 46, page 1; The *Lander Eagle.* December 4, 1914, Fourth Year, No. 45, page 1. UW and Wyoming State Library. https://wyomingnewspapers.org. Accessed April 27, 2022; "City News Notes." The *Lander Eagle.* July 24, 1914. Fourth Year. No. 26. Page 4. UW and Wyoming State Library. https://wyomingnewspapers.org. Accessed Aug. 2, 2024.

13 Pfaff, Betty Carpenter. *Fine Gold.* Private printing. 1998. Chap. 50. Page 3.

14 *WSJ.* Nov. 23, 1917. Vol. 35. No. 7. Page 1. UW and Wyoming State Library. Accessed Aug. 2, 2024; "Atlantic and South Pass." *WSJ.* Nov. 30, 1917. Vol. XXXV. No. 8. Page 7. UW and Wyoming State Library. https://wyomingnewspapers.org. Accessed Aug. 2, 2024.

15 "Fremont County, Defunct Cemeteries," n.d. Unknown who compiled this document. Accessed Sept. 25, 2015. Mount Hope Cemetery. City of Lander.

16 Sherlock, James L. *South Pass and Its Tales.* Private Printing. 1978. Page 130; "Fatal Affray." *The South Pass News.* September 13, 1870. No. 6. Page 3. UW and Wyoming State Library. Accessed Aug. 16, 2016; Lane, Jon. SPCSHS. Probate document. Page 16-17. Sweetwater County. page 32. Accessed Oct. 31, 2015; 1870 US Federal Census. Atlantic City. County of Sweetwater. Sheet No. (stamped) 457. Page No. (penned) 1. Line 26. Digital images. Ancestry.com. www.ancestry.com. Accessed Nov. 20, 2015. Digital images, citing NARA microfilm publication.

17 "Deadwood Affrays." *Laramie Weekly Sentinel.* Feb. 25, 1878. Vol. III. No. 41. Page 2. University of Wyoming and Wyoming State Library. https://wyomingnewspapers.org. Accessed Oct. 31, 2015.

18 Pardon Davis. Ancestry.com. http://person.ancestry.com/tree/3080000/person/1034566173/facts. July 18, 2016; US Federal Census Mortality Schedules Index, 1850-1800, and the family tree on Ancestry.com. Accessed on October 19, 2015; Pardon Harden Davis. Ancestry.com. http://person.ancestry.com/tree/8272891/person/869527491/facts. Accessed July 26, 2016.

19 US Federal Census. Harden Davis. Sept. 8, 1850. Berlin, County of Marquette, Wisconsin. Line 6. National Archives. Record Group Number: 29. Series Number: M432. Roll: 1002. Page 129b. Ancestry.com. Accessed Feb. 14, 2025.

20 Rev. Don A. Sanford, "Pardon Davis: A Prisoner in Louisiana," Seventh Day Baptist Historical Society, Wisc., 1998. Reprinted by permission of the Council of History of the Seventh Day Baptist General Conference.

21 *Richland County Observer*. Richland Center, Wisc. March 11, 1856. Vol. I. No. 17. Page 3. Ancestry.com. https://ancestry.com. Accessed July 18, 2016.

22 1869 Wyoming Territory Census. Carter County. Page 3. Line 214. "Establishing Wyoming Territory." WyomingHistory.org. Wyoming Historical Society. Original data from WSA. Line 1,568. Ancestry.com. https://ancestry.com. Accessed March 7, 2024.

23 "Poll list." Atlantic City. Sept. 2, 1869 election. WSA. Paper copies received from Carl Hallberg. Aug. 19, 2019.

24 Claims. "sp_commerce_carter_co_1868_book_11.pdf" pdf. Pdf pages 580-81, 635. Printed ledger pages 217-19, 327. SPCSHS. Server. Accessed Sept 4, 2024.

25 *Janesville Gazette* (Wisc.). No. 76. June 4, 1870. Page 1. Copyright 2006 Heritage Microfilm, Inc. and Newspaperarchive.com. Accessed July 18, 2016.

26 Note: Doc Harris may be Dr. Harrison, Frank H; *Janesville Gazette*. Vol. 14. No. 76. Saturday, June 4, 1870. Page 1. Ancestry.com. https://ancestry.com. Accessed July 18, 2016; Wyoming Mortality Schedule ending June 1870. Compiled by the ACHS, n.d. Accessed Sept. 26, 2015.

27 Huseas, Marion McMillan. *Sweetwater Gold, Wyoming's Gold Rush 1867-1871*. Mortimore Publishing. Lander, WY. 1991. Page 132.

28 Pdfs from microfilm from original documents are Book 14, pages 93-95. Carter County, held in Sweetwater County. Joseph Powers and Thomas Cook. SPCSHS. Accessed Nov. 18, 2016.

29 Rev. Don A. Sanford, "Pardon Davis: A Prisoner in Louisiana," Seventh Day Baptist Historical Society, 1998. Reprinted by permission of the Council of History of the Seventh Day Baptist General Conference; "Records of Letters of Testimony of Administration, 1868-84." Records of the Clerk of Probate Court for Sweetwater County, Wyoming Territory; Pardon Davis' "land and the buildings thereon, situated near and east of the town of Atlantic). Originals housed at the WSA, Cheyenne, Wyoming. Accessed Oct. 14, 2016; "sp_commerce_carter_co_1868_book_01_b." Carter County. PDF file. Pdf pages 10-11. Ledger pages 48-50. SPCSHS. Server. Accessed Dec. 17, 2019; Townsend, Barbara. "Pardon Davis: An Old West Cold Case." *WRM*. Fremont County Pioneer Museum. November 2019. Vol. 28. No. 2. Pages 4-6.

30 David, Robert Beebe. *Finn Burnett, Frontiersman*. Mechanicsburg: Stackpole Books. 2003. Page 246. For an account of the Hay Fields fight at Fort C. F. Smith on Aug. 1, 1867, and Robert Wheeling's actions on that day, refer to pages 162-195. Fort C. F. Smith is in Montana on the Bozeman trail, 220 miles north of Atlantic City.

31 US Census. Harden Davis. Sept. 8, 1850. Berlin District, County of Marquette, Wisconsin. Line 6. National Archives. Record Group Number: 29. Series Number: M432. Roll: 1002. Page 129b. Ancestry.com. Accessed Feb. 14, 2025; US Census Mortality Schedules, 1850-1885 for Harden Davis. Schedule 2. Milton, County of Rock, Wisconsin. Line 10. Wisconsin Historical Society, Madison, Wisconsin. Archive. Roll Number 4. Ancestry.com. Accessed Feb. 14, 2025.

32 Lenocker, Julia. "Re: Pardon Davis." Email interview. July 18, 2016.

33 1869 Territorial Census. Wyoming Territory. Online display page 206. Lines 1524-1526. WSA. Ancestry.com. www.ancestry.com. Accessed March 29, 2024.

34 1870 US Federal Census. Atlantic City. County of Sweetwater. Wyoming Territory. Lines 29-32. NARA Roll: M593_1748; Page: 457A. Ancestry.com. https://ancestry.com. Accessed April 7, 2024.

35 1880 US Federal Census. Atlantic City. Sweetwater County. Wyoming. Page No. 5. Sheet 299. Lines 28-30. NARA Roll. Ancestry.com. https://ancestry.com. Accessed Nov. 21, 2015.

36 Tract Books, 1880-C. 1955. Dakota Territory. March 12, 1880. Bureau of Land Management. US Land Assessment. FamilySearch.org. www.familysearch.org. Accessed April 7, 2024.

37 "Additional Locals. An Old Pioneer Gone." *Fremont Clipper*. Dec. 31, 1887. Vol. 1. No. 19. Page 2. Lander library microfilm: Box #1. Diazo. Fremont Clipper Sept. 17, 1887-Dec. 26, 1888. Accessed April 30, 2024.

38 "Twenty-Five Years Ago Today." *WSJ*. Jan. 3, 1913. Vol. XXXI. No. 18. Page 2. Fremont County Library, Lander. From microfilm. Accessed April 30, 2024.

39 *Dangerous Duty; A History of Frontier Forts in Fremont County, Wyoming*. John D. McDermott. The Fremont County Historic Preservation Commission. 1993. Page 98; Wyoming Mortality Schedule ending June 1870. Compiled by members of the ACHS. Note: St. Mary's station had originally been called "Rocky Ridge or Foot of the Ridge station until 1865" when Indians burned it down. The station was rebuilt and was a telegraph line station. Service continued until the Union Pacific railroad completed its line elsewhere. Handwritten

(continued) note by Betty Carpenter Pfaff, labeled "Paul H Notes." Fremont County Pioneer Museum. Folder "St. Mary's Station," Cabinet A1, Box 3. Accessed June 5, 2024.

40 *South Pass News.* April 9, 1870. No. 56. Pages 1, 4; *South Pass News.* August 8, 1870. No. 4. Page 2. UW and Wyoming State Library. https://wyomingnewspapers.org. Accessed July 25 and 26, 2016.

41 Note: Doc Harris may be Dr. Frank H. Harrison; "One Dead, Two Frozen." *Rock Springs Miner.* Feb. 25, 1905. Vol. XXV. No. 8. Page 1. Information provided by Sharon Lass Field, October 15, 2021.

42 *Dangerous Duty; A History of Frontier Forts in Fremont County, Wyoming.* John D. McDermott. The Fremont County Historic Preservation Commission. 1993. Page 98; Wyoming Mortality Schedule ending June 1870. Compiled by the members of the ACHS. Accessed Oct. 9, 2015; The *South Pass News.* April 9, 1870. No. 56, page 4; *South Pass News.* No. 4, August 8, 1870, page 2. UW and Wyoming State Library. https://wyomingnewspapers.org. Accessed July 26, 2016.

43 "The Indian Question." *South Pass News.* April 9, 1870. No. 56. Page 1. UW and the Wyoming State Library. https://wyomingnewspapers.org. Accessed July 25, 2016.

44 Betty Carpenter Pfaff. *Fine Gold.* Private printing. 1998. Chap. 28. Page 1.

45 "Advertised Letters." *WRM.* No. 48; August 19, 1896, page 3. UW and Wyoming State Library. https://wyomingnewspapers.org. Accessed Nov. 20, 2015.

46 "Atlantic City, Center of an Exceeding Rich Mining Belt." *The Miner.* Vol. 3. No. 19. Aug. 6, 1909. UW and Wyoming State Library. https://wyomingnewspapers.org. Accessed Feb. 22. 2024.

47 Pfaff, Betty Carpenter. *Atlantic City Nuggets.* Privately published. 1978. Page 131.

48 1900 US Federal Census. Atlantic City. Atlantic Precinct. Sheet (stamped) A, (penned) 1. Line 65. Ancestry.com. https://ancestry.com. Accessed Nov. 20, 2015; 1910 Federal Census Index, page 313, line 7; Atlantic City, Precinct 12, page 1, line 7.

49 "Short News Items of Local Interest." WSJ. Jan. 19, 1912. Vol. 30. No. 21. Page 3. UW and Wyoming State Library. https://wyomingnewspapers.org. Accessed Feb. 22, 2024.

50 Betty Carpenter Pfaff. *Fine Gold.* Private printing. 1998. Chap. 17, page 2; Chap. 29, page 1; and Chap. 52, page 5.

51 *WSJ.* No. 26. April 19, 1918. Page 1; and No. 27, April 26, 1918. Page 6; and No. 28. May 3, 1918. Page 2.

52 "Name on Document." Certificate of Death. WSA. Carl Hallberg. Feb. 21, 2024.

53 Halstead, Philippina. Report in the minutes to the ACHS's annual meeting. August 25, 2007.

54 *South Pass News.* April 9, 1870. No. 56. Pages 1, 4. UW and Wyoming State Library. https://wyomingnewspapers.org. Accessed July 26, 2016.

55 1869 Wyoming Territory Census. Carter County. "Establishing Wyoming Territory." WyomingHistory.org, Wyoming Historical Society. Original data from WSA. Line 1506. Ancestry.com. www.ancestry.com. Accessed March 7, 2024.

56 Excerpt of a private letter printed in the *Wyoming Weekly Leader.* May 22, 1869. Page 6. Accessed Dec. 4, 2016; Handwritten index card, #14. Located at SPCSHS. Carter County 1870 tax assessment roll. Accessed Oct. 12, 2016.

57 1869 Wyoming Territory Census. Carter County. Line No. 1388. WSA. Ancestry.com. Accessed Aug. 3, 2024.

58 "Rocky Ridge." Wyoming Historical Society. Jan. 27, 2017. Accessed Feb. 25, 2024. https://www.wyohistory.org/encyclopedia/rocky-ridge.

59 *South Pass News.* April 9, 1870. No. 56. Pages 1, 4. UW and Wyoming State Library. https://wyomingnewspapers.org. Accessed July 26, 2016.

60 McDermott, John D. *Dangerous Duty; A History of Frontier Forts in Fremont County, Wyoming.* The Fremont County Historic Preservation Commission. 1993. Page 98; Wyoming Mortality Schedule ending June 1870. Compiled by members of the ACHS. Accessed Oct. 9, 2015; *South Pass News.* April 9, 1870. No. 56. Pages 1 and 4; and August 8, 1870. No. 4. Page 2; Federal Census Mortality Schedules Index, 1850-1880; Ancestry.com. www.ancestry.com. Accessed July 29, 2016.

61 Illinois, Databases of Illinois Veterans Index, 1775-1995. Illinois Civil War Muster and Descriptive Rolls. *Databases of Illinois Veterans.* Illinois State Archive. https://www.ilsos.gov/departments/archives/databases/home.html: accessed 5 August 2014. Ancestry.com. Accessed Aug. 3, 2024.

62 Indenture, James Othick and six others to Thomas Bennett. June 25, 1868. Othick signed on July 8, 1868. "Carter County, Book A of Deeds,p. 92 to End, Book B of Deeds through p. 89.pdf." Pdf page 164. Printed book pages 400-401. SPCSHS. Server. Accessed Dec. 17, 2019.

63 Handwritten cards. SPCSHS. The 1869 Liens, Carter County book and 1870 tax rolls located in Sweetwater County; Handwritten cards. SPCSHS. The 1871 County tax roll is located in Sweetwater County; Huseas, Marion McMillan. *Sweetwater Gold: Wyoming's Gold Rush 1867–1871*. Lander: Mortimore Publishing, 1991. Page 96.

64 McDermott, John D. *Dangerous Duty; A History of Frontier Forts in Fremont County, Wyoming*. The Fremont County Historic Preservation Commission. 1993. Page 98.

65 *South Pass News*. April 9, 1870. No. 56. Page 4, and August 8, 1870. No. 4. Page 2; Wyoming Mortality Schedule ending June 1870. Compiled by members of the ACHS. Accessed Oct. 9, 2015; *Cheyenne Daily Leader*. April 4, 1870. Vol. III. No. 193. Page 1. Chronicling America: Historic American Newspapers. Library of Congress. https://chroniclingamerica.loc.gov. Accessed April 18, 2023.

66 "Various Records. Carter County. Wyoming. From Book 6." Pdf page 89. "sp_commerce _carter_co_1868_book _01 _b." PDF. Ledger page 161. SPCSHS. Server. Accessed Dec. 17, 2024.

67 Bates, Charles E. "Early Days at Atlantic City." *Lander Eagle*. March 24, 1911. Vol. 1. No. 10. Page 5. UW and Wyoming State Library. https://wyomingnewspapers.org. Accessed May 27, 2024.

68 *Salt Lake Herald*. November 6, 1884. Page 8. Chronicling America: Historic American Newspapers. Lib. of Congress. https://chroniclingamerica.loc.gov. Accessed April 18, 2023.

69 *Salt Lake Daily Herald*. Sunday. August 3, 1884. Page 12. Chronicling America: Historic American Newspapers. Lib. of Congress. https://chroniclingamerica.loc.gov. Accessed April 18, 2023.

70 *Salt Lake Herald*. January 7, 1885. Wednesday. Page 7. Chronicling America: Historic American Newspapers. Library of Congress. https://chroniclingamerica.loc.gov. Accessed April 18, 2023.

71 Indenture. Frank Lenne and William Giessler to Dr. George H. Raught. Signed Oct. 27, 1885. Recorded Nov. 12, 1885. Quit Claim Record Book A. Pages 146-147. Fremont County Clerk's Office. Land Recording Office; indenture. Dr. George H. Raught to H. A Van Praag. Signed Nov. 10, 1885. Recorded Nov. 27, 1885. Quit Claim Record Book A. Pages 150-152. Fremont County Clerk's Office. Land Recording Office.

72 Handwritten and undated green index card. SPCSHS. The Atlantic Mining District; *Fremont Clipper*. No. 49. August 2, 1888. Page 3. Accessed Dec. 3, 2016.

73 *Cheyenne Daily Leader*. October 22, 1870, Saturday. Vol. IV. No. 30. Page 1. Chronicling America: Historic American Newspapers. Library of Congress. https://chroniclingamerica.loc.gov. Accessed April 18, 2023.

74 Wyoming Mortality Schedule ending June 1870. Compiled by members of the ACHS. Accessed Sept. 26, 2015; Federal Census Mortality Schedules Index, 1850-1880. Ancestry.com. www.ancestry.com. Accessed July 18, 2016; "Fremont County, Defunct Cemeteries," n.d. Unknown who compiled this document. Accessed Sept. 25, 2015. Mount Hope Cemetery. City of Lander.

75 *Fremont Clipper*. March 6, 1891. No. 26. Page 3; *Cheyenne Daily Sun*. March 4, 1891. Page 5. UW and Wyoming State Library. https://wyomingnewspapers.org. Accessed Nov. 15 and 18, 2015

76 "1880 US Federal Census." St. Louis, Missouri. Enumeration District No. 401. Nov. 9, 1880. Page No. 6. Line No. 5. Ancestry.com. www.ancestry.com. Accessed April 17, 2024.

77 Certificate of Marriage. Marriage Records. Book A. 1884-1904. Page 23. Oct. 20, 1885. Fremont County Clerk's Office. Land Recording Office. Accessed April 30, 2024.

78 Stratmoen, Mark R. *Mayhem, and Mystery: Coroner Inquests in Fremont County 1885-1900*. Lenore Wyoming Publications, Riverton, WY. 2010. Pages 111-113.

79 Handwritten card. SPCSHS. Justice of the Peace docket located in the WSA. Accessed Oct. 27, 2016; The *Daily Boomerang*. Laramie, Wyo. No. 298. March 3, 1891. Page 4. UW and Wyoming State Library. https://wyomingnewspapers.org. Accessed Nov. 18, 2015; *Western States Marriage Record Index*. ID#287525. Accessed July 28, 2016. BYU-Idaho. https://abish.byui.edu; *Fremont Clipper*, No. 26; March 6, 1891. Page 3. UW and Wyoming State Library. https://wyomingnewspapers.org. Accessed Nov. 15, 2015.

80 *Marriage Record Book A: Index*. Page 134. Fremont County Courthouse. County Clerk. Land Recording Office. Lander, Wyo. Accessed March 3, 2022.

81 "United States Census, 1850." Entry for Samuel C Stambaugh and Susan D Stambaugh, 1850. Lines 27-29. www.familysearch.org/ark:/61903/1:1:MX3Y-BCC: Thu Oct 05 20:18:45 UTC 2023); United States Census, 1860. www.familysearch.org/ark:/61903/ 1:1:MCG8-CDC : Thu Oct 05 03:53:46 UTC 2023. Entry for Susan Stambaugh and Charles Stambaugh, 1860. Lines 4 and 5. FamilySearch. Accessed Feb. 24, 2024.

82 "Old Folks Interviewed." *Fremont Clipper.* Oct. 22, 1887. No. 9. Page 3. UW and Wyoming State Library. https://wyomingnewspapers.org. Accessed Oct. 27, 2015; *Sweetwater Gold, Wyoming's Gold Rush 1867-1871.* Marion McMillan House. Mortimore Publishing, Lander, WY. 1991. Page 73; *Dangerous Duty; A History of Frontier Forts in Fremont County, Wyoming.* John D. McDermott. The Fremont County Historic Preservation Commission. 1993. Page 100; *Forts, Fights, and Frontier Sites, Wyoming Historic Sites.* Candy Moulton. High Plains Press, Glendo, Wyoming. 2010. Page 40.
83 "Early History of Fremont County." H. G. Nickerson. (Written in 1886.) Quarterly Bulletin. Vol. 2. No. 1. *Annals of Wyoming.* State of Wyoming, Historical Department. Page 4.
84 House, Marion McMillan. *Sweetwater Gold, Wyoming's Gold Rush 1867-1871.* Lander, Wyo. Mortimore Publishing, 1991. Page 79.
85 *Lancaster (Ohio) Gazette,* May 19, 1870, page 3. Find a Grave. https://www.findagrave.com/memorial/205477693/charles-b.-stambaugh. Photo courtesy of Natalie Herdman. Accessed Nov. 15, 2021.
86 "United States General Index to Pension Files, 1861-1934." FamilySearch. www.familysearch.org/ark:/61903/1:1:QJDP-F6QM: Wed Dec 13 19:58:44 UTC 2023. Entry for Charles B Stambaugh and Susan C Stambaugh, 1870. Accessed Feb. 24, 2024.
87 House, Marion McMillan. *Sweetwater Gold, Wyoming's Gold Rush 1867-1871.* Lander, Wyo. Mortimore Publishing, 1991. Page 79; *US Register of Death in the Regular Army, 1860-1880.* Page 132 of 172. Digital images. Ancestry.com. www.ancestry.com. Accessed Nov. 15, 2021. Digital images, citing NARA microfilm publication.
88 Nationwide Gravesite Locator. National Cemetery Administration. US Department of Veterans Affairs. www.cem.va.gov/nationwide-gravesite-locator/. Accessed May 7, 2024.
89 WRM, March 13, 1898, page 2; WRM No. 26, March 14, 1898. Page 3. UW and Wyoming State Library. https://wyomingnewspapers.org. Accessed June 1, 2016; *Wyoming Press.* Vol. II. March 12, 1898. Page 1. UW and Wyoming State Library. https://wyomingnewspapers.org. Accessed July 28, 2016.

Chapter 10: Cadaver-seeking Dogs

1 Irwin, K. T. Interview. *5 Search.* Video. Time stamp: 01:11.Mionczynski, John. ACHS. June 7, 2016.
2 ——. *5 Search.* Video. Time stamp: 5:00. ACHS. June 7, 2016.
3 ——. *2 Search.* Video. Time stamp: 3:50. ACHS. June 7, 2016.

Chapter 11: Dowsing for Graves

1 Barrett, Sir William, and Theodore Besterman. *The Divining-Rod: An Experimental and Physchological Investigation.* 1926. Reprint, University Books, 1968. Pages 1-9, 275; Hester, Ben. G. *Dowsing: An Exposé of Hidden Occult Forces.* Jan. 1, 1984. Pages 13-14, 97-98; Private printing; Bird, Christopher. *The Divining Hand: The 500-Year-Old Mystery of Dowsing.* Jan. 14, 1997. REDFeather Publishing.
2 Nelson, Linda Faye. "Dowsing for Unmarked Graves." Courtesy of and with permission by the Jay Historical Society and Museum (Florida). www.jayhistoricalsociety.org/pioneerstories/Dowsing_for_Unmarked_Graves_by_Linda_Faye_Nelson.pdf. Accessed July 27, 2018.
3 Chumacero, J. R., and S. E. Chumacero. "The Ideomotor Phenomenon." May 11, 2021. *Living Life in Full Spectrum.* www.llifs.com.au/blog/the-ideomotor-phenomenon/. Accessed July 14, 2024; Barrett, William, Sir. *Psychical Research.* Pages 20-31. New York: J. Holt, 1911. Collection of the University of British Columbia; Toronto. Call No. 1661086. Internet Archive. https://archive.org/details/psychicalresea00barr. Accessed July 14, 2024.
4 The American Society of Dowsers. 2024. https://americansocietyofdowsers.wildapricot.org/. Accessed Feb. 12, 2024.

Bibliography

UNPUBLISHED DOCUMENTS:

Benson-Coolidge Funeral Records, 1918–1947, n.d.

Halstead, Philippina. Report. Atlantic City Historic Society's annual meeting. August 25, 2007.

Haugen, Jean Mathisen. "Pioneer Cemetery and Grave Inventory Form" and its associated attachments for the two cemeteries. Unknown author. November 1970.

Hudson Negatives. Donated by Wendell "Dick" Hudson. June 2, 2021.

Meredith, Verne. Borner Family History, n.d.

Meschter, Daniel Y. "An Inventory of Wyoming Cemeteries." (Preliminary.) May 21, 1968.

Oral History Transcripts. South Pass City State Historic Site.

> Booth, Aurlein
> Booth, Jacob
> Carpenter, James Wallace
> Cook, Joseph
> Freeburgh, Melvin
> Fuller, Zoie Green
> Golliher, Alma
> Greig, Dolly and Alexander
> Klover, George
> Mann, Albert
> Marrin, Laura
> Mionczynski, John
> Moerer, Lyle
> Parker, Pearl Tatro and Hugh Tatro
> Pfaff, Betty Carpenter
> Roe, Clarence
> Sherlock, James L.
> Steinbrech, Mary
> Wehrman, Terry

Pfaff, Betty Carpenter. Family history, n.d.

Sommers, Jonita. *Williams Family History*. 2020.

Trevor, Marjorie C. (1954). *History of Carter-Sweetwater County, Wyoming to 1875*. (Master's thesis, University of Wyoming.) ProQuest Dissertations & Theses.

Williams, Emmett. *Williams Family History in Pictures by Emmett Williams*. December 2000.

PERIODICALS:

Annals of Wyoming. Wyoming Historical Society.

Frontier Times. J. Marvin Hunter.

Wind River Mountaineer. Fremont County Pioneer Museum.
Wyoming History News. Wyoming Historical Society.

Books and Articles:

Barrett, Sir William. *Psychical Research*. New York: J. Holt, 1911.

Barrett, Sir William, and Theodore Besterman. *The Divining-Rod: An Experimental and Physchological Investigation*. 1926. Reprint, University Books, 1968.

Beach, Mrs. Alfred H. (Cora May Brown), ed. and compiler. *Women of Wyoming*. Vols. I and II. S. E. Boyer & Company, 1927.

Belcher, Dennis W. *The 11th Missouri Volunteer Infantry in the Civil War: A History and Roster*. McFarland & Company, 2011.

Bird, Christopher. *The Divining Hand: The 500-Year-Old Mystery of Dowsing*. REDFeather Publishing, 1997.

Coutant, Charles G. *History of Wyoming: From the Earliest Known Discoveries. In Three Volumes*. Chaplin, Spafford & Mathison, 1899.

——. "The South Pass Gold Discoveries, 1842–1869." *Wind River Mountaineer*. Vol. X. No. 2, n.d.

David, Robert Beebe. *Finn Burnett, Frontiersman*. Stackpole Books, 2003.

Farlow, Edward J. *Wind River Adventures: My Life in Frontier Wyoming*. High Plains Press, 1998.

Hayden, F. V. *Sixth Annual Report of the United States Geological Survey of the Territories, Embracing Portions of Montana, Idaho, Wyoming, and Utah*. (1872) Washington: Government Printing Office, 1873.

Hester, Ben. G. *Dowsing: An Exposé of Hidden Occult Forces*. Private printing, 1984.

Homsher, Lola M., Ed. *South Pass, 1868: James Chisholm's Journal of the Wyoming Gold Rush*. University of Nebraska Press, 1960.

Howard, Robert West. *South Pass Story*. G. P. Putnam's Sons, 1968.

Huseas, Marion McMillan. *Sweetwater Gold: Wyoming's Gold Rush, 1867–1871*. Mortimore Publishing, 1991.

Lane, Jon, and Susan Layman. *South Pass City and the Sweetwater Mines*. Arcadia Publishing, 2012.

Lindmier, Tom, and Cynde Georgen, eds. *South Pass City: Wyoming's City of Gold*. Donning Company, 2004.

MacCoun, Townsend. *An Historical Geography of the United States*. Silver, Burdett & Company, 1912.

McDermott, John D. *Dangerous Duty: A History of Frontier Forts in Fremont County, Wyoming*. Fremont County Historic Preservation Commission, 1992.

Moulton, Candy. *Forts, Fights, and Frontier Sites: Wyoming Historic Sites*. High Plains Press, 2010.

Nickerson, H. G. "Early History of Fremont County." (Written in 1886.) *Annals of Wyoming*, vol. 2, no. 1 (July 1924).

Pence, Mary Lou, and Lola M. Homsher. *Ghost Towns of Wyoming*. Hastings House, 1956.

Peterson, Samuel E. *Tales & Trails: Stories of Atlantic City, South Pass and the Sweetwater*. Privately published, 1999.

Pfaff, Betty Carpenter. *Atlantic City Nuggets*. Privately published, 1978.

——. *Fine Gold*. Privately published, 1998.

——. *Changes*. Privately published, 2018.

Progressive Men of the State of Wyoming. A.W. Bowen & Company, 1903.

Redford, Robert. *The Outlaw Trail: A Journey Through Time.* Grosset & Dunlap Publishers, 1978.

Russell, Osborne. *Journal of a Trapper: Nine Years in the Rocky Mountains, 1834–1843.* Syms-York Company, circa 1921.

Sherlock, James L. *South Pass and Its Tales.* Vantage Press, 1978.

Stratmoen, Mark R. *Mayhem and Mystery, Coroner Inquests in Fremont County 1885–1900.* Lenore Wyoming Publications, 2010.

Townsend, Robert K., ed. *Atlantic City, Wyoming: Voices From a Powerful Place.* Atlantic City, WY. Atlantic City Historical Society, 2017.

Wister, Fanny Kemble, Ed. *Owen Wister Out West: His Journals and Letters.* The University of Chicago Press, 1958.

Primary Sources:

Abstract Mining Claims, Book F. Fremont County Clerk, Land Recording Office.

Board of Health Records, 1900–1901. Sweetwater County.

Book A. Powers of Attorney of Carter County, W. T. Record. 1869–1880. South Pass City State Historic Site.

Book A of Deeds, 1868. Carter County. South Pass City State Historic Site.

Book B of Deeds, 1868. Carter County. South Pass City State Historic Site.

Book B of Records of Carter County, Dakota (Wyoming) Territory. 1867–1869. South Pass City State Historic Site.

Cheney, Ervin Franklin's diary, 1887.

Election Poll Books. Atlantic City and South Pass City, 1869, 1871 (results only), 1872, 1880, 1881, 1930–1952.

England and Wales, National Probate Calendar (Index of Wills and Administrations), 1858–1995.

Grantee Book B, Book #2, and Grantee Book D–E, Book #5. Sweetwater County.

Grantor Books, 1–11. Sweetwater County.

Halsted and Company. San Diego. No. B-1283. No. 10. "California, US San Francisco Funeral Home Records, 1895–1985."

Indexes, Books 1–3. 1871–1879. District Court, Third District. State of Utah.

Irwin, K. T. Video recordings. Atlantic City Historical Society. June 7, 2016.

Jail Register. Fremont County Pioneer Museum.

Judge's Civil Docket, 1880–1995. South Pass City State Historic Site.

Judge's Docket #1, 1870–1879. Sweetwater County.

Judge's Probate Docket. 1868–1870. South Pass City State Historic Site.

Marriage Index, L-End, Books 1 and 2 or A & B. Sweetwater County.

Marriage Records, Book A. 1884–1904. Fremont County Clerk, Land Recording Office.

Marriage Records, Book B. Jan. 28, 1904–Feb. 29, 1908. Fremont County Clerk, Land Recording Office.

Marriage Records, Book C. March 18, 1908–Nov. 4, 1914. Fremont County Clerk, Land Recording Office.

Marriage Records, Book 1. Nov. 1887–May 12, 1890. Fremont County Clerk, Land Recording Office.

Military Records. 1946. South Pass City State Historic Site.

Mining Records and Land Claims, etc. of Carter County and Sweetwater County. South Pass City State Historic Site.

Mining Records of Shoshonie District by H. B. Hubbell. Book of 1. South Pass City State
    Historic Site. 1868. South Pass City State Historic Site.
Misc. Records, Book A. 1884–1894. Fremont County Clerk, Land Recording Office.
Misc. Records, Book B. 11-5-1894–7-24-1906. Fremont County Clerk, Land Recording Office.
Misc. Records, Book C. 5-5-[19]06–4-9-1908. Fremont County Clerk, Land Recording Office.
Poll Books and Election Returns. Atlantic City. 1869, Wyoming State Archives; 1880-81,
    Sweetwater County Historical Museum; 1921–30, 1962–78, Fremont County Elections Office.
Probate Docket. Carter County, courtesy of Sweetwater County.
Record Book for Atlantic City. 1889–1961. St. Andrew's Episcopal Church.
Record of Assignments, Transfers and Release of Mortgages and Liens. Book A. 1869. South
    Pass City State Historic Site.
Record of Bonds, 1870–1898. South Pass City State Historic Site.
Record of Licenses, 1869–1877. South Pass City State Historic Site.
Record of Testamentary of Administration 1868–1891. South Pass City State Historic Site.
Records of the California Mining District, Organized September 13, 1867. 1867–1868. South
    Pass City State Historic Site.
Soldiers Discharge Record, Book A. Fremont County, 12-19-17–1-30-30. Fremont County
    Clerk, Land Recording Office.
Tax Book. Carter County. Sweetwater County. South Pass City State Historic Site.
"The Atlantic Gold District and the North Laramie Mountains; Fremont, Converse, and Albany
    Counties." Wyoming. Department of the Interior. United States Geological Survey. 1916.
Thompson, H. A., Docket of Probate Judge. 1868–1870. South Pass City State Historic Site.
Tract Book, 1880–c. 1995. Bureau of Land Management.
Wickliffe, Governor Robert Charles. Papers. Louisiana Historical Center. New Orleans, La.

NEWSPAPERS:
Casper Star-Tribune
Cheyenne Daily Leader
Cheyenne Daily Sun
Cheyenne Leader
Clipper (Lander)
Daily Boomerang (Laramie)
Daily Independent (Laramie)
Daily Inter-Ocean (Ill.)
Daily Sentinel (Laramie)
Denver Post (Colo.)
Dubois Frontier
Fayetteville Observer (N.C.)
Fremont Clipper (Lander)
Fresno Morning Republican (Cal.)
Janesville Gazette (Wisc.)
Kemmerer Republican
Lancaster Gazette (Ohio)
Lander Clipper
Lander Eagle
Lander Evening Post

Lander Journal
Laramie Boomerang
Laramie Republican
Laramie Weekly Sentinel
Miner (Hudson)
New York Times (N.Y.)
North Star Dakotan (N. Dak.)
Ogden Standard-Examiner (Utah)
Pine Bluffs Post
Pinedale Roundup
Republican (Sundance)
Richland County Observer (Wisc.)
Riverton Chronicle
Riverton News
Riverton Ranger
Riverton Review
Rock Springs Miner
Rocket Miner (Rock Springs)
Rustler (Bonanza)
Salt Lake Daily Herald (Utah)
Salt Lake Herald (Utah)
Salt Lake Herald-Republican (Utah)
Salt Lake Tribune (Utah)
Sheridan Post
Shoshoni Enterprise
South Pass News
South-Southwestern (La.)
Sweetwater Mines (Fremont County)
Vernal Express (Utah)
Wind River Mountaineer (Lander)
Wind River News (Riverton)
Wyoming Press (Evanston)
Wyoming Semi-Weekly Tribune (Cheyenne)
Wyoming State Journal (Lander)
Wyoming Tribune (Rawlins)
Wyoming Weekly (Cheyenne)
Wyoming Weekly Leader (Cheyenne)
Wyoming Weekly Republican (Sundance)

SITES AND MISCELLANEOUS SOURCES:
Atlantic City Historical Society
Carbon County Clerk
Cemetery
    Atlantic City
       East Cemetery
       West Cemetery

Hudson City Cemetery
Independent Order of Odd Fellows Cemetery, Riverton
Milford City Cemetery
Miners Delight/Hamilton City Cemetery
Mount Hope Cemetery, Lander
Mountain View Cemetery, Riverton
North Fork Masonic Cemetery, Milford
Rock Creek Hollow Cemetery
South Pass City Cemetery
Central Wyoming College
Fremont County
    Clerk
        Elections Office
        Land Recording Office
        Planning Office
    Coroner
    Library System
        Lander branch
        Riverton branch
    Pioneer Museum
    Sheriff's Office
Fremont County Historical Society
Goodstein Foundation Library, Casper College
Legacy of the Plains Museum, Nebraska
McCracken Research Library, Buffalo Bill Center of the West
Riverton Ranger Office
St. Andrew's Episcopal Church
Seismological Society of America
South Pass City State Historic Site
Stephen H. Hart Research Center, Colorado
Sweetwater County
    Clerk
    Clerk of District Court
    Courthouse
    Historical Museum
    Land Recording Office
    Library System, Rock Springs branch
    Planning Office
Sweetwater County Historical Society
University of Wyoming
    American Heritage Center
    Coe Library
Wyoming State
    Secretary of State
    State Historical Preservation Office
Wyoming Grand Lodge of the Independent Order of Odd Fellows
Wyoming Historical Society

ONLINE SOURCES:
GOVERNMENT SOURCES:
US FEDERAL GOVERNMENT:
    Arca Search. https://gov.arcasearch.com/uswyfre/
    Bureau of Land Management, Lander Field Office. www.blm.gov/office/lander-field-office
    Congressional Record. www.congress.gov/congressional-record
US Department of Agriculture. www.usda.gov/
Department of the Interior
    Bureau of Land Management, General Land Office Records. http://glorecords.blm.gov
    National Park Service
        National Battlefields. www.nps.gov/anti/index.htm
        National Register of Historic Places.
            www.nps.gov/subjects/nationalregister/database-research.htm
    US Geological Survey. www.usgs.gov/
Department of State. https://history.state.gov/milestones/1801-1829/louisiana-purchase
Department of Veterans Affairs. National Cemetery Administration.
    www.cem.va.gov/nationwide-gravesite-locator/
    Library of Congress. www.usa.gov
    National Archives and Records Administration. www.archives.gov
National Institute of Health. National Library of Medicine. Department of Health and Human
    Services. www.ncbi.nlm.nih.gov
    US Federal Census Mortality. FamilySearch. www.familysearch.org/search/collection/1420441
US General Index to Pension Files, 1861–1934. www.archives.gov/research/military/pension-
    genealogy/1861-1934.html
US Register of Civil, Military, and Naval Service, 1861–1905. www.loc.gov/item/04018251/
US Register of Death in the Regular Army, 1860–1880.
    www.ancestry.com/search/collections/2128/
US Senate. www.senate.gov/artandhistory/history
US Social Security. www.ssa.gov/
US Veterans Administration. www.va.gov/

STATE OF WYOMING:
Department of Environmental Quality
    Land Quality Division. https://deq.wyoming.gov/land-quality/
    Map Resources. https://deq.wyoming.gov/land-quality/map-resources/
Department of Health
    Vital Statistics Services. https://health.wyo.gov/admin/vitalstatistics/
Department of State Parks and Cultural Resources
    Historic Preservation Office. https://wyoshpo.wyo.gov/
    State Archives. https://wyoarchives.wyo.gov/
State of Wyoming. www.wyo.gov/about-wyoming/wyoming-history
University of Wyoming
    American Heritage Center. http://digitalcollections.uwyo.edu
    Water Resources Data System & State Climate Office. www.wrds.uwyo.edu/
Wyoming Digital Newspaper Collection. University of Wyoming and Wyoming State Archives.
    http://newspapers.wyo.gov

Wyoming State Geological Survey. www.wsgs.wyo.gov/
Wyoming State Museum. https://wyomuseum.wyo.gov/

LOCAL WYOMING GOVERNMENTS:
City of Lander. Mount Hope Cemetery. www.landerwyoming.org/mount-hope-cemetery
Fremont County Government. https://fremontcountywy-recorder.tylerhast.net
Fremont County Mapserver. www.fremontcountywy.org/mapserver
Sweetwater County Government. www.sweetwatercountywy.gov/
Sweetwater County Historical Museum. https://sweetwatermuseum.org/

OTHER STATE AND LOCAL GOVERNMENTS:
California
  Department of Health. www.cdph.ca.gov
  San Francisco Funeral Home Records, 1895–1985.
Colorado
  Colorado School of Mines. https://www.mines.edu
  Denver Public Library. Special Collections and Archives Department.
    www.denverlibrary.org
  State Archives. https://archives.colorado.gov
Idaho State Historical Society. https://history.idaho.gov
Illinois, University of, Urbana-Champaign. www.library.illinois.edu/
Louisiana State Museum. https://louisianastatemuseum.org/
Missouri
  Lewis County. https://lewiscountymo.org/
  Secretary of State. www.sos.mo.gov/archives/resources/military
  State Historical Society of Missouri. https://digital.shsmo.org
Montana Historical Society. https://mths.mt.gov
South Dakota Secretary of State. https://sdsos.gov/general-information/
North Dakota, State Historical Society of. www.history.nd.gov/archives/stateagencies
Utah, State of Utah Archives. https://archives.utah.gov/
Virginia
  Library of Virginia. https://ead.lib.virginia.edu/
  Virginia Humanities. https://encyclopediavirginia.org/entries/libby-prison/

OTHER:
American Battlefield Trust. https://battlefields.org/
American Pioneer & Cemetery Research Project. https://apcrp.org/
Ancestry.com. www.ancestry.com
Antelope Valley Genealogical Society, California. www.avgenealogy.org
Archives West. https://archiveswest.orbiscascade.org/
Arkansas in the Civil War Message Board. www.history-sites.com/
Burial Search. https://burialsearch.com
Civil War Talk. https://civilwartalk.com/
Colorado Encyclopedia. https://coloradoencyclopedia.org/
Cypress Lawn Memorial Park, California. https://cypresslawn.com

Encyclopedia Virginia. https://encyclopediavirginia.org

FamilySearch. The Church of Jesus Christ of Latter-day Saints. www.familysearch.org

Find a Grave. www.findagrave.com

FindLaw. www.findlaw.com/

Genealogy Trails Group. Fremont County, Wyoming, Genealogy and History. https://genealogytrails.com

Gettysburg Foundation. www.gettysburgfoundation.org

J. Willard Marriott Library, University of Utah. https://lib.utah.edu

Jay Historical Society and Museum, Florida. www.jayhistoricalsociety.org

Johns Hopkins Medicine. www.hopkinsmedicine.org

Living Life in Full Spectrum. www.llifs.com.au

Mayo Clinic. www.mayoclinic.org

Mines Repository. Atmire. https://repository.mines.edu/

Missouri Historical Society. https://mohistory.org/

Newspaper Archives. www.newspaperarchive.com

Newspapers.com. www.newspapers.com

Oklahoma University. Law Library. https://digitalcommons.law.ou.edu/

St. Mary Catholic Cemetery, Ohio. https://stmarylancaster.org/2018/cemetery/

Sfgenealogy. www.sfgenealogy.org

Seismological Society of America. www.seismosoc.org/

Seventh-day Adventist. www.sdanet.org/

Smithsonian Institute Archives. https://siarchives.si.edu/

State Historical Society of Missouri. https://shsmo.org/

State Historical Society of North Dakota. www.history.nd.gov/

Statue of Liberty—Ellis Island Foundation, Inc. www.statueofliberty.org/

Trace. www.traceyourpast.com

Utah Digital Newspapers. J. Willard Marriott Library. http://digitalnewspapers.org

Western States Marriage Record Index. Brigham Young University-Idaho, Idaho. https://abish.byui.edu/specialCollections/westernStates/search.cfm

WyoHistory.org. Wyoming Historical Society. www.wyohistory.org

Wyoming Tales and Trails. www.wyomingtalesandtrails.com/atlanticcity.html

Index

Page references in italics denote illustrations and photographs.

Adger, A. M., 185
Adrian, 226
Alberg, John, *42*
Albertson, Mr., 185
Alwes, Franz August, 103, *103*, *104*
Ambler, Marjane, 262n11,16,
    266n12,13,16,18, 267n38,42, 270n87,
    272n5,117, 278n8, 281n58
Andalusia Ledge, 229, *229*
Anderson, James, 105-10, *105-06*, *108*-09
Anderson, John, G., 223
Anderson, Martha Godward, 105-10, *107-09*
Anderton, Anna, 5
Anderton, Mr., 92-93
Anesi, Ed, 218
Anthony building, 75, 272n117
Anthony, John W., *iv*, 2, 15, 272n117
Arapahos, 245
Armbruster, Clara, 195
Armbruster, Fred, 195
Armbruster, Lottie, 195
Atlantic City Historical Society, *4*, 5-6, 32,
    90, 122, *186*, *199*, *247*, 251
Atlantic City Mercantile, 3-4, 18, 48, 111, 197

Baarghoffer, Herman, 171-72, *171-72*
Baillargon, Oliver, *x*, 81, *81*
Bannocks, 171
Barbett, Joseph, 36-38, *36*, 126, 131, 185
Barr, 191
Barrett, Silvester Frank, 173-74, *173*
Barrett, William F., 252-53
Barrows, Brigham, 173
Basco, Joseph, 175-77, *177*
Beer Garden Gulch, 3, 32, *42*
Beers, Bob, 80
Belcher, Alvin, E., 21, *21*, 264n1
Bell, Bob, 88
Bennington, William B., 223
Besterman, Theodore, 252-53

Big Atlantic Gulch, 245, 247
Big Chief Mine, 183
Blair, A. E., *31*, *33*, *55*, *80*, *153*, *173*
Blewett, Charles, 183, *183*, 224-25, *224-25*
Blue, and K. T. Irwin, 7-8, 31-32, *33*, 39, 98,
    119-20, 154, 158, 249-50, *249*, *251*
Booth, Aurlein, 37-38
Booth, Jacob, 8, 36-38, 153-54
Boston, Andrew J., 22
Boston, G. C., 22, *22*
Boston, James R., 22, *22*
Boston, Martha Dunlap, 22
Boucher, Jack E., *25*
Bouck, Henry, 190
Boyd, Michael, 1, 261n1
Brady, Jacob, 207-07
Britannia Mine and Lode, 185, 205
Brother, Doris, R., 226
Bryson, Charles, E., 225
Bucher, Mary, *iv*, 9
Buffalo Chips, 3
Burk, Harry. *See* Baarghoffer, Herman
Burnett, Eliza Ann McCarthy, 178-82, *178*,
    180, 279n29
Burnett, Fincelius G., 178-82, *178*, *180*, 210-
    11, 231
Burnt Ranch, 28, 175

cadaver dog, 7, 31-32, *33*, 39, 75, 88, 92,
    94-95, 98, 101, 119, 123-24, 127-28,
    131, 134, 139, 147, 149, 154, 158-59,
    161, 165, 167, 169, 249-51, *249*, *251*,
    254, 308
California Mining District, 28, 229, *229*
Camp McArthur, Tex., 53
Camp Stambaugh, 1, 33, 41, *54*, 63, 67, 86,
    94, 117, 192, 245
Cariboo Mine, 185, 241
Carissa Mine, 5, 105, 115, 117, 173-74, 176, 237
Carpenter, Albert Wallace, 40, 44, 176, 201

Carpenter, C. E. IV, *40-41, 45, 47, 49, 50-51, 53, 86-87, 90-91, 194*

Carpenter, Clarence Emmett, Jr., 40, *50*

Carpenter, Clarence Emmett, Sr., 40-41, 50, *50*, 95, *237*, 268n48

Carpenter, Edith Lucy, 40

Carpenter, Eleanor Wallace, 6, 39-43, *39-41*, 45, 49

Carpenter, Ellen McKisson, 6, 32, 44-49, *44-45, 47, 50, 55*, 67, 86-87, 90, 102, 120, 184, 187; red-haired woman, 48, 102

Carpenter family monument, 6, 31-32, *33*, 39, *39*, 95, 119-20, 124-25, 250, 254

Carpenter, Gaylin, *196*

Carpenter, Hazel Winifred, 6, 30, *33*, 39, *39*, 40, 50-52, *50-51*, 237

Carpenter Hotel, 33, 41, 43-50, *41-42, 45*, 47, *51, 55*, 86-87, 90, 92, 103, 154, 176, 183, 185, *185*, 224. *See also* Miner's Delight Inn

Carpenter, James Herron, 6, 53-55, *53-55*, 94, 185, *185*, 200-01, 214, 237

Carpenter, James Wallace, 48, 102, 187

Carpenter, Ruth, 40, *51*

Carpenter, William B., 258

Cassie, James, 37, 183-88, *183-88*, 224

Central Wyoming College, 6, 61, 88, 122

Chartier, Louis, 230

Cheney, Eliphalet, 189

Cheney, Elnathan Sanderson, 189-90, *190*

Cheney, Ervin Franklin, 70, 189-93, *190-93*, 203, *203*

Cheney, Lydia, 189

Cheney, Matilda Jane Henry, 192-93, *192-93*

Cheyenne, 80, 87, 107, 239-40, 242-43

Children's Cemetery, 27, 29, 152-54, 161

Christian Science, 77

Christina Lake Mining Company or ditch, 112-13

Clawson, Timothy, 231

Cleaveland Mine, 241

Clipper group or Mine, 184

Collins, Charles, 2, 13, 227

Connell, Emmett, 79

Connell, Katherine Hess Harsch, 62-63, 269n77

Connell, Michael Emmett, 59, 79, 269n77

Connell, Myra, 63, 73-74, 92, 269n77

Cook, Joseph, 67, 172

Cook, Thomas, 230-31

Crandall, H. H. William, 230

Crimmins, Cornelius, 227

Cripple Creek, Colo., 183, *183*, 224

Crowley, Mamie, 154

David, Robert Beebe, 179, 181

Davis, Charles, A., 232

Davis, Harden "Pardon," 228-31, *229*, 239

Davis, Harriet, 232-33, *232-33*

Davis, Jeremiah, 228, 231

Davis, Mercy, 228

Davis, Sidney (father), 232

Davis, Sidney (son), 232

Davison Collection, *112*

De Pass, 59, 79

Dehnert, Charlotte, 50

Dexter Mill or Mine, 5, *42*, 59, 201,

Dexter Mining Company, 218

Diana Lode, 205

Dohm, Martha Armbruster, 194-95, *194*,

Drucker, Sam, 7-8, 154, 158, 163, 165, 167, 253-54, *254*, 255-57, 260

Duggan, Dan, 173, *173*

Duncan Mine, 25, *25*, 179, 182

Dunkerd, Miss, 237

Earliest marked burial, Atlantic City, 158

Earliest marked burial, East Cemetery, 34

Earthquakes, 2, 261n6, 262n7

Ehelen, William Watt, 244

Elder, William, 6, 61, 122, *122*

Encampment, 89, 235

Eventon Lode, 231

Fairview Lode claim, 22

Field, Sharon Lass, *29*

Fitman, John C., 245

Flynn, Lawrence, 235

Fort C. F. Smith, Mont., 181, 231

Fort Leavenworth, Kans., 70

Fort Niobrara, Neb., 40

Fort Robinson, Neb., 53, 95

Fort Sidney, Neb., 40, 44

Fosburg, Eugene, 234

Fosher, 2

Frankie, 9, 262n17

Freeburgh, Melvin, 2, 184

Fremont County, 12, 36, 63, 74, 88, 192, 200, 225-26, 242; government agencies, 13-14, 22, *22*, 56, 68, 110, 115, 185, 243, *243*; Pioneer Museum, 36, 75

French Town, 3-4, 216
Frenchtown. *See* French Town
Fuller, Zoie Green, 5, 37, 45-47, *97*, 98
Garfield Mine, 201
Garrison, Catharine, 56
Garrison, John, 56-58, *56-58*, 127, 129, 132-35
Geible, David, 3, 15
Giessler, Dorothy Dohm, 195, *196*
Giessler, Edna Dohm, 195, *196*
Giessler, Emma Stegmiller, 194-97, *195-96*, 199-200, 202
Giessler, Lawrence L., 21, *42*, 57, 194-97, *198*, 199-202, *199-200*, 235, 241, 264n1
Giessler Mercantile, 195-97, 199-200
Giessler, William, 21, 199, 201-02, 264n1
Glover, William, 15
Godfrey, John, 23, *23*, 30
Godward, Frank, 111
Golconda Mine, 241
Gold Star Lode, 74
Golliher, Alma Williams, 27, 96, 159, 162, 204
Grand Army of the Republic (G. A. R.), 172, 192-93, 205, 217
Granier Ditch, *4*, 13, 105, 200
Granier, Emile, 13-14, 200
Granier Meadow, 111
Granier Placer, 13
Granier Placer Mining Claim, 13-15
Gratrix, William B., *x*, 77, 81, *81*, 203-07, *203-05, 207*
Green, Laura. *See* Laura Green Marrin
Green River, 12, 63-65, 175
Green, Zoie. *See* Zoie Green Fuller
Greenwich Village, N. Y., 86, 90
Griffin, Marg, *247*
Grosvenor, Wallace, 113
Gustafsen, Martha Harsch, 59, *59*, 63, 78-79, *78-79*
Gustafsen, Peter, 59-61, *59*, 79, 201

Hall, Harry, 235
Hallberg, Carl, 9, 220, *221*
Hallsville, 181, 280n41
Halstead, Philippina, 5, *73*, *85*
Hamilton City. *See* Miners Delight
Harris, Doc, 230, 235, 289n32, 290n41
Harris, William, 208-09, *209*

Harrison, Frank H., 210, 286n135, 289n26, 290n41
Harsch, Anna, *59*, 63
Harsch, Caroline Hess, 62-63
Harsch family plot, 29, 31, 61, *61*, 64, 72, 83, 122, 123-29, 134, 137, 144-48, 151
Harsch, Henry William, *59*, 61-63, *61*, 67-68, 172, 201
Harsch, Martha Elizabeth Schulka Hess, *x*, 29, 59, 61-66, *63-66*, 71-72, 77
Harsch, Philip, G., *x*, 59, 61, *61-64*, 66, 67, 69-72, 74, 77, 201
Harsch, Philip, Jr., 45, 63
Haugen, Jean Mathisen, 21, 223, 277n8,21
Hay Field fight, Mont., 231
Hayes, John Hammond, 24, *24*
Hess, Frederick, 62-65, *62*, *65*, *69*, 71
Hester, Ben G., 253
Heyroth, Alvin, *iv*, *x*, 6, 31, *33*, 34, 73-76, *73*, *75-76*, 119
Heyroth, Louiza E., *iv*, 9, 73-74
Hockett, Steve, 82-83, *83*
Hoffman, 211
Holcomb, Harry A., 241
Homsher, Lola, M., 5-6
Hooten, Andrew, 15
Hopper, Mr., 190
Hudson, 200
Huff, Ellen, 159
Huff family, 7, 41
Huff, John, *x*, 7, 41, 203, 205,
Huff, Nellie "Babe," *247*
Hunt, Lenora Angelina Harsch, 59, 61, *61*, 63, 77-79, *77-79*,
Hunt, Reginald Carew, 24, 77-78, *77*
Hyde's Hall, 2, 75, 261n6, 272n117

Independent Order of Odd Fellows (IOOF), 170, 172, 193, 213, 217, 220, 238
Indians, 1, 19, 28, 30, 94-96, 98, 179, 181-82, *152*, 190-91, 210, 213, 216, 223, 226, 233-34, 236, 239-40, 245
Irwin, Frank G., 151, 156, 210-12, *210-12*
Irwin, James, 178, 181
Irwin, K. T. and dog Blue, 7-8, 31-32, *33*, 39, 98, 119-20, 154, 158, 249-50, *249*, *251*, 255
Ivie, Erin, 68, 110

Jackson, Charles, 67, 112-14, *112-14*
Jackson, Eliza, 112, *114*

Jay Historical Society and Museum, Fla., 292n1

John XXII, 253

Jolly, Levi M., 235

Justice, Carole, *85*

Keel, George W., 241

Kellog, Alanson, 236

Kemmerer, 53

Kennedy, 75

Kennedy, Michael, 25

Kile, John, 231

Kime, James, 205-06

Klover, George, 184

Knight, Alexander, 26-27, *26-27*

Knight, Emma, 26-27, *26-27*, 154, 161

Knight, Jesse, 191

Knight, Martha Marechal, 26-27, *26-27*

Knudsen, Semon, 89

Lamoureux, Jules, *iv*, 28, 213, *213*

Lamoureux, Lizzie, 213, *213*

Lamoureux, Oliver, 28-29, 216

Lamoureux, Richard, *28*, 29, 213, *213*

Lander, 24, 29, 36, 44-45, 50, 57, 67, 88, 102-03, 110-11, 151, 170, 172, 175-77, 179, 182, 190, 192-93, 196, 202, 205, 208, 211, 213, 215, 217-20, 222, 225-26, 237-38, 243-44, 247

Lane, Jon, 174, *174*

Last Chance Mine, 241

Lathan, Charles, 236

Lawn, Edward, *iv*, *x*, 74, 205

Layman, David, 33

Layman, Susan, 33

Lee, Steve, *204*

Lee, Tammy, *204*

Leighton, A. C., 181

Leighton General Store, 179, 182

Leighton, James, 179, 182, 227

Lenne, Frank, 241

Lewellyn, Maurice, *50*, 206, 237-38, *237*

Lewiston, 105, 107, 109, 112-13, *112*, *114*, 171, 225, 240

Linn, John, 15

Little Atlantic Gulch, 67

Logan, George, 230, 239

Lowe, Sheriff, 74

Lucerne, 106, 110

Mackie, Thomas, 205

Malvern Battle, Va. 189

Mammoth Quartz Mill, 236

Mann, Albert, 15, 117, 175

Manning, George, 206-07

Map
    East Cemetery, *35*
    Territory of Wyoming, 1879, *viii-ix*
    Township and Range Survey, 1884, *16-17*
    West Cemetery, *157*

Marrin, John, 238

Marrin, Laura Green, 5, *97*, 98, 201

Marsh, Walter, 204, *204*

Martin, Luther, 253

Mary Ellen Mine, 214, 235, 237-38

Mary Germin Lode, 231

Mason, Jerome, 191

Masons, Masonic Lodge #2, South Pass City, 59, 67, 71-72, 182, 192-93, 201, 218

Massie, Michael, 174

McAuley, Lydia May, 14, 27, 152, 156, 158, *158*, 162-69

McAuley, Lydia (mother), *x*, 158

McAuley, Robert, *iv*, *x*, *10*, 75, *75*, 158, 203, 205, 210, 272n117

McCarroll, William, 115-17, *116*, 237

McCarty, Tim, 191

McGlinchy, John, 64

McGovern, Frank D., 227

McGuire, John, 239

McTurk, Jack, 241

Melin, Casimer, *iv*, 15, 34, 80-85, *80-85*, 101, 146, 156, 191, 238, 255, 260

Melin, Lea Lamoureux, 81, *81*

Meschter, Daniel Y., 73, 80, 93, 114, 155

Meyer, Jacob S., 110

Mills, Harry, 214-15, 214-15

Miners Delight, 5, 12, 94, 117, 206, 245

Miners Delight Cemetery, 223

Miner's Delight Inn, 1, 4, 47, 82, 87, 90, *91*. *See* also Carpenter Hotel

Miners Grubstake, 4

Mionczynski, John, 5, 7, *10*, *20*, 32, 111, 153, 205, 251

Moerer, Jeri, 200

Moerer, Lyle, 18, 200

Moore, Carmela, 155

Moore, Frank, 240

Moore, William, *35*, 155, *157*

Morgan, Harvey, 191

Morris, Esther Hobart, 9
Morris Lode, 113
Morris, Robert, 9, 262n17
Moudy, Mabel W. Cheney, 190, 282n78
Mount Hope Cemetery, 21, 24, 28, 172, 172,
    198, 213, 213, 226, 226, 170, 177, 193-
    94, 196, 202, 208, 215, 217, 219-20, 238

National Register of Historic Places, 205;
    Atlantic City Mercantile, 197; Carpenter
    Hotel Historic District, 49; St. Andrew's
    Episcopal Church, 30, 43
Nations, Edna, 45
Neff, W. H., 247
Newman, Georgina Dewey, 82, 86-91, 86-88, 91
Newman, Paul, 82, 86-91, 89-91
Nickerson, Hermon Gould, 1, 74, 199, 220,
    243, 244
Noble, Ann, 7-8, 27, 32, 98, 120-21, 125-26,
    129, 131, 133, 135, 137, 139, 143-44, 148-
    50, 154, 162, 167, 253, 253-60, 255-56
Norman, Laura, 73, 85
North Fork, Masonic Cemetery, 211, 211, 151
North Star Lode, 241
Nottage, Emma Cheney, 189

Old Stage Station, 50
Oriental Mine, 182
Othick, James, 240
"Our Mother," 92-94, 92-93, 114, 124
Outlaw Trail, 4

Pacific Springs, 12, 175, 208
Pence, Mary Lou, 5-6
Penhoel, Lou, 238
Perkins, Mr., 223
Pfaff, Betty Carpenter, 39, 40, 44, 45, 48, 50,
    51, 53-54, 70, 78, 79, 94-95, 102, 112,
    154, 183, 184, 187, 224, 237
Philistine Mine, 42-43
Point of Rocks, 28, 201, 235
Poire, Louis, x, 74
Powers, John, 223
Powers, Joseph, 230-31
Preston, Douglas A., 205

Ratliff, Donna Sue, 64
Raught, George, H., 241
Red Desert, 1, 28, 235
Red-Haired Woman, 48, 102
Redford, Robert, 4-5
Reid, John M., 74
Reynolds, Rick, 18

Richardson, Alonzo, 92, 94, 94, 125-27
Robbenson, F. U., 28
Roberts, Phil, 252
Robinson, Anne Carpenter, 6, 32, 39, 39, 44,
    95, 120
Robinson, Bonnie, 204
Robinson, Montgomery, 95
Robinson, Scott, 204
Rock Creek, 3-4, 4, 17, 13, 15, 18, 37, 48, 97-8,
    158, 185, 187, 230
Rock Creek Gulch, 171, 203
Rock Springs, 21, 40, 78, 224
Rocky Ridge Station. See St. Mary's stage
    station
Roe, Clarence, 37, 46-47, 185
Roeser, C., ix
Ruebelmann, Lorna, 87

St. Andrew's Cemetery, 30, 44, 50, 69, 103,
    105, 107
St. Andrew's Episcopal Church, 30, 41,
    43-44, 49-50, 77, 83, 95, 105, 107-08,
    108
St. Mary Catholic Cemetery, Ohio, 245
St. Mary's stage station on the Sweetwater,
    234, 236, 239, 290n39. See Rocky Ridge
    station
Saltgaver, Patricia, 210
Schepp, August, 50
Schlichting, Annie, iv, x, 9
Schnell, Charles, H., 74
Schoo, J. W. H., 248
Schooley, Don, 7-8, 27, 32, 39, 48, 98, 120,
    143, 145, 149, 154, 159, 161, 252, 253-57,
    259-60, 259
Seven Lakes, 21
Shears, Hi, 268n48
Sherlock family, 78, 279n22
Sherlock, James L., 36, 59, 173-75, 179
Sherlock, Jason, 245
Sherlock, John, 154
Sherlock, Peter, 175
Sherlock, Richard, 174
Sherman, William T., 245
Shoshones, 171, 179, 182, 203
Shoshoni Mining District, 229, 240
Silbers, Emma, 195
Sioux, 94, 179
Slack, Edwin A., 230, 240
Smith, Bill, 227
Smith, "engineer," 238
Smith, Lewis, 103
Smith, Mrs. Granville, 21

Smith, Granville, T., 21, 264n1
Smith, Jennie S., 242
Smith, Lewis, 103
Smith's Gulch, 67, 223, 240
Smoker State Lode, 28
Sommers, Jonita, 7, 254
Sommers, Verla, *10*
Sostmann, Herman, 234-44, *243-44*
Sostmann, Lizzie Richards, 234-44, *243-44*
South Pass City, 5, 9, 12, 48, 56, 59-60, 62-63, *63*, 70-71, 80, 102, 115, 154, 173-74, *173*, 190-91, 201, 217, 224-25, *224*, 227, 237, 240, 261
South Pass City State Historic Site, 3, *3*, *63*, *70-71*, *80*, *103*, 106, *107*, *173-74*, 174-76, *224*
Spangler, Sam, *x*, *42*, 74, 205
Spencer-Hockett, Pam, *85*
Stambaugh, Charles B., 1, 19, 94, 97, 245, 292n81,86
Stephenson, Gertrude Irwin, 210-11, *211*
Stewart, Mrs., 178, 181, 279n27
Stough, 208
Strumlords, 3
Swabes, Ida, 115, 117, *118*
Sweetwater County, 12, 171, 175, 205, 220, 227; government, 15, 64, 81, 192, 220, 230; Historical Museum, 9
Sweetwater River, 28, 97-98, 175, 199, 234, 236, 239
Sypes, Charles L., *4*, *42*, 201, 218-19, *219*
Sypes, Elizabeth, 218-19

Ta Yu, 253
Taylor, H. M., 236, 239
Taylor, Judy, *190*
Teters Patented Mining Claim, 13
Teters Placer, 13
Teters, Wilbert B., 13-15
Thermopolis, 58, 196, 201-02
Thompson, H. A., 13
Thompson, Merritt, 205
Tibbals, Barney N., *31*, *33*, *55*, *80*, *153*, *173*
Timba-Bah Mining Company, 14-15, 18, 30, 218
tinker, 200
Titcomb, Harold A., *31*, *33*, *55*, *80*, *153*, *173*
Townsend, Robert K., vi, 47, 49
Tozier, Charles W., 13
Trumble, Jo, 3
Trumble, Rod, 3

Tschirgi, Loretta, 32
Tweed, Mrs. Dave, 175
Tweed Ranch, "Boss," 50
Tyler, Carolyn B., 89

Van Praag, H. A., 241
Victoria Regina Mine, 205

Walker, Lizzie, 247, *247-48*
Walrath, Martha, *105*, 106, *107*
Walsh, Ed, 174
Ward, Mr., 210
Ward, William, 220
Ware, H., 223
Washington, Charles, 205
Watkins, Henry, 97
Wehrman, Terry, 4
Westfall, Welsey, *42*, 235
Wheeler, Hull & Company Mill, 230
Wheeling, Bob, 231, 289n30
Wickliffe, Charles, 228, 231
Williams, Baby, 14, 27, 99, 152, *153*, 154, 159-61, *159, 161*, 259
Williams, Barbara, 159, *159*
Williams, Emmett, 98, 159, *159*
Williams, Henry, 7, 31, 40, 98, 159, *247*
Williams, Henry family, 7, 27, *44*, 96, *96*, 98, *112, 159*, 286n136
Williams, Jared, 31, *42*, 96-100, *96-97, 99-100*, 126, 129-31, 142, 160, 235
Williams, John, 97
Williams, Maude Huff, *44*, 98, *247*, 159, 286n136
Williams, William, 96-97
Williamson, Rosemary, 159
Wind River Indian Reservation, 171
Wind River Valley, 239
Winn, Infant, 29, *29*
Winn, Mr. John and Mrs., 29
Winter Cemetery, 153
Wiswell, F. W., 178, *178*, 181, 227, 231
Worthen, Effie L., 214
Wygal, Wayne, 154

Yarnell, Mary, 220, *221*
Yarnell, Nelson, 220, *221*

Zerbe, Lynn, *210*
Zimmerman, G. A., 243

About The Author

After retiring from the United States Air Force, Barbara Townsend's writing journey began in earnest at the University of Wyoming. During her first fiction writing class she felt compelled to write a mystery. The twists, turns, red herrings, clues and making them all fit into one story fascinated her. That first short story, *Murder at Wainwright,* she later wrote into a novel, *Clear and Convincing Evidence.*

An internship in the Toppan Rare Books Library led her in another direction. With books dating from the 1800s, her research paper examined women in nineteenth-century Mormon polygyny. The American Heritage Center granted her first place in its student competition. The accumulated research led to her writing her first trade-published historical mystery *Blood Atonement.*

Her writing credits include articles for the university and Air Force newspapers. She was first a student then a faculty member of the graduate-level Wyoming Writing Project. She graduated *summa cum laude* with a Bachelor of Arts degree.

She lives in Wyoming's Wind River Mountains. Her Old West environs inspired her third novel, another historical mystery *Tarnished Gold.*

Here she continued to indulge her fascination for research. She compiled history and submitted nomination packages to the National Register of Historic Places. The Miner's Delight Inn was listed on the register as the Carpenter Hotel Historic District. She later achieved the same success for the town's venerable St. Andrew's Episcopal Church.

For years, she researched local Old West deaths and burials, employed myriad techniques such as a cadaver dog and three dowsers to find forgotten graves, and even discovered a lost 1875 grave marker. For this project, the Wyoming Historical Society granted her its *Outstanding Historical Preservation Award.*

From the interest and requests for her research *Life and Death in Historic Atlantic City, Wyoming* came into being.

Novels by Barbara Townsend

Blood Atonement
Clear and Convincing Evidence
Tarnished Gold

Novels by Barbara Townsend

Blood Atonement

Missouri Territory, 1846 - Thousands of Mormons endure winter's cruelty before they travel to Zion in the following spring. Plural wife Aveline must also endure her new sister-wife's jealousy. Aveline's world shatters when her sister is brutally murdered. Spring approaches and preparations begin for the trek west. With time running out, her husband refuses for her to investigate. She decides to defy him to search for her sister's killer.

Clear and Convincing Evidence

Jennifer Roby, student reporter at a Wyoming college, reports the hoax of a charred skeleton in a ceramics studio kiln. Jenn's instinct prods her to investigate and she discovers the bones are real. While she unravels the murder, proof of a cover-up climbs higher in the college hierarchy. Jenn races to publish the exposé before officials shut down the newspaper or make good on threats to her safety.

Tarnished Gold

Placer City, Wyoming, 1933 - Em Olson struggles to operate her family hotel in a mining town after her father's abandonment and her mother's death. A new lodger, a handsome geologist, brightens her lonely life. He discovers a body and uncovers swindles embroiling the hotel and her father's gold mine. To find the truth, she is forced to re-examine her life as the man Em has grown to love prepares to depart.

Fine Nib Publishing

www.ingramcontent.com/pod-product-compliance
Lightning Source LLC
Chambersburg PA
CBHW051133120626
46547CB00012B/785